Recommended Reference Books for Small and Medium-sized Libraries and Media Centers

American Reference Books Annual
Advisory Board

RECOMMENDED REFERENCE BOOKS

for Small and Medium-sized Libraries and Media Centers

Volume 29

2009 Edition

Shannon Graff Hysell, Associate Editor

LIBRARIES UNLIMITED

A Member of the Greenwood Publishing Group

Westport, Connecticut • London

LIBRARIES UNLIMITED
A Member of the Greenwood Publishing Group, Inc.
88 Post Road West
Westport, CT 06881
1-800-225-5800
www.lu.com

Library of Congress Cataloging-in-Publication Data

Main entry under title:

Recommended reference books for small and medium-
    sized libraries and media centers.

    "Selected from the 2009 edition of American
reference books annual."
    Includes index.
    I. Reference books--Bibliography. 2. Reference
services (Library)--Handbooks, manuals, etc.
3. Instructional materials centers--Handbooks,
manuals, etc. I. Hysell, Shannon Graff
II. American reference books annual.
Z1035.1.R435   011'.02   81-12394
ISBN 978-1-59158-841-2
ISSN 0277-5948

Contents

Introduction

Recommended Reference Books for Small and Medium-sized Libraries and Media Centers (RRB), now in its twenty-ninth volume, is designed to assist smaller libraries in the systematic selection of suitable reference materials for their collections. It aids in the evaluation process by choosing substantial titles in all subject areas. The increase in the publication of reference sources and availability of reference databases in the United States and Canada, in combination with the decrease in library budgets, makes this guide an invaluable tool.

Following the pattern established in 1981 with the first volume, RRB consists of book reviews chosen from the current edition of *American Reference Books Annual*. This nationally acclaimed work provides reviews of reference books, CD-ROMs, and Internet sites published in the United States and Canada within a single year, along with English-language titles from other countries. ARBA has reviewed nearly 64,000 titles since its inception in 1970. Because it provides comprehensive coverage of reference sources, not just selected or recommended titles, many are of interest only to large academic and public libraries. Thus, RRB has been developed as an abridged version of ARBA, with selected reviews of resources suitable for smaller libraries.

Titles reviewed in RRB include dictionaries, encyclopedias, indexes, directories, bibliographies, guides, atlases, gazetteers, and other types of ready-reference tools. General encyclopedias that are updated annually, yearbooks, almanacs, indexing and abstracting services, directories, and other annuals are included on a selective basis. These works are systematically reviewed so that all important annuals are critically examined every few years. Excluded from RRB are regional guides in the areas of biological sciences and travel guides. All titles in this volume are coded with letters that provide worthwhile guidance for selection. These indicate that a given work is a recommended purchase for smaller college libraries (C), public libraries (P), or school media centers (S).

The current volume of RRB contains 540 unabridged reviews selected from the 1,351 entries in ARBA 2009. These have been written by more than 200 subject specialists throughout the United States and Canada. Although all titles in RRB are recommended acquisitions, critical comments have not been deleted, because even recommended works may be weak in one respect or another. In many cases reviews evaluate and compare a work in relation to other titles of a similar nature. All reviews provide complete ordering and bibliographic information. The subject index organization is based upon the *Library of Congress Subject Heading*. Reference to reviews published in periodicals (see page xix for journals cited) during the year of coverage are appended to the reviews. All reviews are signed.

The present volume contains 37 chapters. There are four major subdivisions: "General Reference Works," "Social Sciences," "Humanities," and "Science and Technology." "General Reference Works," arranged alphabetically, is subdivided by form: bibliography, biography, handbooks and yearbooks, and so on. The remaining three parts are subdivided into alphabetically arranged chapters. Most chapters are subdivided in a way that reflects the arrangement strategy of the entire volume: a section on general works and then a topical breakdown. The latter is further subdivided, based on the amount of material available on a given topic.

RRB has been favorably reviewed in such journals as *Booklist, School Library Media Quarterly, Journal of Academic Librarianship*, and *Library Talk*. The editors continue to strive to make RRB the most valuable acquisition tool a small library can have.

In closing, the editors at Libraries Unlimited would like to express their gratitude to the contributors whose reviews appear in this volume. We would also like to thank the members of the Advisory Board, whose ideas and input have been invaluable to the quality of ARBA, ARBAonline, and RRB.

Contributors

Stephen H. Aby, Education Bibliographer, Bierce Library, Univ. of Akron, Ohio.

Anthony J. Adam, Reference Librarian, Prairie View A & M Univ., Coleman Library, Tex.

January Adams, Asst. Director/Head of Adult Services, Franklin Township Public Library, Somerset, N.J.

Michael Adams, Reference Librarian, City Univ. of New York Graduate Center.

Donald Altschiller, Reference Librarian, Boston Univ.

Adrienne Antink, Medical Group Management Association, Lakewood, Colo.

Susan C. Awe, Asst. Director, Univ. of New Mexico, Albuquerque.

Christopher Baker, Professor of English, Armstrong Atlantic State Univ., Savannah, Ga.

Thomas E. Baker, Assoc. Professor, Department of Criminal Justice, Univ. of Scranton, Pa.

Catherine Barr, Editor, Children's and Young Adult Literature Reference Series, Libraries Unlimited.

Joshua Barton, Serials Cataloging Librarian/Bibliographer for Philosophy, Michigan State Univ. Libraries, East Lansing.

Mark T. Bay, Electronic Resources, Serials, and Government Documents Librarian, Hagan Memorial Library, Cumberland College, Williamsburg, Ky.

Leslie M. Behm, Reference Librarian, Michigan State Univ. Libraries, East Lansing.

Michael Francis Bemis, Asst. Librarian, Washington County Library, Woodbury, Minn.

Laura J. Bender, Librarian, Univ. of Arizona, Tucson.

Elaine Lasda Bergman, Bibliographer for Reference and Gerontology, Dewey Graduate Library, Univ. at Albany, N.Y.

Helen Margaret Bernard, Reference and Interlibrary Loan Librarian, Writing Center Director, Southwestern Baptist Theological Seminary, Fort Worth, Tex.

Barbara M. Bibel, Reference Librarian, Science/Business/Sociology Dept., Main Library, Oakland Public Library, Calif.

Sally Bickley, Coordinator of Reference Services, Texas A&M Univ.—Corpus Christi.

Rebecca Blakeley, Government Documents Librarian and Asst. Professor, McNeese State Univ. Library, Lake Charles, La.

Daniel K. Blewett, Reference Librarian, College of DuPage Library, College of DuPage, Glen Ellyn, Ill.

Polly D. Boruff-Jones, Assoc. Librarian, Indiana Univ.—Purdue Univ. Indianapolis.

Alicia Brillon, Reference Librarian, Univ. of Colorado, Boulder—Law Library.

Georgia Briscoe, Assoc. Director and Head of Technical Services, Law Library, Univ. of Colorado, Boulder.

Simon J. Bronner, Distinguished Professor of Folklore and American Studies, Capitol College, Pennsylvania State Univ., Middletown.

Theresa Lynn Bruno, Asst. Librarian, IUPUC, Columbus, Ind.

Frederic F. Burchsted, Reference Librarian, Widener Library, Harvard Univ., Cambridge, Mass.

Mike Burgmeier, Reference Librarian, Northern Michigan Univ., Marquette.

Joanna M. Burkhardt, Head Librarian, College of Continuing Education Library, Univ. of Rhode Island, Providence.

Greg Byerly, Assoc. Professor, School of Library and Information Science, Kent State Univ., Kent, Ohio.

Diane M. Calabrese, Freelance Writer and Contributor, Silver Springs, Md.

Delilah R. Caldwell, Online Services Librarian and Adjunct Instructor, Southwestern College, Winfield, Kans.

Danielle Marie Carlock, Reference and Instruction Librarian, Arizona State Univ. at the Polytechnic campus, Mesa.

Carolyn Carpan, Reference Librarian/Asst. Professor, Olin Library, Rollins College, Winter Park, Fla.

G. A. Cevasco, Assoc. Professor of English, St. John's Univ., Jamaica, N.Y.

Bert Chapman, Government Publications Coordinator, Purdue Univ., West Lafayette, Ind.

Boyd Childress, Reference Librarian, Ralph B. Draughon Library, Auburn Univ., Ala.

Donald E. Collins, Assoc. Professor, History Dept., East Carolina Univ., Greenville, N.C.

Rosanne M. Cordell, Head of Reference Services, Franklin D. Schurz Library, Indiana Univ., South Bend.

Kay O. Cornelius, (formerly) Teacher and Magnet School Lead Teacher, Huntsville City Schools, Ala.

Paul B. Cors, Catalog Librarian, Univ. of Wyoming, Laramie.

Gregory A. Crawford, Head of Public Services, Penn State Harrisburg, Middletown, Pa.

Mark J. Crawford, Consulting Exploration Geologist/Writer/Editor, Madison, Wis.

Alice Crosetto, Coordinator, Collection Development and Acquisitions Librarian, Univ. of Toledo, Ohio.

Cynthia Crosser, Social Sciences and Humanities Reference, Fogler Library, Univ. of Maine, Orono.

Gregory Curtis, Director, Northern Maine Technical College, Presque Isle.

Anamika Dasgupta, Instructor Librarian, York College—CUNY, New York.

R. K. Dickson, Asst. Professor of Fine Arts, Wilson College, Chambersburg, Pa.

Scott R. DiMarco, Director of Library Services and Information Resources, Mansfield Univ., Mansfield, Pa.

Margaret F. Dominy, Information Services Librarian, Drexel Univ., Philadelphia.

Lucy Duhon, Serials Librarian, Univ. of Toledo, Ohio.

Joe P. Dunn, Charles A. Dana Professor of History and Politics, Converse College, Spartanburg, S.C.

Judy Dyki, Library Director, Cranbrook Academy of Art Library, Bloomfield Hills, Mich.

Bradford Lee Eden, Assoc. University Librarian for Technical Services and Scholarly Communication, Univ. of California, Santa Barbara.

Lorraine Evans, Instruction and Reference Librarian, Auraria Library, Denver, Colo.

Benet Steven Exton, St. Gregorys Univ. Library, Shawnee, Okla.

Elaine Ezell, Library Media Specialist, Bowling Green Jr. High School, Ohio.

Ignacio J. Ferrer-Vinent, Science Reference/Instruction Librarian, Auraria Library—Univ. of Colorado at Denver.

Judith J. Field, Senior Lecturer, Program for Library and Information Science, Wayne State Univ., Detroit.

Josh Eugene Finnell, Asst. Professor of Library Science and Reference Librarian, McNeese State Univ., Lake Charles, La.

James H. Flynn Jr., (formerly) Operations Research Analyst, Dept. of Defense, Vienna, Va.

Walter Michael Fontane, Reference Librarian, McNeese State Univ., Lake Charles, La.

David O. Friedrichs, Professor, Univ. of Scranton, Pa.

Brian T. Gallagher, Access Services Librarian, Univ. of Rhode Island, Kingston.

Zev Garber, Professor and Chair, Jewish Studies, Los Angeles Valley College, Calif.

Denise A. Garofalo, Library Director, Astor Home for Children, Rhinebeck, N.Y.

John T. Gillespie, College Professor and Writer, New York.

Caroline L. Gilson, Coordinator, Prevo Science Library, DePauw Univ., Greencastle, Ind.

Larissa Anne Gordon, Librarian, Wilmington College, Dover, Del.

Glenda Irene Griffin, Serials Cataloger, Sam Houston State Univ., Huntsville, Tex.

Sue Ellen Griffiths, Public Services Librarian 1, Pasco County Library System, Hudson, Fla.

Linda W. Hacker, Reference Librarian, SUNY Brockport, N.Y.

Barry Hamilton, Theological Librarian, Assoc. Professor of Theology, Northeastern Seminary, B. Thomas Golisano Library, Rochester, N.Y.

Ralph Hartsock, Senior Music Catalog Librarian, Univ. of North Texas, Denton.

Karen D. Harvey, Assoc. Dean for Academic Affairs, Univ. College, Univ. of Denver, Colo.

Muhammed Hassanali, Independent Consultant, Shaker Heights, Ohio.

Maris L. Hayashi, Asst. University Librarian, Florida Atlantic Univ., Boca Raton, Fla.

Lucy Heckman, Reference Librarian (Business-Economics), St. John's Univ. Library, Jamaica, N.Y.

Mark Y. Herring, Dean of Library Services, Winthrop Univ., Dacus Library, Rock Hill, S.C.

Joseph P. Hester, SRO-Learning, Claremont, N.C.

Ladyjane Hickey, Reference Librarian, Austin College, Tex.

Susan Tower Hollis, Assoc. Dean and Center Director, Central New York Center of the State Univ. of New York.

Sara Anne Hook, Professor of Informatics and Assoc. Dean for Academic Affairs and Undergraduate Studies, UP School of Informatics, Indiana Univ., Purdue Univ., Indianapolis.

Mihoko Hosoi, Public Services Librarian, Cornell Univ., Ithaca, N.Y.

Ann Howington, Librarian, Univ. of North Texas Libraries, Denton.

Ma Lei Hsieh, Librarian, Rider Univ., N.J.

Shannon Graff Hysell, Staff, Libraries Unlimited.

Amanda Izenstark, Asst. Professor, Reference and Instructional Design Librarian, Univ. of Rhode Island, Kingston.

Melissa M. Johnson, Reference Services, Fenwick Library—George Mason Univ., Fairfax, Va.

Richard D. Johnson, Director of Libraries Emeritus, James M. Milne Library, State Univ. College, Oneonta, N.Y.

Chad Kahl, Coordinator for Library Instruction and Information Literacy, Milner Library, Illinois State Univ., Normal, Ill.

Craig Mury Keeney, Cataloging Librarian, South Caroliniana Library, Univ. of South Carolina.

Edmund D. Keiser Jr., Professor of Biology, Univ. of Mississippi, University.

Roxanne M. Kent-Drury, College of Arts and Sciences, Northern Kentucky Univ., Highland Heights.

Amy Koehler, Support Services Librarian, Moody Bible Institute, Chicago, Ill.

Abe Korah, Reference Librarian, Sam Houston State Univ., Huntsville, Tex.

Lori D. Kranz, Freelance Editor, Chambersburg, Pa.

Betsy J. Kraus, Librarian, Lovelace Respiratory Research Institute, National Environmental Respiratory Center, Albuquerque, N.Mex.

Mary Beth Kreiner, Librarian, Cranbrook Academy of Art Library, Bloomfield Hills, Mich.

Marlene M. Kuhl, Library Manager, Baltimore County Public Library, Reisterstown Branch, Md.

George Thomas Kurian, President, Encyclopedia Society, Baldwin Place, N.Y.

Robert V. Labaree, Reference/Public Services Librarian, Von KleinSmid Library, Univ. of Southern California, Los Angeles.

Peter Larsen, Physical Sciences and Engineering Librarian, Univ. of Rhode Island Libraries, Kingston.

Rob Laurich, Head of Reference & Collection Development, The City College of New York.

Martha Lawler, Assoc. Librarian, Louisiana State Univ., Shreveport.

Charles Leck, Professor of Biological Sciences, Rutgers Univ., New Brunswick, N.J.

Michael Levine-Clark, Collections Librarian, Univ. of Denver, Colo.

Tze-chung Li, Professor and Dean Emeritus, Dominican Univ.

Charlotte Lindgren, Professor Emerita of English, Emerson College, Boston, Mass.

Megan W. Lowe, Reference/Instruction Librarian, University Library, Univ. of Louisiana at Monroe.

Sara R. Mack, Professor Emerita, Dept. of Library Science, Kutztown Univ., Pa.

Tyler Manolovitz, Digital Resources Coordinator, Sam Houston State Univ.—Newton Gresham Library, Huntsville, Tex.

Sara Marcus, Asst. Professor of Education, Touro University International, N.Y.

Michelle Martinez, Librarian, Newton Gresham Library, Sam Houston State Univ., Huntsville, Tex.

Melinda F. Matthews, Interlibrary Loan/Reference Librarian, Univ. of Louisiana at Monroe.

John Maxymuk, Reference Librarian, Paul Robeson Library, Rutgers Univ., Camden, N.J.

Kevin McDonough, Reference and Electronic Resources Librarian, Northern Michigan Univ.—Olson Library, Marquette.

Glenn S. McGuigan, Reference Librarian, Penn State Abington, Abington, Pa.

G. Douglas Meyers, Chair, Dept. of English, Univ. of Texas, El Paso.

Robert Michaelson, Head Librarian, Seeley G. Mudd Library for Science and Engineering, Northwestern Univ., Evanston, Ill.

Terry Ann Mood, Professor Emeritus, Univ. of Colorado, Denver.

Paul M. Murphy III, Director of Marketing, PMX Medical, Denver, Colo.

Charles Neuringer, Professor of Psychology and Theatre and Film, Univ. of Kansas, Lawrence.

Matt Novak, Reference librarian, Univ. of Nebraska College of Law, Lincoln.

Herbert W. Ockerman, Professor, Ohio State Univ., Columbus.

Lawrence Olszewski, Director, OCLC Library and Information Center, Dublin, Ohio.

John Howard Oxley, Faculty, American Intercontinental Univ., Atlanta, Ga.

Kristy Padron, Asst. University Librarian, Florida Atlantic Univ., Boca Raton, Fla.

Alan K. Pannell, Reference Librarian, Univ. of Colorado Law Library, Boulder.

J. Carlyle Parker, Librarian and Univ. Archivist Emeritus, Library, California State Univ., Turlock.

Amy B. Parsons, Reference and Catalog Librarian, Courtright Memorial Library, Otterbein College, Westerville, Ohio.

Arthur Quinn, Library Director, St. Vincent de Paul Seminary, Boynton Beach, Fla.

Jack Ray, Asst. Director, Loyola/Notre Dame Library, Baltimore, Md.

Patrick J. Reakes, Journalism/Mass Communications Librarian, Univ. of Florida, Gainesville.

Allen Reichert, Electronic Access Librarian, Courtright Memorial Library, Otterbein College, Westerville, Ohio.

Christine Rigda, Asst. Professor of Library Administration, Univ. of Toledo, Ohio.

James C. Roberts, Asst. Professor of Sociology and Criminal Justice, Univ. of Scranton, Pa.

John M. Robson, Institute Librarian, Rose-Hulman Institute of Technology, Terre Haute, Ind.

John B. Romeiser, Professor of French and Dept. Head, Univ. of Tennessee, Knoxville.

Barbara Ripp Safford, Assoc. Professor at the School Library Media Studies, Univ. of Northern Iowa, Cedar Falls.

Nadine Salmons, (retired) Technical Services Librarian, Fort Carson's Grant Library, Colo.

Richard Salvucci, Professor, Economics, Trinity Univ., San Antonio, Tex.

John Schlinke, Access Services Librarian, Roger Williams Univ., Bristol, R.I.

Diane Schmidt, Biology Librarian, Univ. of Illinois, Urbana.

Ralph Lee Scott, Assoc. Professor, East Carolina Univ. Library, Greenville, N.C.

Colleen Seale, Humanities and Social Sciences Services, George A. Smathers Libraries, Univ. of Florida, Gainesville.

Susan K. Setterlund, Science/Health Science Librarian, Florida Atlantic Univ., Boca Raton.

Ravindra Nath Sharma, Dean of Library, Monmouth Univ. Library, West Long Branch, N.J.

Stephen J. Shaw, Reference/Bibliographic Instruction Librarian, Prairie View A&M Univ., Prairie View, Tex.

Scott Alan Sheidlower, Asst. Professor, York College/City Univ. of New York, Jamaica.

Kay Shelton, Instructor, Kishwaukee College, Malta, Ill.

Brian J. Sherman, Head of Collection Management, McNeese State Univ.—Frazar Library, Lake Charles, La.

Susan Shultz, Reference and Instruction Librarian, DePaul Univ., Chicago, Ill.

Leena Siegelbaum, Bibliographer of Eastern European Law, Harvard Univ., Cambridge, Mass.

Kennith Slagle, Collection Development Librarian, Northern Michigan Univ., Marquette.

Mary Ellen Snodgrass, Freelance Writer, Charlotte, N.C.

Lisa Kay Speer, Special Collections Librarian, Southeast Missouri State Univ., Cape Girardeau.

Kay M. Stebbins, Coordinator Librarian, Louisiana State Univ., Shreveport.

John P. Stierman, Reference Librarian, Western Illinois Univ., Macomb.

John W. Storey, Professor of History, Lamar Univ., Beaumont, Tex.

William C. Struning, Professor, Seton Hall Univ., South Orange, N.J.

Philip G. Swan, Head Librarian, Hunter College, School of Social Work Library, New York.

Corrine C. Syster, Instructional & Information Technology Librarian, Central Pennsylvania College, Summerdale, Pa.

Susan E. Thomas, Head of Collection Development/Assoc. Librarian, Indiana Univ. South Bend.

Mary Ann Thompson, Asst. Professor of Nursing, Saint Joseph College, West Hartford, Conn.

Linda D. Tietjen, Senior Instructor, Arts and Architecture Bibliographer, Auraria Library, Denver, Colo.

Vincent P. Tinerella, Public Services Librarian, Ross Pendegraft Library, Arkansas Tech Univ., Russelville.

Bradley P. Tolppanen, History Bibliographer and Head of Circulation Services, Eastern Illinois Univ., Charleston.

Elias H. Tuma, Professor of Economics, Univ. of California, Davis.

Diane J. Turner, Science/Engineering Liaison, Auraria Library, Univ. of Colorado, Denver.

Robert L. Turner Jr., Librarian and Assoc. Professor, Radford Univ., Va.

Linda M. Turney, Cataloging Coordinator, Sam Houston State Univ., Huntsville, Tex.

Chris Tuthill, Librarian, Newman Library, Baruch College, New York.

Nancy L. Van Atta, Dayton, Ohio.

Leanne M. VandeCreek, Social Sciences Reference Librarian, Northern Illinois Univ., DeKalb.

Vang Vang, Reference Librarian, Henry Madden Library, California State Univ. Fresno.

Stephanie Vie, Asst. Professor of Composition and Rhetoric, Fort Lewis College, Durango, Colo.

J. E. Weaver, Dept. of Economics, Drake Univ., Des Moines, Iowa.

Lucille Whalen, Dean of Graduate Programs, Immaculate Heart College Center, Los Angeles, Calif.

Robert L. Wick, Professor Emeritus, Auraria Library, Univ. of Colorado, Denver.

Charlotte Widomski, Reference Librarian, Herkimer County Community College, Herkimer, N.Y.

Maren Williams, Reference Librarian, Univ. of Louisiana at Monroe.

Mark A. Wilson, Professor of Geology, College of Wooster, Ohio.

Ryan Womack, Data and Economics Librarian, Rutgers Univ. Libraries.

Julienne L. Wood, Head, Research Services, Noel Memorial Library, Louisiana State Univ. in Shreveport.

Louis G. Zelenka, Jacksonville Public Library System, Fla.

Anita Zutis, Adjunct Librarian, Queensborough Community College, Bayside, N.Y.

Journals Cited

FORM OF CITATION	JOURNAL TITLE
AG	*Against the Grain*
BL	*Booklist*
BR	*Book Report*
Choice	*Choice*
JAL	*Journal of Academic Librarianship*
LJ	*Library Journal*
LMC	*Library Media Connection*
RUSQ	*Reference & User Services Quarterly*
SLJ	*School Library Journal*
TL	*Teacher Librarian*
VOYA	*Voice of Youth Advocates*

Part I
GENERAL
REFERENCE
WORKS

1 General Reference Works

ALMANACS

C, P, S

1. **Whitaker's Almanack 2008.** Farmington Hills, Mich., Gale Group, 2008. 1362p. maps. index. $135.00. ISBN 1-4144-3344-1. ISBN 13: 978-1-4144-3344-8.

Whitaker's Almanack is a fact-packed, thorough, and organized work, now in its 140th edition, that primarily covers the United Kingdom but also is a good source of general information on all countries of the world. The text contains standard almanac fare, such as a section with current and upcoming calendars and a general reference section listing, for example, weights and measures, abbreviations, and the periodic table. The primary section of the almanac, of course, covers the United Kingdom, from the structure of the royal family and their employees to the structure, affairs, and personnel of the government and other institutions. A comprehensive world section contains useful statistics and also includes a listing of countries from A-Z with data for each country, which might include climate, history, economy and trade, communications, media, and culture. Current affairs follow the country section with a year in review of 2006-2007. Color maps are a highlight of the volume. The maps begin with the different world regions and then move on to show various indicators, such as refugees by country of asylum to regional gross domestic product. The maps are followed by a color listing of the flags of the world. *Whitaker's Almanack* would be a good addition to any library collection, especially academic. It will be useful for anyone young adult and older. The volume provides a great place to start current affairs research. As the almanac's cover states, *Whitaker's* is "today's world in one volume." Indeed, it certainly is.—**Sue Ellen Griffiths**

BIBLIOGRAPHY

Bibliographic Guides

C, P

2. **Reference Sources for Small and Medium-sized Libraries.** 7th ed. Jack O'Gorman, ed. Chicago, American Library Association, 2008. 329p. index. $80.00pa.; $72.00pa. (ALA members). ISBN 13: 978-0-8389-0943-0.

This book will assist librarians in offering quality reference sources for public libraries and undergraduate students. Arranged by Dewey categories, the entries are further categorized by type, such as almanacs, atlases, yearbooks, and more. Specific subjects are addressed after the general subject; for example, resources in astronomy, chemistry, and engineering are reviewed within the "Science" chapter. Expert contributors indicate the audience best served by the resource. The table of contents makes it easy to navigate. Costs are given in ranges, to assist with decision-making.

The 7th edition is quite different from the 6th see (ARBA 2001, entry 580). Only a small number of reviews are retained from the previous edition and these are completely rewritten. The new edition covers more ethnic and cultural topics, technology developments, and global awareness; outdated categories were dropped. This edition does not include materials for school libraries as does *Recommended Reference Books for Small and Medium-sized Libraries and Media Centers* (2009 ed.; Libraries Unlimited, 2009). Reviews in the Libraries Unlimited book are more thorough, but offer only one recommendation per category in most subject areas.

O'Gorman includes electronic resources, which were not covered in the previous edition. Resources available in print and electronic formats are occasionally reviewed separately. Free resources are not easily distinguished from subscription-based databases in the entries. Readers would benefit from symbols identifying print, electronic or both, and noting free vs. subscription-based electronic resources. This volume is recommended for public and undergraduate libraries.—**Sally Bickley**

BIOGRAPHY

International

C, P, S

3. **Biography Reference Bank. http://www.hwwilson.com/databases/biobank.htm.** [Website]. Bronx, N.Y., H. W. Wilson. Price negotiated by site. Date reviewed: 2008.

Biography Reference Bank is H. W. Wilson's largest online biography database. It combines the biographical entries of *Wilson Biographies Plus Illustrated* with journal articles from *Biography Index* as well as profiles from over 100 H .W. Wilson biographical reference books. Another feature is the recent addition of 5,000 new biographies from the *American National Biography* dataset. Articles include biographical profiles, color photographs, book review excerpts, essays, speeches, text from interviews, and obituaries. There are over 500,000 people and 36,000 images included in this comprehensive database, and entries range from the ancient philosopher Socrates to present sports star LeBron James.

The wide breadth and depth of coverage makes this database useful across academic content areas and through multiple grade levels including middle school, high school, and beyond. *Biography Reference Bank* has two search options, basic and advanced, as well as several other search features intended to help refine and save search strategies. The basic search option is selected from a tab at the top of the homepage where users type their search term in the search box. The advanced search option, the default option, allows students to narrow or expand their searches. Users can limit their searches to those articles that include images, biographical profiles, or obituaries. The advanced search also enables the user to search the text of other articles. Users may refine their searches by name, profession, place of origin, gender, ethnicity, birth/death dates, and titles of works or keywords.

There are four options that enhance searching: Browse, Search Alerts, Search History, and My Wilson Web. The Browse category enables students to review a list of A-Z terms or to select and search for a variation of terms. The Search alerts option enables users to save a search strategy and receive up-to-date current articles that are added to the database. Once users have retrieved articles, they have several options for printing, e-mailing, or saving. The citation options are not only exceptionally flexible, but they are also great for instructing students in the use of differing citation styles as well as encouraging the use of bibliographic citing software. They have citing options of HTML, MLA, APA, Chicago/Turabian, or Chicago/Author, Date.

Biography Reference Bank is a wonderful resource for middle school and high school students, teachers, academic libraries, and public libraries. The many flexible options for searching, saving, and printing citations make this a highly useful instructional tool. Because of its comprehensive nature, it is much like one-stop shopping where students can get most of the information they need in one location. —**ARBA Staff Reviewer**

C, P, S

4. **Biography Resource Center. http://www.gale.cengage.com/BiographyRC/.** [Website]. Farmington Hills, Mich., Gale Group. Price negotiated by site. Date reviewed: 2008.

Gale's online reference database of biographical information includes more than 440,000 biographies on more than 340,000 prominent individuals from around the world in all disciplines. In addition to full-text magazine and newspaper articles, photographs, and a Recent Updates section it features a new interface and enhanced functionality.

This resource will be especially useful in high school and undergraduate libraries where students will be researching specific people for reports and term papers. The database is extremely useful to use and the information is easy to comprehend. This source, however, should be used as a beginning point and not as a sole point of research. School and college and university libraries will find it of great use to their patrons.—**Catherine Barr**

P, S

5. **Newsmakers, 2007 Cumulation: The People Behind Today's Headlines..** Laura Avery, ed. Farmington Hills, Mich., Gale Group, 2008. 674p. illus. index. $226.00. ISBN 13: 978-0-7876-8087-9.

Newsmakers provides short biographies with portraits and lists of additional sources for persons (and some musical groups) prominent in the media. Biographies of living persons are followed by obituaries of people featured in previous volumes. A rough categorization of the 2007 volume shows biographies from the realms of acting, writing, sports, U.S. government, fashion, science/medicine/technology, music, filmmaking, foreign government, photography, media, education, and others. A sample of the people featured in the 2007 edition include: Tiki Barber (professional football player), Wendy Bellissimo (home furnishings designer), Elaine Chao (U.S. Secretary of Labor), Steve Chen and Chad Hurley (creators of YouTube.com), Steve Fossett (aviator), and Anne Hathaway (actress). The 2005 volume includes cumulative nationality, occupation, subject, and names indexes. *Newsmakers* appears quarterly and in this annual cumulation.

Newsmakers is similar in coverage to *Current Biography* (CB; see ARBA 2008, entry 18), although the annual CB has more entries than *Newsmakers*. Unlike CB, *Newsmakers* has often quite lengthy bibliographies, discographies, and filmographies of a subject's work. The "Sources" section is often considerably larger than those in CB and often includes a list of online sources. Even where the "Sources" sections are of similar size, *Newsmakers* and CB often cite different sources. Any library with an interest in current figures should have both *Newsmakers* and CB.—**Frederic F. Burchsted**

C, P

6. **Nobel: A Century of Prize Winners.** Michael Worek, ed. Richmond Hill, Ont., Firefly Books, 2008. 320p. illus. index. $24.95pa. ISBN 1-55407-416-9. ISBN 13: 978-1-55407-416-7.

This reference work provides a concise history of the Nobel Prize as well as one-page short biographies of selected winners from the inception of the award in 1901 up to the present. The book focuses on winners from each of the six Nobel categories: physics, chemistry, medicine, literature, peace, and economics. These categories are color-coded in the bottom right of each page. The selected winners are grouped by decade, and those winners that do not have a biography are listed at the end of each decade's biographies. The book uses color not only to highlight winner's names, but also to illustrate the work on a single page that won the winner the award. For example, Wolfgang Pauli and his Pauli principle are explained, as is Alexander Fleming with a full-color page describing his discovery of penicillin. This volume will be a welcome edition in any public or academic library reference collection. [R: LJ, Jan 09, p. 130]—**Bradford Lee Eden**

United States

C, P

7.   **African American National Biography.** Henry Louis Gates, Jr. and Evelyn Brooks Higginbotham, eds. New York, Oxford University Press, 2008. 3v. index. $795.00/set. ISBN 13: 978-0-19-516019-2.

Containing over 4,100 biographies of African Americans, *African American National Biography* (AANB) will be a long-lasting, regularly used addition to the reference collections of almost all public and academic libraries. As the editors state, "AANB is a work that tells the story, for the first time, of the broadest swath of the black people who, together, created our collective history" (p. xxxv). Designed as a complement to *American National Biography* (see ARBA 2001, entry 17) and as an update to the *Dictionary of American Negro Biography* (Norton, 1982), the AANB increases dramatically the number of biographies of notable African Americans available to students and researchers. Biographies of African Americans included in *American National Biography* are reproduced in AANB, although photographs are often added and the bibliographies are usually abbreviated. In addition, many living individuals are included in the AANB, a significant difference from *American National Biography*. Thus, many prominent individuals, such as Colin Powell, Toni Morrison, Hank Aaron, Oprah Winfrey, and the editors themselves are included. Coverage of women has also been increased, accounting for 28 percent of the total. Over 1,000 photographs are included, giving the AANB an added dimension. The final volume includes useful indexes such as by subject area and realm of renown and by birthplace. A listing of African American prizewinners, medalists, members of congress, and judges concludes the work.

The individual biographies are well written, placing the individual's life within the context of the time and stressing the person's contributions to American and specifically to African American history. The print is easy to read and the photographs are clear and crisp. The only negatives encountered in the examination copy are bad printing on two pages in the indexes and a cracked binding, both of which should have been caught by the publisher's quality control. The AANB is a required purchase. [R: BL, 1 & 15 June 08, p. 132]—**Gregory A. Crawford**

C, P

8.   **Current Biography Illustrated. http://www.hwwilson/Databases/cbillus.htm.** [Website]. Bronx, N.Y., H. W. Wilson. Price negotiated by site. Date reviewed: 2008.

This is a database of more than 25,000 biographies and obituaries that have appeared in *Current Biography* since 1940, as well as updated biographies and articles not in the print edition. The profiles are written in an entertaining and informative style. The biography's remain unchanged, but more than 19,000 illustrations are included on those profiled. Each year nearly 450 new biographies are added. Users can search by name, profession, place of origin, birth or death date, ethnicity, gender, or popular works. A bibliography provides users with new resources for further study. Building on its solid reputation, *Current Biography Illustrated* is an essential purchase for reference collections at all levels.—**Catherine Barr**

DICTIONARIES AND ENCYCLOPEDIAS

S

9.   **Britannica Learning Zone. http://learningzone.eb.com/.** [Website] Chicago, Encyclopaedia Britannica. Price negotiated by site. Date reviewed: 2008.

Encyclopaedia Britannica has made their encyclopedia accessible for the preschool age and just in time for nationally expanding preschool education. The *Learning Zone* is available either as an add-on to other Encyclopaedia Britannica products or as a standalone. This product will fill a niche in library media resources for the youngest set through second grade. Since the audience is beginning readers, as well as beginning writers and keyboarders, an electronic encyclopedia with age-appropriate multimedia content is ideal for their learning. *Learning Zone* has no search box for keyword search, no hierarchical or browse search terms to click on, and no blocks of text on its homepage. In fact the homepage is where the entertainment begins to draw in preschool and primary-age learners without losing them to assumptions that the site might be "boring" or that it looks too much like "learning." Young students will love the rich, colorful design. The top two-thirds of the screen has a beautifully framed horizontal space resembling a widescreen television. The bottom third of the screen has four attractive activity icons labeled with one-word category names: Explore, Play, Read, and Draw. Along the bottom is a continuously scrolling set of thumbnail graphics showing additional activity choices.

To begin, Newton, the dog, greets student immediately with his spoken welcome. Explore is the first choice and has a globe icon. There are 30 video choices accessible in two ways. Moving the mouse over each flag on the map activates an instant pop-up thumbnail image and the location name, such as Amazon or Southwest. At the same time, the set of 30 thumbnail images, representing the videos, continuously scroll along the bottom of the screen. Users can click either place to start the videos. Each video is about two minutes in length and emphasize the people, tourism, or industry of the region. Others discuss animals in their natural habitat.

The Play option is a set of games with quizzes based on the content of the *Britannica Discovery Library* print set. The Read section has 1,000 words and 650 illustrations drawn from *Merriam-Webster's Primary Dictionary*. When the user clicks Read, the dictionary opens on the big screen to a random word and the definition is read aloud. Once finished, the orange arrows on either side of the word card begin to pulsate, indicating to the user the intuitive possibility of moving to the next word, or going back to the previous word. Meanwhile, alphabet letters are continuously scrolled at the bottom of the screen where users can click to learn about different words.

Draw is a simple online art program with 10 crayon colors, an eraser, and the ability to widen or narrow the width of the line. It should be noted that within Draw, the picture can be printed but the "Clear" feature does not have an "Undo" option and the file cannot be saved as a separate file, so once it is cleared, it is gone.

This product has two potential curricular connections. Students could be guided in their exploration to access specific categories or activities that support the curriculum. Second, students could use *Learning Zone* for open exploration either as a class or in a classroom learning center. The real curricular power in this resource may be found by using the Teacher Tools that allow teachers to do three things: a class can be created and students' names listed with assigned logins, teachers can click to show or hide content determined by their curricular goal, or teachers can use a tool to generate reports that show what content each student viewed within each activity.

The combination of the entertainment-style layout, kid-friendly navigation, and interactivity of the site make this product outstanding for young explorers in preschool and primary grades. Students from preschool to the primary age range will not only enjoy this product, but will be capable of navigating all areas independently. Teachers who want to guide or focus students on a specific geographic region or an animal study also have the capability for selectively including and guiding students to specific content.—**Karla Krueger**

C, S

10.   **Marshall Cavendish Digital. http://www.marshallcavendishdigital.com.** [Website]. Tarrytown, N.Y., Marshall Cavendish. Price negotiated by site. Date reviewed: 2009.

Marshall Cavendish Digital brings together 41 of the publisher's highly acclaimed titles into one fully searchable database. Most school and public libraries will be familiar with Marshall Cavendish's wide range of reference materials, many of which are award winning. The majority of the titles included fall under the topics of social studies, history, and science, with the remainder being health and literature related. Some of the most recently added titles include: *Gods, Goddesses, and Mythology*, *The Old West*, *World and Its Peoples: The Americas*, *Exploring Mammals*, *Habitats of the World*, *Wildlife and Plants*, and *Great Writers of the Modern Era*.

One nice aspect of this database is that libraries can customize the collection to meet their individual library's needs. They can order only the titles/products that they need, or they can order the entire digital collection. Another nice feature to this site is that articles have been cross-referenced and hyperlinked to related articles. In addition, users will have access to the *Merriam-Webster Online Dictionary and Thesaurus*, can bookmark and e-mail from the site, and there are photo galleries to each entry. The illustrations used are of high quality and include photographs, diagrams, maps, and drawings. Users can zoom into the illustrations as well. The site is easy to search using either an advanced or quick search, or users can browse by subject or book title. Each entry's page resembles the page layout in the book, with sidebars and illustrations interspersed.

This digital resource will be most useful in middle and high school libraries due to the fact that users can easily use it for reports and research. Due to the fact that libraries can select and build this digital resource to fit the needs of their specific library it will easily serve those libraries that want to build around their current collection of Marshall Cavendish titles as well as those who are looking to build a new, solely digital reference collection. This digital resource is highly recommended and is one that most school libraries and some larger public libraries should consider.—**Shannon Graff Hysell**

P, S

11.   **Spanish Reference Center. http://www.spanish.eb.com.** [Website]. Chicago, Encyclopaedia Britannica. Price negotiated by site. Date reviewed: 2008.

The *Spanish Reference Center* is actually two separate Spanish-language databases, the *Enciclopedia Juvenil* for children in grades K-6 and *PlanetaSaber*, a comprehensive encyclopedia for older children. Each site has its own home page, which allows school and public libraries to tailor the product to their patron's needs. *PlanetaSaber* includes more than 144,00 entries as well as images, maps, and tables. It is best suited for native Spanish speakers, bilingual students, and students of Spanish. *Enciclopedia Juvenil* is designed for elementary-aged students and provides 1,500 entries. Together these resources combine the ready-reference information from an encyclopedia, while also allowing students to hone their Spanish-language skills. Both databases come with a dictionary, atlas, and timelines. —**Shannon Graff Hysell**

S

12.   **World Book Discover. http://www.worldbookonline.com/.** [Website]. Chicago, World Book, 2008. Price negotiated by site. Date reviewed: 2009.

Available from World Book's growing list of resources available online, *World Book Discover* provides encyclopedic entries written at a lower level and with more pictures and illustrations as examples. It is intended for use by students reading below their grade level or ESL students just learning English. It provides many of the same entry topics as *The World Book Encyclopedia* (see ARBA 2009, entry 26) but in simpler terms. The entries were written and developed by a team of educators that specialize in the needs of these students. Unique to this encyclopedia are reading comprehension questions at the end of each entry to ensure students understand the key concepts discussed, a clean interface that will help avert distraction, and a text-to-speech feature that allows users to highlight a word and hear it out loud. This encyclopedia also features a section of life skills that will help students learn health, financial, and housing skills. For research purposes there are timelines, a citation builder, individual accounts where students can save their research results, and a video series that answer students' questions.

Users can search by keyword and advanced search, by broad topics (e.g., people, places, plants and animals), or by "most-viewed" articles. For each entry users will find on the left-hand side a key to the articles with a list of contents and the option to change the article to other languages (14 languages are offered).

This unique resource will be a much-used reference source in most school libraries. Younger users will like the simpler language and abundance of pictures, while students with learning disabilities and ESL students will benefit from the straightforward articles and extra features. This resource is highly recommended.—**Shannon Graff Hysell**

P, S

13. **World Book Discovery Encyclopedia.** Chicago, World Book, 2009. 13v. illus. maps. index. $389.00/set. ISBN 13: 978-0-7166-7415-3.

This is a general encyclopedia written expressly for primary or middle school children. The vocabulary range is carefully limited, but there is no hint of talking down to readers. Certainly a tool to encourage a child's curiosity and independence, it will also enhance alphabetic searching skills and the ability of students to make alphabetic lists of their own. The content of the articles is directed toward the interests of children and the writers/editors have done a good job of outlining events such as World War I, or identifying primary attributes of a subject. It is particularly interesting to note the fairness in treatment of controversial subjects.

Every entry is accompanied by one or more color illustrations that include photographs, drawings, charts, diagrams, and maps. The encyclopedia is an excellent source of illustrations for people of any age. The set will be easy for young people to navigate due to the many features the publisher has added: guide words at the top of each page, cross-references to related articles, section headings within the longer articles, pronunciation guides, and sidebars with special information geared toward kids. The average length of an article is two to three paragraphs, each consisting of two to three sentences, but there are longer articles of two to four pages. This encyclopedia, written for children to enjoy and beautifully illustrated, would be an excellent addition to any educational library for children, at home, at school, or at a public library.—**Shannon Graff Hysell**

DIRECTORIES

P

14. **Government Phone Book USA, 2008.** 16th ed. Detroit, Omnigraphics, 2008. 2519p. index. $285.00. ISBN 13: 978-0-7808-0696-2. ISSN 1091-9643.

The 16th edition of *Government Phone Book USA* is a comprehensive guide to federal, state, and local government offices in the United States. Based on data compiled by Carroll Publishing, it contains more than 256,000 listings and is thus the largest sectoral telephone and address book. While local telephone directories contain the same listing for local and state and some federal offices, this is the only book that comes close to a national telephone directory covering government agencies and departments at all levels. Because *Government Phone Book USA* does not contain names of officials (except in the case of Congress and state legislatures), the fact that the data are already two years old does not materially affect its accuracy. Moreover, both Carroll Publishing and Omnigraphics have regularly updated and revised it in the past.

Government Phone Book USA is divided into three sections—Federal, State, and City and County. All sections begin with quick reference listing and end with a key word index and both these features are among the most useful. Official abbreviations are included wherever necessary. Fax numbers and e-mail addresses are included in a few cases, although their absence in most cases is a serious drawback. The Federal section occupies close to one-third of the 2,516 pages. It includes the Executive Office of the President, cabinet departments, administrative agencies and organizations, Congress, Supreme Court and the federal judiciary, and federal regional offices. The state section is arranged alphabetically by state and within each state by department and elected officials. Likewise, the City and County section follows the same editorial organization.

Government Phone Book USA remains one of Omnigraphics' best reference titles and has become over the years a staple on information desks. This work is recommended for all public libraries.—**George Thomas Kurian**

C, P

15.   **State and Regional Associations of the United States 2008.** Bethesda, Md., Columbia Books, 2008. 1220p. index. $199.00pa. ISBN 13: 978-1-880873-57-1. ISSN 1044-324X.

State and Regional Associations of the United States 2008 is a directory of state and regional trade and business associations, professional societies, and labor organizations. It is well organized and easy to use and provides nine cross-referenced indexes.

The main index is arranged alphabetically by state and contains the full listing for all of the organizations within that state. Each entry provides the year the organization was founded, telephone and fax numbers, mailing address, e-mail and Website addresses, executive directory, total membership, total staff, annual budget, historical note, and annual meeting dates and location.

The subject index is an extremely useful cross-reference that groups associations of the same ilk. Another useful index is the alphabetically arranged acronym index. The remaining indexes provide access by budget, executive name, geographic area, certification acronym, meetings, and a new index by association trends. This is a solid reference tool for business, professional, and academic pursuits as well as general public interests.—**Shannon Graff Hysell**

GOVERNMENT PUBLICATIONS

P

16.   **Guide to U.S. Government Publications.** 2008 ed. Donna Batten, ed. Farmington Hills, Mich., Gale Group, 2008. 1758p. index. $499.00. ISBN 13: 978-0-7876-8422-8. ISSN 0092-3168.

After more than 40 years, the *Guide to U.S. Government Publications* is still a standard reference source for identifying publications produced by the various agencies of the U.S. federal government. This new edition contains over 38,500 entries listed by the Superintendent of Documents Classification System. Each entry provides the title, starting date, frequency, references to previous and subsequent title changes, item number, Dewey Decimal Classification number, Library of Congress Classification number, Library of Congress card number, and annotations when applicable. Cross-references to related documents are also given. A note is added to items that have been discontinued. For ease of access, the work includes an agency index, a title index, and a keyword in title index.

For document collections, this is a required purchase. Other libraries may find it very useful, but the price may be prohibitive. The major flaw of this work is the lack of Internet addresses for those items that are available freely online.—**Gregory A. Crawford**

HANDBOOKS AND YEARBOOKS

C, P

17.   **The Annual Register, 2008: World Events.** D. S. Lewis and Wendy Slater, eds. Bethesda, Md., ProQuest Journal Division, 2008. 682p. illus. index. $233.00. ISBN 13: 978-1-60030-072-1. ISSN 0266-6170.

In publication since 1758, *The Annual Register* provides a concise summary of major events during the year from all fields of human endeavor in a compact 682 pages. Over one-half of the book is devoted to country-level summaries of major political, economic, and social events. Even small countries receive serious treatment. These are followed by reviews of the activities of international organizations, such as the United Nations and the European Union. Topical chapters cover developments in the sciences, law, religion, the arts, and sports. The work concludes with texts of major documents, such as treaties and UN resolutions passed during the year, obituaries, and a day-by-day chronicle of principal events. The index is thorough, providing complete coverage of names mentioned in the text as well as major concepts. Chapters are contributed by specialists in each area, and the work as a whole has an authoritative and reliable feel. The summaries of cultural developments are slanted toward the United Kingdom and United States, with a few nods to our increasingly global culture, such as coverage of Bollywood in film. That said, any review of a year's worth of events in a single chapter will never please everyone, and the authors here make excellent choices and compromises. The writing is crisp and accurately reflects differences of opinion and debate, making for interesting reading. Comparable publications include the *Statesman's Yearbook* (2008 ed.; see ARBA 2008, entry 63), which combines recent political developments with general country surveys, and Facts on File, which provides a listing of specific news items with less editorial perspective.

The Annual Register provides a reliable and authoritative review that would be extremely valuable for any reference collection, and especially significant for history and political science. ProQuest has also developed a database version that includes all content from 1758 to the present. In print or online, this source would be useful to both academic and public libraries.—**Ryan Womack**

P, S

18. **Firefly's World of Facts.** 2d ed. By Russell Ash. Richmond Hill, Ont., Firefly Books, 2008. 320p. illus. maps. index. $29.95. ISBN 13: 978-1-55407-408-2.

Firefly's World of Facts is designed to be a "one-stop" resource for librarians and users wishing to find general information on a wide variety of topics. The work addresses a wide variety of subjects: natural world and life sciences, science and technology, countries of the world, the planet earth, sports, buildings and structures, language and literature, and arts and entertainment. The work is organized into chapters by these broad topics and then further into subtopics. For example, under the life sciences section there are specific topics on the animal kingdom, sea life, pet power, and environmental concerns. The authors interesting text and lists along with the publishers use of colorful photographs and sidebars makes the book one that users will want to browse long after finding the answer to their original question. In fact, the publisher has used more than 1,500 full-color photographs, maps, charts, and illustrations in this 320-page book.

Sure, this information is available elsewhere, and sure, librarians can probably pull the information for patrons from other sources, but this volume is so compact, colorful, concise, loaded with photographs, and so easy to read, that libraries really ought to have this work, especially at the relatively low price of $29.95. Librarians will not want to put it down either. It is a good read and just right for information hounds.—**Shannon Graff Hysell**

INDEXES

P

19. **Book Review Index: 2008 Cumulation.** Farmington Hills, Mich., Gale Group, 2008. 1050p. $427.00. ISBN 13: 978-0-7876-9513-2. ISSN 0524-0581.

This 2008 cumulative volume of *Book Review Index* (BRI) covers book reviews featured in reviewing sources in the year 2007. Over 80,000 titles are covered and more than 135,000 reviews are cited. Reviewing sources that are cited here include reviewing journals/annuals (e.g., *Choice, Library Journal, American Reference Books Annual*), national publications (e.g., *Newsweek, Time*), scholarly journals, and electronic reviewing publications (e.g., *Reference Reviews, H-Net, Humanities and Social Sciences Online*). Each of the 600 publications is listed in the beginning of the volumes with their abbreviation, frequency of publication (e.g., quarterly, biannual), ISSN, postal address, and Website (if available). Reviews are accessed by the author of the book being reviewed or, if the author is unknown, by the title index in the back of each volume. Each citation includes the author's name, book title, illustrator (if applicable), age code or type of book code, abbreviation of the reviewing periodical, volume number or date of issue, page the review appears on, and number of words the review contains. The editor has recently started indicating whether the review is small (1 to 50 words), medium (51-500 words), or large (more than 501 words) as this can be helpful for users of BRI.

The print of this volume is small and the abbreviations for the reviewing journals take some getting used to but, overall, this source is very user friendly. This is a highly recommended resource for academic and public libraries. School libraries (especially elementary and middle schools) may want to consider the *Children's Book Review Index* instead (see ARBA 2005, entry 1032). This title can be purchased in three volumes that come out periodically throughout the year or in this cumulative edition. This resource is available in diskette and online formats as well.—**Shannon Graff Hysell**

PERIODICALS AND SERIALS

P, S

20.   **Cobblestone Online. http://www.cobblestoneonline.net.** [Website]. Peterborough, N.H., Cobblestone. Price negotiated by site. Date reviewed: 2008.

This database, which is especially strong in the areas of history, geography, and social studies—includes the full text of articles from periodicals, including *Cobblestone, Faces, Calliope, Classical Calliope, Odyssey, AppleSeeds, Dig,* and *Footsteps.* Users can search by key work, time period, subject area, or theme. The database includes information in the following subject areas: American history, contemporary world cultures, geography, world history, physical science, astronomy, earth science, archaeology, African American history, California history, and general social studies and science topics. All articles can be printed directly from the site. It is a good addition for school and larger public libraries.—**Catherine Barr**

QUOTATION BOOKS

C, P

21.   **Great Quotations that Shaped the Western World.** Carl H. Middleton, comp. St. Paul, Minn., Paragon House, 2008. 784p. index. $29.95pa. ISBN 13: 978-1-55778-864-1.

By definition this idiosyncratic compilation is not a book of quotations at all, since approximately 40 percent of the 8,000 entries do not have them. It is rather a survey of the major works, events, and authors of the Occidental canon from ancient civilization to modern times, with quotations illustrating the topic as appropriate. Part 1, comprising 75 percent of the book, is divided into 13 sections comprising a chronological breakdown from the Greeks ("Greek Knowledge Explosion") to the computer age ("Turbo-Science in Hyper-Drive") , with some influential Indian and Chinese works sneaking in. The table of contents has been renamed "List of Topics." The entries in the chronological quotations are arranged by the year of the author's birth, a nice feature that collocates contemporaries. Unlike most quotation books, each entry is preceded by a skeletal biography highlighting the author's importance to western civilization. Unlike other quotation books, however, a great many are lacking sources and often the bibliographic detail in the sources does not contain the same degree of consistency.

The second part arranges quotations thematically, a hodgepodge arrangement consisting of short themes, investment wisdom, foreign phrases, and biblical and other religious quotations. Finding quotes in this section is virtually impossible unless the user stumbles on them, as the index indexes only part 1 of the book, and then only by author or event and (oddly) by occupation, but not by subject. Furthermore, several authors cited in the second part are also included in the first part, yet the user has no way of determining that; most of the quotes in the second section are exclusive to that part of the book. In short, the user is being shortchanged from utilizing the book's full potential.

However, this book may make for an attractive addition to the circulating collection for the students and educated layperson for whom it is intended, but for the reference shelf, stick with *Bartlett's Familiar Quotations* (Little Brown, 2002) and the *Oxford Dictionary of Quotations* (6th ed.; see ARBA 2005, entry 61).—**Lawrence Olszewski**

C, P, S

22.   **Little Oxford Dictionary of Quotations.** 4th ed. Susan Ratcliffe, ed. New York, Oxford University Press, 2008. 477p. index. $15.95. ISBN 13: 978-0-19-954330-4.

   This potpourri of quotations comes from a variety of famous people, using newer sources as well as traditional references. We read Gertrude Stein's quote, "Everybody gets so much information all day long that they lose common sense." This observation still rings true with today's Internet overload. Virgil's advice remains sound when he points out, "We can't do everything." In a more modern selection we find J. K. Rowling's character Dumbledorf say "It is our choices, Harry, that show what we truly are, far more than our abilities." This compact volume is ideal for browsing. One is sure to find an insight to make them chuckle or to save to sprinkle into their next networking conversation. As Dorothy L. Sayres remarked, "I always have a quotation for everything—it saves original thinking."—**Adrienne Antink**

C, P

23.   **Oxford Dictionary of Humorous Quotations.** 4th ed. Ned Sherrin, ed. New York, Oxford University Press, 2008. 536p. index. $45.00. ISBN 13: 978-0-19-923716-6.

   Quotation books serve three functions: to clarify the exact wording of a quote, to identify an author of a quote, or to suggest appropriate quotes for a subject. This compendium meets two of the three criteria very well; the only quibble is that, although it will certainly clarify the wording of a quote, most of the quotations included are not that widely known, especially to American audiences. This edition follows the same format as the earlier editions (see ARBA 2005, entry 62, for a review of the 3d edition). The dictionary is organized by over 200 very general themes in alphabetic order, then sub-arranged by author. The name of the author, adjacent to the quote in the margin, is followed by an often very detailed source note as one would expect from a reference working bearing the Oxford imprint. Since many of the quotes are culled from secondary sources, a substantial number, lacking other verification, end up being labeled as attributions. The consecutive numbering of the quotes is an extremely useful feature that greatly facilitates retrieval from the indexes. The editors managed to classify all possible quotes with only a couple hundred topics, some of which list only a handful of entries. Even with cross-references, however, such a subject breakdown may in fact be too broad to be consistently useful; the much more detailed keyword index, comprising almost one-fourth of the book, provides a more effective means of subject retrieval. An equally useful author index refers to the numbered entry under each topic, assuming one knows that said author is the true owner of the quote or that one is looking exclusively for quotes by that person. These represented authors comprise the usual band of suspects: Mark Twain, Dorothy Parker, Oscar Wilde, and others from all walks of professional life.

   As a fitting tribute to the late Ned Sherrin, who edited all previous editions and who expired shortly after completing the editing tasks for this one, this edition continues in the useful vein of providing sources of humor for speeches, papers, or to fit some other setting. The user should beware, however, since humor, like beauty, is in the eye of the beholder, many of the entries, lacking guffaw humor, are merely witty. The work is appropriate for school, public, and academic reference collections.—**Lawrence Olszewski**

Part II
SOCIAL SCIENCES

2 Social Sciences in General

GENERAL WORKS

Catalogs and Collections

C, S

24. **World Data Analyst Online. http://world.eb.com.** [Website]. Chicago, Encyclopaedia Britannica. Price negotiated by site. Date reviewed: 2008.

This site offers statistical data (e.g., demographics, economies) on countries around the world and also allows the user to make customized comparisons between countries and across time in the form of tables, graphs, and charts. Users can also see maps and access information on geographic features. —**Catherine Barr**

Dictionaries and Encyclopedias

C, P

25. **Encyclopedia of Social Problems.** Vincent N. Parrillo, ed. Thousand Oaks, Calif., Sage, 2008. 2v. index. $350.00/set; $435.00 (e-book). ISBN 13: 978-1-4129-4165-5; 978-1-4129-6393-0 (e-book0.

The *Encyclopedia of Social Problems* fulfills the growing need for an interdisciplinary approach to a wide array of issues facing our society. Each entry is presented in its context as a social problem, written by an expert in the field. These experts were carefully selected by editor and renowned sociologist Vincent N. Parrillo and a team of distinguished associate editors.

The outstanding efforts of the editorial team are evident in this work. The articles offer a general overview and are remarkably consistent in style, depth, and scholarly treatment. Each article ends with a short list of further readings pointing to seminal works on the topic and references to related entries in the encyclopedia. Although the encyclopedia itself is arranged alphabetically, a reader's guide organizes the entries under main headings, allowing the user to easily locate all the entries falling under broader concepts, such as "Social Theory" and "Education." Tables, graphs, and images are used only when appropriate, are easy to comprehend, and adequately enhance the presented material.

This thoughtful approach results in a work that is both broadly comprehensive and thoroughly interconnected. Topics are not covered with as much depth as in James Ciment's *Social Issues in America: An Encyclopedia* (see ARBA 2007 entry 52), but each topic's context as a social problem is unique to this work and is an especially valuable resource for students needing background reading for controversial social issues. Recommended for all undergraduate academic libraries, the wealth of information packed into only two volumes makes this work highly recommended for smaller institutions looking for the best value. [R: BL, 1 &15 Jan 09, p. 124]—**Corrine C. Syster**

C, S

26.   **SIRS Researcher. http://www.proquest.com/products_pq/descriptions/sirs_researcher.shtml.** [Website]. Ann Arbor, Mich., ProQuest. Price negotiated by site. Date reviewed: 2008.

Students can access age-appropriate, Lexile-ranked content on topics ranging from politics and economy to science and health, drawing on 1,600 sources such as *MacLean's*, *National Geographic*, *Newsweek*, and *Time*. Users can easily retrieve information by subject heading, topic browse, and keyword searches. The articles are indexed according to Library of Congress-derived subject headings to ensure the best results can be printed, saved, and e-mailed. New state and national standards search helps educators locate standards-aligned articles and other resources, which saves teachers time in the lesson planning process, and ensures that library resources are correlated directly to learning benchmarks. Special features include information on 100 of the most researched social issues, information on terrorism, maps of the world, suggested research topics, and top news stories of the day.—**Catherine Barr**

Handbooks and Yearbooks

S

27.   **Social Issues Firsthand Series.** San Diego, Calif., Greenhaven Press/Gale Group, 2008. 36v. index. $29.95.

Greenhaven Press has several series available to young adults that deal with social issues, including the Opposing Viewpoints series and the At Issues series. This is yet another look at current social issues; however, this series focuses on the human side of society's pressing problems. It presents a collection of personal narratives on the featured issue. For example, the authors of the chapters are participants, witnesses, victims, or involved professionals. The title on drunk driving features an account from a man who's son was killed by a drunk driver, an article by a man who injured a woman and killed her husband while driving drunk, and articles by those taking action against drunk drivers or organizing safe alternative programs for young people to keep them from drinking and driving (e.g., after prom parties). The titles feature lists of organizations to contact for further information as well as lists of resources (mainly books and periodicals) for further research. These books provide a unique perspective to today's social issues. A sample of titles in the series include: poverty, sexual predators, street and runaway teens, bullying, hate crimes, homosexuality, and interracial relationships.—**Shannon Graff Hysell**

3   Area Studies

GENERAL WORKS

P, S

28.   **CultureGrams.   http://www.proquestk12-com/productinfo/culturegrams.shtml.**   [Website]
Ann Arbor, Mich., ProQuest. Price negotiated by site. Date reviewed: 2008.

Explore customs, traditions, and daily life around the world with this rich database with many points of access. The World Edition is for junior high and high school students and the Kids, States, and Provinces Editions are for upper elementary students. Local experts from each country document the unique, intimate details of their country's customs, traditions, and daily life. Unlike many reference sources, each country in *CultureGrams* is given equal attention, with 25 areas of interest being covered for each. Biographies of famous people, a photo gallery, and recipe collections add interest.—**Catherine Barr**

S

29.   **Global Issues in Context. http://www.gale.com/Globalissues.** [Website]. Farmington Hills, Mich., Gale Group. Price negotiated by site. Date reviewed: 2008.

Global Issues in Context is designed to offer global perspectives on issues and topics that are of current interest to the people of the world today. It is designed to be non-U.S. centric so that it can approach worldwide issues from a variety of angles. The focus tends to be on broad issues such as war, terrorism, human rights, world trade, global warming, and poverty. It does, however, use specific examples in the news to show how things happening today affect our world (e.g., genocide in Dafur, changing weather patterns across the world). The site can be searched by keyword, browsing by topic and issue lists, or by clicking on the Google Maps Country Finder. The articles provide a lot of information and are quite thorough. They include a 500-word overview of the topic, links to full-text articles on the topic from international newspapers and magazines, newspaper articles and editorial articles from local papers to provide a regional perspective, multimedia features (e.g., videos, podcasts, interactive maps), links to primary sources, statistics presented in graph and chart format, links to international organizations (e.g., Amnesty International, World Health Organization), and updated material.

This product could easily be used in a high school or undergraduate library for basic research needs. The students will appreciate the cross-linked articles and the multimedia features. It would also be a welcome addition to larger public libraries for patrons researching countries for business needs and travel to foreign countries or patrons interested in current events.—**Shannon Graff Hysell**

UNITED STATES

General Works

C, P

30.   **Encyclopedia of Rural America: The Land and People.** Gary Goreham, ed. Millerton, N.Y., Grey House Publishing, 2008. 2v. illus. index. $250.00/set. ISBN 13: 978-1-59237-115-0.

Grey House publishing has updated the 1997 ABC-CLIO edition of the *Encyclopedia of Rural America: The Land and the People* (see ARBA 98, entry 98, for a review of the 1st edition). This *Encyclopedia* is a unique description of the varied "industries and roles played in the lives of rural people." Some 380 authorities (an addition of 121 contributors from the 1st edition) have penned articles, or updated their previous works, that have incorporated some new subjects and recent concerns. The 305 articles "address the most pressing topics of concern to rural America, from Addiction to Workers' Compensation."

This reference work touches on agriculture, sociology, environmental studies, politics, and education. Yet, some of the main advantages of rural America are the economic ones—Agriculture, Forestry, Fishing, Energy, Mining, Manufacturing, Tourism, and many others. These economic issues are only one aspect of rural America, but are very vital. Typical examples of entries in this two-volume work are: farms, electrification, insurance, public services, religion, drought, and organic farming.

Arranged alphabetically, each article is uniform in its concise definition of the term, followed by an abstract or overview. Some articles have extensive citations taken from data and research and some have fewer citations taken from the public domain. All articles end with a list of references that were cited in the narrative as well as "must read" items. The reference sections serve as a guide and place to start. A general index is provided to cross-reference terms or topics." Also included are graphs, tables, photographs, a timeline, a bibliography, and an index. Overall, this work is extremely useful. It is informative, easy to use, and well written. [R: LJ, Jan 09, pp. 122-125]—**Scott R. DiMarco**

AFRICA

General Works

Dictionaries and Encyclopedias

C, P, S

31.   **Civilizations of Africa.** Armonk, N.Y., M. E. Sharpe, 2008. 5v. illus. maps. index. $399.00/set. ISBN 13: 978-0-7656-8096-9.

This is one volume in a series on civilizations based on the area of the world. It uses an alphabetic, dictionary-type set of entries to write on major historical, current, and future facets of Africa. Examples of these are art and architecture, environmental issues, German colonies, and the Suez Canal. There is a topic finder with headings of civilizations and peoples, culture and language, general topics, notable figures, and periods and events to help guide the user. There are timelines, cross-references, and maps. The book provides special features on turning points, great lives, modern weapons, and "into the 21st century." Each entry provides further readings. Because of the vast and diverse nature of this continent and the time span covered, the entries are necessarily selective. They are brief relative to the material but nonetheless give the reader a basic introduction to the major and relevant aspects of Africa, past and present. It is accessible resource for information on Africa. There is also a glossary, a selected bibliography, and an index.—**J. E. Weaver**

ASIA

General Works

Bibliography

C

32. **Annotated Bibliography on the Mekong.** Charnvit Kasetsiri and Chris Baker, eds. Seattle, Wash., University of Washington Press, 2008. 318p. $40.00pa. ISBN 13: 978-974-8276-30-4.

This bibliography, edited by Kasetsiri and Baker, justifiably organizes published literature on a river, the Mekong, based upon the premise that it ties together and forms a region within Southeast Asia. The bibliography focuses on works that encompass topics beyond the boundaries of specific countries published since 1950. As such, the bibliography does not organize the entries by country. Instead, entries fall into the broad categories of culture, natural resources, economics, social issues, politics, and "other," which serve to divide the book into sections. Under each topical section, the editors further organized the entries by subtopics, such as agriculture, forestry, fisheries, and mineral exploration for the topic of natural resources. The section "Other" includes bibliographies, journals, multimedia, Websites, and organizations. Such an arrangement further emphasizes viewing the Mekong as a physical feature that transcends country boundaries and pulls the region together.

Most researchers should benefit from the editors' inclusion of the works' titles in the published languages. Readers will know at a glance if the cited works are in Cambodian, Chinese, English, French, Japanese, Lao, Thai, or Vietnamese instead of wading through transliterations into Roman script. The editors arranged the subtopics of bibliographies and leading journals in the "Other" section by language. A translation of the title into English follows languages that use their own non-Roman script. Each entry then includes a one- to three-sentence description of the work's scope and main points as applicable.

As a reference work, an index would improve this book for researchers looking for specific information. For example, entries in the culture section close with ethnic groups and subtopic categories as keywords but those do not appear in an index. Researchers searching for entries on a specific ethnic group may find the lack of an index less helpful and would need to skim through all of the entries in the culture section. With a reasonable price for a reference book, however, any library catering to patrons with research interests in Southeast Asia consider purchasing it.—**Kay Shelton**

C

33. **Sources of East Asian Tradition.** Theodore de Bary, ed. Irvington, N.Y., Columbia University Press, 2008. 2v. index. $99.50/vol.; $32.50pa./vol. ISBN 13: 978-0-231-14304-2; 978-0-231-14305-9pa.

Thomas de Bary, editor of *Sources of East Asian Tradition*, has provided selected translated sources from his popular books, entitled *Sources of Chinese Tradition*, *Sources of Korean Tradition*, and *Sources of Japanese Tradition*. There are two volumes, with volume 1 beginning in the year 2852 B.C.E., the "premodern era," and volume 2 continuing through the Post War Asia, the "modern era" of 1945 through 1998.

The reader learns about the Chinese, Japanese, and Korean traditions and culture with the panoramic view of their history from the earliest writings about the Asian social, intellectual, and religious cultures. The assorted Asian topics illustrated are the development of the earliest Chinese dynasties, courts, and the medieval eras; Confucius and the *Analects*; Buddhism; Daoism; Zen; Japanese aesthetics; the evolution of tea; education; and the politics of socialism in modern times. Each of the source materials is preceded with a historical background, explanations, and the translations of the various Asian languages and dialects. A comprehensive index and bibliography of research sources are provided at the end of each volume. This title is recommended for academic libraries for their history and Asian collections.—**Kay M. Stebbins**

Dictionaries and Encyclopedias

C, P

34.   Lyon, Peter. **Conflict Between India and Pakistan: An Encyclopedia.** Santa Barbara, Calif., ABC-CLIO, 2008. 277p. illus. index. $85.00. ISBN 13: 978-1-57607-712-2.

With works already in print on conflicts in Afghanistan, the former Yugoslavia, Korea, and Northern Ireland, the Roots of Modern Conflict series, as all the ABC-CLIO series, is an excellent collection of reference works for the general population. Few places on the globe have a greater potential for catastrophic explosion at any time than India and Pakistan. It can be argued that Kashmir may be the single most dangerous spot on earth with the possible exception of the Pakistan North West Frontier Province, better known as the tribal areas. Three wars, in 1948, 1965, and 1971; nuclear brinksmanship; and the degree of fundamentalist terrorism in both India and Pakistan show why this is such a crucial and unstable area of the world.

The series format, consisting of a preface that outlines the issues and importance, the alphabetically arranged encyclopedia entries, epilogue, detailed chronology, appendixes, glossary, index, and extensive bibliography, are all well done. Unlike many encyclopedias whose entries are supplied by a large number of contributors, all elements of this volume are completed by a single author who brings his impeccable credentials to the task. Peter Lyon is a reader emeritus in international relations and senior research fellow at the Institute of Commonwealth Studies at the University of London and he is a member of the U.S.-based Kashmir Study Group. The volume describes the people, institutions, events, locations, and issues in the troubled relations between these increasingly important countries.—**Joe P. Dunn**

P, S

35.   **World and Its Peoples: Eastern and Southern Asia.** Tarrytown, N.Y., Marshall Cavendish, 2008. 11v. illus. maps. index. $499.95/set. ISBN 13: 978-0-7614-7631-3.

World and Its Peoples: Eastern and Southern Asia is a timely reference work for one of the fastest growing and economically powerful regions of the world. This comprehensive encyclopedia set covers 22 sovereign countries and 5 territories: Taiwan, Hong Kong, Macau, Christmas Island, and the Cocos Islands. Each country is portrayed in a geographic and historical context, with over 1,000 richly colored photographs, illustrations, and 100 maps detailing geographical features, ethnic demographics, as well as historic and modern places.

Countries are divided regionally into 10 volumes: China and Mongolia; India and its Neighbors; Myanmar and Thailand, Cambodia, Laos, and Vietnam; Korea; Japan; Malaysia, Singapore, Brunei, and the Philippines; and Indonesia and East Timor. Each volume begins with a regional overview of the geography, climate, flora and fauna, followed by country-specific sections that overview its government, history, culture, daily life, and economy. Each country's section also includes basic facts, figures, and chronologies. The coverage on Tibet could have been more substantial, as there were only a few pages included within the volumes for China and Mongolia.

Each volume has its own index as well as a guide to further resources. Volume 11 contains a comprehensive index, selective bibliographies, a comparative statistical survey of the region, a glossary, and 6 thematic indexes (place-names index, ethnic and religious groups index, landscape and climate index, historical index, cultural and artistic index, and economic index). This encyclopedia set would be an asset for school and public library collections.—**Rebecca Blakeley**

China

P

36. **China: People, Places, Culture, History.** By Alison Bailey and others. New York, DK Publishing, 2007. 355p. illus. maps. index. $40.00. ISBN 13: 978-0-7566-3159-8.

China has about the same total land area as the United States but there the similarity ends. Whereas Americans think of their country in directional coordinates of North, South, East, or West, China is best described as having 3 "steps." This country starts in the West with the Tibetan-Qinhai Plateau, often called the "Roof of the World," marked by austere monasteries and the origins of China's major rivers; moves east to the semi-arid steppes, gorges, terraced rice paddies, and the bamboo forests that shelter the iconic pandas; and ends with the lowest step where we find tea plantations and major cities like Beijing and Shanghai and finally the rivers end, flowing into the North and South China Seas. In addition to the stunning photographs of China's diverse landscapes, users peek into the daily lives of a cross-section of the Chinese people. As just a few examples, we meet an eight-year-old school girl being raised by her grandparents in rural Shaanxi who rarely sees her parents because they work in a faraway city, a Buddhist monk, a craftsman of Uighur musical instruments, a Beijing cricket seller (an ideal pet in cramped living spaces), a young Musuo woman who in this matrilineal society close to the Himalayas and Mongolia is the head of her family, and a traditional Chinese herbalist. The work is also filled with interesting facts. For instance, did you know China has 1.75 million doctors trained in Western medicine but only 270,000 practitioners of traditional Chinese medicine? This photographic essay is a visual exploration of Chinese historic, philosophic, artistic, and religious traditions and proves yet again that a picture is worth a 1,000 words, especially when teaching us about a culture so different from our own.—**Adrienne Antink**

India

C, P

37. **The Encyclopedia of the Indian Diaspora.** Lal, Brij V., ed. Honolulu, University of Hawaii Press, 2006. 416p. illus. index. $60.00. ISBN 13: 978-0-8248-3146-2.

A team of 60 scholars from all over the world, under that able leadership of Professor Brij V. Lal, have produced an excellent encyclopedia of the Indians who have migrated to the many countries of Africa, Asia, Europe, North and South America, the Caribbean, Australia, New Zealand, and Oceania during the last two centuries. It is the first comprehensive account of the success and contributions of the Indian immigrants to many fields, including politics, medicine, literature, education, technology, science, business, arts, and sports. The encyclopedia is divided into eight parts under the headings of "The India Context," "The Age of Merchants," "The Age of Colonial Capital," "The Age of Globalization," "Indian Leadership and the Diaspora," "Life in the Diaspora," "Voices from the Diaspora," and "The Communities." All articles are signed and authoritative with many beautiful color and black-and-white photographs, maps, and charts. The encyclopedia also includes an extensive bibliography under the chapter headings and a glossary of Indian terms. It is certainly an excellent reference work and increases the awareness of the rich history of the Indian diaspora. It is a good addition to the literature and is highly recommended for all libraries interested in the history of India and Indians.—**Ravindra Nath Sharma**

EUROPE

General Works

C, P

38.   **Biographical Dictionary of Central and Eastern Europe in the Twentieth Century.** Wojciech Roszkowski and Jan Kofman, eds. Armonk, N.Y., M. E. Sharpe, 2008. 1195p. $289.00. ISBN 13: 978-0-7656-1027-0.

According to the editor, Wojciech Roszkowski, a professor at the Polish Academy of Sciences, the idea of this work occurred to him two decades ago. But due to professor Roszkowski's other commitments the actual compilation of this hefty tome only started after 2000 and took 5 years and the work of more than 40 contributors from the countries included in this biographical dictionary to accomplish the work. The editors refer to the countries covered in this work as the "Lands Between"—East and Central European countries which fell to the Communist rule after World War II, plus Belarus and Ukraine, but excluding East Germany. The entries, of which there are over 1,500, focus on politicians but also include names of prominent representatives of culture and clergy, who frequently had a great impact on political opinions of the people. While the work is organized in one single alphabetic arrangement by last name (for the reason that many persons included were active in more countries than one) an appendix at the end lists names arranged by the country. The entries themselves include names, dates of birth, death, place of birth, outline of a person's activities and career, and a short list of sources used. Altogether this is an excellent reference work that provides information in one single English-language work on persons influential in the East and Central European countries but who were frequently little known in the West and sometimes even in the neighboring countries.—**Leena Siegelbaum**

Ireland

C, S

39.   **Ireland and the Americas: Culture, Politics, and History.** James P. Byrne, Philip Coleman, and Jason King, eds. Santa Barbara, Calif., ABC-CLIO, 2008. 3v. illus. index. (Transatlantic Relations Series). $270.00. ISBN 13: 978-1-85109-614-5.

Part of the Transatlantic Relations Series, this three-volume work documents the long history of Irish-North American relations throughout the centuries. This particular work includes a series editor and editors' preface, a topic finder that assists the researcher in locating specific ideas and people by subject, chronologies of Ireland and the Americas, and introductory essays on Ireland and Canada, Ireland and Latin America, and Ireland and the United States of America, all before the chronological entries. The topic finder index is perhaps the most useful, subdividing the entries into various areas such as art and culture, education, race and ethnicity, places, and more. There are black-and-white illustrations and photographs throughout, and each entry includes a short bibliography of resources. This is a useful and well-researched reference work.—**Bradford Lee Eden**

United Kingdom

C, P

40.   Panton, Kenneth J., and Keith A. Cowlard. **Historical Dictionary of the Contemporary United Kingdom.** Lanham, Md., Scarecrow, 2008. 588p. (Historical Dictionaries of Europe, no.61). $125.00. ISBN 0-8108-5091-5. ISBN 13: 978-0-8108-5091-0.

This book covers the political and historical events in the United Kingdom from the years 1979-2007. The political climate changed greatly under the conservative leadership of Margaret Thatcher and then altered once again in 1997 when the New Labour party gained power with Tony Blair. Most of the entries in this dictionary address political and economic issues; and in an introductory volume for this audience, perhaps they should. But it also devotes a good amount of space to spheres like literature, cinema, architecture, and social movement, so that readers with interests beyond great men and big events will also find useful starting point. Skimming through the volume, the level of specificity seems best suited for college undergraduates, and any library that emphasizes the humanities could consider it money well spent.

Besides of its encyclopedic content the volume offers some useful reference tools. For those not familiar with the key acronyms and abbreviations relevant to UK associations and politics, there is a helpful list following the preface. Also included is a detailed chronology. The stylizing of the dictionary entry headings corresponds more to the hyperlink structure, specifically a wiki, of the Internet than the aesthetic needs of published texts, and this text might lend itself to publishing electronically. A concluding bibliography provides a good overview of materials in subgenres such as history, topical studies, travel and handbooks, and references.—**Amy Koehler**

LATIN AMERICA AND THE CARIBBEAN

General Works

C, P

41.　**Encyclopedia of Latin American History & Culture.** 2d ed. Jay Kinsbruner and Erick D. Langer, eds. Farmington Hills, Mich., Gale Group, 2008. 6v. illus. maps. index. $695.00/set. ISBN 13: 978-0-684-31270-5.

This new six-volume set of the *Encyclopedia of Latin American History & Culture* has been updated due to the explosion of Latin American information. The first edition of 1996 was 5 volumes (see ARBA 97, entry 349), whereas the 2d edition has added more than 560 new entries and expanded into 6 volumes. The information has been taken from Spanish and Portuguese sources, and the chronology covers from prehistoric history to 2008.

The entries are arranged alphabetically and provide the information and a bibliography of sources used to research the information with additional bibliographies that provide updated information. A new feature of the 2d edition is the "Mega Essays" written by subject specialists about major Latin American topics. They cover "Race and Ethnicity," "Migration and Migrations," "Democracy," "Hispanics in the United States," "Economic Development," Hemispheric Affairs," "Nationhood and the Imagination," and "Globalization." There are color maps of Latin American countries on the front and back covers of the volumes as well as color photo essays in each of the volumes. There is a thematic outline of the subjects covered with a separate "Table of Biographical Subjects by Profession."

The *Encyclopedia of Latin American History & Culture* is highly recommended for the reference collections of public and academic libraries as their basic Latin American resource.—**Kay M. Stebbins**

Costa Rica

C, P

42.　Mitchell, Meg Tyler, and Scott Pentzer. **Costa Rica: A Global Studies Handbook.** Santa Barbara, Calif., ABC-CLIO, 2008. 357p. illus. index. (Global Studies. Latin America & the Caribbean). $55.00. ISBN 13: 978-1-85109-992-4.

The authors, Meg Tyler Mitchell and Scott Pentzer, provide this handbook about one of the least written about countries, Costa Rica. *Costa Rica* is the latest books in the Global Studies: Latin American and the Caribbean series, whose focus is to acquaint the U.S. audience with its Latin American neighbors. This handbook provides current information about its history, geography, economics, politics, the people, and their culture. Black-and-white photographs and maps are interspersed throughout the chapters. The second half of this handbook is a reference section and lists various appendixes of helpful snippets of Costa Rican historical events, significant personalities, institutions, places, language, food, and etiquette. A chapter on Costa Rican organizations lists the LANIC Website as the most helpful one for Costa Rican information and for other Latin American countries. The Website for maps of Costa Rica is http://www.maptak.com. Current information can be found on the Costa Rican newspapers, *La Nacion* and *TicoTimes*, an English-language Web newspaper.

An annotated bibliography and an index are available for further research. This handbook is recommended for academic and public libraries for their country studies collection.—**Kay M. Stebbins**

Mexico

C, P, S

43.   **World and Its Peoples: Mexico and Central America.** Tarrytown, N.Y., Marshall Cavendish, 2009. 11v. illus. maps. index. $499.95/set. ISBN 13: 978-0-7614-7802-7.

This beautifully produced volume, one of a larger series entitled World and Its Peoples, which covers the nations, peoples, and societies of North, Central and South America and the islands of the Caribbean region, provides abundant information on Belize, Costa Rica, El Salvador, Guatemala, Honduras, Mexico, and Nicaragua. There is a general introduction that treats "Geography and Climate" and "History and Movement of Peoples." Here one finds information of general relevance to an understanding of what is basically Mesoamerica, including maps (relief, geology, rainfall, and habitat), discussions of major preconquest and colonial ethnic divisions; and principal linguistic divisions. All are profusely illustrated. The historical component is especially well done, compressing a great deal of sophisticated material into the space of a few pages. The individual country sections that follow are equally impressive. Each is divided into and introduction, "Government," "Modern History," "Cultural Expression," "Daily Life," and "Economy." In this way, the standardized format encourages explicit comparisons between countries, including between basic demographic and economic features. The data are generally of recent vintage and appear substantially reliable. There is a basic chronology for each country, generally extending from Before the Christian Era to the beginning of the Second Millennium. The summaries to each section are balanced and direct; for example, "[Honduras] for much of the nineteenth century [was] divided by disputes between liberal and conservative factions. In the twentieth century, the nation experienced periods of military rule and authoritarian governments, most recently from 1963 through 1982 . . . It is largely rural and poor . . . Honduras is a country with great inequalities in the distribution of wealth." All is succinctly put.

As one might wish, the treatment of Mexico, the dominant country in the region, is quite good. The historical and economic sections have been written by outstanding specialists, but nevertheless remain accessible to the high school and above audience for which the series is intended. This is clearly the product of skilled editing and careful attention to detail. Even experienced students will find something to interest them here. If the photographs that illustrate the country and its people are not especially surprising or unusual, they are nevertheless well chosen and beautifully reproduced. There is a certain conservatism in discussions of recent cultural developments in Mexico, and virtually no mention of the recent renaissance in Mexican films, some of which have attained international acclaim. There is also considerably more to the musical culture of the country than mariachi, but if the tourist's view occasionally intrudes, it does so infrequently for a work of this kind. There are basic suggestions for further research, including resources on the Internet. The index is adequate.—**Richard Salvucci**

MIDDLE EAST

General Works

Atlases

C

44.   Smith, Dan. **The State of the Middle East: An Atlas of Conflict and Resolution.** updated 2d ed. Berkeley, Calif., University of California Press, 2008. 148p. illus. maps. index. $19.95pa. ISBN 13: 978-0-520-25753-5.

  This is an overwhelming outline of most of the Middle East countries, published by a first-class university press. Its contents are selected and interpreted by the author for "the people who are not experts." However, there is too little to educate the non-experts and hardly anything new for the experts. The author deals with three topics: The Shaping of the Middle East, Arenas of Conflict, and State of the Nations. Each topic includes a number of subtopics, such as colonialism, sources of conflict, and statistics of ethnicity, language, religion, health, education, military spending, human rights, and water, but hardly any information about conflict resolution. A historical narrative, a chronology, and a set of color maps accompany each subtopic. There is a lot of repetition due to the interdependence of the countries that are in conflict. The narrative leaves the impression that colonialism ended in post-World War II, even though it continues to exist in cultural, economic, and political terms. The conflict between Palestine and Israel did not begin in the mid 1960s. It goes back to the late nineteenth century, and becomes violent since the late 1920s, according to my first-hand experience. Morocco, Tunisia, and Sudan are excluded, even though all three are involved in conflict, but Saudi Arabia is included, although it has no conflict. There is a bibliography, an index, and a colorful design, but no footnotes or room for thinking and analysis.—**Elias H. Tuma**

Dictionaries and Encyclopedias

C, S

45.   **Encyclopedia of the Arab-Israeli Conflict: A Political, Social, and Military History.** Spencer C. Tucker, ed. Santa Barbara, Calif., ABC-CLIO, 2008. 4v. illus. maps. index. $395.00/set. ISBN 13: 978-1-85109-841-5.

  This four-volume set is a carefully planned, analytical, and creative encyclopedia on Israeli-Arab relations, with particular emphasis on the history of Zionism and the Palestinian national entity. Featured too are items related to the decades-long belligerency between the State of Israel and its Arab neighbors. The volume contains more than 750 alphabetically organized entries with cross-references and further readings on a wide variety of military, people, political, religious, and social topics. Of particular value is volume 4, a collection of more than a 150 primary documents that pertain directly to the current Israel-Arab culture and territorial conflict, which, incidentally, is assessed with sincerity and candor in the introductory overview by retired four-star general Anthony Zinni. Proper and respectful visions of the other are the way to traverse the crooked path to the "bloodiest, longest running, and most intractable regional disputes in world history." Learning the complexity of the historical, religious, cultural, psychological, and political factors of the Palestinian national movement is imperative for Israelis. Similarly, Palestinians must come to realize that Jewish self-pride as expressed in peoplehood, religion, and the statehood of Israel are answers to Jewish identity, survival, and virulent anti-Semitism. This well informed and balanced reference work details how and why this conflict came to be and continues still today.—**Zev Garber**

Handbooks and Yearbooks

C

46.   Felton, John. **The Contemporary Middle East: A Documentary History.** Washington, D.C., CQ Press, 2008. 729p. index. $115.00. ISBN 13: 978-0-87289-488-4.

This is a good brief documentary history, enriched by the author's overview, chronology, bibliography, and index. In eight chapters it covers the founding of the contemporary Middle East, the Arab-Israeli conflict, Lebanon and Syria, Iran, Iraq and the Gulf, Afghanistan, and Turkey, roughly since 1914. There is a disproportionate emphasis on the Arab-Israeli conflict, occupying about one-half of the volume. The overviews and the "context for documents" are helpful, especially for readers with limited background. However, it is uncertain that Afghanistan and Turkey are part of the Middle East. The former has little to do with the region, and the latter has for almost a century aspired to belong to Europe. It would have been more useful and relevant to cover the North African Arab countries, both as member of the Arab League and as they relate to the Arab-Israeli relations. The selected documents are quite relevant, but they virtually ignore the role of the Palestinians prior to the 1960s. Even so, this volume is a good contribution to the history and understanding of the current Middle East.—**Elias H. Tuma**

Israel

C, P

47.   Reich, Bernard, and David H. Goldberg. **Historical Dictionary of Israel.** 2d ed. Lanham, Md., Scarecrow, 2008. 636p. (Historical Dictionaries of Asia, Oceania, and the Middle East, no.68). $150.00. ISBN 0-8108-5541-0. ISBN 13: 978-0-8108-5541-0.

The making and conduct of the State of Israel are rooted in the theory of Zionism (Jewish nationalism), which includes the country's political, cultural, religious, mystical, socialist, and synthetic make up. This book addresses the state of Israel as pinnacle or aberration of Zionism, politics of statehood, social problems, military issues, the diversified and competitive role of religion-tradition and secularism, contemporary values, and the realpolitik of a sovereign Jewish state in an Arab world. This is clear in Reich's and Goldberg's focused, fact-finding, and objective tome on the state of the third Jewish commonwealth from Palestinian *yishuv* (Jewish settlement) to independence in 1948 to 2008. Following an introductory overview, there are hundreds of cross-referenced entries on significant people, places, and events, as well as political institutions and parties, military battles, and sundry topics. Items on Palestinian nationalism (e.g., history, ideology, shakers, movers, movements) are fairly presented. Novel elements and often minutiae emerge from its pages. Also, a worthwhile chronology and detailed bibliography (57 pages) enhance the importance of this sourcebook. In sum, this is a one-stop, educated reference for learning about the trials, tribulations, and triumphs of Israel.—**Zev Garber**

4 Economics and Business

GENERAL WORKS

Dictionaries and Encyclopedias

C

48. **Encyclopedia of Business Information Sources.** 23d ed. Farmington Hills, Mich., Gale Group, 2008. 1300p. index. $530.00. ISBN 13: 978-1-4144-2022-6. ISSN 0071-0210.

In its 23d edition, the *Encyclopedia of Business Information Sources* is intended to be a convenient and accessible volume for business managers and information professionals to use to locate key sources for a variety of topics. It includes references to more than 35,000 citations grouped into over 1,100 specific topics. The wealth of topics covered by the volume makes it an interesting publication. Many specific types of industries are covered, including the cheese industry, the musical instrument industry, and the greeting card industry, along with professional groups, geographic regions, government and regulatory agencies, and current issues.

A typical entry in the *Encyclopedia* begins with cross-references to other subject entries in the volume. Sources for an entry are then divided into broad categories of types of works, with general works listed first, followed by almanacs and yearbooks, directories, financial ratios, handbooks and manuals, Internet databases, online databases, periodicals and newsletters, statistics sources, trade and professional associations, and other sources. Other categories in entries cover abstracts and indexes, bibliographies, CD-ROM databases, encyclopedias and dictionaries, price sources, research centers, and institutes. The titles and names of individual sources, such as publications or organizations, are then listed under each category in alphabetic order. The information included with these source listings can include contact information, prices, frequency of publication, and a brief annotation. Entries are easy to use and there is also a helpful user's guide at the front of the volume, along with an outline of the contents that alphabetically lists the topics with page numbers.

The final pages of the *Encyclopedia of Business Information Sources* provide an alphabetic listing of the sources cited in the volume. Sources are listed by publication or organization name, with contact information (including e-mail and Website addresses), price, updates, and a brief annotation. This section may be useful for collection development librarians selecting materials for public, academic, and special libraries that cover business, government, financial, and environmental issues. The *Encyclopedia of Business Information Sources* would be a good addition to reference collections in public, academic, and a wide variety of special libraries. It is comprehensive, well organized, attractively produced, and easy to use.—**Sara Anne Hook**

Directories

C, P

49. **National Directory of Corporate Public Affairs, Fall 2008.** Bethesda, Md., Columbia Books, 2008. 759p. index. $249.00pa. ISBN 13: 978-1-880873-58-8. ISSN 0749-9736.

The *National Directory of Corporate Public Affairs* covers the public affairs profession in the United States and identifies key people and about 1,800 companies with corporate affairs programs. The 2008 directory tracks major changes since the publication of the previous edition, including name changes, mergers and acquisitions, spin-offs, and pending mergers and acquisitions. Companies profiled for the first time are also listed. The "Companies Section" is an alphabetic directory and each entry provides a brief description of company's products and services, annual revenue, name of CEO, main headquarters, public affairs personnel, corporate foundation and giving programs, URL of company, and, where applicable, political action committees. If a company donated to a particular political candidate, the names and amounts contributed are listed. The "People Section" is an alphabetic list of leaders in the corporate public affairs profession; for each individual addresses, telephone numbers, and e-mail addresses are included. There is also a section describing the Public Affairs Council and their membership directory. The *National Directory of Corporate Public Affairs* fills a niche for researchers to find out what public affairs activities in which major companies participate. It also provides valuable contact information to get in touch with major players in public affairs. This book is recommended for research and academic library collections. It is valuable for students, research and business people, and political activists, among others.—**Lucy Heckman**

P

50. **National Directory of Woman-Owned Business Firms.** 14th ed. Bethesda, Md., Business Research Services; distr., Farmington Hills, Mich., Gale Group, 2008. 1288p. index. $295.00pa. ISBN 13: 978-0-933527-86-7.

This one-volume directory is arranged by alphabetic company listings and classified by principal North American Industry Classification System. The NAICS numbers are provided for the company's additional lines of business. The criteria for inclusion in this directory are that the company owner must be a woman and is an American resident or who has permanent residence in the United States, District of Columbia, Puerto Rico, Virgin Islands, American Samoa, or Guam.

Each entry provides the company name, mailing, location, and Internet addresses; owner's name; telephone number and fax number; NAICS numbers; incorporation data; and a description of the company's experience. The final section provides an alphabetic list of business firms organized geographically by state and city. This unique business directory is highly recommended for the business reference collections of public and academic libraries.—**Kay M. Stebbins**

C, P

51. **Small Business Sourcebook: The Entrepreneur's Resource.** 24th ed. Sonya D. Hill, ed. Farmington Hills, Mich., Gale Group, 2008. 2v. index. $550.00/set. ISBN 13: 978-1-4144-2175-9. ISSN 0883-3397.

The *Small Business Sourcebook* contains a listing of annotated resources designed to assist present and future small business owners and provides information sources for the United States and Canada. The directory contains four parts within two volumes: Specific Small Business Topics; General Small Business Topics; State Listings; and Federal Government Assistance.

Small businesses represent a wide array of services/products, among which are delicatessen/sandwich shops; disc jockey services; clothing stores; bicycle shops; ski shops; word processing services; travel agencies; and many others. An annotated listings of guides/resources for each business category are provided. SIC codes are provided for each business profiled and a listing of the SIC codes are provided.

Publishers of resources provided are also listed with names, addresses, e-mail addresses, and URLs. A glossary of terms is also presented.

Within each business category, there are annotated guides arranged by category. For instance, the Adult Day Care Center small business category has annotated resources arranged by categories: start-up information; associations and other organizations; reference works; statistical sources, trade periodicals, videocassettes/audiocassettes, franchises, and business opportunities; computerized databases; and libraries and research centers. This section provides a wide variety of material for researching how to start up and maintain a small business within a specific product/service category.

The General Small Business Topics section is an arrangement by specific topics, among which are Buying a Business; Sole Proprietorships; Selling a Business; Remediation; Public Relations; Ethics; Retailing; Government Regulations; and Insurance. Within each general category annotated resources are listed (i.e., the Business Correspondence category contains materials arranged by associations and other organizations, educational programs, reference works, consultants, trade periodicals, computer systems, software, and research centers).

A section on State Agencies is also provided. Within each state, annotated listings are presented arranged by topics: Small Business Development Center Lead Office, Small Business Development Centers, Small Business Assistance Programs, SCORE Offices, Better Business Bureaus, Chambers of Commerce, Minority Business Assistance Programs, Financing and Loan Programs, Procurement Assistance Programs, Incubators/Research and Technology Parks, Legislative Assistance, Publications, and Publishers. A directory section of federal government agencies and resources are also provided.

The *Small Business Sourcebook* contains a veritable treasure trove of information for those researching specific product/service categories and for issues involved in starting up a business. It should be purchased by larger public libraries and academic libraries supporting a business school curriculum. It should find use by all interested in small businesses, including students, beginners starting up a business, and owners of established businesses.—**Lucy Heckman**

Handbooks and Yearbooks

C, P

52. **Business Statistics of the United States, 2008: Patterns of Economic Change.** 13th ed. Cornelia J. Strawser, ed. Lanham, Md., Bernan Associates, 2008. 633p. index. $154.00. ISBN 13: 978-1-59888-182-0. ISSN 1086-8488.

The 13th edition of *Business Statistics of the United States: Patterns of Economic Change* continues to be a valuable, comprehensive source of U.S. economic data gathered from several federal government agencies. The economic and industry statistics comprising this work are largely drawn from the Bureau of Labor Statistics, the Bureau of Economic Analysis, the Board of Governors of the Federal Reserve, and the Census Bureau. These statistics are presented in approximately 3,500 economic time series, with coverage dating back to the 1950s and 1960s for the majority of these; however, 150 of these series date back to 1929.

In addition to the richness of the data, a considerable strength of this work is the explanatory information appearing throughout the volume. The preface describes the history, organization, and design of the work. The "Notes and Definitions" sections supplement each chapter by providing details about sources, explanations of concepts and terms, and information about data revisions and availability. And two lengthy articles help users contextualize the data: "Topics of Current Interest" and "Using the Data: The U.S. Economy in the New Century."

This review was written in December 2008 when the country was experiencing a significant financial crisis impacting many areas of the economy, including housing, industrial production, employment, credit, business investment, consumer spending, and the financial markets. *Business Statistics of the United States* will be an important resource for students, scholars, practitioners, and consumers to understand the historical implications of this recession. This reasonably priced reference work is recommended for public and academic libraries.—**Susan Shultz**

C, P

53.   Hetherington, Cynthia. **Business Background Investigations: Tools and Techniques for Solution Driven Due Diligence.** Tempe, Ariz., BRB, 2007. 288p. index. $21.95pa. ISBN 1-889150-49-5. ISBN 13: 978-1-889150-49-9.

   Business Background Investigations is written for the aspiring business investigator. The book description claims it will teach the reader how to become an accomplished researcher and the author's stated goal is to provide "the insight and education to perform quality business investigations." While these statements may be overly ambitious, the book does provide a good foundation for business research and will be useful for anyone wishing to hone their company research skills. The author holds the MLS and MSM degrees and appears to have a solid background in business research as an independent information broker and as a corporate investigator. Chapters cover topics such as research and analysis fundamentals, dissecting company information to define the research need, investigating corporate officers and employees, finding regulatory information, identifying assets and liens, researching industries, creating a client agreement, writing the report, and tracking costs for client billing. The book chapter on the basics of information gathering includes tips for effectively communicating with information seekers (one's clients) as well as human information sources. The notion of person as information source is a concept that is often omitted in business research guides and it is worth noting the inclusion. The author discusses research methods and shares stories of her experiences—what has, and has not, worked for her in practice—and recommends specific resources for specific information needs from open Web sources (e.g., blogs, trade and industry Websites, state and federal government Websites), and library resources (e.g., directories, periodicals, databases). Appendixes include sample client agreements for the business investigator, U.S. and international sources (most of these are freely accessible Websites, but there are also less helpful lists of information agencies with no contact information), and a recommended reading list. The many grammatical and typographical errors are distracting, still the content is useful for the novice business researcher and the cost is reasonable. *Business Background Investigations* is recommended for public libraries and for undergraduate business libraries.—**Polly D. Boruff-Jones**

C, P

54.   Martin, Jeanette S., and Lillian H. Chaney. **Global Business Etiquette: A Guide to International Communication and Customs.** Westport, Conn., Praeger/Greenwood Press, 2008. 178p. index. $19.95pa. ISBN 13: 978-0-313-35151-8.

   Global Business Etiquette is a practical guide for all those who travel to other parts of the world for overseas work or who attend conferences or other business-related trips abroad. Topics covered in this resource include: how to prepare for the trip and a country-by-country list of what is required for travel (e.g., passports, visas); what to brush up on in advance of the trip; how to greet people; dos and don'ts of socializing; gestures and other nonverbal communication; dining and tipping customs; dress and appearance; conversational customs and manners; cultural aspects; and oral and written communication customs. In each category the author examines country specific customs and etiquette for Canada, China, England, France, Germany, Italy, Japan, Mexico, Netherlands, South Korea, and Taiwan. The authors include such details as in Japan gum chewing is not permitted in public; those in the Netherlands stress the importance of maintaining eye contact; business attire in Mexico is conservative; and chopsticks are used for eating in Taiwan. The authors provide addresses, telephone numbers, and Website addresses of U.S. Embassy and tourism associations for each country. This source includes bibliographic references and index. This is a very helpful guide for travelers and should be purchased by both public and academic libraries.—**Lucy Heckman**

C, P

55.   **PSI Handbook of Business Security.** Timothy Coombs, ed. Westport, Conn., Praeger/Greenwood Press, 2008. 3v. index. $200.00/set. ISBN 0-275-99394-9. ISBN 13: 978-0-275-99394-8.

   This two-volume reference work published by Praeger Security International (PSI) consists of 67 chapters containing articles, case studies, and practical checklists to help all types of organizations and businesses prevent or manage crises. Editor Coombs and seven other contributing experts in the field emphasize best practices for public, private, nonprofit, and major institutional sectors in the United States and worldwide. They endeavor to demonstrate the range and complexity of business security.

The first volume deals with "Securing the Enterprise." It is divided into four sections: Information (Cyber) Protection, Terrorism as a Business Security and Safety Concern, General Safety Concerns, and Uncommon Business Security Concerns. Each chapter ends with a conclusion (summary), and some include notes and bibliographic information for further research. Topics cover cyber threats, portable device security, insider threats, data back-up, and Internet and e-mail policies. The terrorism section offers extensive coverage of ecoterrorism and agroterrism, and an entire chapter on food security. Every organization is strongly encouraged to make available a Food Security Plan, which outlines vulnerabilities on the one hand, and potential security measures on the other: For example, Vulnerability=Access to hazardous materials; and the Potential Security Measure=Regularly Inventoried Materials with Restricted Access.

Volume 2 deals with "Securing People and Processes." It is divided into three sections: Physical Protection, Security on a Global Scale, and Enhancing the Human Side of Security and Safety. Business security is much more than a security guard stationed at the front door, or a password needed to enter a computer system. It involves studying workplace protection and policies, managing organizational culture and change acceptance, and improving team effectiveness. Each chapter offers a background explanation of the issue at hand, examples of innovative or best practices, and insights into emerging trends. Readers will learn where organizations are most vulnerable, how to work with information technology, surveillance and other technology without crossing legal or ethical boundaries, and how to design, develop, and provide psychological as well as physical security. There is thorough, practical information about traveling abroad, with advice about what to do and not do in foreign hotels and other public places. A complete glossary begins on page 697, and the index begins on page 713. Short biographies of the contributors conclude the second volume.

The chapters are written in a clear, authoritative, straightforward style. This reference provides useful information for researchers, students, and laypersons. It is recommended for public, community college, corporate, and academic libraries.—**Laura J. Bender**

BUSINESS SERVICES AND INVESTMENT GUIDES

C, P

56. **Market Share Reporter: An Annual Compilation of Reported Market Share Data on Companies, Products, and Services.** Robert S. Lazich, ed. Farmington Hills, Mich., Gale Group, 2008. 2v. index. $588.00/set. ISBN 13: 978-1-4144-0871-2.

With this, the 19th edition, national and international material are now integrated into a 2-volume set, avoiding the need to consult both volumes to ascertain what market share material for a variety of commodities maybe available, either nationally or internationally. The user will find that the market share information on products have been gleaned primarily from the current trade journals, but newspapers and general purpose sources have also been included. Since these tables are not specifically indexed in the databases, the usefulness of this title is quickly evident. Information will be found on more than 6,200 companies; more than 2,700 brands; and more than 2,200 product, commodity, service, and facility categories. If the user is interested in a historical perspective they will need to review the earlier editions of this title since the current culmination focuses on topics of current interest to the business press. Material is arranged by SIC two-digit codes but an alphabetic table of topics is provided. Each entry includes a citation when the information was found. The set is well indexed and includes a place-name index; a company index; a brand index; a product, service, name, and issues index; and a source index. Additionally, the publisher has included a list of the SIC, NAICS, ISIC, and the Harmonized Code Coverage codes used in this edition.

This title continues to be a necessary purchase for libraries needing to know market share information. Major business libraries will want to acquire every edition; libraries that have a more casual interest could buy every other edition and use the source index as a place to consult in order to locate more recent information. Advertising agencies would find much of the information in this title useful too.—**Judith J. Field**

CONSUMER GUIDES

C, P

57. Russell, Cheryl. **A to Z Guide to American Consumers: Quick Links to Free Demographics.** Ithaca, N.Y., New Strategist, 2008. 232p. index. $59.95pa. ISBN 13: 978-1-933588-97-1.

The *A to Z Guide to American Consumers* collects links to mostly free and some paid sources for demographic information. Authored by demographer Cheryl Russell, the guide focuses on original and up-to-date resources of demographic data. The information is organized by topic, such as body mass index, cell phone demographics, quality of life, or sleep. Various studies are listed under each topic. Many topics have one source of demographic information, while more researched topics having multiple resources. Parents, for example, lists nine different resources, including reports on maternity leave, parental employment, and a survey on family life. Each report provides a link, publisher information, and a brief description of the survey. The guide also provides appendixes on major demographic surveys, contact information for organizations who conduct surveys, and a glossary of demographic terms. A keyword index to assist in finding topics is also included.

Although there are many government surveys that are cited, this guide provides links directly to the report that the user is trying to obtain. This can be an advantage over trying to find information by going directly to the U.S. Census Bureau Website or other government sites. Additionally, this resource provides an advantage over search engines in that it provides more exacting and credible resources. When comparing Web searches versus information in the guide, the guide was a much more efficient tool. The *A to Z Guide to American Consumers* is highly recommended for all libraries and may be a valuable addition to the ready-reference collection.—**Abe Korah**

FINANCE AND BANKING

Dictionaries and Encyclopedias

C, P

58. **A Dictionary of Finance and Banking.** 4th ed. New York, Oxford University Press, 2008. 471p. $18.95pa. ISBN 13: 978-0-19-922974-1.

Whether reading a financial newspaper or working on a research project, readers often come across unfamiliar financial and banking terms. *A Dictionary of Finance and Banking* posits itself as a resource to better understand industry jargon. It also provides an alternative to using search engines, which often lead to conflicting and imprecise meanings. The dictionary, in its 4th edition, provides 5,100 entries, including 200 new listings.

The dictionary presents information in a manner that is fairly easy to comprehend for readers who have a basic understanding of the finance and banking industries. Although there are some UK-specific terms, there is no overall bias toward any country or financial system. There are also entries for many acronyms, which will be a very useful tool for the reader. The dictionary has a "see web links" icon with some entries, such as "federal reserve system." The reader has the option of going to the book's Website (a rather cumbersome URL) for further information. Unfortunately, this added feature, rather than providing additional insight into the entry, only provides links to organizational Websites, which most readers can easily obtain. This feature would have been more valuable if it provided additional insight into entries or added new terms to the dictionary that were not previously published. The dictionary is recommended for academic, corporate, and public library reference collections.—**Abe Korah**

C, P

59. **Everyday Finance: Economics, Personal Money Management, and Entrepreneurship.** Farmington Hills, Mich., Gale Group, 2008. 2v. illus. index. $195.00/set. ISBN 13: 978-1-4144-1049-4.

Use of the term "finance" in the title of *Everyday Finance* may suggest a more limited approach to money and exchange than is actually found in the text. However, the subtitle, *Economics, Personal Money Management, and Entrepreneurship*, provides a broader insight into the scope of the book as well as introducing its three major sections. The sections contain some 300 interrelated topical articles, each composed of five parts: overview, historical background, further details and fuller discussion, recent trends, and sidebar boxes. The result is a readable and understandable introduction to economics and allied issues. The book is particularly helpful in relating theoretical and technical topics to everyday life, while maintaining sufficient rigor to convey essential importance and significance. Table of contents, readers' guide, glossary, bibliography, and an index, each covering the entire publication, are included in both volumes for easy reference. Graphics, brief biographies of key persons, and anecdotes enliven a subject that has been termed "the dismal science." Every effort has been made to encourage economic literacy, both on behalf of readers with limited background as well as those who seek a review or update.—**William C. Struning**

INDUSTRY AND MANUFACTURING

Directories

C, P

60. **American Wholesalers and Distributors Directory.** 17th ed. Farmington Hills, Mich., Gale Group, 2008. 1900p. index. $335.00. ISBN 13: 978-1-4144-0656-5. ISSN 1061-2114.

The wholesale and distributor market has continued to increase over the years. The 17th edition of this title provided details for 30,000 firms operating in the United States and Puerto Rico, about 1,000 more than the previous edition. To manage this vast number of firms 61 subject categories are used to group firms by principal product line. To assist the user, a product line category thesaurus precedes the listing of firms and helps the user to determine which category to consult. Each entry includes a numeric entry number, name, address, a list of principal products, number of employees, estimated sales figures, and e-mail addresses and URLs. In addition to the broad subject category groups, firms can be identified by consulting the SIC index where firms are listed by both primary and secondary SIC codes. The geographical index groups the firms by state and city and provides the entry number to consult for full information on a firm. The alphabetic index provides the name of the firm, address and telephone number, and the entry number for further information.

Information regarding wholesalers and distributors can be hard to locate since many of these firms operate in just one region and are privately owned. If this information is needed, than this is a useful acquisition.—**Judith J. Field**

C, P

61. **Plunkett's Automobile Industry Almanac.** 2009 ed. Houston, Tex., Plunkett Research, 2008. 575p. index. $299.95pa. ISBN 1-59392-122-5.

Plunkett's Automobile Industry Almanac provides an overview of the automobile industry and the key players. It is intended to be a general guide and offers many easy-to-use charts and tables. A CD-ROM version accompanies the volume.

The opening chapters describe the state of the industry and the major trends and technologies affecting the industry; provide statistics from trade associations and government sources; and offer the industry contacts such as government agencies, associations, publications, job-hunting resources, and various information sources related to the industry. Chapter 4 is the core of this publication, and includes ranking charts and leading companies' profiles. The companies were selected from all U.S. and many foreign automobile and related industry segments: manufacturers; dealerships; financial services; and many others, including makers of trucks and specialty vehicles. Alphabetic and geographic indexes are provided for chapter 4. Each company profile includes the following: company name; ranks; business activities; types of business; brands/divisions/affiliations; names and positions of top officers; address; telephone and fax numbers; Website address; key financials; salaries/benefits; number of apparent women officers; growth plans; and office locations. There are two additional indexes at the end of the publications: index of firms noted as hot spots for advancement for women/minorities, and index by subsidiaries, brand names, and selected affiliations. The glossary at the beginning the publication covers basic industry terminology.

This almanac seems especially useful for market research and job hunting. The inclusion criteria of chapter 4 are not clear and the information provided is not in depth, but the volume provides a good overview of the automobile industry. This work is recommended for business reference collections.—**Mihoko Hosoi**

C

62. **Plunkett's E-Commerce & Internet Business Almanac.** 2008 ed. Houston, Tex., Plunkett Research, 2008. 590p. index. $299.99pa. (w/CD-ROM). ISBN 1-59392-105-5.

Plunkett's E-Commerce & Internet Business Almanac is a comprehensive directory and guide to the industry. It is arranged within sections: "The E-Commerce and Internet Industry," an overview of trends (including statistics), a glossary, and a directory of industry contacts including government agencies and industry associations; and the "E-Commerce 400," the directory section of companies. The "E-Commerce and Internet Industry" overview section, other than its narrative of current trends as projections, includes statistics and results of surveys by agencies. The directory section, the "E-Commerce 400" provides information concerning "the largest, most successful, fastest growing firms in e-commerce and related industries in the world." Companies selected must meet the following criteria: U.S. based for profit corporations (also added were about 20 foreign-based companies); publicly held companies (although a number of privately held firms were added to "round-out certain niche sets of companies") ; prominence or a significant presence in the industry; and financial data regarding companies must have been available (either from company itself or other sources). Companies did not have to be exclusively in e-commerce and Internet fields. Each company listing provides: Website address; mailing address; telephone number; industry group code (based on NAIC code); type of business; officers; financials; growth plans/special features; locations; and brands/divisions/affiliates. In addition to the directory section, companies are indexed alphabetically by location, by industry group, and by firms with international affiliates. Additionally, there are two additional special indexes: one of firms noted as hot spots for advancement for women and minorities and the other of subsidiaries, brand names, and affiliations.

Plunkett's E-Commerce & Internet Business Almanac is an excellent and thorough source on the industry. It is especially recommended to academic library collections and larger public libraries.—**Lucy Heckman**

Handbooks and Yearbooks

C, P

63. **International Yearbook of Industrial Statistics 2008.** Northhampton, Mass., Edward Elgar, 2008. 708p. $325.00. ISBN 13: 978-1-84720-743-2.

The *International Yearbook of Industrial Statistics 2008* is the 14th edition of the United Nations Industrial Development Organization's annual publication that provides statistical indicators relating to the manufacturing sector of global industrial activity. Aggregate manufacturing together with subdivisions are identified by designations of the International Standard Industrial Classification (ISIC) system. The book consists of two major parts. The first is comprised of summary tables showing the distribution of and research trends in total world manufacturing as well as indicators of viable characteristic of major subdivisions. The second part presents tables for individual countries, cross-tabulated by types of manufacturing with number of enterprises, number of employees, aggregate wages and salaries, output, value added, gross fixed capital formation, and indexes of change over time. The book also includes explanatory notes and introduction, list of countries and areas included in selected groupings, description of ISIC classifications, and types of data utilized for individual countries. The *Yearbook* draws together a wide spectrum of disparate data, requiring occasional estimates to arrive at aggregate figures. Data are as current as available, as recent as 2006. The *Yearbook* enables comparisons among manufacturing segments and countries, as well as over recent time. It is an authoritative, comprehensive, and useful compilation of indicators relating to world manufacturing.—**William C. Struning**

INSURANCE

Directories

C, P

64. **Plunkett's Insurance Industry Almanac.** 2009 ed. Houston, Tex., Plunkett Research, 2009. 457p. index. $299.99pa. (w/CD-ROM). ISBN 1-59392-133-0.

Plunkett Research is a well-known publisher of industry directories and almanacs. This particular title covers the insurance industry, and is designed for the general reader to compare the top 300 American insurance companies. An overview of the insurance industry trends is provided and graphs and tables are provided for easy interpretation of the information.

The top 300 insurance companies included here are the largest and most successful companies from all areas of the insurance industry. The alphabetic listing of these top companies provides the industry group, types of business, brands, divisions, subsidiaries, plans for growth, current news, contact information for the officers, annual financials, salaries and benefits, and provides an assessment of the company's hiring and advancement of minorities and women. Indexes to the industry, sales, brand names, and the subsidiaries are provided. A CD-ROM accompanies the text for online access.

This work is recommended as a supplement to the Best's and Weiss' Insurance Ratings guides, due to its very general overview of the insurance industry.—**Kay M. Stebbins**

INTERNATIONAL BUSINESS

General Works

Handbooks and Yearbooks

C, P

65.   Ervin, Justin, and Zachary A. Smith. **Globalization.** Santa Barbara, Calif., ABC-CLIO, 2008. 293p. index. (Contemporary World Issues). $55.00. ISBN 13: 978-1-59884-073-5.

This book is an introduction to the concept of globalization and offers different world views on its benefits and problems. The main push for globalization is the rapid development of technology that has "shrunk" the world to a smaller scale than has ever been possible before. It has created problems that are impossible for national governments by themselves to address. Chapter 1 introduces the concept of globalization and offers different definitions of this word that has caused confusion people interested in the concept. It also addresses the history of globalization. Chapter 2 focuses on the controversies and problems associated with this concept. Chapter 3 concentrates on the role the United States plays in this process. Chapter 4 looks at the chronological events in the history of globalization. Chapter 5 looks at individuals who play a central role in the study of globalization. Chapter 6 provides facts and data presented in tables related to the importance and study of globalization. Chapter 7 provides a directory of organizations directly involved. Chapter 8 offers the annotated list of print and nonprint resources to help the reader further understand this concept. Following this is a glossary with a short definition of various concepts. After this is an index to help locate things of interest.

The book should be of interest to anyone looking for international activities and how globalization is causing problems and also solving some of our major concerns. The book binding and font size is adequate and paper is average. This book should be in most libraries that are looking at the world's problems and looking at potential solutions. It would be useful in university libraries and also large libraries where international functions are of interest.—**Herbert W. Ockerman**

LABOR

General Works

Dictionaries and Encyclopedias

C, P

66.   **The Way We Work: An Encyclopedia of Business Culture.** Regina Fazio Maruca, ed. Westport, Conn., Greenwood Press, 2008. 2v. index. $175.00/set. ISBN 13: 978-0-313-33886-1.

In the *Encyclopedia*'s preface, "business culture" is described as that intangible element that can contribute to the success or failure of an organization. *The Way We Work: An Encyclopedia of Business Culture* focuses on trends, definitions, and facts influencing today's "business office culture." Selection of the over 100 entries covered in the *Encyclopedia* was made by a team of people ranging from journalists and academic researchers to business executives, employees, and corporate coaches in various companies. An entry's inclusion was based on its role in the big picture of business culture as a "culture-shaper." The entries are alphabetically arranged in two volumes covering A-L and M-Z. Also included are a selective group of personal narratives titled "Why I Do This," that offer insights into what selective careers (e.g., commercial airline pilot, museum interpreter) might entail on a day-to-day basis. A listing of entries by subject categories ranging from Associations and Organizations to Women, along with an appendix, a bibliography of books and other materials on business culture, and a detailed index are also included. Coverage of each topic varies in length from a page to several pages; each entry ends with a "Further Reading." Some articles are reprinted from *Knowledge@Wharton*, the Wharton School's online business journal.

While the preface explains the criteria for selection, the reader may be surprised by which entries are and which are not covered in the *Encyclopedia*. For example, pop (business) culture entries include *Dilbert*, *The Apprentice*, and *The Art of War*, but *The Office*, a popular television comedy, was not selected for inclusion.

Entries in *The Way We Work: An Encyclopedia of Business Culture* do provide an interesting snapshot of today's American office culture and topics ranging from E-mail to Killer App and Napster show how technology has pervaded our business culture. Although little has been published in this area since the *Blackwell Encyclopedic Dictionary of Organizational Behavior* (1995), for those libraries operating with reduced book budgets this is not a necessary purchase.—**Colleen Seale**

Directories

C, P

67.   **Job Hunter's Sourcebook: Where to Find Employment Leads and Other Job Search Resources.** 8th ed. Bohdan Romaniuk, ed. Farmington Hills, Mich., Gale Group, 2008. 1389p. index. $187.00. ISBN 13: 978-1-4144-0784-5. ISSN 1053-1874.

This work is a comprehensive guide to sources of information on employment leads and other job search resources. Its stated uses are: to identify sources of job listings, to inform readers how to use career resources effectively, and to enhance career resources collections. The 1st edition of this work won the annual "outstanding reference award" from both *Library Journal* and the New York Public Library.

The 8th edition of this work has been completely updated and six new profiles have been added. The book is divided into two parts. Part 1 lists more than 200 specific professional and vocational occupations and sources of information about each job title. These jobs have been identified from the *Occupational Outlook Handbook* (2008-2009 ed.; see ARBA 2009, entry 210) and the Bureau of Labor Statistics listings for jobs with high growth potential. Part 2 provides information on more than 30 topics of interest to job hunters. Profiles in part 1 guide users to sources that provide want ads, placement and referral services, employer directories and networking lists, handbooks and manuals, employment agencies and search firms, online job sources and services, trade shows, and other sources for job listings (e.g., internships, job hotlines). Sources covered in part 2 include reference works, newspapers, magazines and journals, online and database listings, software, and audiovisual aids. These sources cover such topics as interviewing, disabilities issues, electronic job searches, working at home, international job opportunities, freelance and contract work, temporary workers, and résumé writing. A brief user guide will aid the user in understanding the purpose for this work and how to use it. This is followed by an index of profiled professions. Parts 1 and 2 are followed by an alphabetic index of all sources in both parts.

This work is comprehensive, easy to use, current, and informative. The listings are useful in targeting jobs in growing fields. This work will be a useful addition to any career collection and is recommended. —**Joanna M. Burkhardt**

Handbooks and Yearbooks

C, P

68.   **Handbook of U.S. Labor Statistics, 2008: Employment, Earnings, Prices, Productivity, and Other Labor Data.** 11th ed. Eva E. Jacobs, ed. Lanham, Md., Bernan Associates, 2008. 489p. index. $154.00. ISBN 13: 978-1-59888-180-6. ISSN 1526-2553.

The latest edition of the *Handbook of U.S. Labor Statistics*, a reference staple, contains updated information and new features while retaining content from earlier editions. It includes 13 chapters each of which is preceded by a "highlights" page providing information (along with at least one graph) on recent trends for that sector. For example, a highlight from chapter 12, "American Time Use Survey' is that "Women spent more time caring for children, regardless of employment status or age of the children." Notes and definitions also precede each chapter with information in some cases on coverage, concepts and definitions, procedures, comparability, methodology, and sources of additional information.

The standard prefatory material includes contents followed by a list of tables for each chapter (approximately 200 are provided), a list of figures, page about the editors, a preface, and three new articles ("The American Community Survey"; 'Summary of Articles from the 2006 and 2007 Editions of the Monthly Labor Review'; and "Guidance on Differences in Employment and Unemployment Estimates from Different Sources") . A detailed index follows the 13 chapters of data.

New information added to this edition includes: labor force and employment projections to 2016; the conversion of more data series to the North American Industry Classification System (NAICS); experimental indexes on hours and earnings of private sector employees (that account for some 20 percent of nonfarm employment); and in chapter 2, "Employment, Hours and Earnings,' a new table providing private sector job gains and losses by state and selected territory. Also, noting the importance of historical trends in various data series, some tables included in this edition provide statistics back to 1913. While labor and employment data is readily available online from sources such as the Bureau of Labor Statistics, this publication remains a highly useful compilation of recent and historical statistics and presents a complete overview of the U.S. labor market in a single volume. This edition is recommended for all business reference collections.—**Colleen Seale**

Career Guides

Dictionaries and Encyclopedias

C, S

69. **Ferguson's Career Guidance Center. http://www.factsonfile.infobasepublishing.com/.** [Website]. New York, Facts on File. Price negotiated by site. Date reviewed: 2008.

Recently revamped in the spring of 2007, *Ferguson's Career Guidance Center* provides users with in-depth information on more than 3,300 jobs and industries organized by 16 career clusters that were created by the Department of Education. The Website has been given a new, more modern looking interface that gives users easy access to the information within. Along with the Jobs section mentioned above users will also find a new Skills section as well as a new Resources section. The Skills section provides users with information on interviewing, writing résumés and cover letters, and demonstrating professional behavior. Sample résumés and cover letters are provided as well. The Resources section is organized into categories (e.g., women, minorities), which provide specialized information on fellowships, organizations, internships, scholarships, and awards. Articles discussing career assessment tests can be found in this section as well. The content for the site comes mainly from Ferguson's extensive collection of print directories and handbooks on various careers.—**Shannon Graff Hysell**

Handbooks and Yearbooks

C

70. **Careers in International Affairs.** 8th ed. Maria Pinto Carland and Candace Faber, eds. Washington, D.C., Georgetown University Press, 2008. 420p. index. $24.95pa. ISBN 13: 978-1-58901-199-1.

First published in 1967 and now in its 8th edition, this guide is designed to help those who are interested in a career in international affairs. It is published in conjunction with the Georgetown University's School of Foreign Service and is edited by Carland, a counselor to the School, and Faber, a former journal editor and current political officer with the United States Foreign Service. The guide is divided into two sections. The first contains five chapters on strategies for preparing for a career in international affairs and hunting for employment. It begins with an introduction to the international affairs job market, describing job qualifications (such as education, experience, and internships), and factors related to the job search. The following three chapters focus on interviewing, networking, and mentoring. The last chapter, new to this edition, covers choosing a graduate school with useful advice on what factors to seek in graduate schools, what professional opportunities schools can offer, the importance of a personal and social life, and tips on what factors may impact the final choice. The second section has nine chapters focusing on types of employers: United States government, international organizations, banking, business, business-related organizations, consulting, international development and relief, nonprofit and educational organizations, and university research institutes. The employer chapters are written by former graduates of the School of Foreign Service. Chapters begin with an overview on the type of employer, what is expected in positions, career paths, professional development, how jobs are filled, and more. The bulk of each chapter is the one- to two-page organizational profiles that describe its activities and scope, desired skills and backgrounds of job applicants, and contact information. If internship opportunities are available, they are also detailed. Many chapters also include brief, two- to three-page commentary titled "Getting Started in . . ." that describe the personal experiences of recent graduates who entered the field. The list of profiled organizations in each chapter is selective with the exception of the United States and international organization chapters that are meant to be comprehensive, and the chapter on international development and relief that excludes organizational profiles given the vast range of employment possibilities. An index is provided.

Useful information can also be found in more general guides to seeking international jobs, such as *International Job Finder: Where the Jobs are Worldwide* (see ARBA 2003, entry 234), *International Jobs: Where They Are, How to Get Them* (see ARBA 2004, entry 209), and *Jobs and Careers Abroad* (see ARBA 2006, entry 232).—**Chad Kahl**

P, S

71.   Echaore-McDavid, Susan, and Richard A. McDavid. **Career Opportunities in Forensic Science.** New York, Facts on File, 2008. 318p. index. $49.50. ISBN 13: 978-0-8160-6156-3.

The American Academy of Forensic Sciences (AAFS) defines forensic science as "any science used for the purposes of law" (p. ix). This work describes 84 jobs relating to the field. The volume begins with a definition and short history of forensic science, its development in the nineteenth and twentieth century, and the range of jobs that fall under its umbrella today. General information about who employs forensic scientists and the employment outlook for the field are included. A note to high school students as to how best to prepare themselves for a job in the field indicates the target audience for this book. Acknowledgements are followed by a brief section on how to use the book.

Fourteen sections divide jobs into major categories. There are 2-10 job profiles in each category, with each profile being 2-3 pages long. Profiles begin with a job summary. This section includes brief information on: job duties, salary range, job outlook, advancement prospects, general educational requirements and special skills required, personality traits common to job holders, and career path. A second profile section expands on all parts of the summary. It also includes information about unions and associations for workers in the field and tips for finding and preparing for the job (e.g., background skills, certifications required, websites to visit for additional information). Four appendixes include Web resources for educational programs in forensic science, professional certification programs, contact information for unions and associations, and Web resources for more information about specific jobs and job categories. A brief glossary, bibliography, and index complete the work.

The authors have co-authored one other job-search book. Susan Echaore-McDavid has a lot of experience in publishing as well as working with young people. This book is geared for high school and college students looking for career information, although it could be useful to others. The descriptions are complete though brief and the language is not difficult. Specialized terms are defined in the glossary. This title is recommended for public, high school, and career collections.—**Joanna M. Burkhardt**

S

72. **Great Careers with a High School Diploma Series.** New York, Infobase Publishing, 2008. 8v. index. $32.95/vol.

This new series from Ferguson Publishing is designed for high school students needing career advice who do not plan to attend college soon after graduation. Each of the jobs profiled requires only a high school diploma or GED. Each volume within the series explores one of the U.S. Department of labor's career clusters; within each volume several career options under that topic are examined. Included within each book are insider tips on starting a career in the field and guidance for career success. The volumes also discuss certification that may be required as well as the potential for self-employment. For each job the following are included: an overview, a short quiz to find out if the job is for you, specific tasks involved, money, future trends, where you will work, a typical work day, training needed, how to conduct a job search, secrets for success, other jobs to consider, and a few Websites to check out. To date there are eight volumes in the series: Communications, the Arts, and Computers; Health Care, Medicine, and Science; Personal Care Services, Fitness, and Education; Food, Agriculture, and Natural Resources; Hospitality, Human Services, and Tourism; Sales, Marketing, Business, and Finance; Manufacturing and Transportation; and Construction and Trade.

The layout and conversational tone of the book will appeal to high school students. It will allow students allow with their school counselors to explore a wide range of option within their field of interest. For those libraries interested in acquiring this set it will be expensive to invest in the entire series; however, school libraries can selectively chose the titles that are most appropriate for their geographical area that will be most useful for their student population.—**Shannon Graff Hysell**

P, S

73. **150 Best Jobs Through Military Training.** Edited by the Editors of JIST and Laurence Shatkin. Indianapolis, Ind., JIST Works, 2008. 402p. index. $19.95pa. ISBN 13: 978-1-59357-462-8.

The 150 Best Jobs Through Military Training is the latest in the JIST Best Jobs series. It was written to illustrate how the military provides the best training for many civilian jobs. The information is garnered from many familiar career sources, such as the Department of Labor's O*NET database and the U.S. Bureau of Labor Statistics, the Census Bureau, and the U.S. Department of Defense's Website (http://www.todaysmilitary.com).

There are 75 military jobs described that can provide work and job skills for over 150 civilian jobs. Each entry provides a job title, definition or summary of the job, whether it is an officer's or an enlisted military job, personality type, military services that offer the job, training provided, helpful attributes, work environment, opportunities in the military, and civilian occupations for which it provides training. All of this information is available on various government Websites, but the editors of JIST and Shatkin have gathered this valuable information and published in one volume. This is a valuable source for the job-seeker, in the military or out of the military, and I would recommend this book for the armed forces and public libraries to have available for the young job-seeker.—**Kay M. Stebbins**

C, P, S

74. **150 Great Tech Prep Careers.** 2d ed. New York, Ferguson/Infobase Publishing, 2009. 561p. index. $85.00. ISBN 13: 978-0-8160-7733-5.

This work provides job profiles in more than 150 jobs in tech prep careers. The publisher defines "tech prep" as a rewarding career choice that does not require a four-year degree and that uses on-the-job training or apprenticeships, along with a certificate or associate's degree. While the publisher states that this work will be most useful to high school students thinking about career options, it will also be useful to anyone considering work in one of these fast-growing fields field. Some of the jobs appearing here are: automobile collision repair, cosmeticians, firefighters, legal secretaries, plumbers, medical assistants, and graphic designers.

  The first section of each job profile includes an overview of the job, the details of the job, requirements (including high school, postsecondary training, certification, or other requirements), exploring career options, employers, how to start out, advancement, salary, work environment, and where to go for more information.

  Information in the 2d edition has been updated using the latest salary, outlook, and other job information from the U.S. Department of Labor and professional organizations. Bibliographies have been updated as has contact information for professional organizations. New sidebars and several new job profiles have also been added.

  This work will be useful for those seeking to find in-depth information about what career options are available for those not wanting to pursue a four-year degree but still wanting a rewarding career. It will be helpful to any career-related collection in guidance offices and public libraries and is recommended.
—**Joanna M. Burkhardt**

C, P, S

75. **The Top 100: The Fastest Growing Careers for the 21st Century.** 4th ed. New York, Ferguson/Infobase Publishing, 2009. 394p. index. $75.00. ISBN 13: 978-0-8160-7729-8.

  This edition reflects the changes that have occurred in the marketplace since the 3d edition was published in 2001. The profile for each career discussed includes recommended school subjects, personal skills, minimum education level needed, certification or licensing requirements (if any), and the expected work conditions. There is also information included on major employers of workers in the field, how to start out, advancement possibilities, earnings expectations and a section that discusses the long-term employment outlook for workers in the field. The user will also find a list of periodicals to consult, Websites to visit, potential of summer jobs, volunteer opportunities and associations, and government agencies or unions that can provided additional information. The profiles have a uniform layout and are easy to understand. The index assists the user to the correct profile by including alternative job titles and referring the user to the correct profile. This would be a good addition to career collections in high schools, public libraries, and job training centers.—**Judith J. Field**

MANAGEMENT

P

76. **The Safe Hiring Audit: The Employer's Guide to Implementing a Safe Hiring Program.** By Lester S. Rosen, with Michael Sankey. Tempe, Ariz., Facts on Demand Press, 2008. 288p. index. $17.95pa. ISBN 13: 978-1-889150-51-2.

  Safe hiring is critical to every employer since negligent hiring can lead to a lawsuit for negligent hiring, loss of business, and damage to a company's professional reputation. The author stresses just how important safe hiring as follows: "It's a sobering thought, but every time an employer hires anyone, there is the possibility that new hire can put him out of business. This person has access to your assets, your clients, your co-workers, your money, and even your very existence," Lester Rosen, an attorney at law and President of Employee Screening Resources, consultant, writer, and presenter, has written a thorough guide to what employers must do to ensure safe hiring. Rosen defines a Safe Hiring Program (SHP) as "a series of policies, practices, and procedures designed to minimize the probability of hiring dangerous, questionable or unqualified candidates, while at the same time helping to identify those candidates who are capable, trustworthy, and best suited to the job requirements." Core competencies of the Safe Hiring Program are: organizational infrastructure or organizational commitment to the SHP; initial screening practices; in-depth screening practices; post-hire practices; and legal compliance practices. The author describes the steps employers need to take including setting written policies, practices, and procedures and understanding the law notably the Fair Credit Reporting Act (FCRA), Federal discrimination laws, the Americans with Disabilities Act, age discrimination, and privacy laws. Other issues discussed are the application process, interview questions an employer may or may not ask, checking past employment and education records, what happens when a prospective employee has a criminal record, and precautions to be taken in checking a prospective employee's Internet and Social networking sites such as Facebook or MySpace. Appendixes contain FCRA summaries; information about Title VII EEOC Notices; the Application Process Checklist; Verification and Reference Worksheet; the Safe Hiring Timeline; and Description of Pre-Employment Tools.

The Safe Hiring Audit offers practical guidelines and advice to prospective employees providing information on what they need to know. This book should be purchased by human resources departments and public and academic libraries. Those interviewing for jobs and employers should both find the information presented highly informative and practical.—**Lucy Heckman**

P

77.   Sitarz, Daniel. **Greening Your Business: The Hands-On Guide to Creating a Successful and Sustainable Business.** Carbondale, IL, Earthpress/Nova Publishing; distr., Lanham, Md., National Book Network, 2008. 320p. index. $29.95pa. (CD-ROM). ISBN 13: 978-1-892949-46-2.

Every element of a business's impact on the environment is examined in this comprehensive book. It covers such topics as energy and water use, waste, transportation, computers and office equipment, supply chains and purchasing, building practices, and service design. The book is designed in two parts. Divided into five chapters, part 1 covers the basics of making a business "green," such as why it is important in today's market place to be green, the basic concepts of what it means to be green, green business tools, and creating a path to becoming green. Part 2 of the volume is the largest section. It provides business owners with "action plans" on how to change their business practices to create a more eco-friendly atmosphere. Topics in this section include energy use, water use, waste and recycling, business travel, office equipment, building design, buying green products, and environmental regulations. The book includes a CD-ROM that provides the user with worksheets for developing a comprehensive business environmental plan. There are Excel spreadsheets for business carbon emission calculations.

This is a step-by-step guide for the small to medium-sized business owner who needs a plan to becoming more eco-friendly in their business practices. Business owners will find that the practices found here will be good not only for the environment but also for their financial bottom line.—**Shannon Graff Hysell**

REAL ESTATE

P

78.   Abbott, Damien. **Encyclopedia of Real Estate Terms.** 3d ed. London, Delta Alpha Publishing, 2008. 1508p. $165.00. ISBN 13: 978-0-9668946-4-6.

The purpose of the *Encyclopedia of Real Estate Terms* is to provide definitions for real estate terms, but the 3d edition has expanded its coverage to encompass banking, accounting, economics, insurance, taxation, and tort and contract terms. There are over 10,000 defined terms, 15,000 citations, 5,700 cases, and 1,900 statutory of code references. Each of the real estate terms and phrases are defined with clear concise definitions. If the term has been affected by a legal case, the case citation has been included, as well as whether the term is an American, English, Australian, or Canadian real estate or legal term. The editor,

Damien Abbott, states "this 3rd edition is a dictionary, thesaurus, as well as an encyclopedia all rolled into one."

There are six appendixes that include a bibliography, major laws and enactments, professional associations, Imperial or American measurements, financial formulae, and abbreviations and acronyms. This 3d edition of the *Encyclopedia of Real Estate* is highly recommended for academic, public, and business libraries as well as real estate and legal collections.—**Kay M. Stebbins**

5 Education

GENERAL WORKS

Dictionaries and Encyclopedias

C
79. **Battleground: Schools.** Sandra Mathison and E. Wayne Ross, eds. Westport, Conn., Greenwood Press, 2008. 2v. index. $175.00/set. ISBN 13: 978-0-313-33941-7.

This work contains 93 essays on school and education during the past century. Arrangement is alphabetical by topic. Essays are grouped into seven categories: legal issues and legislation; school and classroom practices; school organization and forms of schooling; schools and society; school subjects and disciplines; social, moral, and emotional development; and teachers and teaching. Each essay is signed and attached with a short list of works for further reading. The contributor's biography is given at the end of the book. The book concludes with a general bibliography, list of Editorial Advisory Board members, and an index.

Each essay "summarizes the nature of controversy, including major players and events relevant to the topic" (preface). As its title "Battleground" indicates, the book presents "competing fundamental values and beliefs and how they are played out within schools" (introduction). One of the book's features is its stress on controversy in each topic. But, not all essays cover well controversies in schooling. For instance, the essay on "Head Start" doe not mention Arthur Jensen's work in 1969 that caused huge controversy in his view that the Head Start programs designed to boast African American IQ scores did not work.

The essay on "No Child Left Behind (NCLB)" discusses the Act well. In the Internet age, it would be appropriate to add an essay on Child Online Protection (COPA) and Children's Online Privacy Protection Act (COPPA). These Acts sparked controversies in their constitutionality, which have been fought all the way to the Supreme Court. The book has a nice selection of topics and all topics are well presented.
—**Tze-chung Li**

C, P
80. **Encyclopedia of Bilingual Education.** Josue M. Gonzalez, ed. Thousand Oaks, Calif., Sage, 2008. 2v. illus. index. $325.00/set; $405.00 (e-book). ISBN 13: 978-1-4129-3720-7; 978-1-4129-6398-5 (e-book).

Bilingual education has long been a controversial topic; the recent debate over immigration has thrust it even further into the spotlight. Now more than ever researchers need a resource that will document the history, major trends, and major names of this field. The two-volume *Encyclopedia of Bilingual Education* answers this need masterfully. Its entries range in topic from pedagogical theory to lawsuits, and each entry is followed by an up-to-date bibliography. Six pertinent appendixes relating to the relationship between the U.S. government and bilingual education complete the second volume. Through its entries, bibliographies, and appendixes, this encyclopedia fulfills its purpose: to provide researchers with a solid foundation on which to build their knowledge and pursue further study.

The *Encyclopedia of Bilingual Education* not only provides researchers with foundational information about bilingual education in the United States, but also enables researchers to access that information quickly and effectively. The volumes begin with an alphabetic list of topics and also a subject-divided list of topics, allowing readers to see the breadth of this field at a glance and also to conduct a focused search. Entries are cross-referenced, and both volumes end with a comprehensive index. Readers will find the entries themselves to be admirably clear and easy to read. Refreshingly free of academic jargon, they nonetheless present information that will be valuable both to those in academia and to the general public.

Although at times the entry titles and information given in the entries may be confusing to a reader new to the terms of this field (see, for example, the entry entitled "Affirmative Steps to English," which refers to affirmative action in bilingual education), that slight drawback is easily overcome through the cross-referencing feature. This set will be an invaluable addition to high school, university, and public libraries for the benefit of researchers, journalists, and all other readers interested in the field of bilingual education.—**Helen Margaret Bernard**

C

81.   **Encyclopedia of Education Law.** Charles J. Russo, ed. Thousand Oaks, Calif., Sage, 2008. 2v. index. $325.00/set; $405.00 (e-book). ISBN 13: 978-1-4129-4079-5; 978-1-4129-6391-6 (e-book).

Encyclopedia of Education Law is a two-volume set covering legal topics of interest to educators. It is edited by Charles J. Russo, an expert in both education and law. This new work is intended to supplement and not replace works such as *Education Law* (3d ed.; Lawrence Erlbaum, 2004), which provides extensive analysis of questions of education law, and the *Deskbook Encyclopedia of American School Law* (2008 ed.; Center for Education & Employment, 2007), which describes state and federal appellate court decisions affecting education.

Encyclopedia of Education Law follows a conventional encyclopedia format, with alphabetically arranged signed entries. A list of contributors precedes the entries. The majority of the entries focus on education law in the United States and include topics (e.g., Technology and the Law), individuals (e.g., William Douglas), legislation (e.g., Equal Access Act), and court decisions (e.g., *Brown v. Board of Education of Topeka*). However, there is also some coverage of important international topics, such as the United Nations Convention on the Rights of the Child. All entries provide either references for further reading or legal citations, with most entries providing both. Access is provided through the reader's guide, which lists the entries by under 17 subject areas and the comprehensive index. Users who need to locate an exhaustive list of articles dealing with a particular topic will find the index more useful.

This reference work is especially helpful for academic libraries serving undergraduate and graduate program in education. However, the entries are accessible to the general reader and all academic and public libraries will find this a useful resource.—**Cynthia Crosser**

C

82.   **Encyclopedia of Educational Psychology.** Neil J. Salkind, ed. Thousand Oaks, Calif., Sage, 2008. 2v. index. $350.00/set. ISBN 13: 978-1-4129-1688-2.

The *Encyclopedia of Educational Psychology* is a two-volume work edited by Neil Salkind, Professor of Psychology and Research in Education at the University of Kansas. It contains over 275 signed entries falling within the categories of human development, measurement, and teaching. Entries range from 1,000 words for smaller topics (e.g., Parent-Teacher Conferences, Fluid Intelligence) to 5,000 words for broader topics (e.g., Literacy) that contain subtopics (e.g., Policy Debates, Emergent Literacy). The contributors and their affiliations are provided in volume 1. Entries are arranged alphabetically and followed by sections with references (further readings) and related topics (*see also*). Access is provided in both volumes by an alphabetic list and a reader's guide that precede the entries. Both volumes also provide a comprehensive index at the back.

Comparison with existing resources may be useful for libraries thinking about purchasing this work. Sage's one-volume *Encyclopedia of School Psychology* (see ARBA 2006, entry 756) provides some overlap, but does not cover topics from a human development perspective. M. E. Sharpe's three-volume <I>Encyclopedia of Education and Human Development (see ARBA 2006, entry 275) provides similar coverage. However, the M. E. Sharpe resource is arranged thematically with references provided after each broad section. These structural differences make some topics (e.g., Dyslexia) easier to locate in the *Encyclopedia of Educational Psychology*. Overall, this is a good resource and is recommended for academic libraries, especially for those with departments or programs in educational psychology.—**Cynthia Crosser**

C, P

83.   **Encyclopedia of the Social and Cultural Foundations of Education.** Eugene F. Provenzo Jr., ed. Thousand Oaks, Calif., Sage, 2009. 3v. index. $425.00/set. ISBN 13: 978-1-4129-0678-4.

These three volumes, chronicling the social dimensions and foundations of American education, provide the educator and interested reader with an easy to use A-Z resource of the comprehensive issues and history of American education, including short biographies of many of the key players that have influenced early and present trends in educational development. Encompassing such disciplines as history, sociology, globalization, and technology, this resource also chronicles the environmental conflicts, tensions, and forces in American society. The editors correctly identify the foundations of American education within the complexities of their social, historical, and political context. The qualified writers chosen to write each entry have developed their entries with this complexity in mind and provide additional resources for the reader, as well as cross-referencing to other articles in the three volumes. The purpose of these volumes is to bring these environmental and interdisciplinary resources together to provide an "interpretive, normative, and critical perspective on education." The editors have accomplished this task with a compendium of entries that are clearly written with a minimum of technical language. The student and advanced researcher will appreciate the effort made by the editors to provide a comprehensive index that is plainly cross-referenced, an A-Z list of entries, and a topically organized reader's guide that is also cross-referenced.

These volumes will be a welcomed edition to any college/university and public library. Central and district public and private school offices will be able to use them to support the development of programs and information that will facilitate both professional and public understanding.—**Joseph P. Hester**

Handbooks and Yearbooks

C, P

84.   **Education State Rankings 2008-2009: Prek-12 Education Across America.** Kathleen O'Leary Morgan and Scott Morgan, eds. Washington, D.C., CQ Press, 2009. 469p. index. $65.00pa.; $65.00 (CD-ROM); $99.95 (CD-ROM and database versions). ISBN 13: 978-0-87289-931-5.

The 469- page *Education State Rankings 2008-2009: Prek-12 Education Across America* supplies comprehensively examined data on American public education with table of contents, preface, "Smartest State Award," "District and Facilities," "Finance," "Graduates and Achievement," "Safety and Discipline," "Special Education," "Staff," "Students," a useful glossary, list of sources, and a precise index. The publisher has helpfully displayed the information about the states both by grade and by alphabet. For handy facts on community instruction, the sources section lists additional resources with contact information and Internet addresses. A multipurpose feature is "Smartest State Award" and the "Previous Smart State Rankings," which reveal the outstanding recipients of the "Smartest State Award" from 2002-2003 to 2008-2009. The intended audience for this title is those needing U.S. education statistics specifically or civics statistics in general.—**Melinda F. Matthews**

C

85.   **Handbook of Moral and Character Education.** Larry P. Nucci and Darcia Narvaez, eds. New York, Routledge/Taylor & Francis Group, 2008. 635p. index. $89.95pa. ISBN 0-8058-5961-6.

The work is a compilation of 30 articles grouped into five parts. Part 1 addresses the basic philosophical, historical, and methodological issues on moral and character education; the role of community in forming the moral lives of students; promotion of moral and character education; and the research for measuring the impact of moral education. Part 2 presents the social environments of classrooms and classroom influence on moral and character formation, care theory and cooperative groups on student social and moral development, Social and Educational learning (SEL), and implications of school-peer relations.

Part 3 discusses contemporary approaches to teaching moral and character education and at different grade levels, such as the Child Development Program (CDP) at the elementary school level, and "what works" in moral and character education. Part 4 deals with moral programs for community service and informational learning experiences through the media and other means of learning beyond classroom. Finally, part 5 focuses on the moral development and character education of professionals to prepare teachers to engage in effective moral and character education.

All articles are signed. Each article ends with references. There is a comprehensive index. It is important to educate students during their formative age moral and character development to be good citizens. The work is a valuable source on theory and practice in moral and character education.—**Tze-chung Li**

C, S

86.   **Handbook of School Counseling.** Hardin L. K. Coleman and Christine Yeh, eds. New York, Routledge/Taylor & Francis Group, 2008. index. $89.95pa. ISBN 13: 978-0-8058-5623-1.

The *Handbook of School Counseling*, edited by Hardin Coleman and Christine Yeh, is a comprehensive work dealing with the critical issues facing school counselors today. The book consists of 47 chapters written by scholars in school counseling. The chapters are divided into seven areas: "Introduction to the Field of School Counseling," "Diversity and School Counseling," "Student Development," "School Counselor Competence," "School-Based Interventions," "Working with Socioemotional Challenges," and "Accountability and Professional Issues in School Counseling." The affiliations, qualifications, and research interests of chapter authors are listed alphabetically at the beginning of the book. The back of the book contains both a subject index and an index of authors cited.

The editors have chosen an empirical approach, which means that every chapter contains a review of the literature for the topic covered. Although the primary goal of the handbook is to serve the needs of school counselors through their first five years of professional work, it is also valuable as a guide for research. Readers looking for practical suggestions will be better served by titles such as *Professional School Counseling: A Handbook of Theories, Programs and Practice* (Caps Press, 2004). However, some chapters of the *Handbook of School Counseling*, such as "Cultural Identity Enhancement Strategies," provide appendixes with lesson plans.

This work is well researched and covers issues that are very relevant for school counseling. This is an essential purchase for academic libraries with school counselor training programs. School libraries will also want to purchase this for their school counselors.—**Cynthia Crosser**

C

87.   **Moral Education: A Handbook.** F. Clark Power and others, eds. Westport, Conn., Praeger/Greenwood Press, 2008. 2v. index. $200.00/set. ISBN 13: 978-0-313-33647-8.

Moral Education: A Handbook provides a critical source of information about moral education for parents, teachers, scholars, and students, including religious moral education, moral philosophy, psychology, and character/civics education. The value of this book is its A-Z format offering the reader quick access to topics and information of interest and need. The introduction to this series adds an excellent overview of the history of moral education from colonial times to the present and correctly points out that the Columbine massacre in 1999 began a period of renewed emphasis on moral education in American schools. This short history, outlined in episodic fashion, serves to contextualize the individual entries and provides a reference for continual research and for deepening understanding. Unlike many books on moral education, which limit their material to only classroom materials, the editors cover a wider territory that includes moral philosophy, religion, religious education, reverence, civic education, sports and sports character, and major ethical topics such as respect and responsibility. Although any one of these topics could have encompassed a multivolume encyclopedic work, the authors have narrow their entries for reasons of practicality and to stay within the scope of their purpose as a multiuse source of information for a variety of audiences that provides avenues for continued research and discussion. The entries are clearly written, and are detailed but not burdened with professional jargon. They are relevant, current, and practical. The editors provide an extensive bibliography, an index that is cross-referenced for ease of use and research, materials for additional study, and a biography of editors and contributors.—**Joseph P. Hester**

C, S
88.   Sundem, Garth, Jan Krieger, and Kristi Pikiewicz. **10 Languages You'll Need Most in the Classroom: A Guide to Communicating with English Language Learners and Their Families.** Thousand Oaks, Calif., Corwin Press, 2008. 260p. illus. $38.95pa. ISBN 13: 978-1-4129-3782-5.

Written for the teacher, this work also services the librarian dealing with non-English-speaking patrons. Focusing on the 10 most common languages spoken by immigrants who do not also speak English, rather than simply the 10 most common languages, this work deals with Spanish, Vietnamese, Hmong, Chinese (Cantonese), Korean, Haitian Creole, Arabic, Russian, Tagalog, and Navajo. The work ends with a set of three reading tests written in each language's script, for the first, third, and fifth grade. Each of the 10 chapters focuses on a single language, beginning with an introduction to the culture and cultural facts, a list of phrases in the language itself and transliterations, reproducible pictorial dictionaries by topic, and translated letters to parents. Geared to help communication as well as to assist the librarian or teacher in learning about communicating with new students and patrons, the work is mostly of use to the school librarian but can also be a welcome addition to any library servicing teachers who work with large multicultural populations.—**Sara Marcus**

EARLY CHILDHOOD EDUCATION

C, P, S
89.   Griffith, Priscilla L., Sara Ann Beach, Jiening Ruan, and Loraine Dunn. **Literacy for Young Children: A Guide for Early Childhood Educators.** Thousand Oaks, Calif., Corwin Press, 2008. 233p. index. $30.95pa. ISBN 13: 978-1-4129-5200-2.

Written by four professors at the University of Oklahoma, this work uses vignettes of four diverse children throughout the book as examples of the topics discussed. Each of the 11 chapters has sections on theory to practice, assessment and instruction, centers, diversity, and concludes with a summary. A detailed table of contents along with an extensive index enables quick location of a topic of interest, while a list of references and separate list of children's books referenced will assist in further research. The list of resources for teachers and list of helpful Websites will aid in the implementation of the topics covered in this work. Supported by research and including references to other chapters, the authors also provide call outs with important information as well as numerous illustrations and lists. Addressing the pre-K and kindergarten classroom, the work focuses on child development, language development, phonological awareness, alphabetic principle, writing, comprehension, sharing books with children, integrating literacy across the curriculum, literacy in the real world, and helping parents. This work is of importance to any library servicing an early childhood population or those who work with such a population.—**Sara Marcus**

ELEMENTARY AND SECONDARY EDUCATION

S

90.   Perez, Kathy. **More Than 100 Brain-Friendly Tools and Strategies for Literacy Instruction.** Thousand Oaks, Calif., Corwin Press, 2008. 123p. index. $28.95pa. ISBN 13: 978-1-4129-2693-5.

Written by a professor of education at Saint Mary's College of California, these six chapters are geared to the elementary audience but can be adapted for other levels. Presenting a collection of brain-friendly tools, techniques, and strategies for enhancing literacy across the curriculum and supporting the standards based-curriculum, this volume presents over 100 specific strategies to optimize student learning and achievement. Beginning with the building blocks of "brain-based" teaching, Perez then addresses structures to engage student's thinking before the lesson, followed by a discussion of the importance of and examples of flexible group structuring. Chapter 5 focuses on strategies to adapt the lesson to meet the diverse needs of today's students. The work ends with practices to help both in literacy instruction and elsewhere. A comprehensive index and list of references makes this a book one will go to again and again for assistance in today's constructivist and project-based learning environment.—**Sara Marcus**

P, S

91.   Waller, Raymond J. **Educator's Guide to Solving Common Behavior Problems.** Thousand Oaks, Calif., Corwin Press, 2008. 116p. index. $23.95pa. ISBN 13: 978-1-4129-5766-3.

Written by an associate professor of special education at Piedmont College, the 22 chapters on 20 topics focus on behavior problems in children. Addressing positive behavioral management, the easy-to-implement methods are presented as ways to motivate children and remedy problems. Using numerous parallels to real-life situations, the work is written in the first person and in an easy-to-understand language. Including points to remember and recommended readings in each chapter, the reader will feel as if Waller is talking directly to them. Based on research and theory, *Educator's Guide to Solving Common Behavior Problems* uses short chapters to address each topic by itself, encouraging the user to find the exact section needed at the time, while the writing style enables reading the work cover to cover. An index is provided for assistance in locating all discussion on a topic as well. This work is of great use to any professional working with children, and can also be of use to parents and other adults dealing with children. —**Sara Marcus**

HIGHER EDUCATION

General Works

Handbooks and Yearbooks

C

92.   Lipson, Charles. **Succeeding as an International Student in the United States and Canada.** Chicago, University of Chicago Press, 2008. 365p. $35.00; $17.00pa. ISBN 13: 978-0-226-48478-5; 978-0-226-48479-2pa.

This book is written for the more than 700,000 students from around the world that come to the United States and Canada for a higher education. Along with adapting to a new culture many have to learn a new language, learn the ropes of a new university system, and deal with a fast-paced lifestyle. The work is arranged into three parts that discuss moving to the United States (e.g., what essentials to bring, passports and visas), succeeding at the university (e.g., succeeding academically, work study, plagiarism), and the largest section on living in the United States and Canada (e.g., earning money, transportation, housing and meals, health care, telecommunications). The chapters are written in an easy-to-understand style with plenty of bulleted lists and sidebars for emphasis. The work concludes with two appendixes (a glossary of words and phrases for international students and a list of common abbreviations, holidays, and clothing sizes) and an index. This is not an essential purchase but can serve as a supplemental resource for university libraries.—**Shannon Graff Hysell**

C, S

93.   Phifer, Paul. **College Majors & Careers: A Resource Guide for Effective Life Planning.** 6th ed. New York, Ferguson/Infobase Publishing, 2009. 294p. index. $35.00. ISBN 13: 978-0-8160-7664-2.

A useful guide for the high school student, this work allots approximately 2 pages to profile each of more than 60 college majors or careers, ranging from accounting to philosophy, and from construction to food and beverage management. Each profile includes five sections, the first of which lists high school courses that are pertinent or possible prerequisites to further study. This is followed by a list of related occupations, with an indication of type of degree usually needed to enter that occupation. A third section lists leisure activities of those typically involved in this subject area or career, while a fourth section provides a bulleted list of skills that employers will expect. A final section lists values and attributes associated with those who enter the field in question. Each career option also has an information section that provides projected job outlook up to 2016 and salary ranges for various jobs in the field.

Although these college major and career profiles comprise two-thirds of the volume, they are prefaced by a list of clusters of careers, a basic introduction by the author, and an explanation of how to use the guide. A suite of 40 questions and answers, aimed at further clarifying questions asked by many high school students, supplements the main body of the text. Appendixes include a self-assessment survey, descriptions of selected occupations, definitions of selected skills, and definitions of values and personal attributes. A full index concludes the work.

In addition to its value for students, the work functions as a useful handbook for counselors, parents, and others involved in advising or career counseling. It is highly recommended for high school, public, community college, and other academic libraries.—**ARBA Staff Reviewer**

Financial Aid

C, S

94.   **College Financing Information for Teens: Tips for a Successful Financial Life.** Karen Bellenir, ed. Detroit, Omnigraphics, 2008. 438p. index. (Teen Finance Series). $58.00. ISBN 13: 978-0-7808-0988-8.

This new series from Omnigraphics is similar in format to the publisher's Teen Health Series, only for these volumes the focus is on responsible management of money and finances. The works consist of documents and excerpts written by various government, nonprofit, and for-profit organizations and agencies, including the Department of the Treasury, the United States Securities and Exchange Commission, the American Savings Education Council, the National Association of Securities Dealers, and Visa, Inc.

Joining other titles in the series (e.g., *Cash and Credit Information for Teens* [see ARBA 2006, entry 171], *Savings and Investment Information for Teens* [see ARBA 2006, entry 172]), *College Financing information for Teens* provides information on saving for college, paying for college with federal student aid, college scholarships, national merit scholarships, grants, loans, and student work programs. Some of the most valuable information in this book includes discussion of the various ways to finance an education; how to apply for loans and scholarships; special financial aid for athletes and those entering the health care fields; loan cancellation and deferment options for teachers; and financial benefits for those in the armed forces, Peace Corps, and AmeriCorps. This work concludes with a chapter for more information that includes Websites for more information on financial aid resources and state higher education agencies.

This series will prove useful for high school and undergraduate students. Both school libraries and college reference collections should add this work to their collections.—**Shannon Graff Hysell**

LEARNING DISABILITIES

C, P, S

95.   **The Complete Learning Disabilities Directory, 2009.** 15th ed. Millerton, N.Y., Grey House Publishing, 2008. 560p. index. $145.00pa. ISBN 13: 978-1-59237-368-0.

Although Internet searches will provide considerable amounts of information on a topic such as learning disabilities, this extensive directory brings together lists of public and private agencies, online and print resources and materials, schools, and programs related to various learning disabilities. The organization is clear and the format is easy to read. In the print edition the more than 7,000 listings can be approached through the table of contents, which lists 21 chapters and 100 subchapters, or through the entry name, geographic, and subject indexes. One quirk of the organization is that subchapters are arranged alphabetically, so general resources on a topic are not listed first. The user guide in the front outlines the entry format, which may include up to 14 fields including record number, organization name, address, telephone and fax numbers, e-mail address, Website, the names of key personnel, an organization description, and price, length, and format of publications. The indexes list entry numbers rather than page numbers. No information is given on how organizations or resources are chosen. This publication has been recognized by the National Center for Learning Disabilities and is a 2008 National Health Information Awards Winner in Patient Education Information. The information provided in this *Directory* is also available in an online format from the publisher (http://www.greyhouse.com). Users can search the information by entry name, major category (e.g., Adults, Behavior and Self Esteem), minor category (e.g., Attention Deficit Disorder, Camps and Summer Programs), keyword, executive last name, or state.

Although it is pricey, libraries that have found this directory useful in the past will want to update their copy or renew their online subscription. This work is recommended for academic libraries serving special education teacher preparation programs and public libraries.—**Rosanne M. Cordell**

C, S

96.   Pierangelo, Roger, and George Giuliani. **Teaching Students with Learning Disabilities: A Step-by-Step Guide for Educators.** Thousand Oaks, Calif., Corwin Press, 2008. 173p. index. $31.95pa. ISBN 13: 978-1-4129-1601-1.

Written by an associate professor at Long Island University's Department of Special Education and Literacy and an associate professor and Director of Special Education at Hofstra University's School of Education and Allied Health, this work provides educators and others interested a step-by-step guide and approach to the most effective methods of teaching and reaching students with learning disabilities. Explaining learning disabilities through the eyes of a teacher, the authors help one to work effectively with administrators, parents, other professionals, the teacher, and the outside community to provide each child with the best education possible. Helpful to one trying to understand key concepts of learning disabilities without taking courses in the topic, this work enables one to learn how to be an effective educator when working with students with learning disabilities. While the terminology might be technical for the novice, this is a necessary work for any educator or other knowledge provider who might encounter learners with learning disabilities. A detailed table of contents, along with a glossary and index enables one to use the book as a reference, while the material can also be read cover-to-cover either for personal development or as a text in a course. An extensive list of references can help the reader to find out more.—**Sara Marcus**

NONPRINT MATERIALS

Bibliography

P, S

97.   Barr, Catherine. **Best New Media, K-12: A Guide to Movies, Subscription Web Sites, and Educational Software and Games.** Westport, Conn., Libraries Unlimited/Greenwood Publishing Group, 2008. 237p. index. $50.00. ISBN 13: 978-1-59158-467-4.

Catherine Barr, editor and author of other children and young adult reference sources, has produced this new addition to the publisher's Best Books series. This volume includes over 1,300 entries for films and documentaries on DVD, software (on CD-ROMs, online downloads, interactive books, or handheld devices), computer games, and subscription Websites. The items included were favorably reviewed in library journals, received awards, or were otherwise recommended. Barr intends to provide librarians and media specialists with a tool to evaluate and build collections, provide guidance to library users, or create materials and programming for their libraries. The table of contents lists the subjects covered in order, followed by the listing of Major Subjects Arranged Alphabetically. The main body of this work is divided into Materials for Younger Children (Grades K-3) and Materials for Older Children (Grades 4-12). The numbered entries are short, with an icon for the type of material; the title; recommended level; copyright date; length; publisher, ISBN, computer requirements, or URL; price, and a brief description. Review source or award is listed at the end of each entry. Title and subject indexes follow. While this type of resource is definitely needed in school or public librarianship, one wonders if the publisher is ready to update it often enough for it to remain current. Nonetheless, it is highly recommended for school and public libraries, and academic libraries that support teacher or librarian preparation programs. [R: SLJ, Jan 09, p. 140]—**Rosanne M. Cordell**

Handbooks and Yearbooks

C, S

98.   November, Alan. **Web Literacy for Educators.** Thousand Oaks, Calif., Corwin Press, 2008. 109p. index. $25.95. ISBN 13: 978-1-4129-5843-1.

Written in the first person by an international leader in educational technology to help teachers and students learn more about Web literacy and develop critical thinking skills, *Web Literacy for Educators* serves not only educators but their students as well. November has provided an easy-to-understand work filled will exercises, tips, handouts, and stories from current practitioners around the country. The wide variety of activities provided are labeled for the reader to know which to use with students, which to use for personal or staff development, and which to try out first to determine usefulness for students. The book has a Website that provides direct access to links mentioned within each chapter as well as an ever-changing list of questions for further thought. However, a lack of listing of resources found within the book can cause problems for the reader without current Internet access. Providing knowledge as well as techniques and ideas to try out and expand upon in one's own practice, this work is a valuable tool for any educator seeking to teach both the static Web as well as the dynamic Web 2.0 that students regularly encounter today. Educators and librarians can adapt and select the activities best suited to their population at the time, be it children just starting to use the Web or graduate students coming for an information literacy session in the academic library. Formative multiple-choice assessments are included at the end of each chapter to review skills covered, increasing comprehension for the reader and providing a jumping-off point for use in an educational setting.—**Sara Marcus**

6 Ethnic Studies

ANTHROPOLOGY

C, P

99. **Cultural Encyclopedia of the Body.** Victoria Pitts-Taylor, ed. Westport, Conn., Greenwood Press, 2008. 2v. illus. index. $175.00/set. ISBN 13: 978-0-313-34145-8.

What is beauty? What is erotic? This encyclopedia explores how various parts of the body are viewed, used, admired, and desired. The entries draw from history, fashion, medicine, the arts, philosophy, archaeology, anthropology, and sociology. The author demonstrates the social and political implications of how we see our bodies. These bodily paradigms influence our concepts of self and shape power relationships between men and women. Every culture modifies the body in some way, be it tooth filing, foot binding, corsets, neck stretching, or breast implants. Tattooing is a good illustration of the author's premise. This practice dates back to 10,000 B.C.E. in Japan. It may be done with needles, chisels, gouging, or sewing. For example, tattooing has been used for sacred purposes, mark entry to adulthood, or designate social status. The Ancient Greeks and Romans tattooed slaves. The Russians put facial tattoos on prisoners in the eighteenth century. Long associated with the lower classes, tattooing became popular with the European upper class in the late nineteenth century. It is believed Queen Victoria and Prince Albert had tattoos. The author's comprehensive survey brings home to the reader that what is acceptable and even prized in one culture may be abhorred in another, and that perceptions about beauty can change over time within the same society.—**Adrienne Antink**

C, P

100. Jacoby, Joann, and Josephine Z. Kibbee. **Cultural Anthropology: A Guide to Reference and Information Sources.** 2d ed. Westport, Conn., Libraries Unlimited/Greenwood Publishing Group, 2007. 284p. index. (Reference Sources in the Social Sciences Series). $65.00pa. ISBN 13: 978-1-59158-357-8.

This 2d edition of *Cultural Anthropology* adds Internet sites and new print sources not available in 1991 when the last edition came out. Although the librarians recognize that online searches and electronic anthropological databases have opened access to sources, they make a contribution in this digital age by organizing and annotating the wealth of information under categories of general anthropology reference sources, methods and practice, subfields, research areas, humanities related fields, area and ethnic studies, and supplemental sources. Anthropology is indeed a big disciplinary tent under which many kinds of fields lodge, and this guide can be useful to the student or instructor in taking them all in. Some newer areas of concern such as performance studies, GLBT anthropology, and environmental studies are given more attention than previously. Yet, the boundaries between fields the authors set up do not always hold up well. The chapter on humanities related fields is especially problematic with the authors' correct observation that folklore studies broadly include material and social culture, and yet they restrict references to oral literature. They list Funk and Wagnalls' outdated 1949 reference as a standard text and miss Thomas Green's more current *Folklore: An Encyclopedia of Beliefs, Customs, Tales, Music, and Art* (see ARBA 99, entry 1180) and folklife references that cover material and social culture more comprehensively. Even within oral literature, they appear unaware of a new edition of the *Tale-Type Index* by Hans-Jorg Uther

(2004) supplanting Stith Thompson's 1961 reference. And argument would probably be given by folklorists about the categorization of their field as strictly humanities when it has a strong social science legacy. The sections on area studies are useful for Africa and Asia, but sorely underrepresent European and American ethnography. Prior to the closing section on supplemental sources, there is organization by subject and area, but the last chapter is too much of a catch-all category covering journals, organizations, and publishers. Multiple indexes for subjects, titles, and authors help locate works within the text.—**Simon J. Bronner**

ETHNIC STUDIES

General Works

C, P, S

101.   **Encyclopedia of Race, Ethnicity, and Society.** Richard T. Schaefer, ed. Thousand Oaks, Calif., Sage, 2008. 3v. illus. index. $495.00/set. ISBN 13: 978-1-4129-2694-2.

The wealth of information in the three volumes of the *Encyclopedia of Race, Ethnicity, and Society* is opulent. Volume 1 begins with a list of the Editorial Board, an About the Editors section, a list of contributors, and the introduction. Volumes 1 through 3 provide a list of entries, list of images, the reader's guide, alphabetized entries, appendixes (Data on Race and Ethnicity in the United States, 1820 to the Present, and Internet Resources on Race, Ethnicity, and Society). An index concludes all three volumes.

The list of entries provides an alphabetic list of the contents, while the list of images provides an alphabetic arrangement of pictures and maps, such as maps of countries described and captivating pictures of places and people. For example, a map of The Netherlands and a picture of a celebration in Little Italy adorn the encyclopedia. The reader's guide magnificently directs readers to entries on 18 themes. Appendix A provides 14 tables on such details as people acquiring U.S. residence, ancestors in the predominant cities of North America, and specifics on race to 2050 in the United States. Appendix B provides Internet addresses for extra specifics. Any reader seeking the whole story on race, ethnicity, and society will discover essential information in the three-volume reference source.—**Melinda F. Matthews**

C, S

102.   Messer-Kruse, Timothy. **Race Relations in the United States, 1980-2000.** Westport, Conn., Greenwood Press, 2008. 173p. illus. index. (Race Relations in the United States). $49.95. ISBN 13: 978-0-313-34311-7.

W. E. B. DuBois was quoted in 1903 as saying that "the problem of the twentieth century is the problem of the color line." He correctly predicted race would be a major issue for America in the twentieth century—and remains a challenge in the twenty-first century. Using an encyclopedia format, this book covers significant events, key individuals, important legislation, and media/cultural influences impacting race relations during the 1980s and 1990s. The book's scope includes African Americans, Native Americans, Latinos, and Asian Americans. As a sampling of what is offered to the reader, the author discusses the roots of the current immigration debate, the rise of Hispanics as the nation's largest minority, urban racial tensions, riots like the one sparked by the beating of Rodney King, the recognition of Indian tribal sovereignty with the 1988 Indian Gambling Regulatory Act, and the emergence of crack cocaine that fueled gang violence and severe sentencing laws that put a proportionally high number of African Americans in prison. (By 1990 more African American males were incarcerated than in college.) In the same time period, we see popular culture being heavily influenced by not only African American but also Latino and Asian-American entertainers, athletes, and writers. This volume helps the reader to understand the current state of race relations in America. Although the United States has come a long way since DuBois' 1903 statement, there is still work to be done.—**Adrienne Antink**

African Americans

Dictionaries and Encyclopedias

C, P, S

103.   **The African American Experience. http://aae.greenwood.com.** [Website]. Westport, Conn., Greenwood Press. Price negotiated by site. Date reviewed: 2008.

This is a comprehensive research database that provides reliable information on African American life, history, and culture. Users can browse a wide range of subject areas, from "Arts and Entertainment" and "Business and Labor" to "Sports" and "Women." The Resources section includes the following headings: title list, timeline, image index, primary source index, landmark documents, slave narratives, classic texts, and audio files.—**Catherine Barr**

C, P

104.   **Encyclopedia of African American History, 1896 to the Present: From the Age of Segregation to the Twenty-First Century.** Paul Finkelman, ed. New York, Oxford University Press, 2009. 5v. illus. index. $495.00/set. ISBN 13: 978-0-19-516779-5.

One of the monumental reference resources of the past few decades has finally reached completion with the publication of this new five-volume set, which chronicles African American history from 1896, the year of *Plessy v. Ferguson*, through the present (fittingly, President Obama's face is central on each cover). The previous set, published also by Oxford University Press in 2006, covered the period 1619-1895, and libraries therefore will need both sets for comprehensive coverage (see ARBA 2007, entry 270). This new work features 1,250 scholarly articles on nearly every topic relevant to the period, including politics, sports, entertainment, literature, and education, with separate articles on personalities, organizations, and movements. Articles vary in length, from a single column to around 10 pages, but all articles are well written and well researched, with secondary bibliographies (including Websites) and *see also* references at the end. Some black-and-white photographs are also included, but otherwise the set is not illustrated. Over one-half of the final volume is devoted to a chronology of African American history during the period, followed by a detailed index to the set. Undoubtedly some will discover missing topics, but in general the editors have done a fine job of inclusiveness and breadth. Considering the overall excellence of this work and its companion set, the *Encyclopedia of African American History* is an essential purchase for all academic and public libraries, along with Palmer's equally fine six-volume *Encyclopedia of African-American Culture and History* (2d ed.; see ARBA 2006, entry 329), regardless of the degree of duplication of topics.—**Anthony J. Adam**

C, P

105.   **Encyclopedia of the African Diaspora: Origins, Experiences, and Culture.** Carole Boyce Davies, ed. Santa Barbara, Calif., ABC-CLIO, 2008. 3v. illus. index. $295.00/set. ISBN 13: 978-1-85109-700-5; 978-1-85109-705-0 (e-book).

Davies (professor of African Diaspora Studies, Florida International University) is a leading authority in the area of African Diaspora Studies (ADS) and is well suited for pulling off such a large, potentially unwieldy project. As she notes in her lengthy introduction, the purpose of this set is to "provide in one place a well-documented and readily accessible body of information about the most important historical, political, economic and cultural relations between people of African descent in the world community."

The range is thus international is scope, and Davies has drawn in a wide variety of scholars from across the globe as field specialists. Because of the strength of her home institution's ADS program, Davies has also enlisted many current and former FIU individuals to contribute. The 500-plus articles are approximately 500 words long, signed by the author, with a short secondary bibliography attached. Entries cover a variety of topics, including general and specific subjects, select biographies, regional and country studies, and concepts (e.g., signifying). Cross-references are available throughout, but illustrations are scarce. For such a broad subject, Davies' selections are overall good, as is the writing and scholarship, but omissions are also easily discovered. Why, for example, an essay on "Langston University and Historically Black Colleges and Universities" but not single article on "Higher Education" or "HBCUs"? Still, Davies' encyclopedia is an excellent complement to other broad African Diaspora resources, including Gates' and Appiah's *Africana* from Oxford University Press (2d ed.; see ARBA 2006, entry 328). This work is recommended for all African and African American Studies collections.—**Anthony J. Adam**

C, P

106. **The Oxford African American Studies Center.** **http://www.oxfordaasc.com/public.** [Website]. New York, Oxford University Press. Price negotiated by site. Date reviewed: 2008.

Includes research materials on the history, contributions, and achievements of African American, with primary source documents, biographies, images, maps, charts, and tables plus helpful thematic timelines and browse/search features that allow users to pinpoint eras or subjects of interest. The more than 8,000 entries come from such prominent Oxford titles as *Africana* (2d ed.; see ARBA 2006, entry 3280, *Encyclopedia of African American History, 1619-1895* (see ARBA 2007, entry 270), *Encyclopedia of African American History, 1896 to the Present* (2009), *Black Women in America* (1999), and *African American National Biography* (see ARBA 2008, entry 14). The 1,300 illustrations and 150 maps—all with captions written especially for this product—enhance the entries. The site adds new material and updates old material on a regular basis in order to keep the data as up to date as possible.—**Catherine Barr**

Asians

P, S

107. West, Barbara A. **Encyclopedia of the Peoples of Asia and Oceania.** New York, Facts on File, 2009. 2v. illus. maps. index. (Facts on File Library of World History). $175.00/set. ISBN 13: 978-0-8160-7109-8.

Do you want to know the difference between the Tuvaluans (from the Polynesian state of Tuvalu) and the Tuvans (from the Republic of Tuva, a semiautonomous region in the Russian Federation)? Then this overview of the diverse peoples of Asia and Oceania, targeted at high school and college social studies students, is for you. The editor provides entries for contemporary and historical peoples as well as nationality descriptions. West has selected the peoples she considers most relevant to our current time. For example, all 55 of China's recognized groups are included because of China's importance in today's world. For each people we learn their time period, location, language, religion, culture, history, historical timeline, and ethnic origin. As a sample, the encyclopedia includes a general entry on Aboriginal Taiwanese, one on the Taiwanese nationality and individual descriptions of 6 of the 13 recognized peoples of Taiwan. Useful features include a list of contemporary peoples covered in the book by country, a list of historical peoples described in the reference, a chronology of Asian and Oceanic history, and essays on kinship, subsistence, and religious systems. Reading the entries we quickly appreciate the relevance of studying these peoples to better understand today's political events. To illustrate, one of the issues in the recent conflict between Russia and the Republic of Georgia over South Ossetia hinges on when the Ossetian people moved from their place of origin in the northern Caucasus into the land currently known

as South Ossetia—200 or 2000 years ago. Those who recognize the earlier date support the cause of independence for South Ossetia. Those supporting the later date advocate unification with Georgia.
—**Adrienne Antink**

Indians of North America

Dictionaries and Encyclopedias

C, P, S

108.   Everett, Deborah, and Elayne Zorn. **Encyclopedia of Native American Artists.** Westport, Conn., Greenwood Press, 2008. 267p. illus. index. (Artists of the American Mosaic). $74.95. ISBN 13: 978-0-313-33762-8.

According to a recent headline in *The New York Times*, minorities may be a majority in the United States within a generation. What was once called the American melting pot is more often referred to today as the American mosaic. And Greenwood Press has tapped into the nation's increasingly diverse literary and artistic output by introducing two series: Stories from the American Mosaic and Artists of the American Mosaic. Of the latter, five titles have been or soon will be published on Jewish, Asian, African, Arab, and Native American artists.

The authors of the *Encyclopedia of Native American Artists*, Deborah Everett and Elayne Zorn, are not indigenous, but they have over four decades of combined experience working with and writing about Native peoples, and are educated in the fine arts. The two have selected a diverse group of 70 contemporary Native North American artists from the United States and Canada, and the introduction explains that their goal is to introduce readers to a range of art and artists. They have chosen an eclectic group of artists that represents a wide range of media. Some artists work in the traditional fine arts (e.g., painting, print making, sculpture, photography, film), while others in crafts (e.g., textiles, gold, glass, baskets, masks), and still others in avant-garde arts (e.g., digital, performance, assemblage, multidisciplinary). In their effort to expose readers to a wide variety of art forms and artists and not duplicate the wealth of information already available, the authors have intentionally excluded some of the most prominent indigenous artists.

The *Encyclopedia of Native American Artists* invites comparison with the *St. James Guide to Native North American Artists*, published a decade earlier (see ARBA 99, entry 865). The *St. James Guide* is a more ambitious effort, including 350 artists. This encyclopedia has one-fifth the number of artists, but the entries are longer, running three to five pages instead of one or two. Both titles have black-and-white illustrations and entries that include recommended readings and locations of exhibits. This encyclopedia includes eight pages of attractive color plates that are not in the *St. James Guide*. Although a relatively small number of entries makes indexing less important in this encyclopedia, this reader would have appreciated medium and tribe indexes, both of which are available in the *St. James Guide*. This encyclopedia's index does help, but not all media are included.

Academic or public libraries serving patrons who are interested in the contemporary Native American art scene are encouraged to select this title. Others may rely on the *St. James Guide* or the burgeoning number of Websites related to this subject, such as *ArtNatAm* (http://www.artnatam.com/).—**John P. Stierman**

C, S

109.   Leahy, Todd, and Raymond Wilson. **Historical Dictionary of Native American Movements.** Lanham, Md., Scarecrow, 2008. 205p. (Historical Dictionaries of Religions, Philosophies, and Movements, no.88). $85.00. ISBN 0-8108-5773-1. ISBN 13: 978-0-8108-5773-5.

After reading the unusually lengthy introductory essay (an overview of American Indian history beginning before Columbus arrived), I needed to clarify the definition of " movement." The dictionary definition is: "A group of people working together to advance their political, social, or artistic ideas. A campaign undertaken by such a group." Basically, people working together to achieve a mutual goal.

In the foreword, the editor briefly describes the discrimination, deceit, oppression, and brutality that characterized the interaction of the European newcomers and Native peoples. He then states " . . . that it wasn't until Native American movements emerged, fitfully and painfully, that more notable progress (in retaining their lands, languages, traditions, and tribal sovereignty) has been made."

The writers have endeavored to provide useful tools for the reader. The overview is intended to paint the broad picture of invasion, conflict, and the many efforts to exterminate Indian people. It does provide a structure for understanding the issues for Native peoples but also suffers from too much information crowded into "coverage." A simple map of the location of Native American movements is included. It is not clear why some of these "movements" were selected (e.g., the Red Earth Powwow in Oklahoma City, Oklahoma), but it is nonetheless helpful. Another section presents acronyms and abbreviations, which are necessary for identifying the many Indian organizations. A comprehensive chronology from 12,500 B.C.E. to 2007 is included.

The cross-referenced entries describe important people, places, events, and institutions and political, economic, social, and cultural topics, organizations, leadership strategies, and major issues. Fortunately, the authors recognized that it is critical to include Native voice to capture the importance, determination, and emotion of Native American movements. Although this appendix is brief, it is an important addition to the book. Finally, the authors provided an extensive bibliography, including electronic media. The reference reflects what they believe to the best and most useful works. A quite personal introduction to this bibliography is welcome. This volume will be particularly appreciated by students.
—**Karen D. Harvey**

Handbooks and Yearbooks

C, S

110.   Mathews, Sandra K. **American Indians in the Early West.** Santa Barbara, Calif., ABC-CLIO, 2008. 327p. illus. index. (Cultures in the American West). $65.00. ISBN 13: 978-1-85109-823-1.

The American West has a special allure for students of all ages. Without adequate background reading, we can easily buy into the mythology of the West, which has been successfully neutralized by the "New Western History" scholars, like Richard White. With the Cultures in the American West series, ABC-CLIO adds to the new west history movement, introducing titles such as *Hispanics in the American West* (see ARBA 2006, entry 353) and *Women in the American West* (see entry 293) that highlight minorities and their unique contributions to the history of the land between the Missouri River and the Pacific Ocean.

Each of the titles in the series, according to the series editor, is written by an expert in the subject, and *American Indians in the Early West* is evidence of that. In a thorough preface, Sandra K. Mathews outlines her academic credentials, including a Ph.D. from University of New Mexico; a dissertation on Pueblo Indian land rights; books, chapters, and articles on Native Americans of the West; and an associate professorship at Nebraska Wesleyan University. Although the author was schooled in the southwest and spent her formative academic years researching the native populations of that region, she has recently published a monograph on a life in Alaska, which helped develop her interest in the indigenous population there.

American Indians in the Early West is ideal for the student who needs a chapter-length introduction to indigenous populations and their interactions with non-Indian populations in each of four broad geographic regions: Rio Grande Valley and beyond, from the Pacific to the Gulf of Mexico, from the Saint Lawrence to the Rockies, and from the Aleutians to northern California. In addition, the author has included an informative and lengthy (one-third of the book) chapter that outlines origination and migration theories for all of the distinct regions of the West and a short concluding chapter on historiography. Each chapter includes interesting insets (e.g. "Childhood as a Crow Indian," "The Tlingit Social Structure," "Environmental Consequences of the Fur Trade") , a bibliographic essay, and images. As with the other titles in this series, *American Indians in the Early West* includes maps, a chronology, a selected bibliography, a glossary, and an index.

The main question facing the bibliographer is not whether or not to buy this title, but where they should put it. Because it is text-rich, many selectors will want to add it to the circulating collection, but it also clearly has reference value and will help supplement a student's textbook reading. Since the price is reasonable, libraries serving strong Native American history programs may want to buy two copies. —**John P. Stierman**

Jews

Dictionaries and Encyclopedias

C, S

111.   **Encyclopedia of the Jewish Diaspora: Origins, Experiences, and Culture.** M. Avrum Ehrlich, ed. Santa Barbara, Calif., ABC-CLIO, 2009. 3v. illus. index. $295.00/set. ISBN 13: 978-1-85109-873-6.

The term "diaspora" was first used in the Septuagint (the Greek translation of the Hebrew Bible) referring to the exile of the Babylonian Jews. This 3-volume encyclopedia contains valuable information on the 2,500-year history of the Jewish diaspora. The first volume provides an overview, surveying "themes and phenomena," such as Israel and the diaspora, diaspora languages, and music and culture. The second and third volumes cover regions and individual countries. Since the literature on the major diaspora communities in the United States, France, and Great Britain is so extensive, the editor wisely decided to provide wider coverage to the history of lesser-known communities (e.g., China, India, Kyrgyzstan, Zambia, Iceland). The 400 entries range in length from a few pages to long chapters and were written by scholars. Each entry contains a useful bibliography with frequent references to little-known citations. Photographs and illustrations are nicely interspersed throughout the text; each volume has a cumulative index expediting easy access to the entire text. While Judaica reference works invariably cover the long and textured history of the Jewish diaspora, this outstanding encyclopedia is a unique source.—**Donald Altschiller**

Handbooks and Yearbooks

C

112.   **The Columbia History of Jews and Judaism in America.** Marc Lee Raphael, ed. Irvington, N.Y., Columbia University Press, 2008. 490p. index. $75.00. ISBN 13: 978-0-231-13222-0.

This volume contains 18 essays by leading scholars of Jewish studies and is entitled *The Columbia History of Jews and Judaism in America*, which implies a chronological survey, but it is distinguished, and enhanced, by more than half of the volume devoted to topical essays. To the editor's credit, the essays take culture more seriously than other surveys singling out the great events and figures of the Jewish past. Highlights include Jeffrey Shandler's provocative query of "What is American Culture?" and Jenna Weissman Joselit's probing essay on the American Jewish social club. The editor's purpose is to provide an overview of Jewish experience in one volume and has achieved the goal of providing a thought-provoking set of essays rather than a comprehensive textbook. He addresses often-overlooked areas of Jewish experience such as southern and Pacific Jewry, and gives attention to feminism, politics, and education with separate chapters. Certainly there are areas that could have been given mention (e.g., Sephardim, relations with Israel, sports, music, community center movement), but there is much to ponder here nonetheless. There are thematic continuities among the contributions that the editor lays out in the introduction: Jewish struggle with anti-Semitism until the 1970s, when, debatably, it largely disappeared; the development of progressive Judaism and secular Jewish culture as hallmarks of American Jewish life; and the dramatic socioeconomic rise of Jews as a group since the twentieth century. The result is an engaging text that gives social diversity and cultural experience their due in Jewish studies.—**Simon J. Bronner**

Latin Americans

C, P, S

113.   **Latino American Experience. http://www.greenwood.com/mosaic/lae/.** [Website]. Westport, Conn., Greenwood Press. Price negotiated by site. Date reviewed: 2008.

Encompassing the content of more than 200 volumes—from encyclopedias to biographies—this wide-ranging database focuses on all aspects of Latin American history and culture from pre-Columbian times to the present day. It is designed, developed, and indexed under the guidance of Latino librarians and library directors to meet the research and curriculum needs of students, teachers, librarians, and researchers. Special features include a fully searchable timeline, content on modern-day Latin American countries, Spanish-language content (e.g., folktales, recipes), 25 classroom lesson plans, and primary source materials (e.g., maps, images, audio clips, interviews, music files, speeches, documents, links to vetted Websites).
—**Catherine Barr**

7 Genealogy and Heraldry

GENEALOGY

Bibliography

P

114. Henritze, Barbara K. **Bibliographic Checklist of African American Newspapers.** Baltimore, Md., Genealogical Publishing, 2008. 206p. index. $39.95pa. ISBN 13: 978-0-8063-1457-0.

Bibliographic Checklist of African American Newspapers provides listings of past and current African American newspapers and additional publications such as books, dissertations, and other references sources. This title is easy to use with its organization and appendix. The resources listed are organized by the state where they were published and then arranged by city. One benefit of this work is it includes dates of newspaper publications. Many African American newspapers are regional and published with varying lengths of time, so researchers may be able to identify newspapers that no longer are published. One shortcoming of *Bibliographic Checklist* is it does not provide information on where these sources can be located, although its introduction describes how researchers can do so. This work will best be used in conjunction with the more extensive resource, *African-American Newspapers and Periodicals: A National Bibliography*, edited by James P. Danky (see ARBA 2000, entry 278). *Bibliographic Checklist* was initially published in 1995 then reprinted in 2008 with no changes. This volume is recommended for libraries with focuses in African American history and genealogy.—**Kristy Padron**

Handbooks and Yearbooks

P

115. Carmack, Sharon DeBartolo. **You Can Write Your Family History.** repr. ed. Baltimore, Md., Genealogical Publishing, 2008. 245p. index. $19.95pa. ISBN 13: 978-0-8063-1783-0.

You Can Write Your Family History takes the genealogist beyond the collecting of names and dates by showing step by step how to bring your ancestors to life through the writing of a narrative history. Extremely practical and easy to read, this guide contains excellent guidance on research, writing, and publishing. The author shows how to conduct background research in order to weave social history into the narrative. She discusses plot sequencing and structure, point of view, verb tense, and the other technical aspects of writing. The chapter on citing sources is brief so the reader will probably want to refer to other sources for this important aspect of the writing process. The publishing and marketing chapter provides good insight on the various avenues available for the family history writer, including self-publishing, print on demand, and commercial publishing. All things considered, this is an excellent practical guide for the family historian, and is recommended for public, academic, and genealogical libraries.—**Danielle Marie Carlock**

P

116.   Mitchell, Brian. **Pocket Guide to Irish Genealogy.** 3d ed. Baltimore, Md., Genealogical Publishing, 2008. 83p. $16.95pa. ISBN 13: 978-0-8063-5385-2.

This 7-x-10-inch "pocket" guide is hardly pocket sized. Nevertheless, this guide is an essential source for researchers doing Irish genealogy or family history. The 1st edition contained 63 pages, the 2d edition 77 pages, and the present 3d edition has added another 6 pages of essential research information. The review of the 2d edition recommended that further editions contain an index. There is still no index. Nevertheless, the 3d edition is recommended for all reference and circulating collections as a necessary replacement of its 1st and 2d editions (2d ed.; see ARBA 2003, entry 339).—**J. Carlyle Parker**

P

117.   **The Oxford Companion to Family and Local History.** David Hey, ed. New York, Oxford University Press, 2008. 661p. $50.00. ISBN 13: 978-0-19-953298-8.

In the past few years there has been a growth of interest in local and family history. Although there have been advances in technology, uncovering one's heritage is not easy. *The Oxford Companion to Family and Local History* makes this process easier by offering users a guide to the whole of the British Isles family heritage. This revised edition updates and adds several sections that the 1st edition lacked. The editor correctly describes the new and revised items in his "Notes to the Reader."

The *Companion* begins with 13 thematic contents listings. It is followed by an essay section covering numerous topics of concern to family and local historians. Twenty erudite contributors write these long thematic essays. Next are the more than 2,000 shorter jargon-free entries, written mostly by the editor and arranged in alphabetic order. There are cross-references indicated by an asterisk or by the use of *see* references; *see also* references are used to inform the reader of related subjects and bibliographic references that may be of interest. A dagger indicates a reference to an essay. An appendix lists national and major county and local record offices along with special collections of national importance, with their addresses and Websites.

Although this reference is limited to British Isles local history, it is of interest to anyone interested in uncovering and understanding the past of the United Kingdom.—**Nadine Salmons**

Indexes

P

118.   **Ancestry Library Edition.** http://www.proquest.com/products_pq/descriptions/ale.shtml. [Website]. Ann Arbor, Mich., ProQuest. Price negotiated by site. Date reviewed: 2008.

This site is a partnership with MyFamily.com and provides unparalleled coverage of U.S. and UK genealogical information available today. In addition to investigating their family history and looking for family members, users can research the origin of their names, geographical distribution of their last name, and interesting facts such as average life span. The site has nearly 4,000 databases, such as U.S Federal Census image and indexes, Map Center, *American Genealogical Biographical Index*, and Social Security Death Index. Searching functions including intuitive content organization, image enhancing, and a simplified on-screen navigation. It is accessible to both beginner and advanced researchers.—**Catherine Barr**

HERALDRY

C, P

119.   **Companion to Emblem Studies.** Peter M. Daly, ed. New York, AMS Press, 2008. 632p. index. $225.00. ISBN 0-404-83720-5. ISBN 13: 978-0-404-63720-0.

The *Companion to Emblem Studies* is the 20th work in the AMS Studies in the Emblem series. The stated goal of this particular book in the series is to provide the reader with an introduction to the topic of emblem studies. The variety of topics found in the 21 chapters of this edited work appear to support this stated goal. The book starts with an introduction to the topic of emblems and an essay on emblem theory is also included. The focus of the articles in this work then shift to examining the emblem in specific languages and countries throughout Europe (also including one article about emblems in America). This work then shifts focus again to discuss the emblem in specific contexts, such material culture, the tournament, and in modern logos and advertisements. Black-and-white illustrations can be found throughout this work, and a selective bibliography for further reading is included at the end.—**Larissa Anne Gordon**

8   Geography and Travel Guides

GEOGRAPHY

General Works

Atlases

C, P, S

120.   **The Comparative World Atlas.** rev. ed. Long Island City, N.Y., Hammond, 2007. 104p. illus. index. $11.95pa. ISBN 13: 978-0-843-70952-0.

This resource is a slim volume packed with extremely useful data and maps. Contained in this thin and easily transportable volume are 35 maps of the world. In addition, thematic maps of each continent/region cover climate, temperature, vegetation, population, rainfall, energy sources, and environmental concerns. Global relationship maps cover structure of the earth, atmosphere and oceans, climate, vegetation and soils, environmental concerns, population, languages and religions, standards of living, agriculture and manufacturing, energy and resources, transportation and trade, and global politics. The computer-generated topographical maps are very good and enhance readers' understanding of the relationship between terrain and political boundaries. This edition includes an index of countries, cities, regions, political divisions, and physical features of the world. Colored and labeled tabs at the top clearly identify sections of every continent and enable quick thumbing to a particular region. The fifth ocean has been omitted from the list of oceans and seas. The Southern Ocean was identified and labeled in 2000 by the International Hydrographic Organization (IHO). Overall, this is a very handy resource and quick reference for students.—**Linda M. Turney**

C, P, S

121.   **Hammond Essential World Atlas.** Long Island City, N.Y., Hammond, 2008. 191p. illus. maps. index. $19.95pa. ISBN 13: 978-0-843-70964-3.

This atlas is comprised of five major sections: guidance on using the reference; overview essays on the solar system, the earth, earthquakes, volcanoes, natural disasters, climate, vegetation, world religions, and languages; satellite images showing the Earth's physical features and settlement patterns; political maps by world region and subsets within each region; and a reference component with statistics, world flags, and time zones. The maps use the Hammond Optimal Conformal Projection, a new technique that minimizes shifts in scale and shape for a depicted region. After the cartographer defines the map area, a specialized computer program evaluates the size and shape of the region. Whereas the typical atlas uses one standard projection for all the maps in the collection, with this technique, each map has a unique projection to create a more distortion-free image.—**Adrienne Antink**

C, S

122.   **Oxford Atlas of Exploration.** 2d ed. New York, Oxford University Press, 2008. 256p. illus. maps. index. $50.00. ISBN 13: 978-0-19-534318-2.

This overview of the history of exploration begins with an examination of the earliest known expeditions, which included the Phoenicians, Greeks, and early Europeans. The subsequent sections each focus on particular continents, including Asia, Africa, the Americas, the Pacific islands, Australia, New Zealand, and the Arctic and the Antarctic. A section on the oceans and the field of oceanography is followed by a section on current exploration, which includes scientific examinations of ecological environments (such as the rain forest and the desert) and of the regions outside other earth's atmosphere (the solar system and beyond). Each section is presented chronologically with accompanying historical details and events. Colorful illustrations and detailed maps enhance the concise, informative text and reflect the changes in perception that came with increased knowledge. A listing of individuals involved in the history of exploration is given at the end with brief biographical information and page numbers for corresponding entries within the main text. A timeline of exploration, divided into categories for Asia, Africa, Europe, and the rest of the world is followed by an index. The excellent, concise presentation serves as a beginning point for further study of the history and techniques of exploration.—**Martha Lawler**

C, P, S

123.   **Oxford Atlas of the United States.** New York, Oxford University Press, 2006. 208p. maps. index. $27.95pa. ISBN 13: 978-0-19537236-6.

This atlas continues to be a valuable addition to public and academic libraries needing the most up-to-date geographical information. The work is organized into four sections. "North American Geography" provides statistical information on topics such as politics, energy and minerals, climate and weather, indigenous people, immigration and population changes, urbanization and agricultural uses of land, and languages and religion in North America. Following this is a section entitled "United States," which provides detailed maps of the regions and each of the 50 states in the United States as well as Puerto Rico and the U.S. Pacific Territories. Next is a section of city maps that provides detailed maps of 15 major cities. One of the most useful sections of the atlas is the gazetteer, which provides general information on the state (e.g., nickname, state bird, state flower), a brief history of the state, information on the state's capital, and a side bar with statistical information on the population, businesses, and geography. The index provides access to the 30,000 place-names in the atlas, along with latitude/longitude and letter/figure grid references.

The *Oxford Atlas of the United States* is well-executed and accurate. It should be a useful addition in academic, public libraries, and school libraries.—**Shannon Graff Hysell**

P, S

124.   **World Atlas. http://www.factsonfile.infobasepublishing.com/.** [Website]. New York, Facts on File. Price negotiated by site. Date reviewed: 2008.

The Facts on File *World Atlas* database is an excellent electronic resource of printable maps for teachers, librarians, and students. It provides an extensive collection of 1,500 full-color, original maps that can be reprinted for use by students and teachers. The site provides political, outline, elevation, statistical, and locator maps. Included within are world maps, regional geographic maps, and regional thematic maps. There are also country profiles, U.S. state profiles, and Canadian province profiles. These special profiles provide: descriptions facts and figures for each country or region; government, legal, and economic information; selected country constitutions; information about climate and weather, people and culture, ethnic composition, languages, and religion; biographies; history; chronology; images; and further resources. Unique to this resource is a tool that compares and ranks countries, U.S. states, and Canadian provinces and territories using selected statistics. A special "In the News" section features regularly updated articles organized by country as well as an archive of past articles. This database is highly recommended for all middle and high school libraries and public libraries.—**Shannon Graff Hysell**

Dictionaries and Encyclopedias

C, P

125.   **The Columbia Gazetteer of the World.** 2d ed. Saul B. Cohen, ed. Irvington, N.Y., Columbia University Press, 2008. 3v. index. $595.00/set. ISBN 13: 978-0-231-14554-1.

Since its publication in 1998, *The Columbia Gazetteer of the World* (see ARBA 2000, entry 351) has been the standard geographical reference source, continuing the tradition of its predecessor, *The Columbia-Lippincott Gazetteer of the World*. The new edition will remain in that spot. With over 170,000 entries, the *Gazetteer* is the most comprehensive A-Z listing of geographic locations and features available. There are 7,000 new entries, and numerous revisions reflecting changes to the physical environment, demographic shifts, and human conflict. Hurricane Katrina, the 2004 tsunami, the Three Gorges Dam, various wars, and numerous smaller events and decisions that have altered the geographic landscape are all reflected here. The online version has been updated continually and the changes have now been added to the new print edition. This is still an important source that almost all libraries will need to have in their reference collections, although some may opt for only the online version.—**Michael Levine-Clark**

S

126.   **United States Geography. http://www.usgeography.abc-clio.com/Login/Login.aspx.** [Website]. Santa Barbara, Calif., ABC-CLIO. Price negotiated by site. Date reviewed: 2009.

S

127.   **World Geography. http://www.worldgeography.abc-clio.com/Login/Login.aspx.** [Website]. Santa Barbara, Calif., ABC-CLIO. Price negotiated by site. Date reviewed: 2009.

Designed with the same format as ABC-CLIO's other education Websites, *World Geography* provides more than 18,000 reference entries discussing countries, cultures, environmental overviews, each country's history, and structures of government of countries around the world. Also included are 40,000 primary and secondary sources, 500 maps and flags, 200 country overviews, 1,500 biographies of key political and cultural figures, and "Clioview," an online statistical tool that allows students to make statistical comparisons between countries. Along with the option to search by keyword or perform an advanced search, users can also click on Explore a Country to browse various geographical regions or click on Analyze, a new feature that allows students to find key dilemmas in history and discover different viewpoints or interpretations from academics. Included are political and topographic maps for each country as well as regional maps so students can see where countries lie in relation to each other. The site also features access to a Merriam-Webster dictionary.

United States Geography has much the same format but focuses solely on the 50 states. It presents an overview of each state with a highly visual interface. It provides 19,000 primary and secondary sources, images of state flags and seals, 2,600 images, 150 maps, and even multimedia that includes state songs and statewide events. It also includes "Clioview," which allows students to compare statistical data between states.

These databases, along with all of ABC-CLIO's other databases, have been updated in Release 2.0, which offers cross-database searching if you have access to multiple databases, as well as easy-to-use filters for searches, features stories that connect entries to current events, and MLA citations that can translate to other popular citations styles. Teachers and media specialists will find the sites useful because they allow them to create assignments, tests, and a syllabus on the Staff Edition page. Only teachers and librarians will have access to this page. This feature also allows students to access the Website from home and will allow parents to be aware of their children's homework and future assignments.

These databases, much like the others from ABC-CLIO, will enhance any school's teaching curriculum. They will bring geography to life for many students and provide a new outlet for learning. If used along with other databases from ABC-CLIO, these geography databases will put world history, politics, current events, and geography all in a context that will be easily understood by students.—**Shannon Graff Hysell**

PLACE-NAMES

C, P

128.   Room, Adrian. **African Placenames: Origins and Meanings of the Names for Natural Features, Towns, Cities, Provinces and Countries.** 2d ed. Jefferson, N.C., McFarland, 2008. 218p. $55.00. ISBN 13: 978-0-7864-3546-3.

When studying Africa over time, the problem of changing names arises. This book is designed to help clarify this situation by providing "the origins and meanings of the names for natural features, towns, cities, provinces and counties." It is a revised and enlarged edition of the book first published in 1994. Since then, many names of countries, provinces, states, cities, and other locations have been changed. Here one can find the old and the new names along with some history about them. While the alphabetic dictionary is most of the volume, there is a brief introductory essay on Africa, its exploration and settlement, its languages, and prefixes and suffixes in African place-names. There are seven appendixes: Arabic terms in African place-names; official languages of African countries; locations and populations of African countries; official names of African countries; independence dates; African place-names with biblical connections; and African place-names in the 1771 *Encyclopaedia Britannica*. There is also a select bibliography. It is a useful reference book for people interested in Africa.—**J. E. Weaver**

C, P

129.   Room, Adrian. **The Pronunciation of Placenames: A Worldwide Dictionary.** Jefferson, N.C., McFarland, 2007. 229p. $39.95pa. ISBN 13: 978-0-7864-2941-7.

Adrian Room is the author of many reference titles, including *Placenames of the World* (2d ed., see ARBA 2006, entry 392) and *African Placenames* (2d ed.; see entry 128). This reference dictionary provides a user-friendly pronunciation guide for over 12,000 place-names worldwide. It follows an easy-to-read phonetic alphabet that uses only standard English letters; therefore, avoiding any unconventional characters of the International Phonetic Alphabet. Entries include familiar world place-names, both historic and current, as well as several less familiar names that have uncertain or difficult pronunciations. An appendix provides a useful directory to the most well-known countries, regions, and cities whose native names differ significantly from their English counterparts.—**Philip G. Swan**

TRAVEL GUIDES

General Works

P

130.   Fuad-Luke, Alastair. **The Eco-Travel Guide.** New York, Thames and Hudson, 2008. 352p. illus. index. $29.95pa. ISBN 13: 978-0-500-28766-8.

We live in a time where more people are concerned about the impact their lives have on the environment around them. New markets are emerging from these concerns that promote ecologically friendly business practices. One steadily growing area is eco-travel. *The Eco-Travel Guide* by Alistair Fuad-Luke is a well-organized and contemporary guide focusing on this new genre. This work is good for any well-traveled patron seeking green travel information. The book is broken down into four parts. Part 1 examines the "idea of travel," and what it means in the modern world with all of its challenges such as climate change and population growth. The section examines what man can do to mitigate negative travel-related impacts. Part 2 presents the actual destination reviews broken down by the following types: urban, nature, adventure, leisure, and culture. Each destination is presented in a concise, easy-to-read layout with information on the location's architecture, benefits to the local culture and environment, and activities. Part 3 features reports on eco-products for travelers that are grouped into products for mobility, protection, and comfort. The product information covers manufacturers, materials, and eco-design features. Part 4 contains general information on how to be more eco-friendly with online resource listings, suggestions for further reading, and a glossary. The section also contains contact information for the destinations and products featured in the guide. The destinations represent a diverse, worldwide sampling. Some 800 color illustrations enhance the guide. All in all, the work is a great introduction to green travel destinations.—**Sue Ellen Griffiths**

P

131.   **1001 Historic Sites you Must See Before You Die.** Richard Cavendish, ed. Hauppauge, N.Y., Barron's Educational Series, 2008. illus. index. $35.00. ISBN 0-7641-6044-3. ISBN 13: 978-0-7641-6044-8.

This book is designed with both the casual traveler and the history buff in mind. Similar to other titles in the series that focus on specialized topics (e.g., 1001 natural wonders, 1001 gardens), this title provides visitor information on historic palaces, cathedrals, temples, battlefields, and personal homes of historical figures. The book provides practical information (e.g., hours of operation, contact information, price of admission) as well as a detailed description of each location. Users will find many of the expected locales, such as Stonehenge in England, the Coliseum in Rome, Gettysburg in Pennsylvania, Pear Harbor in Hawaii, and the Empire State Building in New York City, as well as some unexpected surprises, such as Dracula's Castle in Romania, Shakespeare's birthplace, the Plain of Jars in Laos, and the Alhambra in Granada, Spain.

This is a title that will appeal to the armchair traveler as well as the history buff planning their next adventure. Although the descriptions and information are thorough in describing each specific locale, users will need to use additional sources to plan a full travel itinerary. This guidebook is recommended for both large and small public library collections.—**Shannon Graff Hysell**

United States

P

132.   **City Profiles USA, 2008-2009: A Traveler's Guide to Major US Cities.** 9th ed. Detroit, Omnigraphics, 2008. 1074p. $175.00. ISBN 13: 978-0-7808-1025-9. ISSN 1082-9938.

City Profiles USA, 2008-2009 is the 9th edition of a guide to the U.S. cities that represent most likely destinations for travelers. The major portion of the book consists of state-by-state profiles of selected U.S. and a few Canadian cities. Each profile includes a brief overview, popular driving distances, typical weather conditions, information sources, transportation services, accommodations, restaurants, major shopping facilities, media, colleges/universities, hospitals, attractions, sports/recreation, and notable events. Listings contain telephone numbers and, where appropriate, street addresses, fax numbers, and Internet addresses. Profiled cities are indexed by state and by city. An introduction offers further explanation of the information found in the profiles. Useful tables list area codes, airlines, airport codes, AAA offices, business services, car rental agencies, credit card companies, convention centers, visitor information bureaus, hotel chains and reservation services, mileage major cities, American Express travel offices, online travel services, weather information sources, and a calendar of events. The guide provides convenient access to comprehensive and pertinent information on the most popular U.S. cities for travelers and travel planners.—**William C. Struning**

ARCHAEOLOGY

C, P

133.   **The Concise Oxford Dictionary of Archaeology.** 2d ed. By Timothy Darvill. New York, Oxford University Press, 2008. 547p. $50.00. ISBN 13: 978-0-19-953405-0.

The Concise Oxford Dictionary of Archaeology is quite possibly one of the finest single-volume reference works in the field of archaeology currently available. Compiled by Darvill, a professor of archaeology, it covers a wide array of archaeological topics in comfortably sized, easy-to-understand entries. The coverage is very broad, explaining archaeological terms, cultures, people, and artifacts from Asia, Africa, the Americas, and the Pacific Rim in addition to Europe and the Mediterranean area. All of the entries are as current as possible. While some illustrations would have added even more to this resource, without them it is still a great purchase for any library.

The entries are alphabetically arranged, with the term printed in bold face for ease of scanning and the entry written for a non-archaeological audience. Some excellent quick reference resources, including treaties covering the handling of archaeological and cultural artifacts, timelines of major areas of the globe, listings of rulers and emperors, and a complete timeline of ancient Egyptian dynasties and their rulers are included in the appendixes. In the introduction, a scheme is detailed classifying each entry by type (i.e., deity, artifact, biography, equipment, and so forth), and each entry carries an abbreviation telling the user what type of entry they are reading. New to this edition are recommended, up-to-date Web links for over 100 entries on the *Dictionary of Archaeology* companion Website. The publisher plans to regularly update the site to keep links completely current.

The Concise Oxford Dictionary of Archaeology will be useful in all sorts of libraries for all sorts of patrons, from children writing book reports to university students preparing research papers to readers of historical fiction curious about terminology and authenticity. It is recommended as a vital reference resource for all types of libraries.—**Mark T. Bay**

C

134.   Kipfer, Barbara Ann. **Dictionary of Artifacts.** Malden, Mass., Blackwell, 2007. 345p. illus. $124.95. ISBN 13: 978-1-4051-1887-3.

This volume includes more than 2,000 entries defining terms relating to artifacts and archaeology. An artifact is defined as anything made or used by humans. The author states that she has selected terms that are both cross-cultural and "cross-Atlantic." Entries range in length from a single phrase to half a page. Entries cover archaeological sites, eras, processes, plants, artifact analysis and care, decoration, production and technology, and materials. Some entries include drawings or photographs. One large category omitted from this work is architecture. Language is accessible and jargon-free.

While the book is advertised as a lexicon for practitioners as well as for students and general readers, some terms and definitions are too simplistic to be of real value. For example, the word *ball* is defined as "a round object used in games" (p. 26) and the entry includes a labeled drawing of a sphere. Most of the words/terms defined would be useful to an archaeological novice or a general reader, but it is hoped that most practitioners would be familiar with the vocabulary covered. The high price of this volume will make it less desirable for those with limited budgets. The author is both an archaeologist and lexicographer. She holds a Ph.D. in linguistics and has written two other archaeological reference works. This dictionary is recommended for general reference collections in academic libraries. [R: LJ, 1 Sept 07, p. 167]—**Joanna M. Burkhardt**

AMERICAN HISTORY

Atlases

C, P, S

135.   **Atlas of United States History.** rev. ed. Long Island City, N.Y., Hammond, 2007. 72p. maps. $11.95pa. ISBN 13: 978-0-843-70955-1.

In the *Atlas of United States History*, Hammond once again has presented a quality reference resource intended for all audiences, at a very reasonable price. From pre-European contact through the colonial period to the present, the atlas is full of maps that focus on cultural, archaeological, anthropological, and historical features. From maps of Native American linguistic, tribal, and cultural areas to trade routes and military campaigns, along with political and social demarcations, this resource illustrates a great deal of information about the development of the United States. Also included are many useful charts that explain the breakdowns of political party membership from 1789 through 2004, along with maps that show political sectionalism from most presidential elections. Maps and charts of census information chart the growth and change of the U.S. population from the beginning to nearly the present. At the back of the book is a section of flags from history and from the states and territories, and a large map showing states, cities, waterways, and boundaries is included for reference.

The *Atlas of United States History* is an excellent historical and social reference tool. The maps are clear and colorful, and the maps and charts are drawn to show a great deal of information in graphical format. A table of contents aids in finding relevant information quickly, and gazetteer of states, territories, and possessions helps the user locate area, population, admission, and settlement dates at a glance. Being a Hammond product, this atlas is of high authority. My only complaint is the flimsiness of the binding. Being paperback, it will not last long after high use. It keeps the price very low, but many libraries might prefer paying a little more for more durability. Still, its quality and price make the *Atlas of United States History* an excellent addition to any library collection.—**Mark T. Bay**

Biography

C, P

136.   **American Heroes.** Hackensack, N.J., Salem Press, 2009. 3v. illus. index. $217.00/set. ISBN 13: 978-1-58765-457-2.

This biographical encyclopedia of 209 heroes builds off some of the essays found in the Great Lives from History series published by Salem Press in 2006-2008. Each essay is provided in a standard format. It opens with a quote from the individual followed by ready-reference information, such as birth and main contributions to society. This is followed by the narrative essay about the subject's early life, main work, and significance. The individual entry concludes with an annotated bibliography.

The third volume includes a couple of useful indexes, including one based on category (such as sports or social reform) and another on ethnicity. The publisher defines heroes as "a person who has placed others above self" and has courageously undertaken difficult measures to better the world for other people

(p. vii). As the publisher readily notes, the term hero is subjective and they have included some controversial figures, such as Louis Farrakhan and Andrew Jackson. Overall, the entries are good and informative. Many of the individuals are social reformers or involved with government, although sports figures are also well represented. Other fields also come up, such as explorers, scientists, Native American leaders, and educators. Given the limited number of biographies selection is always a question, although in general their coverage is good. The one quibble is with the book's title; "North American Heroes" would have been more accurate. Otherwise, this is a useful, well-designed reference source that is highly recommend. [R: BL, 1 &15 Jan 09, p. 120]—**Allen Reichert**

C, P

137. **Icons of the American West: From Cowgirls to Silicon Valley.** Gordon Morris Bakken, ed. Westport, Conn., Greenwood Press, 2008. 2v. illus. index. (Greenwood Icons). $175.00/set. ISBN 13: 978-0-313-34148-9.

Simply put, an icon is a symbol. The Greenwood Icons series is an attempt by the publisher to present outstanding examples of people, places, movements, and so forth that over time have come to represent larger ideas and ideals. Recent titles include *Icons of Horror and the Supernatural: An Encyclopedia of Our Worst Nightmares* (see ARBA 2008, entry 902) and *Icons of Business: An Encyclopedia of Mavericks, Movers, and Shakers* (see ARBA 2008, entry 150). Although many are billed as being an encyclopedia, these two-volume sets are much more than those, as typically bite-sized entries are dispensed with in favor of 10 to 20 page signed essays. As the series foreword makes clear, the intent is to strike a balance between the concise but superficial treatment of subjects given in standard reference works and the comprehensive but time-consuming bulk of full-length narratives (p. xi). This reviewer finds the approach to be a refreshing and effective alternative.

In the current title, the emphasis is on people (e.g., Chief Joseph, Annie Oakley), although places (e.g., Yosemite National Park) and organizations (e.g., Sierra Club) make appropriate appearances. Cleverly, the editor, a professor of history at California State University (Fullerton) with an impressive body of published work on the American west, separates his subject matter into the old (volume 1), as epitomized by cowboys and Indians, mountain men, and so forth, and the new (volume 2), in which entries treat glittery Las Vegas and the fairy tale estate of Disneyland. The aforementioned length of entries allows the individual authors ample opportunity to strip away the accumulated layers of myth and stereotype to arrive at, if not the truth, at least an approximation of it. The 27 articles in this set are engagingly written, dispassionate in tone, and appear to be well supported by available documentation.

With special features, such as a chronology of major events in the history of the American west, shaded boxes containing excerpts from primary sources, and end-of-entry bibliographies, this set provides an insightful look at what makes the west the west, which to paraphrase the book, is as much a state of mind as a place of residence (p. 228).—**Michael Francis Bemis**

Catalogs and Collections

C

138. **The Early Republic: Critical Editions on the Founding of the United States. http:// earlyrepublic.press.jhu.edu.** [Website]. Charlene Bangs Bickford and others, eds. Baltimore, Md., Johns Hopkins University Press. $500.00 (first year subscription); $250.00 (subsequent annual subscriptions). Date reviewed: Dec. 2008.

Compiled by the First Federal Congress Project and published in 17 volumes by Johns Hopkins University Press, January 2009 will mark the debut of this set in electronic form. The database includes primary documents on the actions, debates, and thoughts of the First Federal Congress and members from the years 1789-1791. The database includes 17,000 annotated pages and 250 images as well as a cumulative index. Future plans for this database include the addition of two new volumes of primary documents as well as the inclusion of some 20 other publications that relate to the Colonial period and the American Revolution. This site will be updated on an annual basis. It will be useful to students and scholars studying and researching this important part of U.S. history.—**Shannon Graff Hysell**

Chronology

C, S

139.   Carlisle, Rodney P. **Civil War and Reconstruction.** New York, Facts on File, 2008. 452p. illus. maps. index. (Eyewitness History). $67.50. ISBN 13: 978-0-8160-6347-5.

This work treats the history of the Civil War and Reconstruction era, covering the years from 1846 through 1877. The story is told through topical and roughly chronological chapters that, taken individually, cover the build-up to the war, secession, emancipation, land and naval warfare, politics, and Reconstruction. While much of this material is available electronically and in print, the combination of narratives, chronologies, maps, and supplementary appendixes brings the story together in an easy-to-use format that should prove useful for individuals unfamiliar with the period.

Carlyle, a widely published historian, treats his subject in well-written and well-reasoned essays that follow generally accepted interpretations of the events covered. Each of the 11 chapters follows a consistent format that includes a historical narrative, followed by a chronology of events, and contemporary eyewitness accounts pertinent to the chapter's topic. Three appendixes provide substantial relevant documentary, biographical, cartographical, and tabular data relative to the period.

Although this is overall an excellent volume, there are criticisms. The atlas adds little to the book. Its brevity and the curious selection of maps add little value to the history of the period. Electoral maps illustrating the presidential vote between 1844 to 1860 omit the major election of 1864 in which Abraham Lincoln came close to losing to George McClellan. Additionally, one might question the inclusion of some battles to the exclusion of others of more significance. On the positive side, the 48 biographical sketches provide a well-rounded selection of significant famous and infamous civilian, military, male, and female persons of the period. A 50-page documentary appendix provides the text of pertinent legislation, speeches, and correspondence. Of particular interest are two charts that provide chronologies of worldwide emancipation of slavery from 1761 to 1962, including state-by-state emancipation in the United States. Due to this books organizational structure, access to the contents is limited primarily to an adequate 15-page index. Overall, this is a good, well-rounded reference work and is recommended for public and academic libraries of all levels that have an interest in the Civil War.—**Donald E. Collins**

C, S

140.   Fredricksen, John C. **Chronology of American History.** New York, Facts on File, 2008. 4v. illus. maps. index. (Facts on File Library of American History). $315.00/set. ISBN 13: 978-0-8160-6800-5.

Chronological encyclopedias have always been an integral reference source for students of historiography. This new four-volume encyclopedia by Professor John C. Fredricksen, is the newest addition to the Facts on File Library of American History series and a rare production that will undoubtedly set the standard in the field. Spanning 12,000 years, the encyclopedia includes almost 8,000 chronological and day-to-day entries, 400 feature boxes, maps, a generous supply of high-quality illustrations, and a number of added features that facilitate its ease of use.

Coverage spans a diverse range of subjects, and the essays are well written and should appeal to a wide audience. One especially notable feature is the abundance and quality of the encyclopedia's biographical sidebar entries. The day-to-day entries are the heart of the encyclopedia, and are extremely comprehensive and interesting. Fredricksen has done an admirable job of including a wide range of entries with engaging descriptions of events. Bound in attractive and durable bindings using high-quality materials, this encyclopedia should serve history students of all levels, and will make a welcome addition to all serious American history collections. Thus, it is highly recommended for all undergraduate, school, and large public libraries serving students, American history buffs, and interested readers.—**Vincent P. Tinerella**

Dictionaries and Encyclopedias

C, S

141. **American History. http://www.americanhistory.abc-clio.com/Login/Login.aspx.** [Website]. Santa Barbara, Calif., ABC-CLIO. Price negotiated by site. Date reviewed: 2009.

This electronic resource from ABC-CLIO is designed specifically with teachers and students in mind. Designed much like the other social studies databases from ABC-CLIO, this Website focuses on American history from the early exploration (1350) to the American Revolution and the establishment of the 13 original colonies. It covers westward expansion, the Civil War, the Industrial Revolution, and the current threat of terrorism, with much more in between. *American History* provides more than 18,000 reference entries discussing cultures, events, inventions, religious movements, and personalities that have had an impact on U.S. history. Also included are 15,000 primary and secondary sources, 3,300 biographies of important figures, more than 100 topical overviews that explore connections to past and present events, and some 150 thematic essays that discuss major themes. The essays on each topic are thorough and will be easy for middle to high school students to understand and the photographs and maps are clear.

Searching this site is straightforward. Along with the option to search by keyword or perform an advanced search, users can also click on Explore an Era to browse various time periods or click on Analyze, a new feature that allows students to find key dilemmas in U.S. history and discover different viewpoints or interpretations from academics. When students find the topic they are researching they will also find related entries located in a sidebar, which will further their research.

This database, along with all of ABC-CLIO's other databases, has been updated in Release 2.0, which offers cross-database searching if you have access to multiple databases, as well as easy-to-use filters for searches, features stories that connect entries to current events, and MLA citations that can translate to other popular citations styles. Teachers and media specialists will find the site useful because it allows them to create assignments, tests, and a syllabus on the Staff Edition page. Only teachers and librarians will have access to this page. This feature also allows students to access the Website from home and will allow parents to be aware of their children's homework and future assignments.

The *American History* Website is a remarkable tool that will give learning U.S. history new appeal to young adults. Students will enjoy using it and it will give teachers the opportunity to teach U.S. history in a new and exciting format. For all of the topics covered and the use it will have in the library, the classroom, and in students' homes this product deserves careful consideration.—**Shannon Graff Hysell**

C, P, S

142. **Daily Life America. http://www.greenwood.com/dailylife/america_info.aspx.** [Website]. Westport, Conn., Greenwood Press. Price negotiated by site. Date reviewed: 2008.

Daily Life America is a database of more than 100 different reference sources focusing on the lives of ordinary Americans from pre-Columbian times to the present, among them *The Greenwood Encyclopedia of American Regional Cultures*, *The Uniting States: The Story of Statehood for the Fifty United States*, *Encyclopedia of American Holidays and National Days*, and *Famous American Crimes and Trials*. There is a lot of information on cultural topics, such as housing, clothing, food, and celebrations. State-by-state resource guides give easy access to state songs, mottos, and other key pieces of information. The ability to browse—by subject, time period, or region—and the primary documents, maps, and photographs make this a useful resource.—**Catherine Barr**

C

143.   **Encyclopedia of American Studies. http://eas-ref.press.jhu.edu/references.** [Website]. Balti-more, Md., Johns Hopkins University Press. $325.00 (annual subscription). Date reviewed: Dec. 2008.

Johns Hopkins Press's online database the *Encyclopedia of American Studies* brings together over 660 online, searchable subject entries and biographical entries on American history and culture from pre-colonial days to the present. Each entry contains a bibliography for further reference. The content is suitable for high school students on up to undergraduates. It will aid those conducting research in Ameri-can history as well as in sociology and ethnic studies. This is an ideal place for researchers to begin their research on a variety of American history topics. This site is edited by Miles Orvell and sponsored by the American Studies Association. It is updated quarterly ensuring it will provide users with up-to-date information.—**Shannon Graff Hysell**

C, S

144.   **Encyclopedia of the Jazz Age: From the End of World War I to the Great Crash.** James Ciment, ed. Armonk, N.Y., M. E. Sharpe, 2008. 2v. illus. index. $199.00/set. ISBN 13: 978-0-7656-8078-5.

F. Scott Fitzgerald coined the phrase "The Jazz Age" to describe the care-free years between the end of World War I and the start of the Great Depression (1918-1929). In our collective perception since, the era is most often remembered fondly by its flamboyant characters—Hemingway, Fitzgerald, Bryan, Landis, Mencken, Capone, Ness, Hearst—its fads and speakeasies, and the prosperity and free-wheeling individualism of the Roaring Twenties. In fact, the immediate post-war years were a complicated period in our nation's history of profound and unprecedented social and cultural conflict pitting agrarian traditional-ist, fundamentalist values against a new urban modernism in nearly every area of life: politics, economics, foreign and domestic policy, religion, ethnicity, race relations, gender, immigration, social class, and morality.

This new collaboration between editor James Ciment and M. E. Sharp notably captures the com-plexity of the period with its in-depth coverage, comprehensiveness, and the engaging and informative narrative of its more than 300 signed articles written by an impressive list of scholars and subject special-ists. The set thus furnishes a distinctive and valuable one-stop reference source for the period. Written pri-marily for senior high school readers and undergraduates, this encyclopedia should make a fine addition to almost any school, academic, or public library collection serving students and history buffs interested in this unique period in American historiography.

The encyclopedia is divided into three main sections. The set begins with a series of thematic essays on a variety of important subjects relative to the period, followed by the main A to Z section, and ending with a section entitled "Cultural Landmarks," which furnishes descriptions and commentary of more than 100 significant art, film, music, literature, and architectural offerings. Notable features include an intro-duction to the period written by Ciment, a topic finder, and bibliographies at the end of articles; a good, easy-to-use main index subdivided by topic; a comprehensive bibliography; cross-references; a list of sidebars; and a generous amount of high-quality illustrations and archival photographs. The *Encyclopedia* will fill an important void in the historical reference literature for most school and undergraduate libraries, and it is therefore highly recommended.—**Vincent P. Tinerella**

P, S

145.   **Exploring American History: From Colonial Times to 1877.** Tom Lansford and Thomas E. Woods Jr., eds. Tarrytown, N.Y., Marshall Cavendish, 2008. 11v. illus. maps. index. $359.95/set. ISBN 13: 978-0-7614-7746-4.

Exploring American History is a fitting title for this middle school encyclopedia of early American history. The reader is enticed by photographs, attractive reproductions of woodcuts, lithographs, maps, facsimiles of documents, and other visual attractions to explore the 219 entries on one of five main themes: culture, society, and economy; government, politics, war, and foreign affairs; laws, treaties, cases, and documents; people; and places. For example, "Architecture, Building and Homes" includes a well-written background summary of the topic, a chronology, six photographs of diverse structures, a facsimile of the title page and frontispiece from a book on cottages by Andrew Jackson Downing, a panel with a quote from Emerson's *Self-Reliance* critical of undue European influence on American architecture, and a sidebar called Jefferson's "Academic Village," which discusses his design of the University of Virginia.

But the 11-volume set's greatest strength is its clear and concise writing, made easily accessible for young readers by an editorial staff. The primary editors are Tom Lansford, who is the chair of the political science department at the University of Southern Mississippi—Gulf Coast and Thomas E. Woods, Jr., who teaches American history at Suffolk County Community College, SUNY, and is best known for authoring the *Politically Incorrect Guide to American History* (2004). According to the editors the articles are written by "accomplished scholars," many of whom are affiliated with an academic institution. Each entry is signed and include see also references. A short list of resources for further study is found, by topic, at the end of each volume, with a larger list in the comprehensive index. Other useful information there includes Internet Resources and Resources for Younger Readers.

Regarding selection of entries, the editors included the standard subjects contained in any general introduction to American history from colonial times (defined as approximately 1550) to the end of Reconstruction (1877). They have also included a generous number of entries on social and cultural history: Arts—Performance, Arts—Visual, Chautauqua Movement, Frontier Life and Culture, Labor Movement and Unions, Literature, Press, and Suffrage. Given that the set has a limited number of entries (219), one should not expect many biographies, but a few prominent African Americans, who are not always included in textbooks, are included here (e.g., Benjamin Banneker, Paul Cuffe).

According to the Editors' Introduction, an editorial staff shaped the scholars' thoughts into language that students and general readers could understand. Only a few examples of questionable word selection were discovered by this reviewer (e.g., *Dred Scott v. Sandford*: "The decision had many ironic consequences, some tragic, some merely droll.") . Readers might also find the gothic-looking font for all headings to be difficult to read. But these are minor criticisms that should not deter any middle school or public librarians from buying this attractive multivolume introductory encyclopedia of early America for their collections.—**John P. Stierman**

S

146. **Issues and Controversies in American History. http://factsonfile.infobasepublishing.com/.** [Website]. New York, Facts on File. Price negotiated by site. Date reviewed: 2008.

This database covers American history from colonial times to the present with regularly updated links to overviews and background articles as well as special features to enhance research, such as timelines, captioned images, full-text primary documents, facts and figures on a wide range of topics, biographies, and so forth. It also provides discussion questions and activities that assist students in understanding the issues, as well as arguments for and against.—**Catherine Barr**

P, S

147. **The Old West: History and Heritage.** Edward Countryman, ed. Tarrytown, N.Y., Marshall Cavendish, 2009. 11v. illus. maps. index. $359.95/set. ISBN 13: 978-0-7614-7829-4.

The history and culture of the North American West still contains rich and diverse themes we mine today in contemporary society. These beautifully illustrated volumes are designed for readers in middle school and above, so effectively they will appeal to teenagers and casual adult readers. Each volume is relatively thin (not much more than 100 pages) and the 193 articles are divided among the first 10 volumes. The last volume is a comprehensive set of indexes with an extensive timeline and long lists of additional resources.

Each article is relatively long—up to about a dozen pages for some—and written by a noted expert on the topic. Most of the illustrations are of the highest quality, including many old photographs, woodcuts, lithographs, and maps. The literature boxes, however, are difficult to read because of a poor choice of background and type colors. Articles often contain their own chronological list, and they always start with a useful summary. The editor and publisher decided to carry a cinematic theme throughout the volumes, so nearly every article has still photographs from movies that may have touched upon the topic. These images include a caption with some discussion of the film's narrative and particular perspective on the story. Sometimes the connections are a bit forced. For example, *The Wizard of Oz* is included in the article about water because of the melting end of the Wicked Witch. (Dorothy's parents, you see, were hard-working farmers in Kansas who knew the value of a bucket of water.)

Considering how hard it is to write history for a younger audience and still retain an appreciation of the complexity, the prose is very readable and remarkably close to current historical perspectives. The many Western groups are treated fairly, including Indians, women, Mexicans, African Americans, and Mormons. The history of western Canada is included in detail, and parts of Mexico are also covered. This encyclopedia set is recommended for libraries serving adolescents and the general public.—**Mark A. Wilson**

C, P

148.　Schroeder-Lein, Glenna R. **The Encyclopedia of Civil War Medicine.** Armonk, N.Y., M. E. Sharpe, 2008. 421p. illus. index. $95.00. ISBN 13: 978-0-7656-1171-0.

This impressive new encyclopedia nicely begins to fill a much-neglected niche in the reference literature of the Civil War. While two-thirds of the Civil War dead lost their lives from disease rather than combat, historians and reference publishers have tended to concentrate on the more glamorous military and political aspects of the war. In every way in which a reference book may be evaluated, Glenna R. Schroeder-Lein provides a volume that is as close to perfection in terms of form, content, access, and accuracy as this reviewer, a Civil War historian and former reference librarian himself, has had the pleasure of using or reviewing.

Although the author limits the content to a seemingly brief 200-plus entries, these cover the field of Civil War medicine surprising well. Included are essays of from one paragraph to several pages in length on such topics as the medical aspects of Gettysburg and other battles, specific diseases common to soldiers, medicines, sanitation, the diet of soldiers and its consequences, amputation, ammunition and its impact on the body, named museums and their contents, medical associations and agencies, and health-related biographies of noted medical workers and others. These and other entries are highly readable, and are easily understood by lay and professional readers alike due to the purposeful exclusion of overly technical terms. All entries include bibliographies for further reading. Access to the contents is excellent through the alphabetic arrangement, the table of contents, a detailed index, and extensive *see* and *see also* references to other articles. A lengthy chronology places medical events in context with significant military, political, social, and other occurrences. The author includes a substantial bibliography and a small number of illustrations. This superb new volume is highly recommended for any person and any library even moderately interested in the American Civil War.—**Donald E. Collins**

P, S

149.　**U*X*L Encyclopedia of U.S. History.** By Sonia Benson, Daniel E. Brannen Jr., and Rebecca Valentine. Farmington Hills, Mich., U*X*L/Gale Group, 2008. 8v. illus. index. $495.00/set. ISBN 13: 978-1-4144-3043-0; 978-1-4144-3274-8 (e-book).

An up-to-date encyclopedia designed specifically for middle school students, this unique set is an essential purchase for school and public libraries serving those students. Eight attractively designed volumes yield approximately 700 alphabetically arranged main entries and more than 400 black-and-white images and maps. The entries reflect the 10 historical eras defined in the 2002 National Council for the Social Studies (NCSS) Curriculum Standards for Social Studies—Middle School. Teachers preparing lesson plans in accordance with these standards will welcome coverage that begins in the pre-1620 period and continues to the present. Within individual entries, terms in bold print serve as cross-references to related entries. Each volume contains the brief "Reader's Guide" as well as the general bibliography and the cumulative subject index in which boldface terms designate main entries and page numbers.

The selection of entries and the bibliography reflect the contemporary and student-friendly tone of this encyclopedia. Entries cover traditional persons and subjects as well as topics as diverse as Beatlemania and Barack Obama, Tobacco and Telephone. Sources cited in the bibliography include books, a surprisingly small handful of periodical articles, and numerous Websites ranging from Sparknotes.com to PBS online, Classicbands.com and Time.com. All Websites were available as of July 21, 2008.—**Julienne L. Wood**

Handbooks and Yearbooks

C, P, S

150.   **American Civil War: Gale Library of Daily Life.** Steven E. Woodworth, ed. Farmington Hills, Mich., Gale Group, 2008. 2v. illus. index. $211.00/set. ISBN 13: 978-1-4144-3009-6.

American Civil War: Gale Library of Daily Life contains some 200 articles arranged thematically. Each volume has an index covering both volumes and a chronology of 1858-1865; each of the thematic topics has its own annotated bibliography. Themes covered are a soldier's life, family and community, religion, popular culture, health and medicine, work and economy, politics, effects of war on freed people and slaves, reconciliation, and remembrance. The editor is the author of most of the overview pieces, with graduate students or professors, historians and others contributing the articles.

Most of the black-and-white illustrations are familiar, but a few, such as "Franklin County Court House" (p.90, v.1) lack complete attribution. *American Civil War: Gale Library of Daily Life* gives short shrift to some topics like popular songs, while being quite thorough in the health and medicine section. Civil War enthusiasts will enjoy browsing the sidebars in these volumes, but serious scholars will note omissions of many people, places, and events and might question some of its scholarship. However, given the continuing popularity of Civil War references, *American Civil War: Gale Library of Daily Life* is a logical addition to such a collection.—**Kay Cornelius**

S

151.   Hillstrom, Kevin. **The Great Depression and the New Deal.** Detroit, Omnigraphics, 2009. 226p. illus. index. (Defining Moments). $44.00. ISBN 13: 978-0-7808-1049-5.

This slim volume on the Great Depression and the New Deal is the latest installment in the Defining Moments series, designed for students grades 8-12, on pivotal events in U.S. history from the twentieth century forward. This volume, like others in the series, is divided into three primary sections: narrative overview, biographies, and primary sources. The narrative overview section provides a factual account of the topic, outlining origin, key players, major events, and impact. In *The Great Depression and the New Deal*, the timeline of events from the roaring twenties and the stock market crash up to the end of the Depression due to the prosperity of World War II is discussed. The author examines the economic problems that caused the Depression, the successes and failures of Roosevelt's New Deal, and how the country got back on track. The biographies section provides sketches of 7 leading figures of the period, including Herbert Hoover, Frances Perkins, Eleanor Roosevelt, and Henry A. Wallace. Sources for further study accompany each sketch. Primary sources include 11 documents ranging from Franklin Roosevelt's inaugural speech to an excerpt from John Steinbeck's *The Grapes of Wrath*. Additional useful materials include photographs, a chronology, a glossary, a bibliography that also includes Websites and videotapes, and a subject index.

The Great Depression and the New Deal is a well-organized, balanced, and approachable reference source for its intended audience, undoubtedly reflective of the composition of the series advisory board (public and school librarians and educators) and hopefully indicative of the quality of other titles in the series.—**Lisa Kay Speer**

C, S

152.   **Industrial Revolution: People and Perspectives.** Jennifer L. Goloboy, ed. Santa Barbara, Calif., ABC-CLIO, 2008. 224p. illus. index. (Perspectives in American Social History). $85.00. ISBN 13: 978-1-59884-065-0.

The United States emerged into the twentieth century as the world's leading industrial giant, and while that remarkable transformation from an agricultural to an industrial nation had accelerated tremendously after 1860, its origins were evident much earlier. This clearly written and carefully researched volume documents those early steps toward industrialization from roughly 1800 to 1860, calling attention to groups—women, ethnic and cultural minorities, laborers—often given short shrift in standard political and economic treatments of America's past. Dealing with free women workers, manufacturers, consumers, and the nascent working and middle classes, editor Jennifer Goloboy, a graduate of Harvard University's American Civilization Program, has written five of the book's nine chapters herself. The other four on white male artisans, slaves, readers and writers, and immigrants were "outsourced" to specialists in their respective fields. One point in particular made by the authors has a contemporary ring. Popular mythology of the self-made man notwithstanding, the Jacksonian era saw the rich getting considerably richer, as the richest 10 percent of the population increased its share of the national wealth, primarily after 1820, from 49.6 percent in 1774 to 73 percent in 1860. And in this pre-Darwinian age, the Protestant ethic offered easy justification for the success of the few and the failure of the many.

Adhering to a fairly standard format for the series on Perspectives in American Social History, this work provides a useful timeline from 1748 to 1860, an abundance of photographs, an assortment of primary documents from Alexander Hamilton's 1791 "Report on Manufactures" and Thomas Skidmore's *The Rights of Man to Property!* to William Gregg's "Practical Results of Southern Manufactures" and T. S. Arthur's "The Factory Girl," a bibliography at the end of each chapter and a topical bibliography at the end of the study, and an adequate index. While certainly useful to scholars, this is a work for a general audience that would be a worthwhile addition to high school and university libraries.—**John W. Storey**

C, P, S

153.   **Milestone Documents in American History: Exploring the Primary Sources That Shaped America.** Paul Finkelman, ed. Dallas, Tex., Schlager Group; distr., Hackensack, N.J., Salem Press, 2008. 4v. illus. index. $385.00/set. ISBN 13: 978-0-9797758-0-2.

Primary documents have always been essential scholarly sources for serious researchers and students of American historiography. Their study, moreover, has become increasingly important for high school and undergraduate-level students. What has been missing in previous attempts at encyclopedias devoted to primary documents has been broad and expressive contextual analysis. This new four-volume encyclopedia from the Schlager Group is the publisher's inaugural publication, the first offering in a larger series of future volumes entitled "Milestone Documents," and a first-rate effort intended to provide students with a comprehensive and scholarly traditional reference source. An electronic version is available from the publisher's companion Website (http://www.history.salempress.com.). It will undoubtedly become the premier reference work devoted to the subject.

What sets this encyclopedia apart is the combination of the full-text of 130 of the nation's most important documents with expert analysis by an impressive list of nearly 100 esteemed scholars and American historians. Edited by Paul Finkelman, President William McKinley Distinguished Professor of Law and Public Policy at Albany Law School (New York), *Milestone Documents in American History* incorporates a number of notable features. Each entry begins with an overview of the document and includes explanation and analysis; an examination of the context in which it was created; a brief biography of the article's author; a glossary; essential quotes; the author's intended audience; the document's historical impact; sidebars; questions for further study; related documents; photographs and illustrations; a bibliography; timelines; and the full-text of the document. The signed essays are comprehensive, the writing is terrific, the research is outstanding, and the depth of analysis noteworthy. Two forthcoming companion sets in the series, *Milestone Documents of American Leaders* and *Milestone Documents in World History* will be offered in 2009, and if they meet the high editorial standards of this first offering, will make for a major contribution to the study of history unmatched in its field. Thus, *Milestone Documents in American History* is highly recommended for all school, undergraduate, and large public libraries serving American history students, researchers, and interested readers.—**Vincent P. Tinerella**

ASIAN HISTORY

C, P

154.   Roy, Kumkum. **Historical Dictionary of Ancient India.** Lanham, Md., Scarecrow, 2009. 431p. (Historical Dictionaries of Ancient Civilizations and Historical Eras, no.23). $105.00. ISBN 13: 978-0-8108-5366-9.

India is home to many religions, cultures, languages, and over one billion people. It is a rising power with a very successful democracy and diversity in the world. Kumkum Roy, a Ph.D. in ancient Indian history, has published the 1st edition of the *Historical Dictionary of Ancient India*. The book has many good features including a thorough introduction, maps, a chronology of the history of India, a selected bibliography under various subject headings, and additional information about the author. The work examines the history of India from the earliest Paleolithic cultures up to 1000 B.C.E., and includes entries on rulers, bureaucrats, ancient societies, religions, gods, and philosophy. Much information on India's role as a crossroad for cultures from China and Europe to the Middle East and Africa is shared. Thousands of entries have been arranged in a dictionary style. They range from a paragraph to five pages in length. This work is certainly an excellent reference book and is recommended highly for all collections.—**Ravindra Nath Sharma**

EUROPEAN HISTORY

General Works

C, P, S

155.   **Encyclopedia of the Age of Imperialism, 1800-1914.** Carl Cavanagh Hodge, ed. Westport, Conn., Greenwood Press, 2008. 2v. index. $225.00/set. ISBN 13: 978-0-313-33404-7.

Students examining the economic, political, social, and technological changes of modern history will benefit from the Greenwood Press 2008 release of the *Encyclopedia of the Age of Imperialism, 1800-1914*, edited by associate professor of political science and director of the International Relations Program at the University of British Columbia-Okanagan, Carl Cavanagh Hodge. Beautifully designed, thoughtfully edited, carefully arranged, and masterfully written, this two-volume reference text is a user-friendly springboard source into the multifaceted subject of Imperialism. Not claiming to be exhaustive but rather comprehensive, not interpretive but descriptive, the *Encyclopedia* comes close to being a one-stop authority on the historical facts as well as a worthy guide to the scholarship published on the key themes of Imperialism. Note the further reading suggestions at the end of each entry as well as the selected bibliography in volume 2.

Both volumes provide lists to the 800 alphabetic entries, to which more than 60 senior and junior scholars contributed, and to the 30 primary documents, which are arranged chronologically. Open volume 2 to actually read Monroe's Doctrine, Bismarck's "Iron and Blood" statement, and Austro-Hungary's threat of war to Serbia, among others. Also included in both volumes is a Guide to Related Topics, such as Battles, Concepts, and Monarchs, and 13 maps of mostly western and eastern Europe, but also of Africa,

Asia, the Ottoman Empire, Russia, and the United States. A wonderful introduction, which provides a definition of imperialism and succinctly explains the complexity of its history, and a nicely laid out chronology, which outlines key events, treaties, and battles, can be accessed in volume 1; whereas the primary documents, selected bibliography, About the Editor and Contributors, and the index can be found at the end of volume 2. The encyclopedia portion of both volumes provides concise entries on topics ranging from the start of the Napoleonic Wars (*see* Waterloo, Battle of [1815]) to the outbreak of World War I (Franz Ferdinand). Within each entry, bold face type indicates cross-references.

This is the first reference work devoted solely to Imperialism. For both its singularity and the text's authority I recommend the source to high school and college libraries. That said, not just novices but even junior and senior scholars of modern history would benefit from the accessibility and content of the encyclopedia as well as the rich list of resources published within. The encyclopedia is available in print and as an e-book and is well worth the $225 cost. [R: LJ, 1 April 08]—**Amy Koehler**

France

C, P

156.   Raymond, Gino. **Historical Dictionary of France.** 2d ed. Lanham, Md., Scarecrow, 2009. 471p. (Historical Dictionaries of Europe, no.64). $110.00. ISBN 13: 978-0-8108-5095-8.

It is impossible to argue that France and its culture have been fundamental influences on western civilization. From the prehistoric caves at Lascaux to the European Union Parliament in Strasbourg, France has been at the center of events. Despite being famously dismissed by former U.S. Secretary of Defense Donald Rumsfeld as part of "old Europe," France's influence on and importance to the world have been profound and ongoing. Raymond, professor of Modern French Studies at the University of Bristol, United Kingdom, has provided in one volume an excellent resource for anybody interested in learning more about the history of France and its influence on politics, art, history, philosophy, and culture. From prehistoric hunter-gatherers to the present day, through centuries at the center of Western civilization, through World War II and the post-war era, this resource defines and explains important events, people, and places in the history of this fascinating and extremely influential country.

The authority of the book is good, and is free from obvious bias. The entries are concise and well written, and are accessible for anyone with an undergraduate reading level. A chronology, map, list of acronyms (and the French are extremely fond of acronyms), and lists of monarchs, presidents, and prime ministers are included as well. There is a bibliography for further reading. One complaint this reviewer has is the lack of illustrations. The map included is small and of indifferent quality, with too much detail crammed into one small map. Also, many of the entries cry out for at least line drawings. The nature of the work mostly restricts it to academic libraries supporting programs in Western European studies, history, philosophy, and cultural areas. The book is recommended for academic libraries, and even though it is fairly expensive, France has been so influential in so many areas that it should be considered essential for the reference collection.—**Mark T. Bay**

Greek

C

157.   **A Dictionary of Greek and Roman Culture.** William Smith, ed. New York, I. B. Tauris; distr., New York, Palgrave Macmillan, 2008. 2v. index. $595.00/set. ISBN 13: 978-1-84511-000-0.

Sir William Smith edited this expansive and still very useful cultural dictionary in 1842 and revised it, with William Wayte and G. E. Marindin, in 1890, because the intervening years had been "a period of quite exceptional activity both in classical research and exploration." Because the years since 1890 have also produced advances in classical scholarship, this re-issue of the 1890 edition is best suited for university libraries. That is not to say that the lay enthusiast would not covet and enjoy these volumes. However, this work is intended for reference rather than browsing, even though the expansive definitions of ancient words read more like encyclopedia entries—thus a "dictionary" of "culture." Typical illustrations are appealing line drawings of artifacts, such as an onyx cup depicting oscilla (masks) referenced in Virgil's *Georgics*. Maps and overviews of ancient sites, such as the theatre of Dionysus in Athens, are also simple but effective. Mammoth works are dangerous, however, because readers will always spend more time in browsing than they will in merely consulting the meaning and cultural context of a word. Nevertheless, Smith's Victorian works are not light reading. More accessible to lay readers and younger students are *Harpers Dictionary of Classical Literature and Antiquities* by Harry Thurston Peck (Kessinger Publishing, 2007) and Catherine Avery's *The New Century Handbook of Classical Geography* (Appleton-Century, 1972), both still available in both hard cover and paperback. Historians familiar with Smith's extensive scholarship will appreciate Christopher Stray's introduction, which within a dozen pages defends the accomplishments of "dead white [Victorian] males," recounts Smith's modest beginnings and impressive career, and tweaks the noses of novelists, movie producers, and shrewd students that have found profit in recycling Smith's works. Stray's essay alone is enough to justify a re-issue. This work is recommended for academic libraries.—**Nancy L. Van Atta**

LATIN AMERICAN AND CARIBBEAN HISTORY

C

158.   Giesso, Martin. **Historical Dictionary of Ancient South America.** Lanham, Md., Scarecrow, 2008. 259p. (Historical Dictionaries of Ancient Civilizations and Historical Eras, no.21). $80.00. ISBN 0-8108-5385-X. ISBN 13: 978-0-8108-5385-0.

This volume is another in the series Historical Dictionaries of Ancient Civilizations and Historical Eras. The scope of the book encompasses the current knowledge of the indigenous people of South America prior to the 1500s when the Europeans arrived. The author is a researcher and authority on the topic. The entries cover a wide range of topics related to the people and the continent, including names of sites, archaeological groups, cultures, architecture, art, religion, tools, agriculture and other means of financial support, funeral practices, and famous archaeologists. The biographical entries include both early anthropologists, such as Francisco P. Moreno, and recent archaeologists, like Jorge Marcos and James Ford. The introductory chronology begins prior to 13,000 B.C.E. when the first humans entered South America and ends with 1571 C.E. with the last independent Inca kingdom in the Eastern Andean valleys. Background material on the geographic regions and peoples is provided in the introduction. The body of the text is the 700-plus topics arranged alphabetically. Most of the entries are approximately 100 words in length with a few exceeding a page in length. *See also* references are provided and topics in bold within the entries indicate a separate listing on the topic. A few pronunciations are given. The eight pages of black-and-white photographs in the center of the book do not enhance the text. There are three appendixes: museums, research institutions, and series and journals. The bibliography is extensive and divided into general terms and information, countries, and historical sources. As the term "dictionary" implies, the information is basic and explanatory. This is a quick reference resource for an area and historical topic covered in most schools. [R: BL, 1 &15 Jan 09, p. 125]—**Elaine Ezell**

MIDDLE EASTERN HISTORY

C, P

159.   Bierbrier, Morris L. **Historical Dictionary of Ancient Egypt.** 2d ed. Lanham, Md., Scarecrow, 2008. 429p. (Historical Dictionaries of Ancient Civilizations and Historical Eras, no.22). $120.00. ISBN 13: 978-0-8108-5794-0.

This volume by a well-known Egyptologist provides the interested reader/researcher with a wealth of information that can serve as a prelude to further research. Opening with a short but solid review of the history of ancient Egypt from Paleolithic times around 200,000 BCE and moving briskly but accurately through to the Arabian conquest of the land in 641-42 CE and then into the period of European contact up to modern times, Bierbrier gives a solid sense of the ebb and flow of this area's fortunes.

The dictionary itself consists of many short entries on people, deities, places, roles, concepts, and much more, providing dates where appropriate and locations with both ancient and modern names, along with other information that will assist the reader/ researcher in her/her understanding. This second edition not only adds the introduction but also adds a chronology and two appendices, one of which gives a detailed dynastic list from the first dynasty of pharaonic Egypt up through Byzantine times including lists of Satraps and Roman prefects, and Alexandrian and Coptic patriarchs, while the second lists museums world wide with Egyptian holdings. Of tremendous value is the extensive set of bibliographies, well over one hundred pages of useful resources, largely, though not entirely, referring to works in English. Such a combination of resources in one modest volume will serve scholars and yet is not so overwhelming as to intimidate the more casual reader. Thus this dictionary belongs in college and university libraries and larger public libraries or parts of county library systems. [R: LJ, Jan 09, p. 126]—**Susan Tower Hollis**

C, S

160.   Brier, Bob, and Hoyt Hobbs. **Daily Life of the Ancient Egyptians.** 2d ed. Westport, Conn., Greenwood Press, 2008. 311p. illus. index. (The Greenwood Press "Daily Life Through History" Series). $49.95. ISBN 13: 978-0-313-35306-2.

This volume, the 2d edition of a book originally published in 1999, is less a book to read cover to cover, unlike similar resources published over the last 15 or so years, than it is a resource to which a reader may turn with a particular interest or question in mind. Thus, instead of presenting exactly "daily life," it discusses specific topics within its 11 chapters that cover aspects of life, some of which are truly daily and some of which are definitely not. The first of these chapters sets the stage with a short précis of ancient Egypt's history, followed by chapters covering religion, government and society, work and play, food, clothes and other adornment, architecture, arts and crafts, technology and construction, warfare, and medicine and mathematics. Each chapter is comprised of subsections that address particular topics; for example, scribes in the chapter on work and play and shipbuilding in that on technology and construction.

The volume concludes with a short glossary, a limited and somewhat dated bibliography save for its list of Websites (but missing a major resource in Donald B. Redford *The Oxford Encyclopedia of Ancient Egypt* [see ARBA 2003, entry 504]), and concluding with an index. It includes many line drawings and photographs within the text.

While some Egyptologists will dispute some statements in the text, overall the volume provides a solid beginning point for the middle and high school student, college students, and interested lay readers seeking a handy, accessible, and generally reliable resource to gain initial information about this ancient culture.—**Susan Tower Hollis**

WORLD HISTORY

Chronology

C, S

161.   Dickson, Keith D. **World War II Almanac.** New York, Facts on File, 2008. 2v. illus. maps. index. (Almanacs of American Wars). $125.00/set. ISBN 13: 978-0-8160-6297-3.

Yet another reference work on the Second World War? How does an author go about establishing originality and freshness in a vast sea of classic, time-honored publications? Keith D. Dickson, a professor of military studies at the National Defense University, has risen to the challenge in some interesting ways in his *World War II Almanac.* The primary advantage of this two-volume work lies in the prescribed format of the Almanacs of American Wars series, which focuses on a minute, almost day-to-day chronology of the major events and decisions of the war. The chronology in fact comprises the largest part of the almanac. The military and diplomatic calendar, beginning in 1922 with Mussolini's famous March on Rome, and ending November 19, 1945, when General Eisenhower replaced General Marshall as army chief of staff and contingency plans were drafted for a nuclear war with the Soviet Union, drives the entire almanac. Yet, and surprisingly so for a war fought on almost every continent, the chronological approach actually enhances our understanding of the immensity of the conflict by grouping within entries for a given date events in disparate, seemingly unconnected theaters of operations. For example, the entry for December 15, 1942, reveals that construction got underway for the Ledo Road in the China-Burma-India theater, the U.S. Coast Guard sank a German U-Boat in the Atlantic, B-17s attacked Tunis and Bizerte in North Africa, and U.S. infantrymen engaged Japanese defenders in New Guinea. Instead of giving a piecemeal impression of the war, the chronology actually heightens and intensifies the drama and strategic challenges in a multi-theater, epochal struggle.

Other useful features of the *World War II Almanac* include an A-Z dictionary of the leading military and political figures and types of weaponry used as well as an extensive bibliography as an aid for further research. Black-and-white photographs, illustrations, and maps also enhance the reference work. Another impressive part of the almanac is the 37-page historical introduction, which, in a cogent and succinct fashion, develops the intricate threads of conflict and cooperation culminating in the outbreak of war in Europe in 1939 and the creation of alliances, some of which would outlast World War II by decades. Much has been written and is known about the attack on Pearl Harbor on December 9, 1941, and the decision of the United State to go to war against Imperial Japan in retaliation. However, less is commonly known about the diplomatic and military game of shuffleboard being played by Japan, China, Great Britain, and the United States in the years preceding 1941. This useful introduction probes the complexity of such prewar maneuvers.

The *World War II Almanac* is a valuable, much-appreciated contribution to a firmer grasp of a conflict that, sadly, is fading with the passage of time and the passing of the soldiers who served and fought during it. It is a highly recommended addition to school, college and university, and public libraries,
—John B. Romeiser

C, P, S

162.   **History of the World in Photographs: 1850 to the Present Day.** New York, Black Dog & Leventhal Publishers, 2008. 512p. illus. index. $50.00. ISBN 13: 978-1-57912-583-7.

This landmark world history reference title brings together the images and scholarship of two well-respected organizations. The book uses more than 2,000 photographs from Getty Images as well as 6,000 timelines entries from *Encyclopaedia Britannica*. The work is arranged chronologically with timelines running across the top and bottom of every page displaying the historical events in categories of science, medicine, and technology; religion; philosophy and education; history and politics; business; social life; and the arts. Additional, more in-depth articles are interspersed throughout to provide deeper knowledge of historical events. What makes this title special, however, are the incredible black-and-white and full-color photographs and illustrations used throughout the volume. By seeing the expressions on peoples faces, the fashion of the day, technology in use, and both city and country landscapes, users will get a glimpse what these historical events truly looked like as they were happening. The book comes with a fully searchable, cross-indexed CD-ROM that includes 20,000 additional photographs from Getty Images as well as free access to an additional 20,000 photographs from the Getty Website and millions of facts on the *Encyclopaedia Britannica* Website.

For a mere $50 (a remarkable bargain in today's world), this title will give students, researchers, and the interested layperson access to hundreds of historical facts and photographs of history in the making. It would be a worthwhile purchase for school, public, and academic libraries.—**Shannon Graff Hysell**

Dictionaries and Encyclopedias

C, S

163. **Daily Life Online. http://www.greenwood.com/dailylife/.** [Website]. Westport, Conn., Greenwood Press. Price negotiated by site. Date reviewed: 2008.

This suite of databases offers various combinations of access to a wealth of materials on history, culture, religion, economics, people, and so forth. The main components currently are *Daily Life Through History*, *Daily Life in America*, and *World Folklore and Folklife*. Access to the site can be purchased as either a basic package or as a premium package. The basic package allows access to 60 single and multivolume Greenwood reference works. The majority of the materials focus on pre-1900 history, with just a small portion covering the twentieth century. The premium package offers all of the materials in the basic collection as well as all of the materials from Greenwood's World Cultures Today series, the entire collection of the Cultures and Customs series, and the history of Modern Nations series. Also included are content from Greenwood's culture cookbooks, holiday titles, and teen life around the world.—**Catherine Barr**

C, S

164. **Encyclopedia of Society & Culture in the Ancient World.** Peter Bogucki, ed. New York, Facts on File, 2008. 4v. illus. maps. index. (Facts on File Library of World History). $360.00/set. ISBN 13: 978-0-8160-6941-5.

This reference work addresses 69 broad topics, such as adornment, social organization, seafaring and navigation, religion and cosmology, sports, household goods, crime and punishment, settlement and migration, language, and metallurgy, by exploring each subject from prehistory to the fall of Rome (476 C.E.) across Africa, Egypt, the Middle East, Asia and the Pacific, Europe, Greece, Rome, and the Americas. Each entry ends with further reading, with both print and nonprint sources. The authors draw from archaeology, physical anthropology, history, epigraphy (study of ancient texts), historical geography, paleobotany, archaeo-zoology, and geology to tell the story of how ancient peoples across the world organized and lived their lives. We learn about the sacred mountains of Jebel Barkal on the Egyptian-Sudanese border, Makade near the ancient city state of Axum in present day Ethiopia, Ayers Rock in Australia, Mount Fuji in Japan, Mount Tai Shan in China, the Hill of Tara in Ireland, and many others across the ancient world. The mineral springs at Bath, England have been visited by humans since 8,000 B.C.E. The first traces of Indo-European and Chinese languages go back to 9000 B.C.E. The Greeks did not have soap. Instead they used soda, potash, and clay for cleansing. The ancient Romans had no concept of exploration for scientific purposes. The Latin word *exploration* refers to military reconnaissance. Excerpts from source documents like Herodotus on mummification and Confucius' analect on children are scattered throughout the volumes. The set ends with a glossary, a chronology by region from prehistory to 500 C.E., and a bibliography by geographic area. [R: BL, 1 & 15 June 08, p. 129]—**Adrienne Antink**

C, S

165.   **Encyclopedia of Society and Culture in the Medieval World.** Pam J. Crabtree, ed. New York, Facts on File, 2008. 4v. illus. maps. index. $360.00/set. ISBN 13: 978-0-8160-6936-1.

The four-volume *Encyclopedia of Society and Culture in the Medieval World* provides coverage of medieval culture, beginning where its companion set, *Encyclopedia of Society and Culture in the Ancient World* (2008), left off with the fall of Rome in 476 up to the start of the Renaissance. Seventy-one alphabetic entries cover specific aspects of medieval society such as building techniques and languages. Of these entries, 14 major topics such as agriculture and religion are explored in more depth. For every article, an introduction is provided and then the topic is examined from the perspective of five centers of civilization: Africa, the Americas, Asia and the Pacific, Europe, and the Islamic World. These centers are sometimes further divided by region or subtopics. The treatment on Islamic medieval culture is removed mostly from the perspectives of Africa and Europe and treated separately. Entries end with materials suggested for further reading and cross-references.

Sidebars provide information on topics outside the scope but which are still related to article topics. Maps, photographs, and translations of primary sources also support the entries. The fourth volume contains a bibliography and a brief chronology by region and is followed by a large index. For information on notable personalities of the medieval world, it should be noted that the content of this set focuses on medieval society and culture and not individuals so coverage of individuals is scattered minimally among entries or sidebars. The content is very readable, and the articles are subdivided in a logical manner. High school students, college undergraduates, and general readers should find this set very useful.—**Brian J. Sherman**

S

166.   **History of the Ancient and Medieval World.** 2d ed. Tarrytown, N.Y., Marshall Cavendish, 2009. 11v. illus. maps. index. $499.95/set. ISBN 13: 978-0-7614-7789-1.

Photographs have a way of capturing our attention and curiosity. Our culture seeks visual stimulation and there are plenty of interesting and captivating photographs in the 2d edition of this set, *History of the Ancient and Medieval World*, from Marshall Cavendish Press. While the photograph of a human skull inlaid with precious gemstones representing the Aztec deity Tezcatlipoca makes my spine shiver, middle grade students would find this "cool." This is fitting since this series, which attempts to cover history from the first humans to the Renaissance in 13 volumes, is geared toward students between the 5th and 10th grades. Students and teachers in these grades will love the ease of use of this series and visually stimulating photographs.

Another strength of this series is its attempt to cover many marginal groups throughout history, such as the Albigensians, a persecuted Christian sect in southern France, and the Basque people, from the Iberian Peninsula. Trying to include "everyone" however, has its drawbacks. Since this series attempts to cover all of human history up to the sixteenth century, it often fails to give the in-depth treatment necessary for a reference work. If a student wanted more in-depth information on the Pueblo Indians or the Roman Emperors, the *Encyclopaedia Britannica* or a subject-specific book would give more detailed information. Despite this shortcoming, *History of the Ancient and Medieval World* is a good introductory resource that will captivate and capture the attention of middle and high school students.—**Theresa Lynn Bruno**

S

167.   **World History: Ancient and Medieval Eras. http://www.worldhistory.abc-clio.com/Login/ Login.aspx.** [Website]. Santa Barbara, Calif., ABC-CLIO. Price negotiated by site. Date reviewed: 2009.

Designed with the same format as ABC-CLIO's other education Websites, *World History* provides more than 10,000 reference entries discussing cultures, events, inventions, religious movements, and personalities that have had an impact on history around the globe. Also included are 6,600 primary and secondary sources, 1,200 biographies of important figures, profiles of countries and regions, and more than 70 in-depth topic explorations that provide overviews of specific time periods. Along with the option to search by keyword or perform an advanced search, users can also click on Explore an Era to browse various time periods or click on Analyze, a new feature that allows students to find key dilemmas in history and discover different viewpoints or interpretations from academics. When students find the topic they are researching they will also find related entries located in a sidebar, which will further their research. The site also features access to a Merriam-Webster dictionary.

This database, along with all of ABC-CLIO's other databases, has been updated in Release 2.0, which offers cross-database searching if you have access to multiple databases, as well as easy-to-use filters for searches, features stories that connect entries to current events, and MLA citations that can translate to other popular citations styles. Teachers and media specialists will find the site useful because it allows them to create assignments, tests, and a syllabus on the Staff Edition page. Only teachers and librarians will have access to this page. This feature also allows students to access the Website from home and will allow parents to be aware of their children's homework and future assignments.

This database, much like the others from ABC-CLIO, will enhance any school's teaching curriculum. It will bring world history to life for many students and provide a new outlet for learning. The price may be a bit high for many schools, but the amount of material found here may make up for the expense.
—**Shannon Graff Hysell**

Handbooks and Yearbooks

C, P, S

168.   Collins, Ross F. **World War I: Primary Documents on Events from 1914 to 1919.** Westport, Conn., Greenwood Press, 2008. 411p. illus. index. (Debating Historical Issues in the Media of the Time). $65.00. ISBN 13: 978-0-313-32082-8.

Collins, Associate Professor of Communication at North Dakota State University, Fargo, has made a fine addition to the Greenwood Press Debating Historical Issues in the Media of the Time Series with *World War I: Primary Documents on Events from 1914 to 1919*. A simple quote by a Boston Judge on January 1, 1799, from the series foreword makes a big impression on the reader who may be grasping for the importance of this series and more specifically this work: "Give to any set of men the command of the press, and you give them command of public opinion, which commands everything."

This book is divided into 22 chapters, each of which has a great many primary documents on the topic of that chapter that illustrate the theme, a set of 3 to 5 questions for the reader to ponder that help place the chapter in a better historical context, and a bibliographic note (in select chapters). There is also a series foreword, an introduction, an excellent chronology, a selected bibliography, and an index.

A typical chapter, " War and the Character of the Soldier," starts on page 327 and lasts 19 pages. It contains a three-page introduction that takes into account modern findings and writings of this topic. It is divided into subsections like "The Beneficial Effects of War on Soldiers," with 12 primary documents of support and "The Destructive Effects of War on Soldiers," with 23 primary documents of support. This work is recommended.—**Scott R. DiMarco**

C, S

169.   **Nations and Nationalism: A Global Historical Overview.** Guntram H. Herb and David H. Kaplan, eds. Santa Barbara, Calif., ABC-CLIO, 2008. 4v. illus. maps. index. $395.00/set. ISBN 13: 978-1-85109-907-8.

As its subtitle title suggests this four-volume reference work aims to provide a global perspective to the topic of nationalism and nation building from 1770 until the present day. Abandoning any attempt to be comprehensive, this work instead aims to be representative, providing students and junior scholars with a cross section of articles that discuss various nations and themes relating to nationalism. Divided chrono-logically, each volume includes a series of nation essays (104 in total), and a collection of slightly longer thematic essays (42 in total). The entries are substantial (4,000 to 6,000 words) and treat each topic in great detail. Each nation essay provides the reader with a chronology, map, illustration, bibliography, and several different sections of content. These sections help to situate the nation in its political and social context, discuss the key actors, institutions, and philosophies of each nation, define the role of ethno-cultural identity in building each nation, and discuss the history of events and strategies used in helping to build and legitimize each nation. The thematic essays, which cover such topics as the arts, religion, education, culture, and technology, provide background information on each theme, discuss its importance to nationalism, the ways in which it impacts different groups in society, and its consequences for nations in the future.—**Larissa Anne Gordon**

C, S

170.   Williams, Robert C. **The Historian's Toolbox: A Student's Guide to the Theory and Craft of History.** 2d ed. Armonk, N.Y., M. E. Sharpe, 2007. 200p. illus. index. $58.95. ISBN 13: 978-0-7656-3026-2.

Williams' concise guide to history and historical analysis is already a standard handbook in libraries and at work stations in schools and colleges. The 2d edition covers current issues and sources, including feminist re-evaluations of gender-charged debate and the objectivity and reliability to researchers of essays on *Wikipedia*. Key to the readability of text is succinct instruction that does not insult student intelligence; for example, an

explanation of the early Greek concept of history, the elements of the Enola Gay controversy, the importance of chronology to a biography of philosopher Margaret Fuller, and a discussion of historical evidence of Pickett's Charge are all discussed. Essential to the guide are charts, photographs, line drawings, citations, and suggested readings. Williams concludes with a seven-page glossary on such essentials as genomes, metahistory, skepticism, and paradigm. Well ordered and indexed, Williams' toolbox deserves a place in public, high school, and college libraries; as a teaching manual for homeschoolers; and as a gift book for students to place alongside their dictionary and thesaurus.—**Mary Ellen Snodgrass**

10 Law

GENERAL WORKS

Chronology

C, P

171. Finkelman, Paul, and Melvin I. Urofsky. **Landmark Decisions of the United States Supreme Court.** 2d ed. Washington, D.C., CQ Press, 2008. 791p. illus. index. $250.00. ISBN 13: 978-0-87289-409-9.

Designed as a ready-reference book providing quick and easy access to succinct case summaries of the most important decisions of the United States Supreme Court, this source offers almost 1,200 cases that influenced America's constitutional and judicial history. Constitutional, judicial, and political historians and scholars will find an additional 150 cases. From 1792 to 2007, there is now at least one case for every year the court met.

Organized chronologically by decade, cases are listed alphabetically at the beginning of each decade and in the case index. For easy research, later cases on a particular point of law are cited within the case. The introduction summarizes the history of the court and is suitable for high school government classes. One appendix contains the list of confirmed nominations to the Supreme Court by nominating president, while another lists the membership changes in the Supreme Court by Chief Justice.

The authors' reputations, expert analysis, and well-written summaries make this an excellent choice. *Landmark Decisions of the United States Supreme Court* is highly recommended for academic and public libraries.—**Ladyjane Hickey**

Dictionaries and Encyclopedias

C, P

172. **Encyclopedia of the First Amendment.** John R. Vile, David L. Hudson Jr., and David Schultz, eds. Washington, D.C., CQ Press, 2009. 2v. illus. index. $240.00/set. ISBN 13: 978-0-87289-311-5.

The first of the 10 amendments that make up the Bill of Rights of the U.S. Constitution is probably the most important in terms of everyday social and governmental interaction. This solid work covers the various significant political, historical, and cultural factors; people; events; and issues related to this amendment. It starts off with seven introductory essays that provide an overview of the clauses of the amendment, how it is viewed around the world, and its future. The more than 1,400 signed entries, arranged in the traditional alphabetic order, are written by 224 expert contributors, and provide authoritative discussions of these issues. At the end of the entries one finds *see also* references and at least one suggestion for further reading on this particular topic. These suggestions are supplemented by the selected bibliography at the end of volume 2. Because the legal interpretations of this amendment are so widespread, a multitude of court cases are dissected for their meaning and impact. A two-page appendix describes appropriate online resources. A 10-page chronology (313 C.E. to 2008) covers the historical development of the basic principles and there are three separate tables of contents: alphabetical, topical, and court cases. This quality set complements the *Encyclopedia of the American Constitution* (2nd ed.; see ARBA 2001, entry 720), and is much more detailed than the *Encyclopedia of Constitutional Amendments, Proposed Amendments, and Amending Issues, 1789-1995* (see ARBA 97, entry 596). It is suitable for the reference collections of law, academic, and large public libraries. [R: LJ, Jan 09, pp. 125-128; VOYA, Feb 09, p. 560; BL, 1 &15 Jan 09, p. 122]—**Daniel K. Blewett**

Directories

C, P

173.   **The Sourcebook to Public Record Information: The Comprehensive Guide to County, State, & Federal Public Records.** 9th ed. Tempe, Ariz., BRB, 2008. 1877p. $89.95pa. ISBN 1-879792-89-3. ISBN 13: 978-1-879792-89-0.

Now in its 9th edition, *The Sourcebook to Public Record Information* remains a valuable resource for locating public records. It has retained the basic layout of the most recent edition (see ARBA 2007, entry 449) with two main sections. Section 1 focuses on helping the reader determine where to find a particular category of public record and how to search for that public record. Included is a section on privacy issues that includes topics on what is considered public information versus private information, and how personal information can enter the public domain. Section 2 contains contact information for both federal and state agencies, arranged in alphabetic order by state. Brief attention is given to U.S. Territories and Canada. Mailing addresses, telephone and fax numbers, hours of operation, Website addresses, fees involved, and other helpful information are provided for each agency.

The 9th edition of the *Sourcebook* includes information on subjects that were not addressed in previous editions, such as Native American court records, military records, excluded parties, and U.S. government watch lists. It also includes fully updated telephone numbers and Website addresses as well as over 500 newly added online sources for record searching.

The *Sourcebook* continues to be updated via PRRS (*The Public Record Research System*), a subscription service available on the Internet. For users who need the most up-to-date information see http://www.brbpub.com for information on subscribing to the online version as well as links to free resources. Overall, the *Sourcebook* remains a highly useful reference resource for finding public records, and is therefore recommended for public and academic libraries alike.—**Alicia Brillon**

Handbooks and Yearbooks

C, P

174.   DeWitt, Larry W., Daniel Beland, and Edward D. Berkowitz. **Social Security: A Documentary History.** Washington, D.C., CQ Press, 2008. 557p. index. $115.00. ISBN 13: 978-0-87289-502-7.

Examining the past is essential to understanding the present and planning for the future. The main objective of *Social Security: A Documentary History* is to depict the development of the Social Security program through various primary source documents, thereby giving readers the opportunity to discover for themselves how the program came into being, how it reached its present state, and how it might continue to evolve.

The book begins with an introduction to the history of the Social Security program in which nine distinct eras of development are identified and discussed. The rest of the book is divided into nine chapters that correspond to these nine eras of development. Each chapter begins with a short preface that explains the main issues at play during that era. The history and development of each era is revealed through the primary source documents that include items such as government pamphlets, letters, congressional hearings and reports, and presidential speeches. Many of the resources come from the Social Security Administration historical archives. Preceding each of the individual documents is a brief statement that explains that relevancy and context of the document. Although the entirety of each document is not always included, enough of each document is provided to give a clear understanding of its content.

In addition to the primary source documents, the book includes several useful and informative appendixes. One appendix lists all public laws that have impacted Social Security and Medicare over the years. Other appendixes provide an overview of political party support for various components of the program, financial issues, and the number of beneficiaries. The inclusion of the primary source documents, many of which are not easily accessible, makes this resource especially valuable to researchers. However, anyone who has an interest in the development of the Social Security program will find this to be an interesting and valuable resource.—**Matt Novak**

C, P

175. **The Manual to Online Public Records: The Researcher's Tool to Online Resources of Public Records and Public Information.** Tempe, Ariz., Facts on Demand Press, 2008. 590p. $21.95pa. ISBN 13: 978-1-889150-53-6.

This book provides information on how and where to search for public records. It consists of seven chapters. The first four chapters include discussion of what is found online and "many facets and techniques about searching for public records and public information" (introduction). The bulk of information is in chapter 5, "State and Local Government Online," which is over 440 pages. The chapter is a state-by-state listing of online resources. Each state covers state public record agencies, state occupational licensing and regulatory boards, courts, and other local or county agencies (e.g., recorders, assessors). It also denotes fee-based or free online access systems. Chapter 6 is on searching federal court records and chapter 7 deals with public record database vendors.

Practically all search engines use free-text searching. To ensure relevancy of search result, qualifiers, such as logical operators, positional operators, and fields (if available), should be used. The book mentions well the use of operators in search engines such as Google. But, the example given on proximity searching of "Cynthia Hetherington" is confusing. A proximity search of "Cynthia Hetherington" (added with * in Google or NEAR in Exalead) results in a larger not smaller recall as suggested in the book (pp. 18, 22).

The book has an index that is sketchy. Many topics are not indexed. The book's back cover gives a listing of online sources that can be "effectively" located, such as Addresses and LLCs & LLPs. It is hard to find those topics without being indexed. The authors have compiled thousands or records with descriptions and good topics of using them. In spite of some flaws, the book is a very useful reference source.—**Tze-chung Li**

C

176. Patrick, John J. **The Supreme Court of the United States: A Student Companion.** 3d ed. New York, Oxford University Press, 2006. 415p. illus. index. $60.00. ISBN 13: 978-0-19-530925-6.

This annual volume reviewing and analyzing selected Supreme Court cases from the 2007-2008 term contains some 11 feature articles, as well as Janice Rogers Brown's "Annual B. Kenneth Simon Lecture" on the First Amendment and a concluding look ahead at the Court's October 2008 term. About one-half of the articles deal with Bill of Rights issues, while the others address business-related cases concerning securities class actions, government interference with contracts, and patent licensing. Among the former are two articles on the Boumediene decision holding that the right of *habeas corpus* extends to the noncitizen detainees at Guantanamo Bay and an approving article ("The Second Amendment Is Back, Baby") on the Heller decision that struck down the District of Columbia's ban on handgun ownership. The authors are all legal professionals and the articles are scholarly and well written. That said, the material is nearly all written from the Cato Institute's perspective, which publisher Roger Pilon describes as "classical Madisonian . . . grounded in the nation's first principles, liberty and limited government" (the exception is one of the Boumediene articles, which offers an opposing point of view). And Editor-in-Chief Ilya Shapiro notes in his introduction that "we are happy to confess our biases," making the point of view explicit. Even so, these critiques are well researched and closely argued, not mere opinion. This title is recommended for most academic and law libraries. (It should be noted, however, that full text of this annual is in LexisNexis Academic.) [R: SLJ, Dec 06, p. 89; VOYA, Dec 06, p. 468]—**Jack Ray**

P, S

177.   Raskin, Jamin B. **We the Students: Supreme Court Cases for and About Students.** 3d ed. Washington, D.C., CQ Press, 2008. 333p. illus. index. $50.00; $32.00pa. ISBN 13: 978-0-87289-760-1; 978-0-87289-761-8pa.

    This book is an outgrowth of the Marshall-Brennan Constitutional Literacy Project, in which law students visit public high schools to teach students about the Constitution. The book aims to "introduce the informal curriculum of school life into the formal curriculum of classes on law, government, and American history." Accordingly, it is organized by topics of particular interest to students: free speech in school, freedom of the student press, religion at school, privacy rights, student discipline, racial and other forms of discrimination, sexual harassment/bullying, and pregnancy/sexuality. Each chapter presents excerpts from Supreme Court opinions, along with a number of editorial features ("What Do You Think?" exercises, "For the Class" group projects using hypothetical cases to stimulate debate, "Dissenting Voices" excerpts from the Court's opinions, and background sidebars on the justices who wrote the opinions). Appendixes include the text of the Constitution, a glossary, and a bibliography. Manifestly, this book is designed as a high school course text rather than a reference book. It is well written, very engaging, and with typically high CQ Press production values. A total of 40 cases are featured, 7 more than the 2003 2d edition (see ARBA 2004, entry 561). This title is highly recommended for high school and public libraries.—**Jack Ray**

CRIMINOLOGY AND CRIMINAL JUSTICE

Chronology

C

178.   Rubin, Barry, and Judith Colp Rubin. **Chronologies of Modern Terrorism.** Armonk, N.Y., M. E. Sharpe, 2008. 405p. index. $99.95. ISBN 13: 978-0-7656-2047-7.

    As terrorism continues to dominate many areas of international politics, the number of terrorism reference books continues to grow as this work demonstrates. *Chronologies of Modern Terrorism* looks at terrorist incidents in many areas of the world during the twentieth century and includes overviews of regional terrorist activities and a chronological listing of key terrorist incidents.

    An introduction describes the multifaceted definitions of terrorism and how terrorist groups have been classified in different regions of the world. The main sections of the book describe historical and ideological origins of terrorism from the Elizabethan era in England to the present; terrorism as social and revolutionary strategies in Europe and North America; and the roles played by terrorism and terrorists in Latin America, Africa, Asia, and the Middle East with Islamist terrorism receiving particular emphasis.

    Individual chapters begin with an analytical overview of the historical origins and ongoing evolution of terrorist incidents within these geographic regions. Highlights of these chapters include chronological enumerations of terrorist incidents (e.g., "April 16, 1993—In the first Hamas suicide bombing, a Hamas terrorist detonates a bomb in the parking lot of a restaurant near the West Bank settlement of Mekholah, killing one") (p. 205). Within these chapters, there are further breakdowns of relevant regional events and related terrorist events, such as "The Fall of the Taliban" in the section dealing with Islamist terror.

The work concludes with a glossary of terrorist organizations, such as the Al-Aqsa Martyr Brigades and a selected bibliography of books, journal articles, and Websites. Both of the authors are prominent and prolific writers on Middle Eastern political issues who have produced a work that will be beneficial for users desirous of having chronologically arranged historical reference work on terrorism with a global coverage emphasis. This work is recommended for academic libraries.—**Bert Chapman**

Dictionaries and Encyclopedias

C, P

179.   **Battleground: Criminal Justice.** Gregg Barak, ed. Westport, Conn., Greenwood Press, 2007. 2v. index. $175.00/set. ISBN 13: 978-0-313-34040-6.

Battleground: Criminal Justice is a two-volume encyclopedia edited by Gregg Barak. Approximately 100 distinguished contributors offer comprehensive insights into the field of national and international criminal justice, enticing readers to actively pursue both volumes. Readers rapidly move through controversial and conflict-oriented content authored by the experts in their perspective fields of study.

Entries address criminal justice from an institutional array of social, political, economic, and legal foundations. Diverse political positions include liberal, moderate, and conservative points of view. The contributors highlight complex, multifaceted controversies that matter a great deal to a nation that advocates human and constitutional rights. Insightful and current issues emerge from the approximately 100 entries that focus on new technologies and laws. Moreover, the evolution of policies, practices, and judicial emerging issues in the criminal justice system represent primary importance in the entries. The varying points of view may polarize public opinion: however, complex social and political controversies persist. The underline values and attitudes create a maze of emotional filters for these controversial societal and cultural issues.

Battleground: Criminal Justice emphasizes core issues that disappear and reassert themselves in continuing patterns of precedent, current, and potential future themes. Perhaps the most interesting are the social justice issues (e.g., prison issues in the Caribbean, the post-apartheid struggle in South Africa). Another interesting article is entitled State Crime Control, which offers a critical criminology perspective on the potential of state criminality. The criminal justice battle remains a struggle of crime control versus human rights, public order versus due process, and legal traditions versus social change. Readers have opportunities to compare or contrast: Homeland Security versus Antiterrorism Laws, Driving while Black and Racial Profiling, and Restorative Justice Versus Prisoner Experimentation.

The volumes' entries are organized alphabetically and classified by general content in six cluster areas: Law and Society; Law Enforcement; Prosecution, Courts, and Adjudication; Punishment and Corrections; Science and Criminal Justice; and Society, Crime, and Justice. Each excellent entry is approximately 200 to 500 words and portrays a similar sequence of section format. The style and format focus the reader's thoughts and provide a smooth transition to related entries.

Battleground: Criminal Justice would serve as an excellent contribution to libraries in the United States and has opportunities for international sales. Community college and university libraries may also welcome this set of encyclopedias in their collection. Secondary schools may consider adopting *Battleground: Criminal Justice* because of student interest in crime and course offerings in criminal justice. The interdisciplinary content and comparative justice issues are exceptional for study in a broad array of social science courses.—**Thomas E. Baker**

C, S

180.   Bell, Suzanne. **Encyclopedia of Forensic Science.** rev. ed. New York, Facts on File, 2008. 402p. illus. index. (Facts on File Science Library). $85.00. ISBN 13: 978-0-8160-6799-2.

Building on the popularity of her 1st edition (see ARBA 2004, entry 573) and continued interest in forensic sciences by the public, Suzanne Bell has released an expanded and revised version of her encyclopedia. The new edition includes 80 new entries in the traditional A-to-Z format as well as 15 new essays discussing more general observations about the field of forensic sciences.

The new entries and essays make this work applicable to a broader audience. Some of the new entries include: *CSI* and the *CSI* effect, Jack the Ripper, the Madrid Bombings, and blood doping in sports. These mass-market entries refer the reader to other entries that have a clearer connection to forensic science such as "identification of the dead" when discussing the Madrid bombings.

Most of the entries are concise, easy to digest, and referenced. Its broad appeal makes it suitable for most libraries. It is more user friendly and less intimidating than the *Encyclopedia of Forensic Sciences* by J. Siegel, P. Saukko and G. Knupfer (see ARBA 2002, entry 565). It is still limited by the fact that it is largely written by one author, but it remains an excellent introduction to and starting point for research into forensic sciences.—**Walter Michael Fontane**

C, P

181.   **Crime & Punishment in the U.S.** Phyllis B. Gerstenfeld, ed. Hackensack, N.J., Salem Press, 2008. 3v. illus. index. $217.00/set. ISBN 13: 978-1-58765-427-5.

Crime & Punishment in the U.S. represents a superior academic endeavor on the part of editor Phyllis B. Gerstenfeld, professional contributors, and Salem Press. This clear and comprehensible three-volume Magill's Choice encyclopedia collection, bound in an enticing criminal justice-themed cover, makes an immediate impression on the reader. The collection is a comprehensive source of basic criminal justice content offered by prominent contributors. The essays engage readers to pursue noteworthy content in numerous criminal justice entries.

This three-volume encyclopedia supplements other Salem Press related publications. The Magill's Choice Series includes content from five other encyclopedia publications. The 257 articles are presented in alphabetic order and permit instant access to the topics. The articles provide insightful content, concise subject substance, summaries, and definitions. Volume 3 offers a detailed general subject index of 60 individual categories and essay topics that include a considerable range of important criminal justice issues. In addition, a glossary with more than 530 criminal justice definitions and terms support the three volumes.

This striking three-volume edition focuses on significant criminal justice issues relating to types of crimes. Entries immediately introduce terms by defining: definition of term, criminal justice issues, and significance. The major subcategories include: apprehension, arraignment, criminal defendants, trial procedures, and types of punishments. In addition, the emphasis describes the criminal population, and the numerous types of crimes they commit. The subject coverage contains four core area and related issues: criminals (70 articles0, law enforcement (120 articles), prosecution and trials (50 articles), and punishment (60 articles). There are a significant number of illustrations: photographs (90), maps (70), graphs (28), charts (16), tables (16), and textual sidebars (60).

Volume 1 has many interesting articles; however, Bigamy and Polygamy, Civil Disobedience, and Animal Abuse immediately appear as captivating reader entries. The article on Capital Punishment represents a superior scholarly endeavor. Volume 2 follows the same reader-friendly format with engaging articles: Hate Crime, Identity Theft, Insider Trading, Justice, and Mail Fraud, to mention a few. Volume 3 continues the same impressive literary tradition by offering additional excellent entries. Racial Profiling, Sports and Crime, and Terrorism are particularly outstanding and knowledgeable entries.

In conclusion, *Crime & Punishment in the U.S.* is a comprehensive source for nonspecialist readers at the middle school, high school, community college, and university levels. This excellent three-volume encyclopedia would certainly make a welcome addition to any of these collections. Moreover, private and international libraries will define this series as a valuable asset in their collections. The content and basic foundations serve as an excellent starting reference for the study of criminal justice.—**Thomas E. Baker**

C, P

182.   **Forensic Science.** Ayn Embar-Seddon and Allan D. Pass, eds. Hackensack, N.J., Salem Press, 2009. 3v. illus. index. $364.00/set. ISBN 13: 978-1-58765-423-7.

Forensic chemistry, forensic science, forensic psychology, and police criminalistics course offerings dramatically impact innovative and contemporary national and international academic programs. Learner interest is widespread, touching all ages and grade levels. Television shows, including *Cold Case*, *CSI: Crime Scene Investigation*, *Forensic Files*, and an assortment of forensic documentaries that highlight captivating case studies, persist in stimulating viewers and motivate career interest in thought-provoking investigations. The editors and contributors have compiled an excellent sequencing of fascinating topics. The accomplished editors made a notable effort to publish a work that serves a meaningful purpose and supports reader requirements to seek reliable and accurate information. *Forensic Science* offers an impressive list of topics and primarily slants themes from a forensic investigator perspective.

This three-volume encyclopedia set stands tall among competitive endeavors to offer readers comprehensive and credible resource texts. In addition, *Forensic Science* serves as a major contribution that supports the scientific, legal, law enforcement, and extensive academic communities. The three brilliant hardbound covers immediately strike a first glance observer, and unquestionably encourage readers to take a journey through the expansive and exciting world of forensic science. The reader's impression of evaluating a "major resource" would not be overstating its significance; this is truly a professional contribution. Investigative skills are multiplied when coupled with excellent scientific knowledge and superior reference materials. *Forensic Science*'s format is easily maneuvered, and includes a pleasant, readable font and numerous photographs that enhance reader interest. Sidebars, a glossary, tables, charts, maps, and related directories support entries in a meaningful and appropriate manner.

Forensic Science serves as a magnificent addition to any library collection and interested individuals would be proud to own such a literary accomplishment. The benefits of easy access would prove most valuable and quickly enhance research goals. The volumes comprise major themes, including forensic investigations, forensic science and the legal system, historical references, high profile cases, and forensic science and the media. The impact of *Forensic Science* is widespread and inclusive. An extensive variety of allied topics include: forensic nursing, forensic odontology, forensic psychiatry, forensic psychology, forensic psychiatry, forensic archaeology, forensic botany, forensic entomology, forensic geoscience, forensic photography, and forensic sculpture, to mention a few.

The three volumes are organized in 465 alphabetically ordered essays; thereby, facilitating easy access to carefully selected book articles. The essays unfold in a uniform format, ranging in length from 500 to 3,000 words. The individual contributions are prefaced by comprehensive definitions, and the conclusion documents further readings and coordinating contributions. Forensic case essays of notable interest include: Beslan Hostage Crisis: Victim Identification, Challenger and Columbia Accident Investigations, and the Sacco and Vanzetti Case.

In summary, numerous venues exist for the *Forensic Science* encyclopedia, including: high schools, community colleges, and university collections; attorneys; law enforcement agencies; and international markets. There are many additional public and private libraries that would find *Forensic Science* a valuable and noteworthy contribution to their collections.—**Thomas E. Baker**

C, P

183.   Mayo, Mike. **American Murder: Criminals, Crime, and the Media.** Canton, Mich., Visible Ink Press, 2008. 425p. illus. index. $24.95pa. ISBN 13: 978-1-57859-191-6.

American Murder: Criminals, Crime, and the Media is an encyclopedic look at America's love affair in the media with lawbreakers, from angels of death like Charles Cullen to well-known serial killers like John Wayne Gacy. Additionally, *American Murder* addresses tangential people (like Dominick Dunne), events (various massacres), and objects (such as the development of the Thompson Submachine Gun). From unsolved mysteries (like the New Orleans Axeman) to well-publicized trials (O. J. Simpson), *American Murder* hits them all.

While *American Murder* is admittedly rather comprehensive, it focuses primarily on white victims and white offenders. It does include such well-known minority offenders as O. J. Simpson and Charles Ng, but it omits George Emil Banks, an African American spree killer from Pennsylvania, whose victims included his own lovers and children, or the Yahweh ben Yahweh cult in Florida, which advocated the killing of white people and defectors from the cult (an exclusively black African American group), although the book does look at Jonestown and Jim Jones. *American Murder* also overlooks significant details of certain cases, such as the role of Frank Bender's forensic sculpture (which was featured in the episode of *America's Most Wanted* that led to List's capture) in the capture of John List, as well as omitting the homosexual relationship between Leopold and Loeb, which was certainly sensational for the time in which the two were caught and tried. Moreover, *American Murder* does not include *see also* or cross-referencing, which would be useful for people who may not know the alias or the names of individuals involved; for example, many people are familiar with the Black Dahlia case but may not remember that her name was Elizabeth Short, or that H. H. Holmes' name was Theo Durrant.

There is, despite these shortcomings, much to praise in *American Murder*. Mayo thoughtfully reaches way back in America's history to pull out such "gems" as Chester Gillette, whose 1906 murder of his pregnant girlfriend prompted Theodore Dreiser to write *An American Tragedy*, and Andrew Kehoe, who blew up a school in 1927 in Bath, Michigan. He looks at the sensational murders, crimes, and unexplained deaths of celebrities in the 1930s, 1940s, and 1950s, a precursor to our modern society's continued fascination with celebrities. He also looks at modern adaptations of historical events, such as the recent Jesse James movie *The Assassination of Jesse James* by the Coward Robert Ford (2007) starring Brad Pitt. Mayo does not limit himself to movies—he also looks at books and music based on events and people, such as Thomas Harris' best-selling novel *Silence of the Lambs*. In addition to his historical thoroughness and his coverage of media forms, Mayo has made the language of *American Murder* accessible to a general audience. Mayo does an appreciable job examining cases, individuals, and events, and exploring their relationship with the media.

Overall, *American Murder* is an excellent resource, and is recommended for public and academic libraries alike, especially academic libraries with criminal justice and mass communication programs.
—**Megan W. Lowe**

C, P

184.   Palmer, Louis J., Jr. **Encyclopedia of Capital Punishment in the United States.** 2d ed. Jefferson, N.C., McFarland, 2008. 623p. illus. index. $95.00. ISBN 13: 978-0-7864-3263-9.

Although the implementation of capital punishment today is a rather infrequent event in the Western world, the death penalty issue retains great importance symbolically and politically. The retention of capital punishment in the United States—for a small sliver of federal offenses, in some states for heinous crimes—sets the country apart from Western nations that have almost wholly abandoned it, and has inspired much criticism of American justice. Some of the traditional majority support for capital punishment has eroded in the face of a growing number of cases that have established, via DNA testing, that some of those on death row could not have committed the crimes that led to the imposition of the death penalty.

The present work updates an edition originally published in 2001 (see ARBA 2002, entry 566). It offers an exceptionally comprehensive coverage of capital punishment in the United States. Rather remarkably for an encyclopedia of this nature, it has apparently been authored by a single individual, Louis J. Palmer, Jr., an attorney for the West Virginia Court of Appeals. This is certainly a prodigious achievement. Perhaps unsurprisingly, coverage of legal dimensions of capital punishment is especially exhaustive. The author makes the credible claim that he has included entries on all U.S. Supreme Court decisions through 2006 on capital punishment, including some 40 such decisions since the publication of the 1st edition. These decisions include a few especially noteworthy rulings, on such matters as mental competence as a precondition for execution, a minimum age, and acceptable methods of execution. The opinions include attention to both concurring and dissenting opinions.

Other entries address the status of capital punishment in some 200 nations, an in all the principal U.S. jurisdictions. The most famous death penalty cases—and some noteworthy but less-well-known cases—are addressed. Entries are devoted to the experience with capital punishment of different human groupings, in terms of ethnicity and gender. There is a long history of active citizen engagement with this issue, so there are entries devoted to organizations that have supported and opposed capital punishment. The preferred methods for carrying out the death penalty have varied over the course of time, from hanging to the electric chair to lethal injections, so there are entries devoted to these different methods. The military has administered the death penalty for certain offenses, and there are entries devoted to capital punishment within a military context. Although the experiences of many victims in death penalty cases are recounted in entries on those convicted in the cases, independent entries are not devoted to primary and secondary victims in such cases.

Altogether, this reference work should be very useful to all students of capital punishment-related matters. It includes many charts, tables, lists, and photographs, and a wealth of statistical data. The style of writing is sometimes stilted and somewhat dry, but the volume has been produced with a lay readership in mind. Useful cross-references are interspersed throughout the volume.—**David O. Friedrichs**

Handbooks and Yearbooks

C, S

185.   Newton, David E. **DNA Evidence and Forensic Science.** New York, Facts on File, 2008. 268p. index. (Library in a Book). $45.00. ISBN 13: 978-0-8160-7088-6.

DNA and forensic science has changed the way policing operates and law enforcement officers prosecute criminals. The computer revolution and suspect linkage allow law enforcement agencies to close dead-end cold case files. Coordinated efforts between investigators and forensic scientists remain essential components to successful arrest and conviction in sometimes decade old unsolved crimes.

DNA and forensic science is essential to due process, conviction of the guilty, exoneration of the innocent, and justice for all. Forensic science staffs provide valuable assistance in that investigative endeavor. The text *DNA Evidence and Forensic Science* is a supreme effort to systemize investigative strategies, theories, numerous concepts, and significant historical personalities who have contributed to the field.

DNA Evidence and Forensic Science serves as a distinguished one-volume source book that offers indispensable insights into the field of study. The text represents a comprehensive starting point for related and essential research. Excellent narratives describe central issues, chronological scientific events, and biographical data. The carefully organized glossary of terms, index, and annotated bibliography, support research efforts and enhance readability.

Chapter 2, "The Law Relating to Forensic Science and DNA Evidence," reviews various federal and state laws, and incorporates related court cases. The appendixes are particularly helpful, especially the court cases and laws. Legal case studies set the foundation for understanding the law and legal decisions. Landmark legal citations, including *Daubert v. Merrell Dow Pharmaceuticals*, *Frye v. United States*, and *United States v. Scheffer*, offer insight into the legal ramifications of scientific evidence.

DNA Evidence and Forensic Science cites historical, analytical, and research germane to understanding of forensic science and practical issues. Captivating topics include DNA research and current topical issues. The text's format and readability favor comprehension and retention. DNA typing and related investigative techniques offer new ways of cross-indexing scientific and criminal information. The purpose of this text is to provide a cogent resource on DNA that synchronizes with investigative strategies. Professors, teachers, and students need to identify DNA and forensic-related data sources promptly. In addition, many learners find fingerprinting techniques, firearms identification, polygraph examinations, and DNA typing fascinating academic content.

Chapter 6, "How to Conduct Research on Forensic Science and DNA Typing," is the best chapter for resourcing scientific information. In addition, it describes the use of library systems, print and electronic resources, and scholarly articles. The related content on Internet links, Websites, and search engines is helpful in the research and information gathering process. Library personnel, teaching staff, and students will find this chapter particularly useful for identifying resources and references.

DNA Evidence and Forensic Science is an excellent resource; it would make a welcome addition to local, state, and federal law enforcement agency libraries. This superb source book is essential to international and U.S. library collections. Moreover, universities, colleges, and community colleges would find the text indispensable to their collections. High schools would likely welcome this excellent resource because of its readability, reader interest, and career track information. The content serves as an excellent reference and resource for the study of crime and related scientific considerations.—**Thomas E. Baker**

ENVIRONMENTAL LAW

C, P

186.   **Environmental Law Handbook.** 19th ed. Thomas F. P. Sullivan, ed. Blue Ridge Summit, Pa., Government Institutes, 2007. 915p. index. $99.00. ISBN 13: 978-0-86587-024-6. ISSN 0147-7714.

Although environmental law in some form has existed for many years, the field has become enormously more complex in the last 35 years or so, primarily because of the greatly increased statutory and regulatory involvement at the federal level. This handbook is intended as an overview of the major areas of the law for persons without a legal background, particularly those who are working in areas in which compliance with environmental laws is necessary. The book succeeds in this objective for two reasons: first, the authors, although they are all attorneys who specialize in environmental law, write in a clear and straightforward style that will be understandable to educated general readers; and second, the book is admirably organized. Each of the 16 chapters is written by one of the handbook's 15 authors and deals with either a general topic (e.g., underground storage tanks, pesticides) or a specific federal act (e.g., Clean Water Act, Toxic Substances Control Act). The chapters are divided into short subparts and sub-subparts, and all of these chapter subunits are listed in the table of contents, making scanning of detailed contents easy. Nearly every page has footnotes to regulations, statutes, and court cases, obviating the need for a lot of flipping around. One understandable limitation that the editor makes clear at the beginning is that this book does not cover natural resource laws (e.g., Endangered Species Act), but only those that are intended to protect human environment, health, and safety. Most public and academic libraries will find this handbook useful.—**Jack Ray**

ESTATE

P

187.   Clifford, Denis. **Plan Your Estate: Protect Your Loved Ones, Property & Finances.** 9th ed. Berkeley, Calif., Nolo Press, 2008. 548p. index. $44.99pa. (w/CD-ROM). ISBN 1-4133-0761-2. ISBN 13: 978-1-4133-0761-0.

This guide, written by Denis Clifford, an estate planning lawyer and author of several self-help legal guides, is designed for those persons looking to write a legally binding estate plan that includes a standard will, living trust, health care directives (i.e., living wills), and children's trusts, among others. The book begins with short chapters discussing setting goals, special property ownership rules for married people, and choosing beneficiaries. It carefully goes over the reasons for creating an estate plan, including providing advanced health care plans for emergencies, avoiding having the state determine who receives your property, and appointing a guardian for minor children and a trustee to administer property to them.

Parts 2-10 discuss the nuts and bolts of planning an estate, including: how to address personal concerns (e.g., providing care for minor children, concerns of unmarried couples); laying the groundwork (e.g., inventorying your property, selecting beneficiaries); dealing with the concerns of your children (e.g., naming someone to care for minors, disinheritance); wills (e.g., types of wills, keeping wills up to date); probate and how to avoid it; understanding estate and gift tax; reducing or eliminating estate taxes; imposing controls over property (e.g., property control trusts for second or subsequent marriages); taking care of personal issues (e.g., making medical decisions when incapacitated, body and organ donation); and family and business estate planning. The remaining parts discuss finding a lawyer, what loved ones should do after your death to begin the process, and finally, sample estate plans. The work concludes with a glossary, appendix with state inheritance tax rules, and an index.—**Shannon Graff Hysell**

INTELLECTUAL PROPERTY

C, S
188.   Caso, Frank. **Censorship.** New York, Facts on File, 2008. 342p. index. (Global Issues). $45.00. ISBN 13: 978-0-8160-7123-4.

Censorship provides the reader with a historical overview of censorship practices from the United States and four other countries, as well as an in-depth look at each country's modern censorship practices. Chapter 1 introduces the reader to the topic of censorship, analyzing subjects such as the motives for censorship and the various methods of implementation. Chapter 2 is devoted to censorship in the United States—from the Alien and Sedition Acts to the USA Patriot Act, landmark events, legal cases, and events in society are explored and analyzed. Chapter 3 provides a global perspective by discussing the censorship practices of four additional countries: China, Egypt, Russia, and Zimbabwe. The methods that each of these five countries use in an attempt to silence political actors, controversial artists, and others provides a comprehensive overview of how censorship is used by those in power as a means to retain their power. Chapter 4 provides a chronology of original documents that illustrate the evolution of censorship in the United States. Included are items such as the bench warrant issued for John Peter Zenger in 1734 and the Smith Act from 1940. Similarly, chapter 5 provides some of the primary documents for the additional four countries covered. From excerpts of China's Measures for Managing Internet Information Services (2000) and Zimbabwe's Public Order and Security Act (2002), a researcher of censorship issues will find numerous useful and enlightening documents consolidated in this one source. Additional resources include: a chapter on how to research censorship, an alphabetic listing of "key figures" who were linked to censorship issues, a listing of U.S. and international organizations that are involved in countering censorship, an annotated bibliography, and a timeline of censorship activity from 443 B.C.E. to 2008.

Censorship would be a very helpful resource for anyone interested in becoming more knowledgeable about the roots of censorship as well as its impact on select societies around the world today. It should also prove useful as a quick reference guide to many of the main primary source censorship documents for the countries discussed.—**Alicia Brillon**

11 Library and Information Science and Publishing and Bookselling

LIBRARY AND INFORMATION SCIENCE

Reference Works

Directories

C, P

189. **American Library Directory 2008-2009.** 61st ed. Medford, N.J., Information Today, 2008. 2v. index. $299.95/set. ISBN 13: 978-1-57387-320-8. ISSN 0065-910X.

Whether you need to contact a fellow subject specialist librarian in your state for advice, or to locate a certain collection of rare books in the library community, just turn to *American Library Directory 2008-2009*. This two-volume tome is edited and compiled by Information Today and is updated every year to reflect important changes in libraries and library personnel.

There are more than 37,000 detailed profiles for public, academic, special, and government libraries and library-related organizations in the United States and Canada. There are more than 40 categories of library information, including addresses, telephone and fax numbers, e-mail addresses, consortium participation, expenditures, significant holdings and special collections, names and contact information of key personnel, and more. The library entries are arranged alphabetically by state and city, and listings of library school programs and library consortia are included as well. Information about each library came from the library itself via questionnaires or from publicly available sources. However, entries on school libraries are not included within this directory.

Volume 1 contains an editorial revision form, sample entry, library count, a list of library award recipients for 2007 (awards for outstanding librarianship or services, grants, and research projects), a key to symbols and abbreviations, and a listing of libraries in the states of Alabama through Rhode Island. Volume 2 contains a listing of libraries in the states of South Carolina through Wyoming, and libraries in Puerto Rico and Canada. Volume 2 also contains information for: networks, consortia, and other cooperative library organizations (e.g., automation networks, statewide networking systems); library schools (entries include entrance requirements, tuition, special courses offered, degrees offered); libraries for the blind and physically handicapped; libraries for the deaf and hearing impaired; state and provincial public library agencies; interlibrary loan codes for the United States; and United States Armed Forces Libraries Overseas. An organization index of all libraries and networks as well as a personnel index are included.
—**Rebecca Blakeley**

C, P

190. **Internet Public Library. http://ipl.org/.** [Website]. Free. Date reviewed: 2008.

C, P

191.   **Librarians' Internet Index. http://lii.org/.** [Website]. Free. Date reviewed: 2008.

These are two of the best all-round library and reference Websites. Both have excellent resources on various aspects of librarianship. In the *Internet Public Library*, click on Arts & Humanities, then Libraries to find everything from Fun Facts to Organizing the Web. The *Librarians' Internet Index* links to 3,374 sites under Librarianship, which is in the Society and Social Science. (It is interesting to discover that two different groups of librarians can choose to place libraries under both Arts & Humanities and Social Sciences.)—**Greg Byerly**

Handbooks and Yearbooks

C, S

192.   George, Mary W. **The Elements of Library Research: What Every Student Needs of Know.** Princeton, N.J., Princeton University Press, 2008. 201p. index. $14.95pa. ISBN 13: 978-0-691-13857-2.

Written with the student in mind, this volume covers the basic steps involved in library research and will prove to be an excellent resource for both teacher and student. The teacher, whose responsibility it is to provide consistent direction and research evaluation will particularly find this volume a useful tool. The introduction is clearly written and in an instructional style beneficial to both teacher and student. Students from the middle grades through college will be able to use this material. The clear divisions of the introduction—moving from the known to the new, reasons for research, varieties of research, and how researchers share their findings—provides a menu from which the teacher can easily choose as points of emphasis, depending on the age-level and needs of their students. The divisions of the chapters provide a four-step plan for research development and project completion that teachers and students will find useful. These include: plan assignment, strategy and tools, finding sources, and a catch-all chapter, insight, argument, evaluation, and beyond. Five appendixes provide helpful hints, timelines, rules to follow, questions to ask, and worksheets that will keep the student researcher on task and prove useful to the instructional task. Coupled with a glossary of library research terms, a selected bibliography, and a useful index, this volume will prove a valuable tool for educators for many years.—**Joseph P. Hester**

C, P

193.   Healey, Paul D. **Professional Liability Issues for Librarians and Information Professionals.** New York, Neal-Schuman, 2008. 236p. index. (The Legal Advisor for Librarians, Educators, & Information Professionals). $85.00pa. ISBN 13: 978-1-55570-609-8.

Written by the author of the seminal 1995 article that is the benchmark of scholarship on the topic of professional liability issues for librarians and information professionals, this work fills a noted gap of writings on librarian liability for torts and related harms in recent years. A preparatory and preemptory work that tackles the jumble of questions that arise when considering liability, immunity, and policy decisions, Healey meets his goal of offering practical opportunities grounded in sound legal scholarship in a way that any librarian can understand. Continuing the pattern set for this series of presenting law and its application through discussion of the law and examples, case studies, bullet-point summaries, and compliance and practice tools, this particular volume focuses on organizing a presentation of legal concepts in specific contexts, such as type of information professional, library or entity, and professional function. The reader, through the examples and case studies, can focus on materials directly related to their own situation, whether the reader is a librarian or another administrator in the entity or organization. Intended to function as a clear, comprehensive guide to professional liability issues, the work explores when and under what circumstances a librarian or information professional might personally face a liability claim for his or her professional activities. Providing a practical, readable work drawing on sound legal analysis, this work is a welcome addition to any library whether or not they are facing such situations, as when the situation arises it might be too late.—**Sara Marcus**

P

194.　Kane, Laura Townsend, Rozalynd P. McConnaughy, and Steven Patrick Wilson, with David L. Townsend. **Answers to the Health Questions People Ask in Libraries.** New York, Neal-Schuman, 2008. 278p. index. (Medical Library Association Guides). $65.00pa. ISBN 13: 978-1-55570-642-5.

　　Answers to the Health Questions People Ask in Libraries was compiled by three medical librarians with medical consultation from a doctor and represents the most commonly asked reference questions in medical libraries. The intention of this work is to provide accurate medical information for the general public who, as the authors note, often search for and find inaccurate information on the Internet. The format, however, makes it doubtful that it will serve as the intended replacement for people seeking medical information through the Internet. Perhaps an online resource linked from a medical library's Website or even from the Medical Library Association Website with appropriate metadata tagging would prove more useful in aiding those seeking accurate medical help from Google searches.

　　The material is presented in a question answer format, first listing the question and then providing a thorough and well-researched answer. A few references are listed at the end of each entry for those who may want additional information. The questions are arranged by broad topics such as Women's Health, Nutrition and Fitness, and Drug Information. Use of either the table of contents or index is necessary to find relevant information. The questions are pre-defined so unless a health question fits one of the questions listed, answer to health and medical issues will not be answered by this resource (i.e., a search for information on memory loss provides no entries).

　　While the writing is clear, well researched, and easy to understand, the usefulness of this resource for the general public may depend on how easy it is to access the resource. The print format will require finding this resource in a library or bookstore, or being directed to it by a librarian. Given the author's acknowledgement that most people find (inaccurate) medical information from the Web, this work may be more beneficial to reference librarians directing patrons to accurate information.—**Susan E. Thomas**

P

195.　Landau, Herbert B. **The Small Public Library Survival Guide: Thriving on Less.** Chicago, American Library Association, 2008. 159p. index. $38.00pa.; $34.20pa. (ALA members). ISBN 13: 978-0-8389-3575-0.

　　Written for the small public library structured as an independent, not-for-profit corporation that receives only partial government support, others can also benefit from the tips provided in this work by Herbert B. Landau—although, as stated in the book, legal guidance might be of use before implementing any ideas. Upon becoming a director of a small public library, the author realized there were many things not learned in library school, and so this book was born to help small public libraries facing challenges such as a decrease in public funding, competition from technology and the Internet, and a de-emphasis on library visits and reading in general. Designed to guide small public library administrators in fighting an often losing battle for sufficient support and recognition, these 12 chapters provide practical tools, guidelines, and strategies that have been tested in a real-world situation. The eight appendixes provide samples to use in one's own library, while a selected bibliography enables one to find more information on topics covered in the brief chapters. An extensive index encourages use of the work as a reference, while the chapter headings enable locating the area of interest in general as well. Many subheadings in the chapters ease the reading and locating of specific information, while the writing style encourages reading from cover to cover. While the intended audience is small, others can also gain from the knowledge presented so as to implement similar ideas into other situations. [R: VOYA, Feb 09, pp. 563-564]—**Sara Marcus**

P

196.　Moyer, Jessica E. **Research-Based Readers' Advisory.** Chicago, American Library Association, 2008. 278p. index. (ALA Readers' Advisory Series). $50.00pa.; $45.00pa. (ALA members). ISBN 13: 978-0-8389-0959-1.

As the number of reference questions in libraries has decreased, the role of readers' advisory has increased. Further, as readers' advisory has become more important, the service has expanded. This guidebook discusses examples of readers' advisory changes based on resent research, serves as an accessible resource for reviewing everyday interactions with readers, and discusses bookgroups and other readers' advisory related topics along with collection development and management. This title would be useful to librarians working in a readers' advisory position everyday as well as for students learning the ins and outs of readers' advisory services. Jessica Moyer has created an indispensable tool for librarians. All libraries should purchase a copy of this work. [R: BL, 1 & 15 June 08, p. 142]—**January Adams**

C, S

197.   **The Portable MLIS: Insights from the Experts.** Ken Haycock and Brooke E. Sheldon, eds. Westport, Conn., Libraries Unlimited/Greenwood Publishing Group, 2008. 296p. index. $50.00pa. ISBN 13: 978-1-59158-547-3.

Writing for the layperson or the beginning librarian, Haycock and Sheldon bring together the insights of 18 leading educators and practitioners in the field of librarianship. Separated into three parts, this is the first published broad overview of the competencies of professionally trained librarians. Finally answering the age-old questions asked of many librarians—"What is it that you do?" and 'Why do you need to go to school?"—*The Portable MLIS* introduces the continually evolving, changing, and oftentimes exciting universe of librarianship. Beginning with 5 essays on foundations, values, and context of the field, followed by 11 entries on functions and competencies of librarianship, the third section presents 2 essays focusing on moving beyond the boundaries. The volume ends with 12 appendixes of importance to librarians and their field. Notes for each entry are presented in a culminated list at the end of the work, along with an extensive index to assist the reader in locating the area of importance to them. A welcome addition to a public or academic library, this might also be a useful book for those in a school or other small library where the importance of a trained librarian needs to be emphasized. [R: BL, 1 &15 Jan 09, p. 127]—**Sara Marcus**

P

198.   Simpson, Jack. **Basics of Genealogy Reference: A Librarian's Guide.** Westport, Conn., Libraries Unlimited/Greenwood Publishing Group, 2008. 176p. index. $40.00pa. ISBN 13: 978-1-59158-514-5.

This book contains excellent information to assist librarians in serving patrons seeking help with their genealogical or family history research. It includes many good illustrated samplings of genealogical and family history records and research techniques. Chapter 13, "Professional Toolkit" (pp. 141-148), contains essential suggestions for professional growth and development of reference librarians serving genealogists and family historians. Bibliographic citations are provided throughout the work and indexed by title in its six-page general index.

Simpson is incorrect in his use of "convert" in the second paragraph on page 115. The tenets of the Church of Jesus Christ of Latter-day Saints are that several of the ordinances of the Gospel of Jesus Christ must take place on earth. For ancestors who died before they received those ordinances in life. LDS members are encouraged to perform those ordinances by proxy for their ancestors who may, in heaven, accept or reject the ordinances of their own free will and choice.

This work is recommended for all reference collections, with circulating copies for library patrons. Libraries should provide free personal copes for each reference librarian to mark up for themselves for use during consultations with genealogical or family history patrons.—**J. Carlyle Parker**

P

199.   Spatz, Michele. **Answering Consumer Health Questions: The Medical Library Association Guide for Reference Librarians.** New York, Neal-Schuman, 2008. 142p. index. (Medical Library Association Guides). $65.00pa. ISBN 1-55570-632-0. ISBN 13: 978-1-55570-632-6.

Written for the general librarian, omitting medical jargon or other technical terms unfamiliar to the MLS, this work helps the health and medical librarian as much as it helps the nonmedical librarian to provide needed information to patrons. Including features such as italicized vignettes to illustrate concepts discussed in a real-life situation as well as tips, recommended resources, and templates, Spatz provides a well-organized and superbly indexed work of value to any library. Providing a summary and list of references in each chapter, the work also includes suggested readings in selected chapters. Beginning with a discussion of understanding and reaching out to the health information seeker, this book addresses issues such as how health reference questions differ from other questions encountered at a reference desk; and common emotions and concerns one might encounter, and how to respond to such situations. The work next addresses professional interactions, including communication guidelines and strategies for verbal and nonverbal communication, reference interview techniques, how to present unpleasant news, and guidelines on how to deal with e-mail and virtual references and telephone reference interactions. The third chapter deals with professional ethics of providing health information (both of the librarian and of the patron), and special issues to consider when working with the young and the mentally challenged. Next covered are legal issues in health information delivery by the nonmedical professional. Chapter 5 addresses the needs of diverse individuals such as disabled, youth, minority and culturally diverse, LGBT, and those with mental health disorders. Chapter 6 is of use to any reference librarian, discussing the difficult patron—the various persona one might encounter, and how to deal with such patrons. The work concludes with ways to deal with stressful situations that arise when dealing with health information reference; methods that can help with any stressful situation. [R: BL, 1 &15 Jan 09, p. 126]—**Sara Marcus**

PUBLISHING AND BOOKSELLING

Directories

C, P

200.   **American Book Trade Directory 2008-2009.** 54th ed. Medford, N.J., Information Today, 2008. 1750p. index. $299.95. ISBN 13: 978-1-57387-317-8. ISSN 0065-759X.

This 54th edition lists nearly 25,500 retailers and wholesalers in the U.S. and Canada. E-mail addresses are included for nearly half of the entries and Websites are included for at least that many. The *American Book Trade Directory* is the only complete public source for bookseller standard address number (SAN). Following the preface is a statistical section based on compiled data from responses to a questionnaire mailed to all booksellers. Comparing the statistics in this edition with the statistics from previous editions will indicate industry trends. This edition is organized the same way as previous editions and provides the same basic information: store or company size, specialties, years in business, owner and key personnel, contact information, and notations for those businesses that also handle audiocassettes, software, and other sidelines. This book is an excellent standard reference for everyone involved in the industry and for all public and academic libraries.—**Ladyjane Hickey**

C, P

201.   **International Literary Market Place 2009: The Directory of the International Book Publishing Industry.** Medford, N.J., Information Today, 2008. 1750p. index. $259.00pa. ISBN 13: 978-1-57387-325-3. ISSN 0074-6827.

C, P

202.　　**Literary Market Place 2009: The Directory of the Book Publishing Industry.** Medford, N.J., Information Today, 2008. 2v. index. $309.00pa./set. ISBN 13: 978-1-57387-329-1. ISSN 0000-1155.

The 2009 edition of <I>Literary Market Place provides users with directory information for nearly 12,500 publishers, editorial services, associations, trade magazines, book marketing specialists, book manufacturing companies, sales and distributions companies, and services and suppliers. In each new edition *Literary Market Place* provides contact information for new publishers, deletes those no longer in business, and provides thousands of updates to existing entries. Volume 1 provides information for publishers (including Canadian and small presses); editorial services and agents; associations, events, courses, and awards; and books and magazines for the trade. Volume 2 provides information on service providers to the book industry, including advertisers and marketing, book manufacturers, sales and distribution, and suppliers. Directory information includes the name of the company; address; telephone, fax, and toll-free numbers; e-mail and Website addresses; names of key personnel with titles; company reportage; branch offices; brief statistics; and a short description of the company. When appropriate Standard Address Numbers (SANs) and ISBN prefixes are provided. A variety of indexes will help users expedite their search. They include company and personnel indexes, a toll-free directory, an index to sections, and an index to advertisers. The directory also includes a list of book trade acquisitions and mergers that occurred between June 2006 and July 2008.

This 2009 edition of *International Literary Market Place* (ILMP) lists more than 15,000 entries from some 180 countries. Publishers account for two-thirds of the information provided. There are six sections to this volume: "Publishing," "Manufacturing," "Book Trade Information," "Literary Associations & Prizes," "Book Trade Calendar," and "Library Resources." Within the chapters companies are listed first by their country, then by keyword. The directory information in ILMP remains the same as in previous editions: name of company; address, telephone number, and fax number; names of key personnel; subjects the publisher specializes in; parent company (if any); imprints; ISBN prefixes; and address of where to order from. Indexes facilitate easy of use throughout the volume. The volume is updated throughout the year with the use of questionnaires and public sources.

The information provided in the print versions of these directories are as accurate as one will find. The LMP staff contacts each publisher directly for updates on an annual basis and is continually researching to find new publishing or publishing-related companies. Those libraries considering either of these titles should note that there is an online version available, which includes access to the information in both volumes. Both are highly recommended for public and academic libraries.—**Shannon Graff Hysell**

12 Military Studies

GENERAL WORKS

Chronology

C, P, S

203. Marley, David F. **Wars of the Americas: A Chronology of Armed Conflict in the Western Hemisphere.** 2d ed. Santa Barbara, Calif., ABC-CLIO, 2008. 2v. illus. maps. index. $195.00/set. ISBN 13: 978-1-59884-100-8.

Of the many reference books on the history of warfare, this is clearly the most comprehensive chronology in print. Beginning with Columbus's skirmish with the native Caribs just off present-day Dominican Republic in January 1493, the two-volume set treats all conflicts in the Western Hemisphere up to the present. The first volume covers the period through the undeclared Hispano-Portuguese Conflict, 1775-1777. The second volume begins with the American Revolutionary War and ends with the Mexican government's crushing of 70,000 striking teachers by military force in October 2006. The entries, organized by chronology and topical headings list events by month and day and the entries are quite comprehensive. For large events, such as the American Civil War, the entries are often daily. Throughout the volumes are more than 271 pictures and illustrations, over 90 maps, and more than 200 sidebars that immeasurably enhance the value of the project. The topical bibliographies are impressive, and the books include a glossary, and geographical and general indexes. In sum, this is a very large and valuable undertaking.

Because the volumes concentrate on warfare in the hemisphere, a global conflict such as World War II gets somewhat less attention than it would in other collections. However, this source covers small and relatively unknown battles, skirmishes, and mini-wars throughout the Americas that are overlooked in almost all other sources. The 2d edition not only brings the volumes up to date but includes expanded coverage about drug cartel wars, international terrorism, and other contemporary issues of import.

The compiler is a naval historian who has completed previous volume on *Historic Cities of the Americas* (see ARBA 2006, entry 845) and *Pirates and Privateers of the Americas* as well as the 1st edition of *Wars of the Americas* (see ARBA 99, entry 629). The compiler's knowledge of pirates and privateers is quite evident in the inclusions in this volume. In every sense, this is a marvelous reference work that would be valuable for any library.—**Joe P. Dunn**

Dictionaries and Encyclopedias

C, P

204. Clodfelter, Micheal. **Warfare and Armed Conflicts: A Statistical Encyclopedia of Casualty and Other Figures, 1494-2007.** 3d ed. Jefferson, N.C., McFarland, 2008. 831p. index. $245.00. ISBN 13: 978-0-7864-3319-3.

Clodfelter, a Vietnam veteran and the author of several books, including *Vietnam in Military Statistics* and the *Dakota War*, offers the reader a unique and interesting approach to the causalities of war through the use of statistics. Armed conflicts between groups have existed since the dawn of time, but this work focuses on the period of 1494 to 2007 and provides seldom seen insights into lesser-known and older conflicts from around the world.

The publisher describes this work the best as "the most comprehensive and accurate statistical compendium of modern armed conflict available, the author has incorporated newly discovered data, offering more information… Arranged roughly be century and subdivided by world region, the entries proceed chronologically and vary from paragraph to chapter-length. Also, each entry provides the name and date of the conflict, precursor events, strategies and details, the outcome and its impacts."

A good example of a typical entry is on page 354—The Irish War of Independence: 1919-21. This entry is a column and a half or half the page in length. A brief background of the conflict is given and so are key players and events. The focus is on the statistical data including those wounded and dead. It is succinct, but informative. Overall, this is a very well-organized and instructive effort. This work is recommended for all collections.—**Scott R. DiMarco**

C, S

205.   **The Encyclopedia of North American Colonial Conflicts to 1775: A Political, Social, and Military History.** Spencer C. Tucker, ed. Santa Barbara, Calif., ABC-CLIO, 2008. 3v. illus. maps. index. $295.00/set. ISBN 13: 978-1-85109-752-4; 978-1-85109-757-9 (e-book).

In three volumes, Spencer C. Tucker presents a close and detailed look at the conflicts that existed within the colonies on the American continent before the Revolutionary War. In so doing, he fills a gap in reference works. While there are numerous books detailing the battles and conflicts of the Revolutionary era, such as *Revolutionary War* from Facts on File (see ARBA 2004, entry 448), most books on the Colonial era have a wider focus, showing the struggles of living in a wilderness, of survival, of building an economy and a way of life. Studies such as *Daily Life in the Early American Republic* by David S. Heidler and Jeanne T. Heidler (see ARBA 2005, entry 449) give details of daily life. The conflicts inherent in these efforts form only part of the study.

Tuckers' three volumes concentrate solely on fighting, military conflict, and wars before the culminating war of the Revolution. Spanish, French, and English colonies and forces were all in conflict with native peoples, and often with each other. The first two volumes consist of encyclopedia entries, often of about a half page, of specific battles. The entries all have brief bibliographies attached for further reference and reading. Ample illustrations from contemporary sources complement the articles.

The third volume is one of primary documents arranged chronologically. They include charters granted by rulers, journal entries, letters, accounts written by explorers and settlers to send back to funding and supporting entities, memoirs, and early attempts at establishing governments. These documents articulate the efforts to shape communities from a new, unknown, and harsh land. Supplemental material includes a glossary, a chronology, maps, a general bibliography, and an index. Tucker also provides a section of "Statistical Information," which gives quick information and facts about various colonies, such as land area and the population at various dates. In addition, a general essay titled "Overview of the North American Colonial Period" provides context for the encyclopedia entries.

The Encyclopedia of North American Colonial Conflicts to 1775 is a good companion purchase and lead-in to ABC-CLIO's earlier *American Revolutionary War: A Student Encyclopedia*, edited by Gregory Fremont-Barnes and Richard Alan Ryerson (see ARBA 2008, entry 392), which details the battles of the war era. High schools, colleges, and public libraries with a history inclined clientele will find this a valuable source.—**Terry Ann Mood**

C, S

206.   McCallum, Jack E. **Military Medicine: From Ancient Times to the 21st Century.** Santa Barbara, Calif., ABC-CLIO, 2998. 383p. illus. index. $95.00. ISBN 13: 978-1-85109-693-0.

In the introduction to this well-written guide to the history of military medicine the author, a historian and former physician, notes the rapid progress that has been made in this area in the past century as opposed to the limited advances of the previous 4,900 years. This progression in the history of military medicine is traced in the ensuing 242 alphabetically arranged entries that range from the earliest efforts in the field to the current wars in Iraq and Afghanistan. Topics covered in the volume include disease (e.g., cholera, plague, yellow fever), individuals (e.g., nurses, physicians, surgeons, other pioneers in military medicine), types of wounds and injuries (e.g., blast injuries, bullet wounds, cold injury), weapons (e.g., chemical and biological warfare), medical procedures and techniques (e.g., Phlebotomy, Venesection), time periods and national histories (e.g., Biblical military medicine, British military medicine, Roman military medicine), instruments, organizations (e.g., Red Cross, Red Crescent), international agreements (e.g., Geneva Conventions, Nuremberg Code), and events (e.g., Great Plague of Athens). Selected wars that are discussed in individual entries include major conflicts, such as both of the world wars, as well as those that are of note from a medical perspective, such as the Haitian Campaign and the Madagascar Campaign, the latter war having the highest death rate from malaria of any campaign in history. The entries range in length from one to four pages and are cross-referenced. The entries are supported by an introductory essay that provides an overview of the evolution of military medicine and by a 111-item annotated bibliography. This interesting book is recommended for all libraries.—**Bradley P. Tolppanen**

WEAPONS

C, P, S

207.   Marguilies, Phillip. **Nuclear Nonproliferation.** New York, Facts on File, 2008. 355p. index. (Global Issues). $45.00. ISBN 13: 978-0-8160-7211-8.

Part of Facts on File's Global Issues series, this title is designed as a "first-stop resource" for students interested in nuclear proliferation. It is divided into three parts. The first is an overview of the nonproliferation issue in three chapters. The first chapter is an excellent, 40-plus page introduction that examines the historical development of nuclear weapons, the vertical and horizontal proliferation, peaceful uses of nuclear energy, potential for nuclear war, differing views on the utility of nuclear weapons, and a history of nuclear nonproliferation efforts and strategies. Chapter 2 focuses on the interaction between the first two nuclear powers, the United States and the Soviet Union/Russia. The last chapter focuses on nuclear proliferation and nonproliferation in South Asia, Middle East, and Northeast Asia, with historical overviews, profiles on key state actors, and international responses. Part 2 consists of U.S. documents and international documents. The U.S. documents are subdivided into nuclear policy, Iraq, and North Korea sections. The international documents include texts of international treaties, United Nations resolutions, and more. Each document notes the online or print source and clearly notes deletions with ellipses. The last part covers research tools in five chapters: "how to research . . .", facts and figures, key players, organizations and agencies, and annotated bibliography. The research chapter reviews types of resources, need for awareness of bias, importance of credentials, and key sources for beginning research. Facts and figures are provided on the international weapons stockpile, nonproliferation, Iraq, and North Korea. Profiles of over 50 key players include civilian and military leaders and theorists, scientists, and whistle blowers. Details for nearly 50 international and national governmental and nongovernmental organizations and research and educational institutions consist of contact information, Website address, and a brief description of activities. The annotated bibliography lists books, articles, and Websites in 12 categories, such as "Nonproliferation History." A list of acronyms, chronology (December 1941 through March 2007), glossary (over 100 terms from "ABM Treaty" to "Zionism") , and subject index are also provided. This work is highly recommended for high school, public, and academic libraries.—**Chad Kahl**

C, P
208.   Murphy, Justin D., and Matthew A. McNiece. **Military Aircraft, 1919-1945: An Illustrated History of Their Impact.** Santa Barbara, Calif., ABC-CLIO, 2009. 348p. illus. index. (Weapons and Warfare). $85.00. ISBN 13: 978-1-85109-498-1.

More a descriptive and historical text than an encyclopedia, this new volume in the publisher's Weapons and Warfare series complements Murphy's earlier volume on military aircraft through World War I (see ARBA 2006, entry 678). Following introductory chapters on military aviation during the interwar period and World War II, the authors document fighter, bomber, auxiliary, and naval aircraft. They conclude with an overview of aircraft development in sections on the United States, Britain, France, the Soviet Union, Germany, Italy, and Japan, as well as brief coverage of aircraft of lesser powers. These chapters are designed for the general reader with just enough technical description for historians and other researchers. The text is not documented and there is an overall listing of sources. The volume concludes with a listing of aircraft by country, a glossary, a useful index, and nearly 80 pages of individual aircraft information, including nation of origin, manufacturer, technical notes, total production, and a brief descriptive summary and photographs.

Considering the emergence of air power following World War I, this is a handy reference volume and fits well with the design of the series. While numerous other books on World War II aircraft are readily available, this volume with a textual emphasis provides more than those heavily illustrated selections.
—**Boyd Childress**

13 Political Science

GENERAL WORKS

Dictionaries and Encyclopedias

C

209.   Daid, Lynda Lee, and Christina Holtz-Bacha. **Encyclopedia of Political Communication.** Thousand Oaks, Calif., Sage, 2008. 2v. illus. index. $350.00/set. ISBN 13: 978-1-4129-1799-5.

The *Encyclopedia of Political Communication* is a wonderful tool for researching the various roles that communication plays in the political processes in the United States and internationally. It is made up of two volumes. With 600 entries, this set discusses the theoretical approaches to the field (e.g., agenda-setting, sociological, framing and priming), the importance of political speeches, political advertising and posters, political debates, and the rise in Internet sites and new technologies. This encyclopedia was put together by a group of scholars. The articles are in the traditional A-to-Z format for each volume. The articles vary in length. They have *see also* references and a bibliography of books, journals, and some Internet sites. Some articles are accompanied by maps and black-and-white photographs. Some key entry topics include: Election, Legal and Regulatory, News Media Coverage of Politics, Women in Politics, and Media Outlets and Programs. There is a general bibliography that covers books, journals, and Internet sites in English.

This set will be a wonderful addition to academic libraries that need reference works on world politics. It will be of interest to undergraduates as well as members of the general public. Professionals involved in politics, such as lobbyists, government officials, and political organization leaders will find there is much to be found within these two volumes.—**Benet Steven Exton**

S

210.   **Gale Encyclopedia of World History: Governments.** Farmington Hills, Mich., Gale Group, 2008. 2v. illus. index. $220.00/set. ISBN 13: 978-1-4144-3152-9.

What strikes most about this encyclopedia is that it bears a confusing title. History and government are two discrete and different fields of study and both are so vast that it will take several volumes to deal with even one of them. It turns out that the encyclopedia is about neither. It is about nations and therefore properly belongs in the field of country studies.

In this context, the work is extremely informative and brings new perspectives with an unusual array of categories and rubrics. However, it is organized not in alphabetic order but by periods and eras. This might make it difficult for a reader who wants to look up India or Germany, to go directly to the entry. National histories overlap chronological eras and sometimes nations merge, morph into something else, or disappear altogether. Therefore, a chronological division of the counties can be the least user-friendly arrangement in an encyclopedia. For some reason Nepal appears just before United States of American and this is extremely counterintuitive for any reader. The term Republic is used with some countries but not with many others that are in fact republics.

Each entry is organized according to a logical scheme. It traces the development of nations (governments is the term used throughout as a synonym for nations) in nine chronological chapters from 4,000 B.C.E. to the present day, covering 270 nations. Each entry has the following subsections: Type of Government, Background, Government Structure, Political Parties and Factions, major Events, Aftermath, and Bibliography. This structure does not always work well. For example, political parties came into being in the West only in the seventeenth century. How many political parties did Carthage and Babylonian Empire have? Uniformity is good, but when it becomes rigidity, the reader is not well served. Each entry presents a snapshot, and does not reflect the dynamics of world history nor the evolutionary process and incremental changes.

The encyclopedia is the result of a bold concept and was designed to be compatible with the National Council for Social Studies high School World History Curriculum Standards. Yet, the work does not convey the excitement that history should bring into the classroom.

There are a number of useful features, such as a brief chronology of 11 pages, a glossary of two pages, and a bibliography. There are many black-and-white illustrations that are of such poor quality that they actually detract from rather and add to the value of the book. This work is recommended for school libraries with the qualifications noted above.—**George Thomas Kurian**

Handbooks and Yearbooks

C

211.   **A Companion to Contemporary Political Philosophy.** 2d ed. Robert E. Goodin, Philip Pettit, and Thomas Pogge, eds. Ames, Iowa, Blackwell Publishing Professional, 2007. 2v. index. $350.00/set. ISBN 13: 978-1-4051-3653-2.

After the 1960s political philosophy emerged as a major field with the work of figures such as John Rawls and Jürgen Habermas. Even in the last decade political philosophy has developed enough to warrant expanded treatment in a 2-volume 2d edition of *A Companion to Contemporary Political Philosophy*. This companion aims to provide an overview of worldwide political philosophy as it is currently practiced in each of its major modes. While the editors have particular interests in normative analysis—determining what kinds of political institutions ought to be strived for—these volumes also include significant input from fields that suggest what kinds of institutions are feasible. Hence, the companion has contributions from experts in analytical and continental philosophy, political science, sociology, history, economics, and more.

The companion is organized into three parts. Part 1, "Disciplinary Contributions," discusses the contributions to the field from 9 disciplines, some of which were just mentioned. Part 2, "Major Ideologies," provides insight on certain political schools of thought, such as Conservativism, Liberalism, and Socialism. Part 3, "Special Topics," covers 38 areas of interest, including just war, intellectual property, democracy, environmentalism, and toleration. The first two parts consist of substantial, article-length entries. The entries in part 3 are slightly briefer. Each entry is followed by references and recommendations for further reading. The organization allows the reader to refer to topics within the context of a discipline or ideology in parts 1 and 2, or to refer to topics as isolated issues in part 3.

The *Companion* will serve as a useful resource for undergraduates and researchers alike. The diverse selection of expert contributors is impressive, although there is little representation from outside the Western academic tradition. The expanded coverage since the 1st edition reflects an attempt to address research on issues raised by increased globalization and other recent world developments.—**Joshua Barton**

C, P

212.   Maddex, Robert L. **Constitutions of the World.** 3d ed. Washington, D.C., CQ Press, 2008. 518p. index. $125.00. ISBN 13: 978-0-87289-556-0.

This title does not contain the texts of the national constitutions, which can be found in other reference works and over the Internet (e.g., *Constitution Finder*, from the University of Richmond, http://confinder.richmond.edu/). Nor should it be confused with the microfiche serial set of constitutional texts produced by K. G. Saur Verlag, *Constitutions of the World: 1850 to the Present* (2002-). This 3d edition examines 20 new constitutions, and updates and revises the information about the governing instruments of other countries. Arranged alphabetically by the country name, each of the 119 entries consists of a brief introduction; a historical overview of the development of the national legal and constitutional systems; various influences on the constitution; important dates; and discussion of the amending process, fundamental rights, and the basics of the legislative, executive, and judiciary branches. At the front of the book one can find "Constitutions at a Glance," which is a quick reference table that shows the type of state, government and legislature, the date of the most recent constitution, and whether or not provisions are made for an ombudsman or constitutional or judiciary review. The glossary is only four pages, and the bibliography lists only one source per country, so this work is only intended for quick beginning information, not long in-depth study of the intricacies of a constitution or government powers. Facts on File published a similar three-volume work edited by Gerhard Robbers entitled *Encyclopedia of World Constitutions* (see ARBA 2007, entry 444). Maddex, an international law attorney, is the constitutional expert for CQ Press, and previously compiled for CQ the *Illustrated Dictionary of Constitutional Concepts* (see ARBA 97, entry 594), which can supplement other works on constitutions. The title under review is appropriate for the reference collections of academic and large public libraries, although those that already own the Facts on File title may not desire to duplicate the information here.—**Daniel K. Blewett**

C, P
213. **Political Handbook of the Americas 2008.** Washington, D.C., CQ Press, 2008. 629p. maps. index. (Regional Political Handbooks of the World). $135.00. ISBN 13: 978-0-87289-903-2.

The *Political Handbook of the Americas 2008* consists of four parts: an introduction, "Governments," "Intergovernmental Organizations," and appendixes. It is one title in the Regional Political Handbook of the World series. Other handbooks deal with the Middle East, Africa, Asia, and Europe.

The introduction presents a historical setting of the United States, relations with the United States, migration, race and class, and an overview of history and current events of South America, Central America, North America, and the Caribbean. The main part of this title is "Governments." It has 39 entries arranged by states and colonial states in alphabetic order. But, Aruba, a Dutch colony, is listed separately—not under the entry of Netherlands Territories. The length of each entry varies from four pages for Aruba to 34 pages for United States and related territories. A typical entry includes a map, information on government and politics, political parties, legislature, communications, and intergovernmental representation. Two entries are given extra items: Falkland Islands in Argentina and Panama Canal Zone in Panama. Falkland Islands is found respectively in entries of Argentina and United Kingdom Territories.

"International Organizations" has over a dozen organizations, including Agency for the Prohibition of Nuclear Weapons in Latin America and the Caribbean (OPANAL), Andean Community of Nations (CAN), Organization of American States (OAS/OEA), United Nations (UN), and so on. The appendix consists of a chronology of major events in the Americas 2007 (arranged by government) and a serials list. There is a personal name index, but it is far from complete. Names of most cabinet members are not indexed. The index would enhance its usefulness if proper names and subjects are indexed. Overall, this book is an excellent reference source.—**Tze-chung Li**

C, P
214. **Political Handbook of the World 2008.** Arthur S. Banks, Thomas C. Muller, and William R. Overstreet, eds. Washington, D.C., CQ Press, 2008. 1827p. maps. index. $240.00. ISBN 13: 978-0-87289-528-7. ISSN 0193-175X.

After an astounding amount of research and work by the writers, the *Political Handbook of the World 2008* shares information using a Contents, Governments, Intergovernmental Organizations,

Appendixes, and Indexes. A helpful Intergovernmental Organization Abbreviations and Preface precede the informative entries for Government and Intergovernmental Organizations. The inside back and front covers allure readers with detailed world maps.

Revelation of country territories, number of people in the country, type of government, size of the country, largest cities with population, languages, currency, past politics, dealings with other countries, present incidents, political affiliations, legislature and public officials, journalism and reporting, and diplomats enlighten readers. Uncovered are the foundation of the international organizations, the goals, locations, Web page, chairperson, countries participating, spoken languages, growth of the organization, who meets and how often, and actions by the international organizations. Appendix A is a timeline of affairs from 1945-2007. Appendix B lists the United Nations' conferences from 1946-2007. Disclosed in appendix C are the nations contributing in the United Nations and 17 other organizations. Appendix D, Serial List, is a directory of periodicals and catalogs the past editions of *The Political Handbook* (1927-2007). The geographical and organizational names and personal names indexes are all-inclusive.—**Melinda F. Matthews**

POLITICS AND GOVERNMENT

United States

Dictionaries and Encyclopedias

C, S

215.   **Congress A to Z.** 5th ed. Washington, D.C., CQ Press, 2008. 704p. illus. index. $85.00. ISBN 13: 978-0-87289-558-4.

The 5th edition of this title uses an expansive format that permits a traditional dictionary style A-to-Z arrangement, with allowance for some entries that are more encyclopedic in length and depth. The alphabet does not confine itself to either strict biographical emphasis or subject/topic arrangement either. Instead, entries are interspersed so that, for example, three-fourths of a page about "Ervin, Sam J., Jr." is bookended by a paragraph about "Equality of the Houses" and an 8-plus page entry entitled "Ethics." Numerous sidebars, tables, photographs, an extensive cross-referencing mechanism urging one to "find more on this topic," cartoons, and other graphics, promote a visually interesting text, which could be even more interesting if any of the value-added graphics were in color. This is something for editors to consider for the next edition, particularly since this is not an inexpensive title.

Congress A to Z is part of the CQ Press American Government A to Z Series, which includes *The Supreme Court A to Z* (4th ed.; see ARBA 2007, entry 446), *Elections A to Z* (3d ed.; see ARBA 2008, entry 628), *The U. S. Constitution A to Z* (2d ed.; CQ Press, 2008), and *The Presidency A to Z* (4th ed.; see entry 221). The series thus addresses the three federal governmental branches: Congress (legislative); the Presidency (executive); and the Supreme Court (judicial), plus the cornerstone legal document, the U. S. Constitution, and a manual on elections.

This compendium of all-things Congressional represents a skillful balance of history, biography, and primary source materials. Only the most senior and current Congressional leaders receive entries; for example, Bill Frist, Nancy Pelosi, Harry Reid, and Ted Kennedy. Selected major or historical Congressional leaders, such as John C. Calhoun, Denny Hastert, Tom Daschle, Al Gore, and Newt Gingrich, are also included. Notably absent are current minority leaders John Boehner and Mitch McConnell. Topical entries include: Appropriations Bills; Blue Dog Democrats; Filibuster; Readings of Bills; Scandals, Congressional; Subpoena Power; and Women's Suffrage (cross-referenced to a complete list of Women Members of Congress, 1917-2007).

The body of this dictionary contains 600-plus pages. Preceding A-Z entries are a comprehensive table of contents and substantial, chronologically arranged introductory essay, "Historic Milestones." Pages 621-672 contain reference materials, including organizational charts for both the U.S. House of Representatives and the U.S. Senate, a ubiquitous "How a Bill Becomes a Law," diagram, Congressional information on the Internet, writing to a member of Congress, and an extensive bibliography of Congress-related readings, arranged topically. Rounding out the dictionary is a detailed back of the book index.

The 5th edition of this dictionary is highly recommended for the reference collections of undergraduate and graduate academic and law libraries. It also deserves consideration for a place on the reference shelves of high school libraries able to afford it.—**Linda D. Tietjen**

C

216. **Encyclopedia of U.S. Campaigns, Elections, and Electoral Behavior.** Kenneth F. Warren, ed. Thousand Oaks, Calif., Sage, 2008. 2v. illus. index. $250.00/set; $315.00 (e-book). ISBN 13: 978-1-4129-5489-1; 978-1-4129-6388-6 (e-book).

This encyclopedia contains more than 450 individual entries covering all aspects of American campaigning, electioneering, and electoral behavior. The scope of coverage for each of these areas of analysis are described in the introduction of the *Encyclopedia*. The first volume also begins with a list of entries by category or theme, an alphabetic list of all entries, a directory of contributors, and a chronology of key historical events shaping the development of American campaigns and elections. The alphabetic list of all entries is repeated in the second volume and both volumes conclude with a comprehensive subject/name index, which is particularly helpful for locating references to specific topics or people mentioned anywhere in the work. Pictures and reproduction can be found in both volumes. Written by 129 scholars, the entries provide succinct descriptions and analysis of issues, events, and people associated with the American campaign landscape. There are entries covering each presidential campaign from 1790 to 2008. Additionally, there are entries that provide an overview of contemporary politics and campaigns for each state. Entries include *see also* references and a bibliography to journal articles, books, and Websites that lead the reader to further information. Some references are more complete than others, however. For example, the bibliography for "Election Outcome Forecasting Models" includes references to seven useful articles form the journal *PS: Political Science and Politics*, whereas the bibliography for "Colorado" only includes a reference to *The Almanac of American Politics* and election data from *The Washington Post* and CNN (with a URL listed only to the general Website), thus missing the opportunity to guide readers to *Colorado Politics & Government: Governing the Centennial State* by Thomas E. Cronin and Robert D. Loevy (University of Nebraska Press, 1993). The work is decidedly focused on presidential campaigns and electoral behavior, although the influence of local politics is mentioned in the state entries and many of the profiles are of political leaders, such as Huey P. Long. Overall, this work provides a comprehensive descriptive analysis of the federal campaigns and elections and is a very useful resource for any student seeking concise information about virtually any aspect of American electoral behavior on the federal level.—**Robert V. Labaree**

P, S

217. Ford, Lynne E. **Encyclopedia of Women and American Politics.** New York, Facts on File, 2008. 636p. illus. index. (Facts on File Library of American History). $76.50. ISBN 13: 978-0-8160-5491-6.

The *Encyclopedia of Women and American Politics* provides a solid first step in researching this topic. The author, Lynne E. Ford, has published in this area before and has now produced a one-volume encyclopedia with introductory-level information on a variety of subjects significant to the entrance of women into American politics. Subjects were selected that represented major social and political reforms that helped establish women as separate legal and political entities.

The list of contributors is included and many entries are signed. The text is arranged in A to Z fashion and topics include biographies, organizations, political issues, decisive legal cases, and political movements. Entries range from one paragraph to several pages with many also having further reading sections.

Some entries contain cross-references, but not many. While concerned primarily with the United States, prominent English women are included, namely Mary Wollstonecraft. The text is written in clear, jargon-free language. The appendixes contain primary documents, including significant speeches, a section with empirical statistical information on the number of women in American politics, as well as lists of women past and present who served in Congress. The monograph concludes with a helpful bibliography to facilitate further research. Lastly, the comprehensive index contains a useful demarcation system to guide users, but the text size is noticeably smaller and slightly hard to read.

Like many books by this publisher the binding is sturdy and will stand up to heavy use. The pages are thick and the typeset is clear. All images are in black and white. This will be a valuable addition to media centers, from middle school to high school, and public libraries.—**Melissa M. Johnson**

C, P, S

218.   **Gale Encyclopedia of U.S. History: Government and Politics.** Farmington Hills, Mich., Gale Group, 2008. 2v. illus. index. $220.00/set. ISBN 13: 978-1-4144-3118-5.

This two-volume encyclopedia chronicles the history of government in the United States from "The Precolonial Era (1450-1620)" to "The Internet Age (1980-Present)" in 11 chapters designed to be compatible with the National Council for Social Studies High School U.S. History Curriculum Standards. Each chapter is divided into six sections: Introduction; How They Were Governed; Important Figures of the Day; Political Parties, Platforms, and Key Issues; Current Events and Social Movements; Legislation, Court Cases, and Trials. There are several subsections within each of the sections. As an example, in the chapter titled "The Watergate Era (1968-1979)" the Current Events and Social Movements section includes subsections about the Black Panther Party, the environmental movement, Watergate, Three Mile Island, and the Iran hostage crisis. The authors have done a great job of capturing and including the various threads of events and multiple influences of any given event or period. The thorough explanations of complicated events and detailed descriptions of the important people of the day (and why they were significant) provide a rich context for the development of U.S. government and politics. The encyclopedia includes many illustrations and photographs from the time period being covered with bibliographic references after each chapter. Each volume is prefaced by a table of contents, general introduction, chronology, and glossary and ends with a list of further readings and an index. Also available as an e-book, the *Gale Encyclopedia of U.S. History: Government and Politics* is highly recommended for public, high school, and undergraduate academic library collections.—**Polly D. Boruff-Jones**

S

219.   Genovese, Michael A., and Lori Cox Han. **Encyclopedia of American Government and Civics.** New York, Facts on File, 2009. 3v. illus. index. $250.00/set. ISBN 13: 978-0-8160-6616-2.

This overview of the complex organization and function of the U.S. government is arranged by larger areas of discussion and then subdivided with individual entries arranged alphabetically. The larger topics include the foundations and background of U.S. government, the pursuit of civil rights and civic responsibilities, the necessity of participation in the political process, each of the three branches of government (legislative, executive, and judicial), the conception and application of public policy, the structure and approach of state and local government, and important aspects of international politics and economics. Individual entries are presented in a series of informative, concise, well-written essays—each of which are followed by a brief bibliography. At the end of the third volume is a larger bibliography, followed by appendixes containing copies of the Declaration of Independence, the Articles of Confederation, the Constitution, Bill of Rights, and other amendments. These are followed by an overall index. The entries are somewhat enhanced by black-and-white illustrations. The information presented serves as an excellent overview for the study of the basic structure and function of the U.S. government. [R: VOYA, Feb 09, p. 560]—**Martha Lawler**

C, S

220.   Grossman, Mark. **Political Corruption in America: An Encyclopedia of Scandals, Power, and Greed.** 2d ed. Millerton, N.Y., Grey House Publishing, 2008. 2v. illus. index. $195.00/set. ISBN 13: 978-1-59237-297-3.

Lord Acton's dictum that power corrupts and absolute power corrupts absolutely is borne out every day in all countries. Despite its claim to be the greatest democracy on earth, America is not exempt from this corruption. Corruption is the underbelly of every political regime, whether democratic or not. As Publius wrote in the *Federalist* 200 years ago, "if men were angels there would be no corruption" and since men are not angels, corruption is a fact of life. In fact, it is surprising that we do not have a branch of politics devoted to this phenomenon known as "corruptionology."

Since history textbooks refer to corruption only peripherally, it is good that Mark Grossman has stepped in to provide a comprehensive chronological of the scandals that have pockmarked American politics from the earliest times. In this 2d edition, the first from Grey House, he has updated his earlier list. Although he has done his best to update the book it is an indication of how frequently politicians fall that he does not include Governor Spitzer of New York or John Edwards. Corruption comes in all forms; there are sexual misdeeds, nepotism, misuse of power, greed, perjury, lying, cheating, electoral fraud, bribery, embezzlement, influence peddling, ticket fixing, drunken driving, ethical lapses, and other offenses that go beyond the Ten Commandments. Corruption is an equal opportunity phenomenon; Republicans and Democrats have vied for full representation in this black book.

The number of corrupt public officials is so large that Grossman may be excused in being selective. There are few judges included. It is also not clear why he has left out all but a few of our presidents (the exceptions are Clinton, Garfield, and Nixon). Even the most obvious candidates for this distinction, such as Harding, Kennedy, and that most corrupt of all presidents, Ulysses Grant, do not appear here. Readers who need information on presidential corruption need to go to Jeff Schultz's *Presidential Scandals* (see ARBA 2001, entry 747).

Making up for the missing entries are a number of useful special features, such as a chronology; documents; entries on corruption as portrayed in films, literature, cartoons and television; expulsion; censure and condemnation in the Senate and House; independent counsel investigations; Governors and Senators; Representatives and mayors; tried and convicted; and impeachments.

These are cautionary tales that need to be read by every U.S. political office holder and every citizen. Corruption will never go away even though the mighty fall, but history always has the last word. This work is recommended for all political science collections.—**George Thomas Kurian**

C, P, S

221.   **Presidency A to Z.** 4th ed. Gerhard Peters and John T. Woolley, eds. Washington, D.C., CQ Press, 2008. 673p. illus. index. (American Government A to Z Series). $85.00. ISBN 13: 978-0-87289-367-2.

Now in its 4th edition, *Presidency A to Z* has been updated and reformatted. New entries, such as those on John Kerry, Hurricane Katrina, and signing statements, cover some of the issues related to the presidency that have arisen since the last edition was published in 2003 (see ARBA 2004, entry 718). Other entries, such as those on George W. Bush, Richard B. Cheney, and the Iraq War, now include coverage of events up to the beginning of 2007. Beyond the content updates, the book has a new look and feel. A wide single column of text has replaced the double columns from the previous edition, making it harder to skim down the page. Grey margins, pulled out quotes, and "closer look" boxes give the book a busier look and sometimes distract from the text. Boxes with cross-references to "more on this topic" have replaced the cross-references in the text from the previous edition and make the book easier to navigate. Another significant change is to the price, now $40 less than the previous edition.

The essays are clearly written, and although they do not include references for further research, collectively they provide a nice overview of the topic. Despite the quibbles about format, this is a useful tool for quick reference and one that will be useful for high school, public, and academic libraries.—**Michael Levine-Clark**

Directories

C, P

222.   **United States Government Internet Manual 2008.** Lanham, Md., Bernan Associates, 2008. 643p. index. $62.00pa. ISBN 13: 978-1-59888-188-2. ISSN 1547-2892.

More than 90 percent of federal depository library documents are now distributed online and much of that material is only available online in electronic format. The *United States Government Internet Manual* is an essential finding aid to these many online documents and federal government Websites. Finding this information using open Web search tools (search engines and Web directories) can be a challenge since often it is necessary to know the site's title, or at least know that a site definitely exists, to be able to search for it effectively. This manual provides an intuitive arrangement by topic, agency or organization, and publication title (for some government documents) and is intended to be a companion guide to the *United States Government Manual* (Bernan Press). Revised each year with new entries added, and sites deemed to be less useful removed, the 2008 manual contains more than 2,000 entries in 20 chapters plus a quick guide to primary agency Websites and organizational charts for those agencies, two appendixes (Members of Congress and Congressional Committees), and four indexes (Sponsor Name/Site Name Index, Publication Index, Spanish Web Site Index, and a Master Index of Subjects, Sponsors, and Site Names). Chapter 1 is devoted to online finding aids developed specifically for government information; chapters 2-20 are arranged by broad subject heading with several subdivisions. Each entry is composed of the entry number, site title, URL (usually one, but occasionally one or more alternate URLs are listed), site sponsor (agency or organization), a description of the site, subject headings, and a list of publications available through the Website if appropriate. The introduction includes standard information regarding scope, organization, content, and "How to Use this Book." The *United States Government Internet Manual 2008* is recommended for all libraries—public, academic, school, and special libraries.—**Polly D. Boruff-Jones**

Handbooks and Yearbooks

P, S

223.   **Electing Congress.** 2d ed. Washington, D.C., CQ Press, 2008. 175p. illus. index. $45.00pa. ISBN 13: 978-0-87289-956-8.

Electing Congress provides a wide-ranging introduction to American voters and how they elect their representatives. Information is provided on just who votes, the political process and political parties, who gets elected, campaign financing, and reapportionment and redistricting. The historical perspective provides an overview of how the election process has changed over time. Also addressed is the question of why only 50 percent of eligible voters actually vote in major elections. The information is clear and understandable, and presents fundamentals about the American legislative election process useful to students and the general public.—**Denise A. Garofalo**

C, P

224.   Freedman, Eric, and Stephen A. Jones. **African Americans in Congress: A Documentary History.** Washington, D.C., CQ Press, 2008. 574p. index. $115.00. ISBN 13: 978-0-87289-385-6.

This new title from CQ Press is the first single-volume reference to provide the complete story of African Americans making U.S. political history. The authors have compiled a collection of original essays as well as 120 important historical documents tracing African Americans in U.S. politics, especially the history of African American legislators in the Senate and House of Representatives. Notable people that receive attention in this title are Shirley Chisholm, the first black woman to serve in Congress; Hiram Revels, the first African American senator; and Barack Obama, the only African American senator in the

110th Congress. Although its subject matter may seem limited, it actually broadly and fairly covers both African American history and African American political history. This title should not be overlooked in the purchasing decisions of academic and public libraries.—**ARBA Staff Reviewer**

C, P, S

225.   **How Congress Works.** 4th ed. Washington, D.C., CQ Press, 2008. 248p. illus. index. $45.00pa. ISBN 13: 978-0-87289-955-1.

The 4th edition of CQ Press's *How Congress Works* continues to be an excellent resource for all collections. While the chapters are unsigned and there is no list of contributors the monograph provides a comprehensive introduction into the workings of Congress. The text covers the hierarchy of both the House and Senate and depicts the distinct personalities of each. The monograph also outlines the legislative process, demystifying the procedures for students and the general public. Written in six chapters, this is a dense monograph for such a slim volume that packs a lot of useful information. The chapters conclude with a notes section as well as a selected bibliography section that will point researchers toward other helpful sources. Its structure precludes it from being a ready-reference type resource, but its versatility will help high school students needing to understand how laws are made to researchers tracking the history of Congress. Educators, including librarians, will find the reference materials at the end of the book very valuable. This section contains a nice graphic on how a bill becomes a law. The section also includes where to find congressional information online. The text concludes with a functional index.

The monograph is not built to last. Since it has a simple paper and glue binding it will not stand up to heavy use. Overall, however, this is an excellent reference source for media centers, public, and academic libraries.—**Melissa M. Johnson**

C, P, S

226.   **The Presidency, the Public, and the Parties.** 3d ed. Washington, D.C., CQ Press, 2008. 237p. illus. index. $45.00pa. ISBN 13: 978-0-87289-957-5.

This is the 3d edition of *The Presidency, the Public, and the Parties*, bringing the text up to date with the current presidential administration. This dense text deals with all aspects of presidential interaction with political and nonpolitical groups. Although slim in appearance, the monograph is full of information. Comprised of six essay chapters broken into subsections, the text was written by academics teaching and researching in the field of political science, and incorporates overviews and scholarly research to provide readers with quality information. Authors are listed for each chapter with credentials provided at the beginning of the monograph. Topics discussed include the changing image of the President, and his interaction with the media, political parties, and interest groups. Also discussed in the book is the President's place in popular culture and need, as well as, use of popularity. Each chapter wraps up with endnotes and a selected bibliography. While an excellent reference source this is not a ready-reference book. The information is not structured to provide quick answers. The monograph concludes with a standard index.

The text is a paperback with glue binding and will not stand up to heavy use over a long period of time. Overall, this is an excellent resource for high school media centers and public and academic libraries.
—**Melissa M. Johnson**

C, S

227.   **Student's Guide to Congress.** Bruce J. Schulman, ed. Washington, D.C., CQ Press, 2009. 379p. index. (Student's Guide to U.S. Government, v.2). $75.00. ISBN 13: 978-0-87289-554-6.

C, S

228.   **Student's Guide to Elections.** Bruce J. Schulman, ed. Washington, D.C., CQ Press, 2008. 394p. illus. index. $75.00. ISBN 13: 978-0-87289-552-2.

Student's Guide to Elections, meant to educate junior and high school students about U.S. elections, consists of a table of contents, list of illustrations, reader's guide, preface, "Historical Milestones of U.S. Elections, 1787-2008: A Timeline," "Essays," "Elections A to Z," "Primary Source Library," "Using Primary Sources," glossary, selected bibliography, and a general index.

The attention-grabbing and educational illustrations include charts, graphs, tables, maps, and photographs such as a photograph of an authentic "I Like Ike" button advertising the 1952 Dwight D. Eisenhower presidential campaign. The reader's guide arranges 360 topics by 11 headings composed of "Amendments," "Elections and Election Campaigns," "Electoral Process," "Federalism and Politics," "National and State Powers," "Political Parties," "Principles of Government," "Public Policies," "The Constitution," "Three Branches of Government," and "Voters and Voting Rights." The preface provides a short summary of how-to-use the book.

The Essays section consists of three essays on the election process and electoral college, why political parties are utilized, and the features that create a democratic United States. Elections A to Z has 153 topics in relation to elections. Primary Source Library discloses 38 actual pieces belonging to past elections.

Student's Guide to Congress consists of three parts: Essays, Congress A to Z, and Primary Source Library. The essays include: "Member of Congress: Who Gets Elected? Who Elects Them?"; "The Way Congress Works: How Does an Idea Become a Law?"; and "Who Is Running America—Congress or the President?" The A to Z section provides encyclopedia-type entries on a variety of topics (e.g., Ad hoc Committees, Bill of Rights, Civil Rights Act, Pork Barrel Spending). Interspersed throughout are "Spotlight" sections that provide in-depth discussions on some important themes in Congress. The Primary Source Library reprints several articles of the constitution, amendments, and impeachment records. The work concludes with a glossary, selected bibliography, and an index.

All persons wanting to learn about elections or Congress will discern these publications are two of the easiest and finest assets.—**Melinda F. Matthews**

Middle East

C, P

229.   **Political Handbook of the Middle East 2008.** Washington, D.C., CQ Press, 2008. 595p. maps. index. (Regional Political Handbooks of the World). $135.00. ISBN 13: 978-0-87289-574-4.

This book contains a brief introduction to the region, entries for each country, a section on intergovernmental organizations, a chronology of 2007 events, and an index. There is not, however, a bibliography, a list of references, or footnotes, which is a major drawback to this book. Many of the entries include direct quotes with no citations, and that sets a poor example for college students who might consider using this book for research, and who need to include citations in their own work. Another flaw is that the introduction has a significantly smaller font size than the entries, perhaps as though the publisher does not expect anyone to read the small print. Despite the small print, the introduction provides a short, general introduction of different ethnic groups in the area, which provides hints for the reader about the diversity of peoples in the Middle East. There is a brief history, focused on recent events, often seen in the historical context of the United States.

Generally, the writing style remains focused, clear, and free from jargon; additionally, abbreviations receive explanations. For the entries on the countries, each includes an overview of the country, a basic map, a short description of the government, foreign relations, current issues, major political parties, and a list of key current government officials. Entries can function as ready reference and one clever feature is the use of all capital letters for the last names of people the first time they appear in the entry, so the reader can find that person's name within the text quickly. Some entries include sections on communications and the media. The entry on Qatar includes criticism of the news agency Al Jazeera that appears subjective. Including references or footnotes would be helpful in such an example. Lastly, one strong feature of this book is the section with entries on intergovernmental organizations, including brief descriptions of bodies within the United Nations targeted specifically to issues in the Middle East. Some of those organizations may be lesser known to nonspecialists in the Middle East.—**Kay Shelton**

INTERNATIONAL ORGANIZATIONS

Dictionaries and Encyclopedias

C, S
230.   Pubantz, Jerry, and John Allphin Moore Jr. **Encyclopedia of the United Nations.** 2d ed. New York, Facts on File, 2008. 2v. illus. index. (Facts on File Library of World History). $112.50/set. ISBN 13: 978-0-8160-6913-2.

This book is a comprehensive guide to the United Nations' procedures, politics, specialized agencies, personalities, initiatives, and involvement in world affairs. It is organized in dictionary style and entries range from a short paragraph to several pages in length. This book describes major world events and the role the United Nations played in them. Subsections include a preface, an introduction, a list of contributors, a list of acronyms, and A-Z entries. This is followed by appendixes that cover the charter of the United Nations, universal declaration of human rights, United Nations member states, Secretary General of the United Nations, statue of the international court of justice, United Nations' resolutions (including uniting or peace resolutions), and declaration on the establishment of the new international economic order. Concluding the volume are lists of conventions, declarations, and other instruments contained in general assembly resolutions; a United Nations chronology; United Nations Websites; a selected bibliography; and an index. The book has above average paper and binding, and the font size is average. This encyclopedia should be in all major libraries and would be particularly useful for people interested in international politics and world peace.—**Herbert W. Ockerman**

INTERNATIONAL RELATIONS

Dictionaries and Encyclopedias

C
231.   Weatherbee, Donald E. **Historical Dictionary of United States—Southeast Asia Relations.** Lanham, Md., Scarecrow, 2008. 436p. (Historical Dictionaries of U.S. Diplomacy, no.7). $95.00. ISBN 0-8108-5542-9. ISBN 13: 978-0-8108-5542-7.

The story of American relations with the nations of Southeast Asia is not always tasteful, given the imperialism of the Spanish-American War and the Vietnam catastrophe. For a long time this has been an area of Great Power expansion and rivalry. Reading about this topic can be confusing, which is why a dictionary such as this one is so useful. Here one can find the meanings of military codewords, definitions of terms, explanations of events, the importance of different locations, a brief narrative of what went on in a country, and the role of various individuals in this region's history. In the front one finds a 7-page list of acronyms and abbreviations, and a 12-page chronology (1833-2007). The 27-page bibliography, in addition to arranging citations by country, also has sections on document collections and official publications, biographies and memoirs, and Internet resources (which is disappointedly limited to 10 official sources). Appendix A is a list of U.S. Presidents and Secretaries of State (1945-2007), while appendix B is a list of Assistant Secretaries of State for East Asian and Pacific Affairs (1950-2007). No index or photographs are included. There are plenty of very helpful cross-references (in heavy type) and *see* references, along with a two-page map of the region, which can be supplemented by *The Palgrave Concise Historical Atlas of South East Asia*, by Robert Cribb and M.C. Hoadley (Palgrave Macmillan, 2003). The companion volumes in this series are Robert Sutter's work on U.S.—China relations (see ARBA 2007, entry 639), and the one on U.S.—Japan relations (see ARBA 2007, entry 666). Weatherbee (emeritus, University of South Carolina), previously published *International Relations in Southeast Asia: The Struggle for Autonomy with Raif Emmers* (Rowman & Littlefield, 2005). This is a required item for Asian collections, and is certainly suitable for other academic and large public libraries, where it will sit near *A Political and Economic Dictionary of South-East Asia*, by Andrew T.H. Tan (Europa, 2004), Michael Leifer's *Dictionary of the Modern Politics of South-East Asia* (3d ed.; see ARBA 2003, entry 731), and *Southeast Asia: A Historical Encyclopedia*, by Keat Gin Ooi (see ARBA 2005, entry 92).—**Daniel K. Blewett**

PUBLIC POLICY AND ADMINISTRATION

C

232.   **Evolution of U.S. Counterterrorism Policy.** Yonah Alexander and Michael B. Kraft, eds. Westport, Conn., Praeger/Greenwood Press, 2008. 3v. index. $299.00/set. ISBN 13: 978-0-275-99529-4.

Finding the primary research material for a topic can always be problematic. Most library patrons do not know how to search for such items, nor do they have the time and patience to learn how to do it correctly. In today's dangerous world there is heightened interest in the threat from terrorists. The title under review provides important excerpts from many pertinent U.S. government documents, such as policy studies, strategy outlines, position papers, executive orders, commission findings, secret reports, official testimony, editorial opinions, public interviews, and press statements. So one can use these three volumes instead of searching for the texts in numerous other printed and online resources. These items make for interesting and sometimes troubling reading, but by examining these publications one can trace the frustrating search for both public and covert policies that might be effective against a nontraditional and amorphous enemy. The introduction and first chapter provide a historical background narrative for the subject and a critical analysis of present policy. The time period covered is from the Nixon Administration to the present day. Bibliographic citations and Internet URL addresses are frequently included for the excerpted item as well as related items. There is a 17-page selected bibliography that includes links for 77 Internet sites, and an index. The only minor quibbles with this product are the lack of a chronology and glossary. James J. F. Forest has edited a related collection of articles titled *Countering Terrorism and Insurgency in the 21st Century: International Perspectives* (Praeger Security International/Greenwood Press, 2007). The National Security Archive has compiled an Electronic Briefing Book with public and declassified government documents that complement these articles, *The September 11th Sourcebooks: Volume I, Terrorism and U.S. Policy* (http://www.gwu.edu/~nsarchiv/NSAEBB/NSAEBB55/index1.html). This set under review is suitable for the circulating collections of academic and large public libraries, or special libraries concerned with this topic. Professors should be informed as to its availability in the library, as it could be used as a reader for appropriate criminal justice and political science courses. An electronic version is also available.—**Daniel K. Blewett**

C

233.   **International Security and the United States: An Encyclopedia.** Karl DeRouen Jr. and Paul Bellamy, eds. Westport, Conn., Praeger/Greenwood Press, 2008. 2v. index. $200.00/set. ISBN 13: 978-0-275-99253-8.

This work examines human security issues in 48 entries on countries or regional country groupings in various global locations. Entries are written by a panel of international scholars representing multiple countries and disciplinary backgrounds with lengths ranging from approximately 15 to 25 pages.

An introduction stresses the role the United Nations Development Programme's Human Development Index (HDI) plays in defining three measures of human development—living a long and healthy life as reflected in life expectancy, educational attainment measured by adult literacy and school enrollment, and possessing a decent standard of living measured by purchasing power parity. The introduction goes on to stress that countries with higher HDIs are likely to achieve higher levels of human security.

Entries for individual countries such as Afghanistan, Australia, Brazil, and Ethiopia and regional country groupings such as former Soviet Republics and Pacific Island States encompass the bulk of this work. These entries begin with background historical information on these countries and demographic data such as its population and ethnic composition, military size, governmental data, and a summary of relevant human security issues, such as Afghanistan's dealing with warlords, drug trafficking, human rights abuses, and resurgent Taliban. These entries go on to include analysis of domestic political conditions, law and order issues, relations with adjacent countries, and country's overall national security environment, justice and human rights, and a concluding summative assessment of the overall human security assessment. A bibliography of scholarly books, journal articles, and Websites concludes most entries.

The cumulative effect is a product with succinctly written entries and a laudable inclusion of countries such as Taiwan and groupings of countries such as Former Soviet Republics and Pacific Island States. Sidebars and statistical tables also enhance the quality and usability of this work, which is recommended for undergraduate library reference collections.—**Bert Chapman**

C, P

234.   Rovner, Julie. **Health Care Policy and Politics A to Z.** 3d ed. Washington, D.C., CQ Press, 2009. 314p. index. $75.00. ISBN 13: 978-0-87289-776-2.

CQ Press always does a great job of covering political and policy issues objectively and this book is no exception. It was necessary to publish a 3d edition of *Health Care Policy and Politics A to Z* because of the significant changes in the area of health policy since the publication of the 2d edition in 2003 (see ARBA 2004, entry 1411). With close to 300 entries (from AARP to Zidovudine) this book provides information on all dimensions of health policy issues currently on the national agenda in an understandable, but not overly simplified, manner. The stated purpose of this book is to provide information that will enable U.S. citizens to engage in the national conversation on health care policy and politics. The content is current, but historical information is provided as background where appropriate. The "Reference Materials" section includes a Health Policy Time Line covering the period from 1796 (the first successful vaccine to prevent smallpox) to 2007, Health Care Policy Acronyms (essential for understanding policy documents and regulations), a list of Congressional Committees Responsible for Health Care Policy with contact information, and Suggested Readings and Sources of Further Information that will allow the reader or researcher to find more in-depth coverage of the health care topics of interest. A complete index includes photographs and illustrations, keywords, and main entry topics. This book is recommended for high school libraries (upper-level students), college and university libraries, and public libraries. [R: LJ, Jan 09, p. 126]—**Polly D. Boruff-Jones**

14 Psychology and Occultism

PSYCHOLOGY

Biography

C, P

235. Stewart, William. **A Biographical Dictionary of Psychologists, Psychiatrists, and Psychotherapists.** Jefferson, N.C., McFarland, 2008. 325p. index. $75.00. ISBN 13: 978-0-7864-3292-9.

Stewart, a counselor, lecturer, and author in the United Kingdom, compiled a list of over 400 individuals in this volume who have contributed significantly to the fields of psychology, psychiatry, and psychotherapy since 1700. Each entry of entries includes summaries of personal life, career highlights, major contributions to the field, and the individual's chief publication in theory and practice.

The book is written in common language that can be enjoyed by both professionals and the general readers. The entries are concise but provided the readers with sufficient information to engage in critical reflection of the life and work of the individuals. The referenced publications in each entry are helpful for further study of the figure. Besides a general index, additional features include a timeline that details each individual's year of birth and death, full name and specialty, and a list of the specialists arranged by disciplines of psychology, psychiatry, and psychotherapy. The volume is well written and organized for a glimpse of the important people in the history of psychology-related fields in the western world. This title is recommended for both academic and public libraries.—**Ma Lei Hsieh**

Catalogs and Collections

C, P

236. **Counseling and Psychotherapy Transcripts, Client Narratives, and Reference Works.** **http://asp6new.alexanderstreet.com/psyc/psyc.index.map.aspx.** [Website]. Alexandria, Va., Alexander Street Press and Thousand Oaks, Calif., Sage. Price negotiated by site. Date reviewed: 2009.

Designed by two well-known publishers in the reference world, Sage Publications and Alexandria Street Press, this new database is a collection of reference works, first-person narratives, and transcripts of real therapy and counseling sessions. It provides users with a comprehensive look at the experience of mental illness, counseling, and therapy. It is the first of its kind to bring together actual therapy sessions with clear illustrations of therapeutic techniques. By using these first-hand experiences along with reference works, users will find a one-stop source to help provide insight into the process of therapy, oftentimes from the point of the patient. When completed the site plans on offering more than 2,000 transcripts of therapy sessions, 40,000 pages of client narratives, and 25,000 pages of reference works. The sources used include diaries, autobiographies, oral histories, and personal memoirs and all come from real-life people and patients. New material is being added on a bi-weekly basis. The publisher is working with an advisory board of eight specialists in psychology. The site can be searched through the use of Boolean operators and searching appears to be straightforward and reliable.

This site is groundbreaking in its field. The access to real-life examples of therapeutic techniques and patient accounts will be a boon to practicing psychologists and students of psychology.—**Shannon Graff Hysell**

Dictionaries and Encyclopedias

C, P

237.   **The Encyclopedia of Psychological Trauma.** Gilbert Reyes, Jon D. Elhai, and Julian D. Ford, eds. Hoboken, N.J., John Wiley, 2008. 720p. index. $160.00. ISBN 13: 978-0-470-11006-5.

The Encyclopedia of Psychological Trauma brings together in one definitive resource the most valid and credible scientific knowledge available from leaders and authorities in the fields of psychological trauma and post-traumatic stress disorder (PTSD). Psychological trauma, PTSD, and related factors are defined and discussed in relation to causal agents, risk assessment, symptoms, cultural elements, treatments, and preventions. Additionally, experts offer information on relevant research, professional organizations, training, and programs.

Trauma affects both children and adults, and the subject matter has evoked increased public interest in recent years. Beneficial to researchers, clinical specialists, scientists, students, counselors, and consumers, this resource furnishes timely and instructive facts, details, and guidelines. As the name discloses, this extensive work delivers its evidence by topic headings arranged encyclopedia-style with subtopics contained within main entries. Most entries are followed with references, and some include suggestions for further reading as well as pointers to related content elsewhere in the encyclopedia.

Almost any topic associated with psychological trauma appears in this work, including marital therapy, memories, domestic violence, dissociative and personality disorder, childhood trauma, child abuse, rape, and telemedicine. In addition to the significant information presented on the psychological impact of overwhelming stress and negative experiences, this resource also offers details about the involvement of the physical body. For instance, facts are presented on the brain and the limbic system as well as description and detail regarding somatic complaints and malingering.

The impressive lists of qualified editors, contributors, advisors, and editorial assistants validate this scholarly work. A subject index and an author index conclude the encyclopedia.—**Glenda Irene Griffin**

C, P

238.   **Gale Encyclopedia of Mental Health.** 2d ed. Laurie J. Fundukian and Jeffrey Wilson, eds. Farmington Hills, Mich., Gale Group, 2008. 2v. index. $360.00/set. ISBN 13: 978-1-4144-2987-8.

Not intended to replace consultation with a health care professional, the information presented here serves as a basic educational reference tool for both laypersons and health care students. There is little use of medical jargon and more of everyday terminology. An alphabetic list of entries is followed by the individual entries. Topics are arranged alphabetically with boldfaced terms and cross-references leading to other entries. Each topic is examined by following a specific format, which includes basic definitions and descriptions. For disorders, the information also includes causes and symptoms, demographics, diagnosis, treatments, prognosis, and prevention. For medications, the information also includes the purpose for the drug, recommended dosage, precautions, side effects, and interactions. A list of resources for further study and the contact information for related organizations and support groups follow each entry. There are insets throughout that list the definitions of key terms and a general glossary and a general index are found at the end of volume 2. The information presented here is thorough, well written, and concise.—**Martha Lawler**

Directories

C, P

239.   **The Complete Mental Health Directory 2008.** 6th ed. Millerton, N.Y., Grey House Publishing, 2008. 597p. index. $165.00pa.; $215.00 (online database); $300.00 (print and online editions). ISBN 13: 978-1-59237-285-0.

The sixth edition of *The Complete Mental Health Directory* is Grey House Publishing's latest version of their unique reference that provides information for clients, families, and mental health professionals. The organization of the book can be confusing for the uninitiated but the information it provides, once located, is very useful. Users will need to use the table of contents. Also, it is important to bear in mind that each piece of information is given a number, although the number does not appear in front of the mental health disorder descriptions in sections one and four. The indexes are comprehensive but are not really very helpful.

The content is divided into eight sections. The first section is designed for clients and their families. It contains alphabetic entries written for lay people of 27 mental health disorders. The descriptions include a brief introduction followed by symptoms, associated features, prevalence, and treatment options. Following the description are resources for family members and clients. The resources are arranged alphabetically within the areas of associations and agencies, books, periodicals and pamphlets, support groups and hot lines, Websites, and directories and databases. The mental health descriptions are following by a subsection listing resources dealing with pediatric and adolescent mental health issues.

Sections two, three, four, five, six, seven, and eight provide fairly straightforward reference information on associations and organizations, government agencies, professional resources, publishers, facilities, clinical management, and pharmaceutical companies. This information will be most useful for mental health professionals. These sections are all numbered and arranged alphabetically within areas and sub-areas. This resource will be useful for any public, academic, or hospital library.—**Cynthia Crosser**

C

240.   Norcross, John C., Michael A. Sayette, and Tracy J. Mayne. **Insider's Guide to Graduate Programs in Clinical and Counseling Psychology.** 2008/09 ed. New York, Guilford, 2008. 387p. $25.95pa. ISBN 13: 978-1-59385-637-3.

Updated details on clinical and counseling psychology programs assist readers of *Insider's Guide* in choosing and applying for doctoral programs. Information on programs includes research areas, theoretical orientation of faculty, entrance requirements, student characteristics, acceptance and attrition rates, and other useful facts. The *Insider's Guide* focuses on the complete application process with sample documents, worksheets, and timelines. Advice, warnings, and an easy-to-read format give this book an edge over resources providing program descriptions only, such as the American Psychological Association's *Graduate Study in Psychology* (41st ed.; see ARBA 2003, entry 763) and *Peterson's Graduate Programs in the Humanities, Arts, and Social Sciences* (42d ed.; Peterson's Guides, 2008). The text is supplemented with helpful statistics and the worksheets assist readers in defining the most important criteria for choosing schools. There are few substantial changes from the previous edition (2006-2007 ed.; see ARBA 2007, entry 661), although the program information is updated.—**Sally Bickley**

Handbooks and Yearbooks

C, P

241.   **Adult Psychopathology and Diagnosis.** 5th ed. Michel Hersen, Samuel M. Turner, and Deborah C. Beidel, eds. Hoboken, N.J., John Wiley, 2007. 730p. index. $110.00. ISBN 13: 978-0-471-74584-6.

The 5th edition of this work reflects the advancements made in the assessment of psychopathology, documented in the text's 17 chapters, and compiled by experts in their respective fields. The chapters are divided into two parts. Part 1 is an overview containing 4 chapters. Part 2 discusses specific disorders in its 13 chapters. Tables serve to illustrate the text, which has comparisons and references to this American Psychiatric Association's DSM III and IV throughout.

Part 1 deals with issues in classification and diagnosis, including race and ethnicity. Part 2 deals with the major diagnoses found in hospitals, clinics, and private practice (e.g., schizophrenia, mood and personality disorders). In general, each chapter contains a description of the disorder, a case study, epidemiology, clinical picture, course and prognosis, psychological and biological assessment, and diagnostic and etiological considerations. Chapters in both parts have a summary and an extensive list of references. Author and subject indexes complete the informative volume. [R: LJ, July 07, p. 122]—**Anita Zutis**

C, P

242.   **Comprehensive Handbook of Clinical Health Psychology.** Bret A. Boyer and M. Indira Paharia, eds. Hoboken, N.J., John Wiley, 2008. 482p. index. $125.00. ISBN 13: 978-0-471-78386-2.

John Wiley's *Comprehensive Handbook of Clinical Health Psychology* is an outstanding reference source in the field of health psychology. Rather than attempting to touch upon all possible topics, the authors have intentionally limited coverage to conditions and trends they consider most prevalent to the field today, and for which health psychology may contribute valuable insight.

The text is organized into four parts. Part 1 presents an overview of theoretical models of health psychology. Part 2 utilizes obesity and smoking cessation as a lens through which to analyze health psychology's role in disease prevention. Part 3 contains chapters on conditions practitioners are most likely to encounter in practice, such as cancer, HIV/AIDS, diabetes, and cardiovascular disease. Part 4 is comprised of special topics, like reproductive health and pediatrics. Case studies, illustrations and other graphics, and plentiful reference lists citing current empirical research round out the densely packed chapters. Additionally, the authors present a new model—the Model for Integrating Medicine and Psychology (or MI-MAP)—meant to guide readers through practical application of the biopsychosocial model. MI-MAP is presented in detail in chapter 1 and then used throughout all of the chapters in part 3.

Chapters on insurance and managed care as well as substance abuse in medical settings are worth noting. Frequently skimmed over or omitted altogether in texts, these areas are major concerns faced by professionals in the field, and thus should be a vital part of today's graduate curricula. Written to be a graduate school text, students and practitioners alike will benefit from this detailed and well-researched volume.—**Leanne M. VandeCreek**

P

243.   **Depression Sourcebook.** 2d ed. Sandra J. Judd, ed. Detroit, Omnigraphics, 2008. 646p. index. (Health Reference Series). $78.00. ISBN 13: 978-0-7808-1003-7.

Like other Omnigraphics' Health Reference Series sourcebooks, this is a compilation of previously published consumer-oriented health information from government agencies, health providers, and organizations on depression and related conditions. The 2d edition updates the content of the 1st edition, published in 2002 (see ARBA 2003, entry 767). This edition covers introductory information about depression, "other medical concerns" that may be linked to depression, risk factors and symptoms, pharmacological and nonpharmacological treatments, and suicide. Notable inclusions are articles for those supporting others with depression, and a section on alternative medicine provides an overview and discussion of specific treatments and their efficacy. An "Additional Resources" section includes a glossary, index, and directories for information on depression and mental health. This title is recommended for public libraries.—**Amanda Izenstark**

C, P

244.   **Handbook of Clinical Psychology.** Michel Hersen and Alan M. Gross, eds. Hoboken, N.J., John Wiley, 2008. 2v. index. $150.00/set. ISBN 13: 978-0-471-94676-2.

Editors of this handbook bring together scholarly information and research from major contributors and professionals in two volumes that span the age spectrum. The work integrates prominent aspects of psychological practice, specifically ethics, legal issues professional roles, and cross cultural psychology. These topics are discussed throughout the sections in each volume.

The first volume, dedicated to adults, opens with chapters dealing with general issues on professional practice, clinical training, and ethical and legal training. The following two sections present theoretical models (e.g., applied behavior analysis) and research contributions (e.g., treatment research). Diagnosis and treatments are also presented in the second volume, which deals with children and adolescents. Other relevant topics in this volume include diagnosis and evaluation of children and special concerns (e.g., cultural concerns, children of divorce).

Both volumes dispense timely, illuminating, and comprehensive information on complex mental health and psychological issues. Included in discussion are matters concerning certain populations such as older adults, married couples, intellectually disabled individuals, and neglected and abused children. Focus is also provided for special challenges such as autism, psychopathology, and cultural issues.

This handbook, aimed at students as well as practitioners, offers prime information in a well-structured format and includes clearly written prefaces and detailed tables of contents, well-defined sections with relevant headings, and summaries and references at the ends of chapters. Subject and author indexes conclude each volume.

Clear, easy-to-follow writing enables the reader to assimilate knowledge unhampered by overly complicated terminology. The user-friendly delivery of information marks this work as a valuable teaching tool and allows the reader to appreciate the interesting and professionally written subject matter. Students, researchers, practitioners, and others interested in these topics will find this resource valuable and worthwhile.—**Glenda Irene Griffin**

OCCULTISM

C

245.   **The Encyclopedic Sourcebook of Satanism.** James R. Lewis and Jesper Aagaard Petersen, eds. Amherst, N.Y., Prometheus Books, 2008. 774p. index. $105.00. ISBN 1-59102-390-4.

Few subjects are as likely to incite the public as Satanism. To the mainstream American mind, Satanism is synonymous with weird and bloody rituals, hedonism, horror movies, ritual abuse, heavy metal music, and teenagers running wild. Although most people have heard of Satanism, few actually know anything about the phenomenon. Certainly very little academic study has been conducted. In *The Encyclopedic Sourcebook of Satanism* the editors have assembled much of the scholarly research devoted to the topic, and attempt to provide users with real information that goes beyond the sensationalism of the topic. This book pulls together scholarly articles and primary source materials, and focuses on two main areas: Satanism as organized religion and the myth of satanic ritual abuse of the 1980s and 1990s. In the introduction the editors define their understanding of modern Satanism. They then go on to provide academic studies, divided into the following major topics: satanic ritual abuse as a moral panic; satanic ritual abuse as demonology; Satanism and the media; modern Satanism; and primary material. Within each section contributors provide exploration of specific topics.

The Encyclopedic Sourcebook of Satanism is an excellent resource within its very highly specialized area of coverage. The editors and contributors are all acknowledged experts, and the treatment of the topic is fair and balanced. Entries are all well researched, well documented, and contain a bibliography of cited works. The few illustrations are reasonably well rendered and add to the discussion they support. The primary sources included are all useful to the study of the topic, and include gems like the "Report of the

Ritual Abuse Task Force" and the "Investigator's Guide to Allegations of 'Ritual' Child Abuse." In summary, this book would be useful for academic libraries supporting programs in psychology, anthropology, folklore, and media. The specialized nature of the topic makes it unnecessary for public or school libraries to acquire.—**Mark T. Bay**

C, P

246.   Guiley, Rosemary Ellen. **The Encyclopedia of Witches, Witchcraft and Wicca.** 3d ed. New York, Facts on File, 2008. 436p. illus. index. $85.00. ISBN 13: 978-0-8160-7103-6.

Guiley is the author of more than 20 books, most dealing with aspects of Eastern and Western metaphysics. Her books are shining examples of professionalism in fields plagued by books that are poorly researched and written. The book focuses on the magic and witchcraft in Western culture, covering classical to modern witchcraft. Classical witchcraft is a term often applied to the medieval conception of witches who worshipped Satan and performed vile deeds. The encyclopedia applies modern research to the concepts and cases of medieval witchcraft. Modern Neo-Pagan Wicca is a nature religion centering on the worship of a mother Goddess, her consort God, and the practice of self-empowering and transformative white magic. Another category of articles are on folk magic and include topics such as village wise women and Pennsylvania Dutch hex witches. Guiley also covers related religions such as Santeria and Vodoun (or Voodoo), which are usually treated by the media as inaccurately as it treats witchcraft. This new edition includes Wicca-related material that was not included in the previous editions.

The articles are arranged in alphabetic order. There are many *see also* references. Most of the articles include a further reading list, and the book has an extensive bibliography. The index looks rather sparse, but is adequate to an encyclopedia that is already organized alphabetically.

The 3d edition adds new articles and updates many of those from the 2d edition, published in 2000. This new edition has 480 entries, many of which have been added or are updated from previous editions. New material include entries on: amulets, magic and Wicca, Wicca practices and rituals, witches as portrayed on television and in film, and folklore relating to witchcraft. *The Encyclopedia of Witches and Witchcraft* is highly recommended. It is a comprehensive source of accurate information concerning topics too often misunderstood. [R: LJ, Jan 09, p. 126]—**ARBA Staff Reviewer**

15 Recreation and Sports

GENERAL WORKS

C, P

247. Mitchell, Nicole, and Lisa A. Ennis. **Encyclopedia of Title IX and Sports.** Westport, Conn., Greenwood Press, 2007. 199p. index. $59.95. ISBN 13: 978-0-313-33587-7.

Title IX legislation mandating equality in all educational programs that receive federal funds has had a dramatic effect in the realm of sports over the last 35 years, particularly at the high school and collegiate levels. This encyclopedia aims to provide "an overview of Title IX and its impact on sports." While that broad intent is admirable, the reality falls a bit short of how good of a resource it could have been.

The main body of the work consists of just 110 pages of entries on significant court cases; relevant organizations; and prominent athletes, politicians, and media members. The criteria for the selection of these 60 people aspired to reflect those involved in the original legislation, longtime advocates for equity in sports and examples of what women can achieve in sports. It is this last category that proves to be a real weakness. How do you include soccer great Michelle Akers, but ignore her more famous teammate Mia Hamm? Where are Jackie Joyner-Kersee, Florence Griffith Joyner, Theresa Edwards, Janet Evans, and Chris Evert? If you are going to include pre-Title IX athletes like Babe Didrickson Zaharias and Billie Jean Moffitt King, why not trailblazers Wilma Rudolph and Wyomia Tyus? In fact, of the top 100 women athletes chosen by *Sports Illustrated* in 2000, only 17 appear here—only 6 of the top 20.

Another element missing from this work are entries on specific sports that have felt the full impact of Title IX, such as the striking growth of soccer in the past three decades. In addition, more attention should have been paid to how controversial Title IX continues to be with an examination of the perceived negative effects of the legislation, particularly towards boys' sports programs.

Nearly half the book is taken up by Title IX regulations, administrative interpretations, and clarifications and a list of resources, and that is too high a percentage of content. What is included is well done and welcome, but much more could have been added to make this book an essential overview of Title IX and women's sports.—**John Maxymuk**

BASEBALL

P

248. Selter, Ronald M. **Ballparks of the Deadball Era: A Comprehensive Study of Their Dimensions, Configurations and Effects on Batting, 1901-1919.** Jefferson, N.C., McFarland, 2008. 190p. illus. index. $45.00. ISBN 13: 978-0-7864-3561-6.

The aesthetics of old time baseball parks has long been a topic of interest to baseball fans, but the form also has a function, and that is what this study is about. Both the size and layout of a field have a strong effect on how the game is played there. In the first two decades of the twentieth century, the fields were large, the ball was not resilient, and the time became known as the Deadball Era in which hits and runs were hard to come by. This study quantifies where the batting was toughest.

Each of the 13 cities in which major league baseball was played during the era has its own chapter, and each of the 34 ballparks used is analyzed in depth. The complete field dimensions and fence heights are listed, and the author even confirmed the data by checking it against Sanborn fire maps from the time. Batting park factors are figured against the league average for doubles, triples, home runs, batting average, and slugging percentage. Home runs are further broken down into over the fence (OTF), inside the park (ITP), and bounce categories. Both OTF and ITP home runs are detailed according to whether they were hit to right field, center field, or left field. All of this data puts the records of the players from that time into a new perspective and can help in their evaluation.

The topic is very much an "inside baseball" one for rabid baseball historians, especially those of a statistical bent. The writing is somewhat dry, but this is a statistical study unlike any other. There is a short summary chapter to conclude the volume that should have been longer and livelier, expounding on the overall effects from the parks of the time with year-by-year details. However, the unique quality of this book recommends it to any baseball research collection.—**John Maxymuk**

BODYBUILDING AND WEIGHT TRAINING

P

249.   Evans, Nick. **Bodybuilding Anatomy.** Champaign, Ill., Human Kinetics, 2007. 193p. illus. index. $19.95pa. ISBN 13: 978-0-7360-5926-8.

P

250.   Nelson, Arnold G., and Jouko Kokkonen. **Stretching Anatomy.** Champaign, Ill., Human Kinetics, 2007. 147p. illus. index. $19.95pa. ISBN 13: 978-0-7360-5972-5.

These two volumes are like having an X ray of each exercise or stretch one uses in their fitness program. The full-color, detailed illustrations show users how a change in position can alter the muscle emphasis or improve safety and effectiveness.

Bodybuilding Anatomy is organized into six sections according to body part: Shoulders, Chest, Back, Arms, Legs, and Abdominals. For each exercise users will find: a detailed illustration listing the muscles in use; step-by-step instructions on how to execute the exercise; primary and secondary muscles involved; and variations on the exercise to influence and fine tune results.

Stretching Anatomy is arranged in a similar style as the *Bodybuilding* title. It is arranged by the following sections: Neck; Shoulders, Back, and Chest; Arms, Wrists, and Hands; Lower Trunk; Hips; Knees and Thighs; and Feet and Calves. For each stretch there is a detailed illustration with muscles outlined; description of technique; list of muscles stretched; and a commentary section that provides further information on variations that can affect results.

The illustrations in both volumes are beautifully executed and well labeled. The layout of the volumes provides a lot of whitespace and lends itself to either browsing or finding specific information. Both volumes provide a short index at the end. These titles will be useful for public libraries, academic libraries with sports medicine programs, and in the personal libraries of fitness trainers.—**Shannon Graff Hysell**

CAMPING

P

251.   Stilwell, Alexander. **The Encyclopedia of Survival Techniques.** new ed. Guilford, Conn., Lyons Press, 2007. 192p. illus. index. $19.95pa. ISBN 13: 978-1-59921-314-9.

Author Alexander Stilwell is a British army survival specialist. His practical, handy guidebook of survival techniques is filled with essential information and good advice. In the introduction he writes of surviving by quickly getting over the initial trauma of your situation and then using your native built in qualities of "determination, perseverance, ingenuity and humour." This book will go a long way toward enhancing those native abilities.

The first half of the book has chapters on surviving in challenging physical regions like deserts, seas, tropics, mountains, as well surviving natural disasters like earthquakes or hurricanes. Chapters in the last half give more detailed information on survival skills like firemaking, navigation, ropes and knots, first aid, fishing, trapping, and river crossing. Every page of the book offers large pictures, line drawings, or informational boxes to make comprehension of exactly what is required to survive as easy as possible. The writing is concise and practical. The occasional use of unique British terminology (e.g., abseil, plaster, chilblain, heliograph) stimulates the reader. All chapters offer bolded, clear paragraph divisions such as "preparation, shelter, action, hazards, finding water, finding food."

The new and revised 2007 edition of the original 2000 printing adds a chapter on "Urban Survival" in place of the appendix on foreign travel. Another useful addition is how to handle a car in a flood. This book is recommended for anyone interested in surviving natural or man-made, life-threatening situations.—**Georgia Briscoe**

CHESS

P

252. Gelo, James H. **Chess World Championships: All the Games, All with Diagrams, 1834-2004.** 3d ed. Jefferson, N.C., McFarland, 2006. 875p. illus. index. $45.00pa. ISBN 0-7864-2666-7.

This is the sixth volume from author Di Felice in McFarland's Chess Results series. This chronological reference work lists the results of men's chess competitions all over the world from 1941 through 1946. It comprehensively lists both tournaments and matches. Compiled from newspapers, periodicals, tournament records and match books, this work contains 810 tournaments and 80 match scores. Entries note the location and oftentimes the sponsor. First and last names of players are included whenever possible. Published sources are cited. It is indexed by events and by players. Excluded in this volume are women's and correspondence competitions; however, the author states in the preface that they may be added in future editions or separate works.—**Shannon Graff Hysell**

FITNESS

C, P

253. **Essentials of Strength Training and Conditioning: National Strength and Conditioning Association.** 3d ed. Thomas R. Baechle and Roger W. Earle, eds. Champaign, Ill., Human Kinetics, 2008. 641p. illus. index. $79.00. ISBN 13: 978-0-7360-5803-2.

The *Essentials of Strength Training and Conditioning* is a research-based volume that focuses on the structure and function of the body systems, testing and evaluation, exercise techniques, program design, and organization of exercise facilities. It organized into topical sections, which are then broken down into subject-specific chapters. The work is organized into five parts: Concepts and Applications of the Exercise Sciences; Testing and Evaluation; Exercise Techniques; Program Design (which is further arranged into anaerobic and aerobic exercise programs); and Organization and Administration. The work uses chapter objectives, key points, key terms, and study questions to provide a structure for students using this volume. The work uses many illustrations, charts, and graphs to explain topics. The volume concludes with study questions and answers for the CSCS exam, references, and an index.

This volume is designed as a preparation tool for the CSCS exam as well as a reference for strength and conditioning professionals and sports medicine professionals. This volume is essential for college and university libraries offering sports training and sports medicine programs. It will also be a good addition to the circulating reference collections of medium and large-sized public libraries.—**Shannon Graff Hysell**

P

254.   Howley, Edward T., and B. Don Franks. **Fitness Professional's Handbook.** 5th ed. Champaign, Ill., Human Kinetics, 2007. 558p. illus. index. $72.00. ISBN 13: 978-0-7360-6178-0.

This 5th edition of the *Fitness Professional's Handbook* (formerly titled *The Health Fitness Instructor's Handbook*) has been substantially updated to reflect new understanding of the role physical activity plays in a client's quality of life. The book is arranged into six parts, with corresponding chapters: "Activity, Fitness, and Health," "Fitness Evaluation," "Exercise Prescription for Health and Fitness," "Special Populations," "Exercise Programming," and "Scientific Foundations." Three new chapters have been added and older material has been updated for this new edition. Other updates include a revised chapter on health appraisal that focuses on the sequence of steps to follow while screening clients; updates based on the current dietary guidelines; a discussion of how to develop effective exercise prescriptions for strength and endurance in small spaces; and a new chapter on yoga and Pilates and the mind-body connection.

This book is ideal for students studying the American College of Sports Medicine (ACSM) guidelines, certified fitness professionals looking to stay up to date on their profession, and instructors needing a updated text. For instructors there is a Website offering a new instructor guide, a test bank, and a PowerPoint presentation package (http://www.HumanKinetics.com/FitnessProfessionalsHandbook). —**Shannon Graff Hysell**

C, P

255.   Manocchia, Pat. **Anatomy of Exercise: A Trainer's Inside Guide to Your Workout.** Richmond Hills, Ont., Firefly Books, 2008. 192p. illus. index. $35.00. ISBN 13: 978-1-55407-375-7.

Anatomy of Exercise is a fascinating book that illustrates how the body's muscles work during specific exercises. Using side-by-side illustrations and photographs users can see what specific muscles are being targeted during each exercise as well as learn the name of each muscle in the body. The book is organized by body areas: legs and hips, back, chest, shoulders, and core, and shows the common sequences in the progression of a typical workout. If used correctly the book can help the reader benefit from each exercise and improve their fitness level. Highlights of the book include the detailed, full-color anatomical illustrations, annotations identifying active and stabilizing muscles, suggestions for modifications to vary intensity of an exercise, and a visual index of exercises that allows for easy navigation through the book.

This book would be useful to anyone interested in enhancing their fitness routine as well as fitness instructors who want to visually show their clients the benefits of each exercise. Therefore, it can be recommended to medium-sized and large public libraries as well as high school and undergraduate collections. There are other books available with this same focus (e.g., Human Kinetics' *Bodybuilding Anatomy* [see entry 249]); however, this title will be useful for the general public, whereas the Human Kinetics' title will be more useful for trained professionals.—**Shannon Graff Hysell**

MOUNTAINEERING

P

256.   Venables, Stephen. **First Ascent: Pioneering Mountain Climbs.** Richmond Hills, Ont., Firefly Books, 2008. 192p. illus. index. $45.00. ISBN 1-55407-403-7. ISBN 13: 978-1-55407-403-7.

Many books have chronicled mountaineering adventures throughout the world but this book is unique in telling the often harrowing stories of those who made the initial ascent of peaks both large and small. The individual stories of those who had the courage to go where no one had gone before can be viewed as inspiring or insane, selfishly egocentric or generous. However, it makes for exciting reading.

The daring feats of the men and women who were lured to the unknown to make it to the top the first time is covered with flair and amazing photography on every page, including archival footage. Historians and mountaineers, both armchair and actual, will find the book hard to put down.

True to history, the book starts with the first recorded crossing of the Karakoram by a Chinese Buddhist Pilgrim, Fa Hian, in 399 C.E. It includes major climbs in all the mountain ranges of the world and ends with modern climbs of unique areas such as sea cliffs and water falls in places like Baffin Island and Venezuela. The pioneering climbs, which include classic mountaineering as well as climbing on rock, ice, and big-walls, expose the development of climbing technology and climbing styles.

Author Stephen Venables is a world class climber who has published a dozen popular mountaineering books. He has many first ascents on his résumé: Everest via a new route on the Kangshung face from Tibet, plus several others in the Himalaya and South America. He admits to a slightly British bias in his latest book, but this is probably justified because Brits have played a major role in "exploring new ground and experimenting with notions of what is possible" on a peak. This book is a joy to read cover to cover, is a fine reference book, and it would make a great coffee-table book to peruse anywhere throughout.
—**Georgia Briscoe**

16 Sociology

GENERAL WORKS

C

257. Encyclopedia of the Life Course and Human Development. Deborah Carr, ed. New York, Macmillan Reference USA/Gale Group, 2009. 3v. illus. index. (Macmillan Social Science Library). $395.00/set. ISBN 13: 978-0-02-866162-9.

This work examines in detail the life course paradigm. This studies human development by looking at lives at the individual level as well as macro-social influences that affect that development. Key assumptions, which influence the questions researched, include the following ideas: lives are influenced by historical context; the meaning of a life event is dependent on when it occurs (i.e., marriage at age 15 versus age 30 can have dramatically different personal, social, and economical outcomes); lives are intertwined by social and generational relationships; and people construct their individual lives through their choices and decisions, which are influenced by social and historical circumstances. Life course scholars look at lives in the context of time and place.

This encyclopedia is divided into three volumes corresponding to three major divisions in one's life. Volume 1 deals with childhood and adolescence; volume 2 deals with adulthood; and volume 3 deals with later life. However, several topics appear in all three volumes since the approach to the topic changes over the life course. For example, for the topic of education most of the articles are in volume 1 but there are also articles in the other volumes.

The articles in each volume are arranged alphabetically. They are well written, using current as well as classic sources, giving a good overview of the topic. Each article has a bibliography. In volume 1 there is a listing of all articles in all volumes, a list of contributors with their qualifications, and a listing of which articles they authored. There is also a thematic outline that lists 32 major themes and then lists articles in each volume that correspond to that theme. Volume 3 contains appendixes, which include a glossary, an article on research methods, an annotated bibliography, and an index.

This encyclopedia is well written and well researched. It should become a starting point for those interested in the life course and will be useful in most academic libraries.—**Robert L. Turner Jr.**

AGED

C, P

258. Handbook of Health Psychology and Aging. Carolyn M. Aldwin, Crystal L. Park, and Avron Spiro III, eds. New York, Guilford, 2007. 450p. index. $55.00. ISBN 1-59385-057-3. ISBN 13: 978-1-59385-057-9.

According to this handbook, the field of health psychology explores the "psychosocial etiology of disease and treatment compliance." The topics in this handbook relate to the question: what are the social and psychological impacts of the physical decline associated with aging (and vice versa)? Health psychology, as it relates to the aged, is a relatively new research area and this handbook provides a thoughtful and informative introduction to the latest findings in this field. Topics such as age discrimination, stereotypes of the elderly, coping strategies, and religion and spirituality are covered, as well as detail about physical changes such as shifting hormone levels and the effects of stress on one's physical health. The chapters cover theoretical, biological, psychosocial, and clinical issues. They are not comprehensive overviews of these aspects, but rather more deeply explore the most significantly relevant findings of current research. In addition to the information about aged populations, there is also significant content related to caregivers—an important aspect of gerontological study. The language of this book is geared toward the researcher or practitioner. Overall, this is an excellent work that brings foundational conceptualizations and research trends of an emerging field into one concise volume. It is highly recommended for academic, research, and health science/medical libraries.—**Elaine Lasda Bergman**

C, P

259.   **Older Americans Information Directory, 2008.** 7th ed. Millerton, N.Y., Grey House Publishing, 2008. 1160p. index. $165.00pa. ISBN 1-59237-357-7. ISBN 13: 978-1-59237-357-4.

This comprehensive directory includes information about resources of interest to older Americans and those who assist the elderly. Most sections deal with health-related topics, such as diseases, medical equipment, and assisted living facilities. Other sections focus on travel, education, and research. The volume lists contact information for a wide selection of government agencies, associations and other not-for-profit organizations, and businesses providing services to older Americans. Caregivers may be interested in the section on continuing education programs. Librarians will find the information about publications, multimedia, and Websites helpful for collection development. Some of the entries provide only the organization name and contact information, which may not be sufficient for some readers. Other entries provide a more thorough description, and Web links are often included. A section of topical NIA reprints are informative, but seem out of context. There is no section on consumer protection, although there is a Legal Aid section. This publication is also available as an online database. Overall, this is a thorough collection of organizations and resources, particularly with regard to the health care needs of the elderly. It is recommended for academic and public libraries.—**Elaine Lasda Bergman**

DISABLED

P

260.   **The Complete Directory for People with Disabilities, 2009.** 17th ed. Millerton, N.Y., Grey House Publishing, 2008. 901p. index. $165.00pa. ISBN 13: 978-1-59237-367-3.

The 17th edition of this directory of resources for the disabled is not much changed from the 2008 edition. The only changes are that there are new resources added and many of the existing entries have been updated. There are about10,000 entries covering resources, products, and services organized into 26 chapters and 100 subchapters. Major chapters cover national and state agencies, numerous associations and organizations, assistive devices, travel, sports and camps, education, media (print, audiovisual, and electronic), assistive computer devices, and rehabilitation centers. Subchapters further divide the topics into specific areas by type of resource and disability.

There are sections covering visual and hearing aids, kitchen and bath aids, and four types of wheelchairs. The media and print section has subdivisions covering periodicals, books, and audiovisual material. Bibliographic information includes ISBN number, publisher, and publication date. All entries are numbered sequentially and contain as many as 14 fields. Contact information is provided and includes e-mail, fax number, and Websites.

The most extensive sections deal with state departments of aging and education, veterans' hospitals, camps, and learning disabilities. Often hard-to-find information on ADA compliant construction and architecture is included, although the agencies and organizations listed are primarily for the professional.

The disabled and their caregivers seeking advice on adapting a home will have to look elsewhere since useful organizations such as the National Resource Center on Supportive Housing and Home Modification and the federal government's Eldercare.org (http://www.eldercare.org) are not included. These omissions point out the problem of a directory created from survey responses. Valuable agencies not contacted or not returning the survey do not appear. Some of the many useful entries that are included are difficult to find despite the table of contents and three indexes (geographical, entry name, and disability/subject). A search for entries on service dogs required going through the list of entries to find appropriate organizations. The same is true for services for amputees. Even though there are frustrations for directory users those must be weighed against the comprehensive coverage of disability resources. Public librarians at busy information desks may find an Internet search provides quicker access when looking for specific information. Hospitals, rehab centers, and social workers will want to have this directory to use when assisting clients.

The information provided in this *Directory* is also available in an online format from the publisher (http://www.greyhouse.com). Users can search the information by entry name, major category (e.g., Camps, Education, Independent Living Centers), minor category (e.g., Aging, Aids for Classroom), keyword, executive last name, or state.—**Marlene M. Kuhl**

C, P, S

261.   Haugen, David M. **Rights of the Disabled.** New York, Facts on File, 2008. 296p. index. (Library in a Book). $45.00. ISBN 13: 978-0-8160-7128-9.

According to the author of this volume in Facts on File's Library in a Book series, the disabled make up the largest minority group in the United States. At one time or other, most human beings will be physically disabled in some way, if not through genetics, accident, or injury, at least in old age, especially as our life spans increase thanks to modern medicine.

Haugen's book is an excellent introduction and guide to the rights of disabled people. The first part, approximately one-half of the book, is devoted to an overview of the topic: the movement for rights of the disabled, its movers and shakers, pertinent legislation, and medical and social issues surrounding disability, including the difficulty of defining the term itself. A chronology and biographical sketches are included in separate chapters. The second part is a guide to research, first explaining how to do research online, then providing a topically organized, annotated bibliography of print and electronic sources and a descriptive list of state, national, and international agencies with full contact information. Eight appendixes make up the third part, supplying excerpts from important legislation and statistical data. The index is coded to main topics and book chapters to ease access for the reader.

Rights of the Disabled is a source with wide appeal, current as of January 2008, and one hopes it will be updated regularly. The Americans with Disabilities Act, the foundation of disability rights, was signed into law in 1990, but if state and federal court dockets are any indication, this issue will be with us for a long time.—**Lori D. Kranz**

FAMILY, MARRIAGE, AND DIVORCE

P

262.   **The International Handbook of Stepfamilies: Policy and Practice in Legal, Research, and Clinical Environments.** Jan Pryor, ed. Hoboken, N.J., John Wiley, 2008. 611p. index. $90.00. ISBN 13: 978-0-470-11458-2.

Are stepfamilies different from other families? It depends. This work looks at stepfamilies from many different perspectives. There are 23 chapters written by family scholars from Japan, France, Belgium, Australia, New Zealand, England, Canada, and the United States. The chapters are arranged under four sections. The first looks at the international, demographic, and culture contexts of stepfamilies with articles that deal with families in the United States, France, Japan, and an examination of Mexican-American families in the United States. The second section looks at dynamics with stepfamily households, including articles on stepfathers, resident mothers, sibling relationships in blended families, a look at the child's appraisals of relationships within the stepfamilies and first families, the distribution of tasks in stepfamilies and first families, and communication in stepfamilies. The third section looks at influences and relationships beyond the household, including kinship issues, the diversity of stepmothers, and intergenerational relationships in stepfamilies. The forth section looks at clinical and legal issues, including adjustments problems in stepfamilies, the legal structures of re-formed families, and the U.S. family and probate laws as related to stepfamilies.

Each article is well written and heavily researched with current article citations. This allows one to find, in a convenient source, a wealth of information on stepfamilies that should generate questions for further research. This will be of interest to most libraries supporting studies in the family.—**Robert L. Turner Jr.**

P

263.   Turner, Jeffrey S. **American Families in Crisis: A Reference Handbook.** Santa Barbara, Calif., ABC-CLIO, 2009. 307p. index. (Contemporary World Issues). $55.00. ISBN 13: 978-1-59884-164-0.

Families cross all cultures and time frames. They are impacted by our social and political institutions, yet also influence these same institutions. The enormous body of literature on the topic demonstrates an interdisciplinary interest and a vibrant area of research. *American Families in Crisis* discusses the times in family life when there is extreme stress, such as divorce, traumatic events, military deployments, and teen suicide. Transformation in the structure and life of the American family, as seen through a historical perspective, is a common theme in this handbook. The authors note the tremendous variety of traumatic events a family can experience and how people cope (or don't cope); it also offers primary resources and statistics on family life in America. These transformations and features that define the family are discussed in a historical and cultural context.

Major issues of current concern, such as domestic violence, family members with chronic disease, and the effect of unemployment on the family, are included. If your library has the *Family in Society: Essential Primary Sources* from Gale (see ARBA 2007, entry 703) there is some overlap, as would be expected, but the unique topics and the historical focus in this work make this a worthwhile addition. *American Families in Crisis* is written for a broader audience and does not have the scholarly depth some other reference titles on family life. It would be appropriate for high school students, undergraduates, and the general public. The entries are well written, clear, and interesting. Additional resources include a chronology, biographical sketches, selected print and nonprint resources, and a directory of organizations to contact for more information.—**Lorraine Evans**

GAY AND LESBIAN STUDIES

C, P

264.   Eaklor, Vicki L. **Queer America: A GLBT History of the 20th Century.** Westport, Conn., Greenwood Press, 2008. 274p. illus. index. $65.00. ISBN 13: 978-0-313-33749-9.

A great deal has been written about twentieth-century U.S. history as well as about the history of gay, lesbian, bisexual, and transgendered (GLBT) people, but this excellent volume is unique in combining the two as a survey of GLBT twentieth-century American history. An outstanding reference that belongs in every academic and public collection, *Queer America* is written for the general reader with a view to documenting how fully in the last century GLBT history is U.S. history. It examines themes of sexuality, class, race, ethnicity, and gender from the turn of the twentieth century to the turn of the twenty-first with a timeline from 1890 (the Battle of Wounded Knee) to 2005 (*Brokeback Mountain*).

Roughly divided into 10-year periods, chapters are informative and well organized, with headings effectively orienting readers to process a massive amount of information. Each chapter concludes with a "debate" representing a diversity of scholars' interpretations of an issue discussed in the chapter; the chapter focused on the Cold War period, for example, has a debate on "What Did The Kinsey Studies Prove?" and the debate in the chapter on the 1970s interrogates "Assimilation or Liberation?" Fine bibliographies appear at the end of each chapter and at the end of the book, and thorough indexing allows readers to locate information quickly. Although more images would have brought the facts and ideas to life even more successfully, *Queer America* is eminently successful in accomplishing its goal of being a one-stop handbook to U.S. GLBT history of the twentieth century.—**G. Douglas Meyers**

PHILANTHROPY

C, P

265.   **Annual Register of Grant Support 2009: A Directory of Funding Sources.** 42d ed. Medford, N.J., Information Today, 2008. 1425p. index. $259.00. ISBN 13: 978-1-57387-326-0. ISSN 0066-4049.

This essential resource, now in its 42d year, is a crucial tool for finding grant support from private foundations, corporations, government sources, and federated organizations. The 2009 edition lists more than 3,200 sources, many of which grant multiple awards annually. Of these, close to 100 are new entries and about the same amount are programs renamed since the last edition.

Information Today has taken over the publication of this title from R. R. Bowker, but the content and format remain the same. The book is broadly arranged by discipline, with programs alphabetically listed in each section. There are 11 major subject categories and 61 subcategories. The helpful introductory material, including a guide to proposal writing, is the same as in previous editions. The indexing—by subject, organization and program, geography, and personnel—is the same as well.

Entries, too, follow the same familiar format, providing contact information, fields of interest for each program, financial figures, data on the numbers of previous applicants and grants, and details on how to apply. Where a single organization supports multiple programs, all are listed with separate application instructions for each. The *Annual Register of Grant Support* is recommended for all libraries.—**Michael Levine-Clark**

P

266.   Miner, Jeremy T., and Lynn E. Miner. **Proposal Planning & Writing.** 4th ed. Westport, Conn., Greenwood Press, 2008. 201p. index. $39.95. ISBN 13: 978-0-313-35674-2.

As in earlier editions, this book discusses funding from government, foundation, and corporate sponsors. The title includes practical advice and examples on developing proposal ideas, identifying funding sources, creating systems and procedures to support grantseeking activities, developing procedural components, budget forecasting, submission procedures, and follow-up techniques. This latest edition includes more extensive information on family foundations; 25 percent more than Websites than in the past editions; examples of successful proposals, including nine sample letters complete with annotations; expanded instructions on evaluation and outcomes assessments; and guidance on project sustainability after grant termination. This standard resource helps grantseekers navigate the funding process and helps grantseekers pinpoint why grants proposals fail or succeed. The volume also includes checklists and a bibliography.—**ARBA Staff Reviewer**

SEX STUDIES

C, P
267.   **Handbook of Sexual and Gender Identity Disorders.** David L. Rowland and Luca Incrocci, eds. Hoboken, N.J., John Wiley, 2008. 671p. index. $95.00. ISBN 13: 978-0-471-76738-1.

The editors of this volume, a professor of psychology at Valparaiso University in Indiana and a radiation oncologist and sexologist at Erasmus Medical Center in The Netherlands, provide information on the diagnosis and treatment of three sexual and gender identity disorders—sexual dysfunctions, gender identity disorder, and paraphilias/atypical sexual behaviors. The editors have pulled together a group of international contributors/scholars to write the chapters and essays within this volume.

Organized by three sections according to the disorders listed above, the book is then organized into individual chapters contributed by experts within this field of study. Covered within are articles on aging and sexuality, gender and sexuality, cross-cultural issues in gender identity disorders, paraphilic sexual disorders, sexual addiction, and legal and privacy issues surrounding paraphilias, just to name a few. The book is intended for use by psychologist and medical professionals needing the most up-to-date information on these disorders and their treatments. This title is written at a high level and uses many psychological and medical terms. It will be most useful for upper-graduate level students studying in this field or practicing mental health and medical professionals who consult patients with these disorders on a regular basis. The *Handbook* is recommended for medical and psychiatric collections.—**Shannon Graff Hysell**

SOCIAL WORK AND SOCIAL WELFARE

Directories

P
268.   **Government Assistance Almanac 2009.** 21st ed. Detroit, Omnigraphics, 2009. 1201p. index. $240.00. ISBN 13: 978-0-7808-0702-0. ISSN 0883-8690.

The *Government Assistance Almanac 2009* provides useful and understandable information on all federal domestic assistance programs in the United States. These domestic assistance programs, including Department of Homeland Security programs, represent nearly $2 trillion work of federal assistance that students, veterans, senor citizens, or parents, as well as civic and organizational leaders, can have access to. This edition provides information to 1,796 federal financial and other domestic programs, 227 more than were in the last edition.

This reference source is user friendly, authoritative, and informative for it has an extensive referencing and cross-referencing index that will enable the user to find the program they are looking for with ease. For example, programs providing financial assistance are italicized. Also, there is a section of "Field Office Contacts" that gives addresses and telephone numbers for more than 3,000 field offices. This 21st annual edition covers every program described in the *Catalog of Federal Domestic Assistance* (CFDA) including programs for state and local government, and since the federal government no longer distributes free printed copies of the CFDA, the *Government Assistance Almanac* is a reference source no public or academic library can do without.—**Vang Vang**

Handbooks and Yearbooks

C, P, S
269.   Gilbert, Geoffrey. **Rich and Poor in America: A Reference Handbook.** Santa Barbara, Calif., ABC-CLIO, 2008. 275p. index. (Contemporary World Issues). $55.00. ISBN 13: 978-1-59884-056-8.

From a social science perspective, the existence and persistence of economic inequality in this country is not to be taken for granted, but rather requires an explanation. This particular volume, written by an economics professor, is a superb review of some of the key questions and data that are relevant to understanding the causes, consequences, and trends related to economic inequality. As with other books in this series, the first few chapters are devoted to framing the issue and documenting both its extent and its consequences. The author distinguishes between inequalities of income and wealth, and demonstrates the widening gaps between rich and poor. He also addresses the consequences of such inequalities (such as health care), the intractability of inequality, racial and ethnic differences, the limited nature of intergenerational social mobility, globalization, and the limitations of education as a great equalizer of inequality. There is also a substantial section discussing various social practices and policies that might impact inequality, such as unionization, the minimum wage, wealth taxes, the earned income tax credit, and more. Subsequent chapters provide a chronology of landmark events dating to the seventeenth century, biographical sketches of notable individuals, data and documents on various features of inequality, a directory of organizations, and a substantial annotated bibliography of print and nonprint resources on the topic. There is also a brief but effective glossary of terms, as well as a subject and name index. Overall, this is a remarkably effective introduction to a complex set of problems. It would be an excellent starting point for students and interested general readers, and it would be well suited both to public and academic library collections.—**Stephen H. Aby**

C, S

270. Whitman, Sylvia. **World Poverty.** New York, Facts on File, 2008. 404p. index. (Global Issues). $45.00. ISBN 13: 978-0-8160-6807-4.

The latest addition to the Facts on File 11-volume Global Issues Series is the title *World Poverty*. The first third of this volume is devoted to intensively documented essays on world poverty (Introduction), the United States (with focus on the United States), and global issues (global perspectives).

The subject of world poverty is limited in the book to the countries of the United States, India, Syria, the Democratic Republic of the Congo, Guatemala, and the Ukraine. Without trying to second guess the authors logic, this reviewer believes less on the United States and more on international issues would have served the reader better.

The primary documents section is certainly eclectic. The U.S. documents include excerpts from Isaac Goodwin, Maureen Berner, the Children's Defense Fund Action Council, and the U.S. Commission on Civil Rights—also a letter to Eleanor Roosevelt and the Populist Party Platform of 1892. The usefulness of these materials is dubious.

The strength of this title is the latter part that is labeled "Research Tools." They cover the topics: "How to Research World Poverty," "Facts and Figures," "Key players A to Z," and "Organizations and Agencies." These tools will be useful to a high school researcher. Facts on File's *World Poverty* is best suited for a public or high school library. I would not recommend purchasing this title for academic or research libraries.—**Rob Laurich**

SUBSTANCE ABUSE

C, P, S

271. Gwinnell, Esther, and Christine Adamec. **The Encyclopedia of Drug Abuse.** New York, Facts on File, 2008. 380p. index. (Facts On File Library of Health and Living). $75.00. ISBN 13: 978-0-8160-6330-7.

Part of the Facts on File Library of Health and Living series, *The Encyclopedia of Drug Abuse* presents important and timely information on drug abuse and related social issues, treatment concerns, prevention initiatives, and law enforcement strategies. The encyclopedia's 200-plus entries cover a wide range of drugs and drug issues affecting countries around the globe, including the United States. While this reference book explores a number of key issues surrounding drug abuse, such drug legalization and the treatment of drug addicts by criminal justice practitioners, it does not seek to resolve these issues. Rather, the intention of *The Encyclopedia of Drug Abuse*, as noted in its preface, is to provide further clarification and understanding of these issues.

In addition to exploring key issues and debates surrounding drug abuse, numerous entries in the *Encyclopedia* explore common myths and misconceptions surrounding drug use and abuse. One myth explored in this book is that minorities are disproportionately represented among drug abusers. Several entries attempt to dissect this myth by examining racial and ethnic differences in drug abuse. A second myth explored in this book is that adolescents are disproportionately represented among drug abusers. Several entries explore differences in substance abuse among adolescents, college students, and young adults. A third myth is that alcohol is a safer drug than illicit substances such as marijuana and cocaine. Several entries focus on injuries and illnesses caused by alcohol and illicit drugs. Another myth explored in this book is that most people take illegal drugs or abuse prescription drugs simply to get "high." Several entries explore psychiatric problems, such as antisocial personality disorder and attention deficit hyperactivity disorder, which are related to substance use and abuse. A final myth explored in this book is that frequent marijuana use is harmless. The *Encyclopedia*'s entry on marijuana examines several associated myths, including beliefs that marijuana is not addictive, that marijuana makes users mellow, that marijuana is useful in treating cancer, that marijuana is less popular among teens than other drugs, that purchasing marijuana does not hurt others, that the government sends otherwise innocent people to prison for casual marijuana use, and more. Other topics explored this book include accidental overdose deaths, barbiturates, opiates, narcotics, club drugs, pregnancy and substance abuse, gangs and drugs, date rape drugs, and drug laws, just to name a few.

The Encyclopedia of Drug Abuse begins with a very thorough "Introduction to the History of Drug Abuse," which provides a useful context for understanding the entries that follow. Included in this historical overview are insights into drug use and abuse in the eighteenth, nineteenth, twentieth, and twenty-first centuries. The encyclopedia ends with an equally helpful grouping of appendixes, including contact information for various state and territorial substance abuse treatment offices, state mental health agencies, state controlled substances scheduling authorities, and state health departments. Also included in the appendixes is important information on admissions to substance abuse treatment centers, types of illicit drug use in lifetime and past year among persons ages 12 and older, federal trafficking penalties for scheduled drugs, medications used to treat alcohol dependence, and state laws on child abuse in relation to drug abuse. The *Encyclopedia* also boasts a topical index designed to assist users in locating key terms and issues found throughout its entries. As with other entries in the Facts on File Library of Health and Living series, *The Encyclopedia of Drug Abuse* provides an objective overview of essential facts and related social ramifications. It is recommended for anyone wishing to learn more about the important issue of drug abuse and is appropriate for inclusion in both academic and public libraries.—**James C. Roberts**

YOUTH AND CHILD DEVELOPMENT

C, S

272.   **Abuse and Violence Information for Teens: Health Tips About the Causes and Consequences of Abusive and Violent Behavior.** Sandra Augustyn Lawton, ed. Detroit, Omnigraphics, 2008. 411p. index. (Teen Health Series). $58.00. ISBN 13: 978-0-7808-1008-2.

Violence is a serious problem for teens. In 2003 more than 5,500 youth between the ages of 10 and 24 were murdered. In 2004 more than 750,000 young people were treated in emergency rooms for injuries resulting from violence. Some 30 percent of teens, 5.7 million, are involved in bullying—either as bullies or as a victim or both. Teen bullies are 4 times more likely than non-bullies to be convicted of a crime by age 24. This level of violence is staggering and has physical and emotional results that affect these youth, and society, for the rest of their lives. This book covers bullying, neglect, domestic violence, elder abuse, child abuse, sibling abuse, stalking, sexual abuse, sexual exploitation, self-injury, suicide, dating violence, physical fights, hazing, gangs, hate crimes, and school violence. The chapters on these topics outline contributing factors, prevention suggestions, warning signs, information on how to find medical and support services, and an explanation of victim rights. The book ends with a resource section that includes a statistical summary, directory of abuse and violence hotlines and support services, as well as sources for further reading. This resource gives teens the information they need to face potential threats and get help—either for themselves or for their friends.—**Adrienne Antink**

C, P

273.   **Children and Consumer Culture in American Society: A Historical Handbook and Guide.** Lisa Jacobson, ed. Westport, Conn., Praeger/Greenwood Press, 2008. 195p. index. (Children and Youth: History and Culture). $49.95. ISBN 13: 978-0-313-33140-4.

This series, Children and Youth: History and Culture, puts children and youth at the center of research, and as such, focuses our attention on those groups that, for the most part, have been ignored. According to one of the essays in the first part of this work, the mass marketers spent $15 billion in 2004 to target this segment of the market, which spent $100 billion on consumer goods and had great influence on another $188 billion of family spending. This work gives the reader a history of how this occurred. It is divided into three parts. The first part has essays written by experts on topics such as mass merchandising and the children's consumer culture, children's media consumption and the struggle to regulate that in the nineteenth and twentieth centuries, discussions on how children were targeted in order to induce brand loyalty, the effects of mass entertainment on children, the connection between schools and mass marketing, and society's varied responses to and attempts to regulate the new consumer culture. The essays in the first part often refer to documents in the second part, which are reprints, either in part or in total, of primary source documents. Related topics are introduced in the second part, with examples from the marketing literature that shows what appeals were used to attract youthful consumers. Thus, one can be studying the essays in the first part and then look at the examples of advertisements and appeals that are shown in the second part. The third part of this work is a very detailed current bibliography on the topics. This will be valuable for those trying to understand how the consumer culture targeted children and the effect that children's desires now have on purchasing decisions.—**Robert L. Turner Jr.**

C, P

274.   **The Greenwood Encyclopedia of Children's Issues Worldwide.** Irving Epstein, ed. Westport, Conn., Greenwood Press, 2008. 6v. maps. index. $599.95/set. ISBN 13: 978-0-313-33614-0.

This work looks at children worldwide in a format that allows ready comparison between countries. Although it tries to be comprehensive, it does leave out some countries simply because experts who could get the required information were not found for every country. For example, Myanmar (Burma), which is one of the world's closed societies, is not included. Each country chapter has the same format so that a comparison can be made easily.

Topics covered in each chapter include the following: a national profile; an overview of children's issues; education; play and recreation; child labor; family; health; laws and legal status; religious life; child abuse and neglect; growing up in the twenty-first century; a resource guide; and maps and indexes. Most of this information could be obtained from a variety of sources. Here it is gathered in one very convenient place.

The six volumes are broken down by place. The first covers Asia and Oceania; the second, Central and South America; the third, Europe; the fourth. North America and the Caribbean; the fifth, Sub-Saharan Africa; and the final volume covers North Africa and the Middle East. Each has a map of the area covered on the inside covers. The countries included are listed in alphabetic order. It would have been helpful if the publisher had numbered the volumes so as to make it easy to determine how the set is organized. There is an index for the total set in the last volume. Each volume has the same series preface and then there is an introduction written by the volume editor discussing the region of the world and the general trends. Each country essay is heavily documented with current sources, both print and online.

This is a major work that will be a very good starting place to learn about children's issues. It is highly recommended.—**Robert L. Turner Jr.**

17 Statistics, Demography, and Urban Studies

DEMOGRAPHY

Chronology

C, P, S

275.   Wright, Russell O. **Chronology of Immigration in the United States.** Jefferson, N.C., McFarland, 2008. 202p. index. $30.00pa. ISBN 13: 978-0-7864-3627-9.

The introduction to this title is a concise history of immigration in the United States, explaining the various periods of time and shifting attitudes toward immigration. The substantial chronology, covering 1600 through 2007, includes entries for legislation, court decisions, articles, news reports, and demonstrations on the various opposing sides of the immigration issue. Six appendixes provide statistical and legislative details, including one that focuses on the contract labor program that ran from 1942 to 1964.

In his introductory essay, Wright identifies the pattern of unrestricted immigration followed by restrictive legislation. Although each act designed to restrict the flow of immigration was initially restrictive, the laws existed only to have exclusions added to them. Eventually, the exceptions would make the act unenforceable. Then the flow of immigration would continue unrestricted until the next legislation was passed. The first attempt to regulate immigration was the Alien and Sedition Acts of 1798; the pattern has continued to the present. The *Chronology* highlights the details that make the pattern.

Wright also chronicles the changes in attitude during recent history. Immigration acts passed from 1965 to September 11, 2001 consider immigration to be a civil rights issue, focusing on compassionately helping those less fortunate; however, acts passed after September 11, 2001 consider immigration to be a security issue. Wright identifies the distinction made by the public between legal and illegal immigration in 2005-2007.

This well-organized and well-written text is easy to understand. This chronology is suitable for high school and undergraduate students to use, while historians and faculty would use it as an easy reference to verify facts. This titled is highly recommended for all libraries.—**Ladyjane Hickey**

Dictionaries and Encyclopedias

C, P

276.   **Immigration in America Today: An Encyclopedia.** James Loucky, Jeanne Armstrong, and Larry J. Estrada, eds. Westport, Conn., Greenwood Press, 2006. 380p. index. $89.95. ISBN 0-313-31214-1. ISBN 13: 978-0-313-31214-4.

Intended as a guide to contemporary immigration topics, this single-volume encyclopedia provides 81 entries by 52 authors on social, economic, legal, political, and cultural aspects of migration to the United States. The essays, generally of two to six pages in length, are written for an undergraduate audience, and include bibliographies for further reading. Entries cover a wide range of topics, such as adoption, diasporas, employer sanctions, food, informal economy, migration processes, residential patterns, and temporary protected status. Because the focus of the book is on immigration today, most of the entries provide only current coverage of the topic with historical context when necessary. Because of this, *Immigration in America Today* will likely need updating fairly often.

There are already several good reference sources about immigration in the United States available. John Powell's single-volume *Encyclopedia of North American Immigration* (see ARBA 2006, entry 824) provides a historical perspective on the topic. James Ciment's four-volume *Encyclopedia of American Immigration* (see ARBA 2002, entry 874) is much more comprehensive, but is already seven years old. *Immigration in America Today* nicely updates some of the topics covered in this earlier work and serves as a nice supplement to either. *Immigration in America Today* would be a nice addition to public and academic reference collections. [R: LJ, 15 June 07, p. 102]—**Michael Levine-Clark**

Handbooks and Yearbooks

C, P

277.   **American Generations: Who They Are and How They Live.** 6th ed. Ithaca, N.Y., New Strategist, 2008. 459p. index. $89.95pa. ISBN 13: 978-1-933588-95-7.

American Generations is a work that uncovers vital details about the five generations; World War II, Swing, Baby Boom, Generation X, and Millennial. The well-researched publication consists of a table of contents, list of tables, list of charts, introduction, "The Generations," "Attitudes," "Education," "Health," "Housing," "Income," "Labor Force," "Living Arrangements," "Population," "Spending," "Time Use," "Wealth," a glossary, a bibliography, and an index.

Interesting and useful facts revealed are that Millennials have greater ease of use of computers, technology, and digital telephones because the Millennials were born into that system. Generation X has the most children but the least number of people. Baby Boomers and Millennials are numerically the biggest. The newer generations accept more readily sex before marriage, gays, lesbians, and wives working. The 273 tables provide valuable facts for each chapter topic. Anyone who needs information on the existing generations will profit from one of the best publications on the area of interest, *American Generations*.—**Melinda F. Matthews**

C, P, S

278.   Wepman, Dennis. **Immigration.** New York, Facts on File, 2008. 476p. illus. maps. index. (American Experience). $72.00pa. ISBN 13: 978-0-8160-6240-9.

Immigration presents the American experience in the words of those who came to this country as aliens in addition to government documents, newspaper accounts, and speeches. It pulls information together so the novice researcher or patron has it in one source.

The work is divided into 11 chapters, each covering a significant time period. Each substantive chapter follows the same pattern with an essay of the historical time period, a chronology of events, and brief excerpts of eyewitness testimony with citations. Appendix A contains 21 state and federal laws, treaties, speeches, U.S. Supreme Court decisions, and excerpts from reports governing or addressing immigration. Appendix B contains 106 brief biographies of major personalities whose words were included. Appendix C contains five maps showing various types of immigrant distribution across the continental United States. The first listed map depicts U.S. distribution of immigrants from six different countries. Appendix D contains 11 graphs and tables. The bibliography is not placed in each section or chapter but has been placed together at the end of the volume.

This book was originally published in the eyewitness history series, so libraries collecting that series will want to consider this a duplicate. This title is highly recommended for all libraries.—**Ladyjane Hickey**

STATISTICS

General Works

C, P

279.   **Oxford Dictionary of Statistics.** By Graham Upton and Ian Cook. New York, Oxford University Press, 2008. 453p. $18.95pa. ISBN 13: 978-0-19-954145-4.

The *Oxford Dictionary of Statistics* is part of a series of dictionaries published by the Oxford University Press that are distinguished by the fact that they are edited by senior and outstanding professionals and carry the signet of authority. The 2d edition of this title is edited by two notable statisticians—Graham M. Upton, author of over 100 publications, and Ian Cook. There are 2,000 entries, including 200 biographies of key figures in the discipline. The 2d edition has more than 500 new entries, including 60 new biographies. There are also major revisions of topics (such as multiple comparison tests) that draw related single entries into larger multiple entries. The definitions are clear, jargon-free, and lucid for a complex subject and are accompanied by charts, diagrams, work examples, and equations. They also cover the related fields of economics, politics, mathematics, probability, operational research, and market research. Many entries have recommended Web links that are continuously updated.

Among the most unusual features of the *Oxford Dictionary of Statistics* are the 17 appendixes. These include a brief chronology of the discipline and profession of statistics (from 1657 when the first book on statistics was published), a bibliography, and a list of major statistical prizes and prizewinners.

Oxford Dictionary of Statistics is probably the best one-volume dictionary of statistics now available. It is highly recommended.—**George Thomas Kurian**

United States

C, P

280.   **Datapedia of the United States, 2007: American History in Numbers.** 4th ed. George Thomas Kurian and Barbara A. Chernow, eds. Lanham, Md., Bernan Associates, 2007. 736p. index. $125.00. ISBN 13: 978-1-59888-083-0.

Now in its 4th edition, this series has become a standard reference work in many libraries. The current volume includes historical statistics of the United States from 1790 to 2007 and also provides demographic and other data projections through 2050. It is divided into seven sections: demographics; environment; industry and services; health, social welfare, and law enforcement; education, society, and leisure; economics; and politics and defense. Each section begins with a timeline of significant events and "Highlights," which emphasizes the changing nature of the United States through time. Each chapter ends with a topical essay that is relevant to the current time. For example, this edition includes essays on identity theft, labor productivity, the development of alternative fuel sources, health insurance, corporate accounting scandals, and African Americans and women in the U.S. military. Most of the more than 345 tables combine data drawn from *Historical Statistics of the United States from Colonial Times* with more current data available in the annual *Statistical Abstract of the United States* (128th ed.; see entry 282). Thus, this work provides a ready source of both historical and contemporary statistics that will fill many reference needs.

Due to its scope and comprehensiveness, this is a work that is recommended for purchase for almost all reference collections, except for the smallest public libraries. Although most of the data are available elsewhere, by compiling it together in such a way, the compilers have made the statistics more useful and accessible.—**Gregory A. Crawford**

C, P

281.   **State Rankings 2008: A Statistical View of America.** Kathleen O'Leary Morgan and Scott Morgan, eds. Washington, D.C., CQ Press, 2008. 604p. index. (CQ Press's State Fact Finder Series). $105.00; $65.00pa.; $99.95 (CD-ROM and database). ISBN 13: 978-0-87289-926-1; 978-0-87289-927-8pa.

Now in its 19th edition, now published by CQ Press but edited by the same editors as previous editions, this series continues to provide a wealth of data from a wide variety of sources focused entirely on the individual states. As the editors state, the mission of the work is to translate complicated and often convoluted statistics into meaningful, easy-to-understand state comparisons. This they have done in an admirable fashion.

The organization of the 2008 edition remains the same as in previous editions, although most of the statistics have been updated to reflect newer data. The work is organized into 15 sections: agriculture; crime and law enforcement; defense; economy; education; employment and labor; energy and environment; geography; government finance: federal; government finance: state and local; health; households and housing; population; social welfare; and transportation. Each section contains a variety of related topics with each one presented using two different tables. The first table gives the states in alphabetic order and the other gives the states in rank order on that particular topic. Full source information is given for each chart. The work also includes a listing of additional sources of information along with relevant Websites and a sparse but useful index.

For libraries that seek to provide current statistical comparisons for the states, this is a useful purchase. The main advantage of this work compared to standard reference sources such as the *Statistical Abstract of the United States* (128th ed.; see entry 282) is its presentation of data at the state level, especially of comparative information. No other work provides such a wide variety of information in such a straightforward manner.—**Gregory A. Crawford**

C, P

282.   **Statistical Abstracts of the United States 2009: The National Data Book.** 128th ed. Lanham, Md., Bernan Associates, 2009. 1000p. index. $74.00. ISBN 13: 978-1-59888-284-1. ISSN 1063-1690.

The *Statistical Abstract of the United States* is the motherlode of U.S. statistics. The annual revision of the work is the most anticipated event for data crunchers, policy wonks, and statisticians of all stripes and persuasions. There is no study of the U.S. economy or society that does not need to refer in some form to the data contained in this volume. The subtitle, "National Data Book," says it all. Bernan Associates has produced a very user-friendly large print edition of the annual in the standard 8 ½-x-11-inch format with a typeface that is 25 percent larger than the GPO edition on quality, acid-free paper with a durable binding.

Although it is the oldest statistical reference source in the United States, the *Statistical Abstract of the United States* makes serious efforts to improve on its collection efforts and organizing principles. Every year there are improvements in the structure of the tables, their scope, their format, and mode of presentation. Most importantly, there are 72 new tables covering a variety of topics, such as learning disabilities in children, people impacted by hurricanes, alternative work arrangements, adult Internet and computer users, cruise industry, women- and minority-owned businesses, and obesity. Twenty-first-century society and economy change almost daily, and new hot-button issues arise that need to be captured in statistical tables. New topics in this edition include the religious composition of the U.S. population, statistics on assisted reproductive technology, the military retirement system, labor violations, aquaculture products sold, homeowner ad rental vacancy rates by state, and expenditures for wildlife-related recreation. The *Statistical Abstract of the United States* is a mirror that paints a portrait of America in numbers. Every table yields some insight into the way the United States is changing.

Almost as important as the tables that are added are the tables that are deleted from each edition. For data-watchers this means that there will be a break in continuity in many of the older series. The word "indispensable" may be applied to few books in this age, but the *Statistical Abstract of the United States* is one of them.—**George Thomas Kurian**

URBAN STUDIES

P

283.   **America's Top Rated Cities, 2008: A Statistical Handbook.** 15th ed. Millerton, N.Y., Grey House Publishing, 2008. 4v. index. $225.00pa./4-vol. set; $65.00pa./individual volume. ISBN 13: 978-1-59237-349-9.

Now in its 15th edition, this work has become a staple of the reference collection. The 4 volumes of the set present profiles of 100 American cities with populations of over 100,000. This edition added 16 new cities, including: Augusta, Georgia; Oakland, California; Spokane, Washington; South Bend, Indiana; and Toledo, Ohio. Each entry follows a strict format: background, rankings, and statistical tables. The background section provides a brief history, recent events, environment, politics, employment, cultural facilities, and climate. The rankings section summarizes rankings that can be found in 238 books, articles, and reports and include such categories as business and finance, health and environment, women and minorities, sports and recreation, and dating and romance. The statistical tables are derived from a variety of sources, most of which are governmental, and are organized into two major sections: business environment and living environment. The business environment encompasses such topics as city finances, demographics, employment, taxes, hotels, and event sites, while the living environment provides data on the cost of living, education, public safety, recreation, climate, and hazardous waste.

Although it may be expensive for the smallest libraries, this set will prove very helpful in most reference collections. As a resource for those contemplating moving to one of these cities, this will be an invaluable tool. Much of the data presented in the set are readily available from other sources, but the strength of the set is that it pulls this information together into one easy-to-use, authoritative product. —**Gregory A. Crawford**

P

284.   **Cities and Water: A Handbook for Planning.** Roger L. Kemp, ed. Jefferson, N.C., McFarland, 2009. 231p. index. $39.95pa. ISBN 13: 978-0-7864-3469-5.

This work is comprised of journal articles that focus on examining specific issues and best practices associated with water management in America's cities and towns. The chapters are arranged in three parts. The first part contains chapters that introduce the topic of cities and water to the reader. Issues covered include America's aging water-related infrastructure, water regulations and land use, and the relationship between water and city growth. The second set of chapters, comprising the bulk of the handbook, are case studies that describe best practices of cities and towns and, by extension, the water planning of the states in which they are located, that have confronted the challenges of urban, suburban, and rural growth. The areas selected as case studies provide examples of best practices applied to a particular aspect of water planning. For example, the city of San Francisco is selected to show how it is enhancing its water quality by using storm water pollution prevention plans. Smaller towns are also cited for their best practices. Delphos, Ohio was selected to demonstrate how smaller cities can improve their aging water waste systems. Considered collectively, the case studies in this handbook provide a diverse set of examples of how city planners have addressed the complex problems of water planning in America's cities. The third part of the handbook consist of chapters focusing on future trends in water planning, including the riverfront conservation movement, smart growth and water benefits, and restorative development. The book concludes with six appendixes: a list of journals and magazines focused on water management, a glossary of key terms, a list of acronyms and abbreviations, a resource directory of local agencies for each of the cities and towns covered, a national resource directory, and a water Webliography. There is also a list of contributors and an index.

For students and researchers who need information about how city and state planners have addressed the challenges of water needs in their growing communities, this is an essential work that should be consulted often. Most of the reprinted articles were written during the past 10 years and, therefore, remain relevant.—**Robert V. Labaree**

P

285.   **County and City Extra, 2008: Annual Metro, City, and County Data Book.** 16th ed. Deirdre A. Gaquin and Katherine A. DeBrandt, eds. Lanham, Md., Bernan Associates, 2008. 1v. (various paging). index. $126.00. ISBN 13: 978-1-59888-183-7. ISSN 1059-9096.

County and City Extra, 2008 is the 16th annual edition of a guide to key demographic and economic data applied to geographic subdivisions of the United States. Data have been grouped into five basic sections or parts of the book: states, states and counties, metropolitan areas, cities, and congressional districts. This volume is limited to cities with populations of 25,000 or more in 2000. A companion volume, *Places, Towns, and Townships* (4th ed.; see ARBA 2008, entry 771), includes data on places with fewer than 25,000 persons. Presentation is largely in the form of statistical tables (e.g., cross tabulations of geographic subdivisions and demographic/economic concepts). However in order to highlight major trends and significant developments, each of the five basic parts contains an introductory summary, several charts illustrating points of importance, and tables that rank the subdivisions in each part of the book in order of magnitude. Column headings, or titles, for each of the tables in a given part are summarized to facilitate searching for a specific subject. The book contains a general introduction, an overall list of subjects covered with references to relevant tables in all five parts, 16 full-color maps of U.S. counties illustrating geographical distribution of significant concepts, detailed information on geographic concepts and codes, source notes, and explanations of concepts. This is an immensely useful guide for anyone who needs gross demographic and economic data distributed into geographic subdivisions; for example, political analysts, marketing managers, or students of the U.S. political and economic scenes.—**William C. Struning**

18 Women's Studies

BIBLIOGRAPHY

C, P, S

286. McVicker, Mary F. **Women Adventurers 1750-1900: A Biographical Dictionary, with Excerpts from Selected Travel Writings.** Jefferson, N.C., McFarland, 2008. 216p. index. $55.00. ISBN 13: 978-0-7864-3205-9.

The women included in this list were chosen for their independent approach to life, particularly in relation to the expectations of society and, in some cases, their own families. An introduction describing how the list was chosen and arranged is followed by the individual entries. Each woman's full name is given, along with her dates and nationality. A brief synopsis of her life, accomplishments, significant events and relationships is often accompanied by sometimes lengthy excerpts from her own writings (e.g., letters, essays, diaries). Since available information was more prevalent for some individuals than others, some entries are longer than others. At the end of each entry are brief bibliographies listing sources of information, as well as works by and about the individual. A more complete bibliography and an index are found at the end. This interesting concept is somewhat spoiled by awkward writing, and in some cases, a disappointing scantiness of information; for example, the entry for "Hon. Mary Georgiana Emma Dawson Damer" only has a citation for her diary and no other information. A complete absence of illustrations is also disappointing. However, the selection of individuals listed and the additional examination of the culture within different societies and time periods would serve as a beginning point for further research.
—Martha Lawler

DICTIONARIES AND ENCYCLOPEDIAS

C, P, S

287. **A to Z of Ancient Greek and Roman Women.** rev. ed. By Marjorie Lightman and Benjamin Lightman. New York, Facts on File, 2008. 398p. index. (A to Z of Ancient Green and Roman Women). $54.00. ISBN 13: 978-0-8160-6710-7.

This well-researched dictionary, which gathers scattered references to women in primary and academic secondary sources, is a fun but trustworthy read from Facts on File. Now in its 2d edition, with more than 100 new entries, these "mini-histories" describe the ancient Greek and Roman world, with each woman taking her turn on center stage. In fact, women never occupied such a position, but the vantage point makes even familiar stories seem fresh and more intriguing. Many entries are familiar to scholars and to students—and even to fans of popular print and celluloid historical recreations such as "I, Claudius." The scope of an essay naturally depends upon the information to be found and how well connected the woman was. For example, the essay for Messalina Valeria, the third wife of the Roman emperor Claudius, recounts the politics and players of the period that surrounded her, that were manipulated by her (and by her even shrewder mother), and that ultimately destroyed her. Although the dictionary is an accurate and sober history, the editors do not squelch the potboiler-drama aspect here; the "occupational title" listed under Messalina's entry is "power broker." This dictionary is itself a valuable general history of ancient Greece and Rome that simply does not leave out the women, as most do. Scholars and laypersons alike may be surprised that in any society the disenfranchised can still play powerful roles, by their own force of character or, more commonly, by their connection to those in power. A comparable dictionary is not available, but students may also find useful the histories of average women in Mary Lefkowitz's and Maureen Fant's *Women's Life in Greece and Rome: A Source Book in Translation* (Johns Hopkins University Press, 2005) as well as their follow-up, *Pandora's Daughters: The Role and Status of Women in Greek and Roman Antiquity*. *A to Z of Ancient Greek and Roman Women* is recommended for school, public, and university library collections.—**Nancy L. Van Atta**

S

288.   **American Women's History Online. http://www.factsonfile.infobasepublishing.com/.** [Website]. New York, Facts on File. Price negotiated by site. Date reviewed: 2008.

Designed for use by middle school and high school aged students, this resource is an authoritative database on American women's history. All of the material has been pulled from Facts on File's extensive list of historical reference sources. It provides biographies, historical entries, maps and charts, images and videos, and timelines for the past 500 years of women's history. The site is filled with Learning Centers that handpick entries within each era, which can serve as starting points for research. Users can search by keyword or phrase, or they can browse by topic or era (nine historical time periods have been chosen). Biographies can be browsed by occupation and primary sources can be searched by type. Some other useful features for students doing research are persistent record links and tabbed search results that show relevant results. Along with biographies, users can also find relevant information on key topics and historical events, such as legal cases, social issues, and organizations. Special features include an "Editor's Selection of the Month" section that highlights an event tied to each month and a "Focus On" feature that spotlights a specific topic, such as women in politics. The more than 60 historical videos cover topics that will be fascinating to students, including fashion and the history of working women. Overall, this database is very useful for students, teachers, and librarians.—**Shannon Graff Hysell**

C, P

289.   **Battleground: Women, Gender, and Sexuality.** Amy Lind and Stephanie Brzuzy, eds. Westport, Conn., Greenwood Press, 2008. 2v. index. $175.00/set. ISBN 13: 978-0-313-34037-6.

Battleground: Women, Gender, and Sexuality is a two-volume reference work describing hot topics surrounding females. Both volumes 1 and 2 include an all-encompassing contents and a guide to related topics. The guide to related topics aids researchers in choosing from areas like body politics; families and parenting; feminisms; gender equity and sexual rights; gender identities and expressions; global political economy; media, visual arts, and communication; politics and social movements; religion and society; sexual identities and practices; social stratification; violence against women; and women's health and reproductive practices. Volume 2 features an extensive bibliography, information about the editors and contributors, and an index. Each section has a researched background and history, news items, a conclusion, *see also* references, and a further reading section.

An example of the eye-opening material found here is eugenics carried out in Singapore gives poverty-stricken females money to stop their reproduction so there are children only from financially capable parents. Malthusians, girls being aborted not boys, who are measured only of substance, is shockingly revealed. Another reprehensible revelation is military women exclusively are citizens.

Battleground: Women, Gender, and Sexuality is a great reference tool that has a large number of themes of females. Anyone seeking new information as well as recognized subject matter on females will, without any hesitation, find the area under discussion in *Battleground: Women, Gender, and Sexuality*. Clearly, it is vital to women's studies.—**Melinda F. Matthews**

C, P

290.   **The Oxford Encyclopedia of Women in World History.** Bonnie G. Smith, ed. New York, Oxford University Press, 2008. 4v. illus. index. $495.00/set. ISBN 13: 978-0-19-514890-9.

The Oxford Encyclopedia of Women in World History, an ambitious project led by Rutgers history professor Bonnie G. Smith, required 4 volumes and more than 900 authors from 50 countries to successfully complete its mission "to survey the history of women of the world." The encyclopedia begins with a chronology, providing a snapshot of the important events and women included here. A topical outline of entries, found in volume 4, explains the conceptual categories found in the encyclopedia. Alphabetic entries include articles about the history and status of women in countries around the world, articles about prominent women in world history, and topical entries about issues like health, religion, government and politics, family and household, culture and society, and women's organizations and movements. Topics include abortion, spiritualism, food, witchcraft, fertility, marriage, widowhood, property rights, sexuality, labor, hunting and gathering, midwifery, poverty, and misogyny. Biographical entries are brief and selective, since biographical information can be found in other sources, such as Gale's 17-volume set *Women in World History*. This set is highly recommended for public and academic libraries.—**Carolyn Carpan**

C, P, S

291.   **Women in the American Civil War.** Lisa Tendrich Frank, ed. Santa Barbara, Calif., ABC-CLIO, 2008. 2v. illus. index. $245.00/set. ISBN 13: 978-1-85109-600-8.

The idea that war is men's work has been around as long as war itself; but the essays included in *Women in the American Civil War* project a different image of war and the women whose lives the war influenced. Rather than simply "glorifying [women] for the sake of noticing them," this encyclopedia presents a view of women that better explains how they "survived, contributed to, undermined, and lived through" the ordeal of warfare and wartime conditions (p. xix). The reality that emerges from this nuanced view of women's roles in wartime, challenges the myth of the self-sacrificing feminine woman propagated following the war. Overall, the essays reinforce the central theme of the work: women played central roles in the war and in determining its outcome. Fourteen contextual essays in two categories—the common experiences of women and specific female groups—provide the framework for the two volumes. The remaining 300-plus, alphabetically arranged entries fall into several common categories, including military affairs, social life, labor, politics, culture, biographical sketches, and events. Significant wartime events, like battles, are included, but the participation and contributions of women in those instances are the focus of the sketches. Related entries are cross-referenced and suggestions for additional readings are included with most entries. The encyclopedia contains a chronology of events between 1831 and 1894 that includes not only milestones in the American Civil War, but also in suffrage and civil rights for women and African Americans. Selections of 24 primary documents written by or about women of the era complete the work. One of the most impressive features is the encyclopedia's extensive 28-page bibliography of scholarly books, journal articles, and published primary resources, like diaries and journals. This bibliography is certain to be a useful tool for students, researchers, and educators. While certainly developed with an academic audience in mind, the encyclopedia entries are approachable and are enhanced with many interesting illustrations. Along with the additional features this set offers (e.g., chronology, primary documents), this set may appeal to a wider audience, including general and high school users.—**Lisa Kay Speer**

HANDBOOKS AND YEARBOOKS

C, S

292.   **Women, Science, and Myth: Gender Beliefs from Antiquity to the Present.** Sue V. Rosser, ed. Santa Barbara, Calif., ABC-CLIO, 2008. 502p. illus. index. $85.00. ISBN 13: 978-1-59884-095-7.

Every so often, a book encapsulates a subject so well that one is at a loss to say anything bad about it. Rosser has edited such a book. Whether by chronology or thematic order, the place of women in the sciences and the myths surrounding the facts of the female place in these subjects is outlined and discussed in this intelligent, historical, and contemporary title in women's studies. Readers get a history of women's place and contributions from what little are known about these before pre-Modern times. We see what disciplines women have been drawn to and the specific research they have accomplished. Of interest are the various defined societal institutions that women have participated in and the growth of females in them. Of course, there is the assumption that the reader has some background in the language that all of these subjects are argued in, but, that is why this book needed to be published; to put in one place the multitude of threads that have led us to this cross-disciplined subject. The book, itself, is well made and will survive many readings. Its 25- page glossary is invaluable to those new to the subject and unfamiliar with its specific language use and definitions. The 11-page bibliography may seem short for a subject with so much to say; however, this is balanced out by the specific topic references and further reading lists following each of the titles 49 essays. There are graphs showing the growth of women's achievements in education and the workforce and a 19-page index that makes it easy to find specific references. Throughout the text are black-and-white photographs chronicling the advance of and changing view of what women do and can do in a world that does not relegate them only to domestic subjects. This title is recommended for upper-division undergraduates, graduates, and anyone who wants to know what woman working in the sciences have done, are doing, and will do in the future.—**Kennith Slagle**

C, P

293. Woodworth-Ney, Laura E. **Women in the American West.** Santa Barbara, Calif., ABC-CLIO, 2008. 387p. illus. index. (Cultures in the American West). $65.00. ISBN 13: 978-1-59884-050-6.

Women in the American West, part of ABC-CLIO's Cultures in the American West series, examines the development of women's history in this region as well as introduces readers to the modern-day opinion of how women influenced the expansion of the West. The title offers profiles of women in an array of professions: pioneers, teachers, nurses, immigrants, prostitutes, and even soldiers. The chapters are arranged chronologically and discuss such topics as marriage, political participation, home life, wages, and war. The chapters include sidebars that highlight key people, events, and historical interpretations. Nearly 30 black-and-white photographs support the text. This book will be useful in high school and undergraduate libraries looking for materials on the history and cultural influences of women on American culture and history. It is a unique look at the history of women in U.S. history and proves to be both insightful and unique.—**Shannon Graff Hysell**

Part III
HUMANITIES

19 Humanities in General

GENERAL WORKS

C

294.   **Electronic Links for Classicists. http://www.tlg.uci.edu/index/resources.html.** [Website]. By Maria C. Pantelia. Free. Date reviewed: 2009.

Among humanities scholars, those dedicated to the study of the classical world have taken to the Internet in large numbers. This Website is the best mega-site available on the subject of classical literature. Originally published in the February 1994 issue of the *New England Classics Journal* and regularly updated since then, this comprehensive site is well maintained by Maria Pantelia, a Classics professor at University of California, Irvine. Only a few links are broken, and the rest are well screened and annotated. This Website is an excellent place to begin any search for resources pertaining to the classical world.

The site is organized hierarchically; the left-hand frame lists major categories, which are hyperlinked to second-level pages. Clicking on a link brings up the corresponding page in the right-hand frame. Major categories include "Gateways," "Links to Classics Resources," "Databases and Web Projects," "Home Pages," "E-Publications," "Publishers and Journals," "Bibliographical Indexes," "Bibliographies," "Images," "E-text Archives," "Course Materials," "Author Specific Sites," "Fonts and Software," "Software Developers," "Professional Organizations," "Classics Departments," "On-line Seminars," "K-12 Resources," and "Discussion Groups."—**Roxanne M. Kent-Drury**

C, P

295.   **Intute: Arts and Humanities. http://www.intute.ac.uk/artsandhumanities/.** [Website]. Free. Date reviewed: 2009.

This site has now merged with *Humbul Humanities Hub* to form a free online service that provides access to the best Web resources for education and research. There are more than 21,000 Web resources listed here that are freely available to the public. Users can search by keyword, by conducting an advanced search, or by new material. The site can also be searched by subject. Subjects are arranged first by broad topic—Arts and Creative Industries, Humanities, and Modern Languages and Area Studies. Under Arts and Creative Industries are subtopics such as architecture, dance, design, and fashion and beauty. Under Humanities users will find archaeology; museums, archives, and libraries; religion and theology; and manuscript studies. And, under Modern Languages and Area Studies users will find the subtopics of Spanish, South Asian, Chinese, Italian, and many more languages. When clicking on a subtopic users are taken to a page of Web bibliographies that provide a short annotation of the site, a link to the site, a link to more details about the site, and the option to save the site. Other features include detailed Internet research tutorials for teachers and students, as well as presentation materials that teachers can download for use in their own courses.—**Shannon Graff Hysell**

20 Communication and Mass Media

GENERAL WORKS

Dictionaries and Encyclopedias

C, P
296.   **Battleground: The Media.** Robin Andersen and Jonathan Gray, eds. Westport, Conn., Greenwood Press, 2008. 2v. index. $175.00/set. ISBN 13: 978-0-313-34167-0.

Few things are as pervasive within modern culture and society as the mass media. As a result there is no shortage of controversy associated with it as well, thus the term "battleground" in the title of this book. The topics here have been drawn from within the broad, interdisciplinary definitions of media and media studies, focusing on the "underlying issues and concepts" of the field. Defining "controversial" is a somewhat subjective undertaking, but the editors have generally done well in the selection of the entries. While it is never possible to include all the topics that might be considered for inclusion when compiling a resource of this nature, this provides a good cross-section of both long standing issues and recent developments.

The book contains approximately 100 entries in encyclopedic format, generally ranging from 5 to 10 pages. Each is comprised of an explanation of the controversy, the full entry, and extensive cross-references to other entries along with suggested further reading. Entries also include useful sidebar information such as tables/graphs, brief case studies, timelines, and examples that help illustrate issues related to the topic. It should be noted that the entries often include the opinion of the author and are not necessarily intended to be neutral or objective. A guide to related topics provides a list that gathers entries into general categories, such as "audiences, citizens and consumers," "international media," "regulation," "commercialism and promotion," and more. A bibliography and index are also provided. This work is recommended for both public and academic libraries, especially those supporting undergraduate programs in communication and mass media.—**Patrick J. Reakes**

Handbooks and Yearbooks

C
297.   Bisbort, Alan. **Media Scandals.** Westport, Conn., Greenwood Press, 2008. 232p. illus. index. (Scandals in American History). $45.00. ISBN 13: 978-0-313-34765-8.

Written in a breezy tone, *Media Scandals* offers breadth over depth. Bisbort aims to provide an overview of scandals in the media. The book itself is broken into two parts: "Recurrent Themes" and "Media as Industry." Part 1 focuses on the following themes: politics, race and religion, and sexuality and morality. Part 2 shifts to center on the various media themselves: books, newspapers and magazines, broadcast journalism, and the Internet. The goal of this book is impressive, yet the reader is left with a sense that too much has been covered and not in enough depth. Similarly, some media scandals receive lengthy discussion, while others are merely a few brief sentences. Finally, the book ends with a section on Internet scandals, yet the chapter itself is only 11 pages. The overall impression is of a hasty introduction to a myriad of media scandals, which could provide a nice jumping-off point for undergraduates interested in learning more about particular examples. The author relies on student-friendly offerings such as timelines of media scandals, brief lists of suggested readings (without descriptions, critiques, or discussions of why these books are suggested), and clever, pun-heavy titles like "Dan Would Rather Not" and "How Weird Hughes." Students may enjoy the inclusion of up-to-date pop culture references like Britney Spears and The Drudge Report. Indeed, this tome seems best suited to an undergraduate survey course in media studies where the aim is to expose students to an expansive discussion of scandal.—**Stephanie Vie**

C, P, S

298.   **Representative American Speeches 2007-2008.** Brian Boucher, ed. Bronx, N.Y., H. W. Wilson, 2008. 192p. index. (The Reference Shelf, v.80, no.6). $50.00pa. ISBN 13: 978-0-8242-1083-0.

For libraries that subscribe to The Reference Shelf, this annual special issue of speeches culled from the contemporary media will arrive automatically. For all others, however, this anthology will promote access to a sampling of current U.S. political and sociological thought. The speeches are divided into five categories— "Electing a President: The 2008 Campaign," "Race in America," "The Mortgage Meltdown," "The Same-Sex Marriage Debate," and "The Obesity Epidemic." The speechmakers themselves also represent the spectrum of contemporary U.S. thought. Not only the expected are found here (e.g., Barak Obama, George W. Bush, Alan Greenspan), but also Sarah Palin, Richard Simmons, and Jeremiah Wright, among others, have their say. Because most of the speeches were not delivered at events with extensive media exposure (no States of the Union or inaugurals here), the volume provides samples of lesser-publicized but equally timely oratorical output from prominent dignitaries. All the topics are timely and the selections are well balanced. *Representative American Speeches* is a valuable resource in any library.—**Lawrence Olszewski**

AUTHORSHIP

General Works

Directories

P

299.   **Writer's Market, 2009.** 88th ed. Robert Lee Brewer, ed. Iola, Wis., F & W Publications, 2008. 1170p. index. $29.99pa. ISBN 1-58297-541-8. ISBN 13: 978-1-58297-541-2.

The 88th edition of *Writer's Market* is an invaluable resource both for aspiring writers and libraries that support aspiring writers. This book is affordably priced, user-friendly, and informative. Its stated purpose is to be a "guide" for writers who are seeking to be published. It accomplishes this goal by giving easy-to-follow principles of submitting a manuscript and a useful introduction to the field of publishing. It is organized efficiently into three main parts: first, general principles of publishing and stimulating narratives by published authors; second, a guide to literary agents; and finally, a guide to publishers. The publishers themselves are organized by genre and then, when applicable, by topic. Within these categories, publishers are arranged in alphabetic order for easy access. A subject index and topical index at the end of the book allow readers to find publishers, awards, and organizations related to publication quickly.

Not only is the information presented in the guide organized and indexed effectively, it is also comprehensive. It contains over 3,500 listings of publishers and agents. The publisher listings include types of material published by the company, number of manuscripts by new authors published each year, manuscript submission requirements, and the editor(s) to whom submissions should be made (when available). These features give writers an overview of the publishing options that are available and allow them to make informed decisions about submissions. *Writer's Market* also offers encouragement and practical advice to new writers. Through the essays of published authors, it gives a realistic picture of the challenges and rewards of attempting to get a manuscript published for the first time. This combination of comprehensive information and encouraging advice makes the *Writer's Market, 2009* a foundational work for writers who are seeking to submit their manuscripts.—**Helen Margaret Bernard**

Style Manuals

C, P

300.　Booth, Wayne C., Gregory G. Colomb, and Joseph M. Williams. **The Craft of Research.** 3d ed. Chicago, University of Chicago Press, 2008. 317p. index. $17.00pa. ISBN 0-226-06566-9. ISBN 13: 978-0-226-06566-3.

Dense and rich with no-nonsense how-to information, *The Craft of Research* is the ideal weapon to have in one's armory when matching wits with research. The authors have thoughtfully arranged the book using the natural progression of the process: simply put, they start by describing the different kinds of documents one might use as a venue for their assertions; doing the research (and documentation); then move on to planning; how to formulate arguments and use logic; and drafting and revisions.

In addition to their linear and logical progression, the authors have not neglected to discuss drafting introductions and conclusions for the end-product of research, nor do they ignore the importance of documentation, from basics such as making notes to utilizing the appropriate style guide. The authors also address the importance of considering one's audience, and one's role in the transmission of information in a research project; they consider the many ways one might work research tidbits into one's work, with regard to how the work is being presented and to who. Research is not simply about finding resources; it is also about the appropriate (and sometimes creative) use of those resources, and Booth, Colomb, and Williams have not forgotten that. Moreover, the intrepid authors do not shy away from discussing the ethics and issues (such as plagiarism) related to research—an important point, especially for those who intend to make a living in research, from English majors to pharmaceutical research scientists.

The one complaint to be made regarding *The Craft of Research* is that the authors attempted to use graphics and illustrations to make their points visually stand out. Unfortunately, the graphics and illustrations detract since they are in black and white and not as visually appealing as they could be. Furthermore, the graphics seem cumbersome and messy.

Despite this minor hitch, this reviewer highly recommends *The Craft of Research*. Although dense, the work is by no means onerous; it provides great examples and quick tips to those searching to better understand research and those who seek to be better researchers. Its bibliographic resources direct readers to more resources, and, to this reviewer, a good resource never hesitates to guide its users to other helpful tools. This work is very highly recommended for public and academic libraries.—**Megan W. Lowe**

C

301.　**MLA Style Manual and Guide to Scholarly Publishing.** 3d ed. New York, Modern Language Association of America, 2008. 340p. index. $32.50pa.; $37.50 (large print edition). ISBN 13: 978-0-87352-297-7; 978-0-87352-298-4 (large print edition).

Many changes have occurred in the area of scholarly publishing since the 2d edition of this work was published in 1998. In the past 10 years electronic publishing has come to the forefront, more online resources are cited in publications, and copyright laws have been updated. This 3d edition of the *MLA Style Manual and Guide to Scholarly Publishing* reflects these changes. The work is arranged into eight chapters: "Scholarly Publishing," "Legal Issues in Scholarly Publishing," "Basics of Scholarly Writing,"

"Preparation of Scholarly Manuscripts," "Preparation and These and Dissertations," "Documentation: Preparing the List of Works Cited," "Documentation: Citing Sources in the Text," and "Abbreviations." The work is clearly laid out with a thorough table of contents and subject index to help users find information quickly. Revisions to this edition include the new MLA documentation style, simplified citation formats for electronic sources, and new information on copyright and fair use laws. It also includes new information concerning the publishing process, including guidelines on preparing electronic files and submitting them to the publisher, issues to consider when submitting a dissertation electronically, and the review process used by scholarly presses.

Academic libraries and larger public libraries should certainly have a copy of this new edition behind the reference desk. At the cost of $32.50, it would also be affordable to put copies in the circulating collection if needed. A large print edition is available for the cost of $37.50.—**Shannon Graff Hysell**

JOURNALISM

C

302.   **Encyclopedia of American Journalism.** Stephen L. Vaughn, ed. New York, Routledge/Taylor & Francis Group, 2008. 636p. index. $195.00. ISBN 0-415-96950-6. ISBN 13: 978-0-415-96950-5.

This is the first comprehensive encyclopedia focused on American journalism since Donald Paneth's 1983 encyclopedia of the same name, although there are substantial differences between the two in format, entry length, and content. Initially proposed as a broader three-volume set titled "Encyclopedia of Journalism History," the final published version is a single volume comprised of just over 400 entries ranging in length from approximately 500 to 5000 words. Ably edited by Stephen Vaughn, it features an impressive list of contributors, including some of the preeminent scholars in the field of journalism history.

While the requisite historical coverage expected in a resource of this nature is evident, there is also more extensive treatment of topics from the second half of the twentieth century than generally available in other journalism reference sources. Examples of this include minority and women's issues, the impact of new technologies, and issues associated with the growth of the "image industries" of public relations, advertising, and entertainment. Both thematic and alphabetic lists of entries are provided, along with an analytical index. Topic areas cover seven major themes, including: associations and organizations; historical overview and practice; individuals; journalism in American history; laws, acts, and legislation; print, broadcast, newsgroups, and corporations; and technologies. Further reading lists are included for each entry, although these have been treated somewhat unevenly by the contributors, with some providing extensive references to supplemental literature while others have fairly brief lists for entries that seem to justify more timely and comprehensive suggestions. This work is suggested as a core reference resource for undergraduate programs supporting either journalism/mass communication or history curricula.—**Patrick J. Reakes**

RADIO, TELEVISION, AUDIO, AND VIDEO

C

303.   Cox, Jim. **This Day in Network Radio: A Daily Calendar of Births, Deaths, Debuts, Cancellations and Other Events in Broadcasting History.** Jefferson, N.C., McFarland, 2008. 251p. index. $49.95pa. ISBN 13: 978-0-7864-3848-8.

Similar in content to the History Channel's popular "This Day in History" (http://www.historychannel.com/tdih/index/html), this small book provides a day-by-day account of events in radio broadcasting history. Logically arranged by month and day, the entries highlight interesting events that occurred on that day—dating back as far as the 1920s. Arguably, some important events are omitted, but no such book can be exhaustive and yet be reasonably priced.

Entries include special occasions, practices, or decision that left a mark on the industry; debuts and cancellations of significant programs; and births and death dates of people in the industry (both those well known and those lesser known). What is most significant about this volume is the amount of detail the author provides. He does not just give one-sentence descriptions of each event, but instead provides detailed analysis on why the person or event discussed is important. This feature adds significantly to the reference value of this title. A 10-page index is a useful addition. This work is recommended for public libraries, academic libraries with communications programs, and ready-reference collections in larger libraries. —**Shannon Graff Hysell**

C, P

304.   Sies, Luther F. **Encyclopedia of American Radio, 1920-1960.** 2d ed. Jefferson, N.C., McFarland, 2008. 2v. index. $195.00/set. ISBN 13: 978-0-7864-2942-4.

With iPods at every elbow and Blackberries on every ear, we forget what the experience of new technology is really like. We expect and demand it when former generations were held spellbound by it. Radio appeared and brought disembodied voices along with music from nowhere. It also brought a kind of sorcerer's necromancy when owners removed the so-called "cat whiskers" about to increase reception, or warmed radio crystals in ovens to make them work.

Almost no review of the current subject, American radio, could begin without the customary genuflection to the palmary Welles and his "War of the Worlds.' The show, now mythopoeic in stature and legendary in scope, is the benchmark of what great radio should be. It is really too bad, not to mention completely unfair. Welles' show remains a testament to his towering ego, so much so that it overshadows remarkable shows throughout the period. But lest I be thought a *laudator temporis acti*—a praiser of old things because they are old—new biographies only now appearing substantiate my claim: the Welles phenomenon was largely manufactured by the irrepressible, egocentric, quintessential Orson.

Too many other shows remain as the bright cynosure in the galaxy of great radio programming. A generation of young people, now octogenarians and older, remain scared witless by "The Shadow' and its bone-chilling, "Who knows what evil lurks in the hearts of men…" opening. Five generations of American opera lovers were born and bred on the fabulous and still marvelous Saturday showcase: "The Metropolitan Opera.' And our memories are lacerated by Moran and Mack, a blackface vaudeville act that appeared regularly on the "Majestic Theater Hour." Only a handful of folks loyal to the old Dick Van Dyke Show recall Morey Amsterdam. But almost none of them remember his radio show from 1948-1950, where he honed to a fine art his fast-talking comedy writer routine. Amsterdam co-hosted *America at Night*, television's first late-night show, and the nucleus of what became television's *The Tonight Show*. All this and more are available in this wonderful tool.

American Radio is really more than names, places, people, shows, and products. It is also a history. More than a dozen and half lengthy articles appear throughout this volume (e.g. "Opera," "Religious Broadcasting," "News on Radio") and inform readers with a delightful style in detailed and panoramic surveys of the subject matter under review. Indexes of stations, programs, or names make locating whatever one is looking for easy. Appendixes of radio chronology and broadcasters alone are worth the price of these tomes, but add to that the 200-plus entry bibliography and you have a tool that belongs on just about every shelf in every library.—**Mark Y. Herring**

21 Decorative Arts

COLLECTING

Antiques

P

305.   **Antique Trader Furniture Price Guide.** 3d ed. Kyle Husfloen, ed. Iola, Wis., Krause Publications, 2008. 382p. illus. $19.99pa. ISBN 0-89689-670-6. ISBN 13: 978-0-89689-670-3.

The 3d edition of this unique resource provides detailed listings and price guides for a variety of antique furniture. There are almost 1,200 items, in full color, featured in this catalog. Most are American-made, but there are examples of other major furniture styles from many other countries as well. There are also a number of tools included: a furniture dating chart, an illustrated black-and-white table of American furniture terms with examples, a short select bibliography, an appendix of major auction services in the United States, and another appendix with full-color photographs of the major stylistic guidelines for identifying American and English furniture.

Each entry in the catalog features a full-color photograph, a detailed description of the item with dimensions, and the current going price for the item. While this price guide would probably not be considered a reference resource in an academic library, it could be of use in a public library setting.—**Bradford Lee Eden**

P

306.   Gaston, Mary Frank. **English China: Patterns & Pieces, Identification & Values.** Paducah, Ky., Collector Books, 2008. 191p. illus. index. $29.95. ISBN 13: 978-1-57432-581-2.

English china is valued by collectors not only for the variety of patterns and decorations available, but also for the china piece's use. Many collectors are often interested in collecting china that was designed for a specific function; for example, teacups and saucers, plates, or platters. In the Victorian era, many of the items available then are no longer being manufactured and may be unfamiliar to collectors today. In *English China: Patterns & Pieces* the author's unique focus is to introduce the reader to these often unusual and diverse items. The china pieces are listed alphabetically by use, from "Apothecary jar" to "Wine jug," with "Cheese keeper," "Invalid Feeder," and "Mustache cup" in-between. Each piece is illustrated in color and with at least one, but often several, examples. Although there is an occasional blurry, dark, or over-exposed photograph, on the whole the 500 color illustrations in this book are clear and useful. The author identifies patterns on pieces that were not included in her previous book on English china, *Collector's Encyclopedia of English China: Identification & Values* (Collectors Books, 2002), which concentrated mainly on identifying English china patterns. *English China* includes a value range for each piece that is determined by comparing auction and dealer prices. Mary Frank Gaston herself is a collector of china and the knowledgeable author of several books on different types of china and porcelain. This book would be appropriate for public libraries and libraries with decorative arts collections.—**Mary Beth Kreiner**

P

307.   Miller, Judith. **Antiques Price Guide 2008.** New York, DK Publishing, 2007. 752p. illus. index. $40.00. ISBN 13: 978-0-7566-2843-7.

This work is designed with convenience of use in mind. Color-coded, top-of-the-page tabs identify main category headings. Each category and subcategory (for example, subcategories of ceramics are porcelain, pottery, and oriental) has an introduction with key facts about factories, makers, styles, and identification points. Advice on fakes is also offered. Over 8,000 high-quality, full-color photographs illustrate items along with a generalized price guide. This is one of the few price guides with illustrations and prices for commemorative ceramics featuring British royalty. Noteworthy are the numerous fine examples of china commemoratives of the coronation of Edward VII and Alexandra. Some of the many overlooked areas of coverage in most guides are featured in this work. There are sections on American and Canadian folk art, bronzes, art deco ceramics, and silhouettes and miniatures. Thoroughness of this guide may be seen in that the usual section of clocks and watches also includes scientific, surveying, microscopic, and medical and telescopic instruments. A whole new trend in collecting objects made and manufactured within the lifetime of our senior citizens is well represented in a section of "modern classics." Illustrations here include modern furniture, lighting, and ceramics. A brief section on posters reflects ships, trains, and tourist travel destinations. A directory of auctioneers that conduct regular sales is a useful inclusion. The work is well indexed by subject including subheading entries. This annual guide should be a part of the fine arts reference collection in public libraries and in appropriate special collection libraries.—**Louis G. Zelenka**

P

308.   Reed, Robert, and Claudette Reed. **Antique and Collectible Dictionary.** Paducah, Ky., Collector Books, 2008. 238p. illus. $24.95pa. ISBN 13: 978-1-57432-580-5.

This is a nice collection of over 5,000 terms used to describe antiques and collectables. If you ever wonder what a *catmallison* or a *hanap* is, then this is the book for you. Each double-page spread of the book contains four illustrations that relate to terms described in the general alphabetic area of the item. The illustrations are not always on the same page as the term in the dictionary so users will have to hunt around to find the definition. For example on page 212 there is a picture of the "Tucker Alarm Till," but there is no information on the item listed under "Tucker"; however, if you look under "till" on page 211, you will find that it is a term for a hidden compartment in a piece of furniture.

Robert and Claudette Reed have operated the *Antique and Collectable News Service*, an international news bureau for the antiques trade since 1988, published several antique books, and work in Knightstown, Indiana. As this volume was being prepared Claudette Reed died but as the introduction states "her contribution . . . remains." The volume is a very attractively designed paperback with many illustrations. There are occasional minor glitches; for example, the "Amos and Andy" Taxicab illustration on the title page appears to be printed backwards (it reads "somA 'n ydnA") , overall the book is easy to use and contains a wealth of general information on collectables. Reference collections will find it a handy addition for general antique identifications. Librarians will no doubt delight that if you Google "catmallison" or "hanap" you get no results, proving there is some information that can still only be found in books.—**Ralph Lee Scott**

Books

P

309.   **Antique Trader Collectible Paperback Price Guide.** By Gary Lovisi. Iola, Wis., Krause Publications, 2008. 302p. illus. index. $19.99pa. ISBN 0-89689-634-X. ISBN 13: 978-0-89689-634-5.

Collectors of vintage paperbacks will appreciate the wide variety of titles and authors found in this book. An introduction is followed by a brief discussion of vintage-era, mass market paperbacks and tips on how and what to collect. An examination of differences in condition and values includes an explanation of the books chosen for review and is followed by essays on budgets, the significance of cover art, and the importance of paperback originals, first editions, and rarities. The book titles are arranged into seven basic categories: fantasy, mystery, western, sports, media-related (e.g., tie-ins with movie and television productions), social issues (e.g., juvenile delinquency, drugs), and miscellaneous (e.g., puzzle books, cookbooks, jokes). Listings in each category are arranged alphabetically by author and then by title. The price for each book is given according to good, very good, and fine condition. A camera icon with selected entries indicates an accompanying picture of that book's cover. Several very good color representations of book covers are included. Within each entry are the author's name, the title of the book, the publisher and/or series name and number, and a very brief synopsis. Most useful is an essay on by-lines, which includes a listing of authors along with their pseudonyms. A glossary of collecting terms, a discussion of foreign paperbacks, a list of recommended book dealers, and a list of trade shows are followed by an index of authors' names. Not only useful for collectors, this source also provides an interesting overview of the history of mass market paperbacks.—**Martha Lawler**

P

310.   Jones, Diane McClure, and Rosemary Jones. **Encyclopedia of Collectible Children's Books: Identification and Values.** Paducah, Ky., Collector Books, 2008. 344p. illus. $29.95. ISBN 13: 978-1-57432-575-1.

This book is a listing of what the editors have determined to be the most-desirable of collectible titles from the 1800s to the present is presented with brief identifying information and an indication of possible values. An introduction serves as an overview of collecting in general and of the intention and scope of the information presented here. It is followed by guidelines on pricing and an examination of the significance of the 1st edition. Background information on the history and progress of various publishing companies is followed by the actual book entries in two separate listings, one arranged by author and the other by series, with titles arrange alphabetically under each author's name or series title. Brief discussion of such aspects as the development of a series, interesting aspects of a book's publishing history, or an author's biography are included at the head of some lists. Color illustrations of book covers enhance the textual information. A list of Newbery and Caldecott winners, arranged chronologically from earliest to latest, is followed by a glossary and list of abbreviations and a bibliography of additional resources. Not all children's authors or series have been included, but the choice of titles is still significant and will serve as an excellent introduction to the topic.—**Martha Lawler**

Coins and Paper Money

P

311.   **Standard Catalog of World Coins 1901-2000, 2009.** Colin R. Bruce II, ed. Iola, Wis., Krause Publications, 2008. 2207p. index. $60.00pa. (w/CD-ROM). ISBN 13: 978-0-89689-630-7.

P

312.   **Standard Catalog of World Coins 2001-Date, 2009.** Colin R. Bruce II, ed. Iola, Wis., Krause Publications, 2008. 432p. illus. $35.00pa. (w/CD-ROM). ISBN 0-89689-631-5. ISBN 13: 978-0-89689-631-4.

The 36th official edition of the *Standard Catalog of World Coins, 1901-2000* is essentially the same as previous editions with updates typically in the valuations. Countries are listed alphabetically. Each country entry includes a brief history and map along with coinage listed in denomination order. Sample images of the coins are provided in half-tones. The *Standard Catalog of World Coins 2001-Date* is in the same format of previous editions but includes accurate pricing for the most recent coins produced and sold by today's mints, central banks, and distributors.

What makes these editions different from previous editions is the addition of a DVD containing the entire content of these rather hefty books. This DVD, compatible with PC and Mac, offers much expanded usability. The entire content opens into a .pdf file and loads rather quickly, but, if necessary, the content is also divided into several smaller files. There are several features that the electronic version has that make it better than the print. First, the ability to electronically search the content instantly enables the user to re-cover information not possible before. For example, if the user is interested in coins bearing images of tur-tles or monkeys or airplanes, regardless of where they come from, they can now search on these terms to discover the coins of interest. The page is displayed with the term highlighted for easy finding. Another feature is the capability to electronically bookmark pages for future quick reference, similar to bookmarking favorite Websites. Thirdly, for those of us with tired eyes, one can now enlarge the page im-age for easier reading. And, finally, one can copy the coin images to a file for use in documenting personal coin collections or want lists.

Avid coin collectors of all ages will appreciate the extended usability of these venerable resources in their DVD formats. This resource is appropriate for public library collections.—**Margaret F. Dominy**

P

313.   **U.S. Coin Digest, 2009: The Complete Guide to Current Market Values.** 7th ed. Dave Harper and Harry Miller, eds. Iola, Wis., Krause Publications, 2008. 277p. illus. index. $16.99 spiralbound. ISBN 0-89689-628-5. ISBN 13: 978-0-89689-628-4.

The *U.S. Coin Digest* is a guide to United States coinage and valuations. The first 60-plus pages are packed with information on the history of American coinage, mechanics of coin production, grading, and so on. Following these initial chapters, coins are listed by denomination starting with the smallest, the half-cent, then within a denomination, coins are listed by year of production. Each denomination or type of coin is shown with a half-tone photograph, both obverse and reverse, and in some cases sections may be shown magnified to highlight a special feature. A short paragraph describing the coin and any interesting historical bit of information is included in the entry.

The primary use of a guidebook like this is the assignment of market valuations. What distinguishes this guide from others is the number of grades listed for each coin, typically 4 to 6 grades. Other guides may give 3 or 4. A grade is the code numismatists use to reflect the condition of the coin. Although the code is a standard, applying it is still a subjective process. The advantage to having more grades gives the collector an improved chance of accurately evaluating a specimen in hand, which translates to improved valuation accuracy. Grading and valuations are not linear. Therefore, trying to estimate grades and valuations between those listed can be problematic.

The main section of this guide is allotted to the standard United States Mint issues. There are addi-tional sections, however, covering U.S. commemoratives, colonial coinage, territorial gold, and a small section on Hawaii, Philippines, and Puerto Rico coinage. These fringe coinages seldom get extensive treatment in other guides. The index is adequate for a guide like this. This guide is suitable for public li-brary reference collections. This edition provides users with a CD-ROM that can be used with a PC or Mac. Users can search by using a find box or by using the browse feature. A plus to using the CD-ROM is the option to enlarge images of the coins up to 400 percent.—**Margaret F. Dominy**

Firearms

P

314.   Quertermous, Russell, and Steve Quertermous. **Modern Guns: Identification & Values.** 17th ed. Paducah, Ky., Collector Books, 2008. 591p. illus. $19.95pa. ISBN 13: 978-1-57432-603-1.

This ready-reference guide to firearms provides pricing information for new and used weapons produced since the start of the twentieth century. Small arms are the focus of this book, with emphasis on civilian versions and a limited discussion of military examples (those older weapons that can be legally owned). Over 3,000 different weapons models are described along with their current collector's value. Coverage is comprehensive. The illustrations are in monochrome and reasonably sized, but many of those depicting older models are rather faded engravings. Overall, accuracy standard is high, with no misprints noted.

The major problem with this volume is that it is not all that easy to use. Because entries are organized by manufacturer, then by weapon action (e.g., single-shot, bolt-action), and then chronologically, those using this reference must be familiar with what it contains to retrieve any specific item. The volume is sturdily perfect-bound in a lay-flat binding, and clearly printed on good-quality paper. Competing reference tools like *Standard Catalog of Firearms, 2005: The Collector's Price & Reference Guide* (see ARBA 2006, entry 905) and *Standard Catalog of Military Firearms 1870 to the Present* (see ARBA 2007, entry 804) should be carefully considered as alternatives to the title under review.—**John Howard Oxley**

CRAFTS

P

315. McCulloch, Graham. **The Woodworker's Illustrated Encyclopedia.** Iola, Wis., F & W Publications, 2008. 288p. illus. $24.99pa. ISBN 13: 978-1-55870-834-1.

Like every hobby woodworking has its own lingo that those new to the hobby will need to understand. Without a guide to the vocabulary woodworking as a hobby can quickly become frustrating. The concepts covered in *The Woodworker's Illustrated Encyclopedia* include tree species, architectural features, furniture components, tools, and more. The book uses full-color, clear photographs and illustration to illustrate key terms. The use of these illustrations will help users fully understand the oftentimes confusing concepts. More than a valuable quick reference tool, this comprehensive guide also offers a brief education in woodworking just by flipping through the pages. At only $24.99 this title would be a useful addition to many public libraries, either in the reference collection or possibly the circulating collection where users can take the book home for further reference.—**Shannon Graff Hysell**

FASHION AND COSTUME

P, S

316. Ambrose, Gavin, and Paul Harris. **The Visual Dictionary of Fashion Design.** Switzerland, AVA Publishing; distr., New York, Watson-Guptill, 2007. 288p. illus. index. $24.95pa. ISBN 2-94037-361-2. ISBN 13: 978-2-94037-361-1.

Graphic designer Gavin Ambrose and freelance journalist Paul Harris collaborated to create *The Visual Dictionary of Fashion Design*, a pocket-sized reference describing terms and trends in the fashion industry. Published in 2007, this volume contains 153 fashion terms fashionistas as well as regular folks should know to navigate through the stylish landscape. Each entry contains a brief definition of the term with a practical explanation given in visual form. There is also a cross-reference feature at the bottom of the page when a relevant term exists in another part of the volume. The final 12 pages of the book is a timeline of trends that dominated the direction of global style. This is a dictionary for modern fashion, and although the timeline goes back to the 1500s, it does not go by decade until the twentieth century. This book is easy to use, but is produced by a British publisher and therefore uses British terminology that some may find difficult to understand. The bright pictures and sketches provide the user with an understanding of the term in a practical sense, but does contain some nudity; therefore, those dealing with younger populations should be cautioned. Furthermore, the definitions are far from comprehensive and some are no more than a sentence. *The Visual Dictionary of Fashion Design* is a fun reference for high school or early college students or anyone who requires a very basic knowledge of fashion terminology, but not for those who crave an in-depth reference.—**Charlotte Widomski**

C, P, S
317.   DeMello, Margo. **Encyclopedia of Body Adornment.** Westport, Conn., Greenwood Press, 2007. 326p. illus. index. $79.95. ISBN 13: 978-0-313-33695-9.

Cultural anthropologist Margo DeMello has written the *Encyclopedia of Body Adornment* to create a context for the many types of body modification and adornment found both in societies throughout history and in various subcultures in the modern world. She skillfully describes practices rooted in tradition as well as contemporary variations on ancient customs. The 207 alphabetic entries, along with a table of listings and a companion guide to related topics, lead the reader through branding, corseting, implanting, piercing, scarification, tanning, and tattooing. While probably not for the faint of heart, the text is neither sensational nor overly sanitized and although some of the descriptions are graphically discomforting, they remain clinically detached. There is some bias toward ways in which traditional practices have been reinvented in the recent past by Euro-American subcultures, but entries on both countries and societies of origin as well as innovators, popularizers, and contemporary groups do a good job of connecting old and new without overly privileging the new. A resource guide, thorough bibliography, and detailed index make the book a good research tool. There are a few tasteful black-and-white illustrations, plus a section of color plates. Each entry includes both specific references and cross-references to other entries. There was certainly potential to make this volume exploitative and provocative, but a professional, matter-of-fact tone makes it a good guide to both social and cultural research into the impulse behind some of today's radical makeover reality shows and fascination with extremes of behavior and body.—**R. K. Dickson**

C, P
318.   **The Thames & Hudson Dictionary of Fashion and Fashion Designers.** 2d ed. By Georgina O'Hara Callan. New York, Thames and Hudson, 2008. 296p. $19.95pa. ISBN 13: 978-0-500-20399-6.

This easily accessible book is itself a wonderful example of engaging fashion design. A consistent, simple page format coupled with easy-to-read entries makes referencing the book a pleasure. This title offers more than 1,200 entries covering the life and work of designers from 1840 to the present, including costume designers and jewelers. In particular, issues of fashion media, photographers, fashion terms, accessory style, technical processes, and fabrics are included. The text is supported by well-chosen, black-and-white illustrations that are necessarily small, but crisply reproduced. Cross-referencing encourages readers to make connections between entries. Bibliographic citations are provided at the end of many entries, and these are supplemented by a bibliography of often-cited texts at the book's conclusion. This is an ideal resource for designers, students of design, and fashion enthusiasts. It is inexpensive enough that most academic and public libraries can add a copy to their decorative arts collections.—**John Schlinke**

INTERIOR DESIGN

P
319.   Berman, Alan. **Green Design: A Healthy Home Handbook.** London, Frances Lincoln, 2008. 208p. illus. index. $24.95pa. ISBN 13: 978-0-71122-834-4.

Over the past 15 years the blossoming interest in green design has yielded a variety of directions in reference publications. Many take a performance-based approach focusing on specific products, materials, and assemblies. Others, like *Green Design: A Healthy Home Handbook*, look at the subject more holistically, emphasizing the overall goal of achieving a healthy home environment. For a person considering building a new home or renovating their existing space, the book is a good starting point, with the caveat that more detailed information will certainly be necessary to bring a project into being.

In the introduction and first chapter, design of a living space is situated in the context of the larger environment, while the three successive chapters discuss more specific aspects of home design including: light, heat, and air; materials; and home energy systems. Each chapter provides examples of design solutions that demonstrate the larger principles of achieving a healthy environment. A directory at the conclusion of the book contains explanations and guidelines regarding electrical appliances, eco-labeling, chemicals, and a checklist of simple steps to achieve a better home environment and improved energy efficiency. A list of Internet resources is also included, but its brevity tends to undermine its usefulness.

Color photographs are used throughout to illustrate the principles discussed, and the book's clear, spare design supports its central theme of simple design being the heart of good green design. The many examples provided will challenge and inspire readers who wish to create a better environment for themselves and others. While not a comprehensive resource, the work is a good introduction to the principles of green design.—**John Schlinke**

22 Fine Arts

GENERAL WORKS

Atlases

C, P

320. e'Avennes, Prisse. **Atlas of Egyptian Art.** paperback ed. New York, The American University in Cairo Press; distr., Sterling, Va., International Publishers Marketing, 2007. 159p. illus. $29.95pa. ISBN 13: 978-977-416-120-9.

This volume, introduced by Maarten J. Raven with captions by Olaf E. Kaper, makes available the work of Emil Prisse d'Avennes, a nineteenth century Frenchman who in two trips to Egypt (1827-1844 and 1858-1860), documented many of the monuments of ancient Egypt, ancient Nubia, and the Islamic world, particularly around Cairo. Although d'Avennes is generally not well known save for the Papyrus Prisse, which is in the Louvre, the drawings, paintings, squeezes, and notes along with the photographs from his second trip that Prisse brought back to Paris in 1860 and soon began to publish have preserved in great detail illustrations of monuments and scenes from temples and tombs. As Raven has written, "Many concern monuments now lost or wall-paintings damaged beyond recognition, thereby constituting precious information for present-day Egyptology . . . (and) excel in their meticulous precision . . ." (p. vi). The volume thus provides materials and information not otherwise available to the reader, researcher, and scholar.

Each illustration is accompanied by a caption, occasionally cross-referenced to another, which includes commentary about destruction and loss where applicable. In addition, each is cross-referenced to the standard topographical bibliographies used by Egyptologists. The volume thus provides a useful tool as well as a delight to the eyes for the Egyptologist as well as for the general reader, the student, and the researcher with an interest in ancient Egypt and its architecture, drawings, sculpture, painting, and industrial art (e.g., tools, vessels). Along with its content, the volume's reasonable price makes it appropriate for acquisition by public, high school, college, and personal libraries of artists and other interested persons.
—**Susan Tower Hollis**

Catalogs and Collections

C, P, S

321. **Art Museum Image Gallery. http://www.hwwilson.com/Databases/artmuseum.htm.** [Website]. Bronx, N.Y., H. W. Wilson. Price negotiated by site. Date reviewed: 2008.

Art Museum Image Gallery boasts 155,000 attractive, high-quality images of artwork. The sheer number of images in this database has nearly doubled in six years. Two outstanding features are apparent: the high-quality, high-resolution reproductions and the opportunities for users to analyze the artwork. Images are available in three sizes: the thumbnail version appears in a search results list, a mid-sized version with full bibliographic data about the image, and a high-resolution image. The site continues to provide opportunities for users to explore the content of over 1,800 worldwide museums of fine and decorative art form 3000 B.C. E. through the 20th century. The full bibliographic information includes most of the following for each image: the object type, title of work, date the work was created, artists(s), nationality, description of work, museum Website, copyright information link, accession number, subjects, key terms, and a persistent URL link to the image. The description of work varies, with some images having no more than the title, while others include a paragraph description content note. The content note may include background information about he painting, the style, additional information about when it was created, and what experts view as significant about the work. Users can do a browse search by such field as birthplace, date of birth, date of death, location of work, object type, nationality publication year, and subject. Unfortunately, no clickable list of any of these options is available; however, entering simply the letter "a" constitutes a search, which then allows the user to begin to browse and scroll through the possibilities.

A final outstanding feature of this database is the Content Discovery Keys sidebar that relates to a search results list form any type of search (basic, advanced, or browse). The Content Discovery Keys are hyperlinked subject terms related to the current results list. These links perform a subject search on the related term and activate a new results list. The *Art Museum Image Gallery* provides a number of learning and teaching opportunities.—**ARBA Staff Reviewer**

Dictionaries and Encyclopedias

C, P

322.   **The Grove Encyclopedia of Materials and Techniques in Art.** Gerald W. R. Ward, ed. New York, Oxford University Press, 2008. 828p. illus. index. $150.00. ISBN 13: 978-0-19-531391-8.

A condensed version of the *Dictionary of Art* (see ARBA 98, entry 947), this work brings together in one volume over 400 articles and 1,000 entries in traditional art forms as well as new media techniques. The work is arranged alphabetically with several of the articles running to several pages. The entry for dyes runs to over four pages. The work is extensively illustrated, with over 180 of the illustrations in color. A bibliography for further study accompanies the longer articles with recommendations for further reading. A comprehensive subject index with cross-references completes the volume.

The work will find use in any library fielding questions on art. The work is recommended for its extensive coverage of all media and techniques, from traditional lost-cast waxing and quilting to new media on magnetic tape.—**Gregory Curtis**

C, P

323.   Hall, James. **Dictionary of Subjects and Symbols in Art.** 2d ed. Boulder, Colo., Westview Press, 2008. 364p. illus. index. $42.00pa. ISBN 0-8133-4393-3. ISBN 13: 978-0-8133-4393-8.

It is hard to figure that less than 100 years ago the prevailing art philosophy taught that the subject of pictures, sculptures, and so on occurred only randomly and had no bearing in the artist's mind or the product of final creation. Subjects, or so it went, were chanced upon, picked conveniently at hand but did not figure into the calculus of the artist's composition. This struck me more profoundly recently after I spent six weeks in Italy chasing the mind of Dante's *Commedia* around as it remains about in churches, murals, and bric-a-brac in Tuscany and all of Italy. One example will suffice: the façade of the Duomo in Orvieto. What we see today is the work of the Sienese Lorenzo Maitani who in the thirteenth century created the magnificent façades, themselves virtually the whole of the Bible from creation to the final judgment. No churchgoers attending there, even illiterate ones, could enter and not know what awaited them for right or wrong living.

The book before us, a revision of the 1974 edition, could not have come at a better time. Not only do many in the present generation not know the Bible (not even easy stories like Adam and Eve) but they have never even heard of the more complex mythologies penned by Ovid and his ilk. Furthermore, even the most literate of readers may not have spent time with (or have ever heard of) de Voragine's *The Golden Legend*, Apuleius's *The Golden Ass*, or any of Erwin Panofsky's works and so do not understand why gridirons (having nothing to do with football), combs, peacocks, goats, roosters, or any number of other mysterious-seeming clues appear in paintings from about 1200 to as late at the nineteenth century.

No longer will this be a problem with this handy vade mecum at your side. No matter what an artist is likely to throw at you, this volume will explain, and in detail, with enough information to satiate you on put you on the right trail for more. The book focuses largely on Christian and classical images, but additional non-Western ones have been added. Most entries are identifications (e.g., "Jester," "Four Evangelists") , others are "signpost" articles (e.g., "flora") , while others still identify themes (e.g., "shooting a dead body") . In every case the definitions are an education in and of themselves. Those who remain print-allergic will be saddened to learn that not even the Web holds all these clues, although, it is true, that is not likely to remain so for many more years.—**Mark Y. Herring**

C, P

324.   **The Oxford Dictionary of American Art and Artists.** By Ann Lee Morgan. New York, Oxford University Press, 2008. 537p. $17.95pa. ISBN 13: 978-0-19-537321-9.

The newly released paperback edition of this impressive work provides a wealth of information in succinct entries about the scope, history, and depth on American art from the colonial times to the present day. "Close to 100 entries" cover not only the artists but also the movements, techniques, and curators that have played a significant role in the evolution of this sector of the art world. Illustrations would have been nice, but as indicated in the introduction, many are available online as the majority of works discussed are held by public institutions.

The largest detractor from this text, however, is the scope of the coverage, which is left to the imagination. Only by circumspection do we discover that simply the plastic arts are represented. Although significant contributors not only to their field, but, it can be argued, American art as a whole, major players are absent: Merce Cunningham (mentioned only briefly in the entry for John Cage), Martha Graham, and Philip Glass just to name a few. The narrow scope would be more than acceptable if a descriptive phrase in the introduction had explained the logic behind it. But even this emphasis has gaps: surely we would expect to find Art Spiegelman and Andres Serrano in this category, not to mention the Stuckist movement, which while originating in Britain, has a strong American presence as well.

This is an important text, but more useful as a supplement to existing reference titles on this topic with larger coverage. It should be of interest to select undergraduate libraries, most community colleges, and special interest libraries (museums and galleries).—**Stephen J. Shaw**

Handbooks and Yearbooks

P

325.   Scheller, W. G. **America: A History in Art.** New York, Black Dog & Leventhal Publishers, 2008. 336p. illus. index. $40.00. ISBN 13: 978-1-57912-779-4.

This beautiful book uses paintings, photographs, sculpture, and architecture to show the history of America. Arranged chronologically by time periods (e.g., "First Americans," "The American Revolution," "The Gilded Age," "Into the Millennium") , the title provides well-written text alongside illustrations of historic art to show how America's history has evolved—and how art has evolved right with it. The focus here is less on history and more on the art. Each illustrated piece of art provides full bibliographic information, including name of the piece, date created, the museum in which the piece is currently displayed, with what materials the piece was created, and a paragraph description of the piece. One of the interesting aspects of this book is that it displays how art transitioned alongside history. Users will see how paintings dominated early America, how the invention of photography showed real-life history (e.g., Native American life), and how the industrial age was dominated by utilitarian structures of architecture (e.g., the Empire State Building). Users can also see how important historical events, such as the World Wars, the Great Depression, and the Cold War, affected the mood and type of art created. This title allows students and layreaders to observe America's history through the eyes of artists and demonstrates how politics, social changes, and economics affect art.—**Shannon Graff Hysell**

ARCHITECTURE

Biography

C, P

326.   Allaback, Sarah. **The First American Women Architects.** Champaign, Ill., University of Illinois Press, 2008. 265p. illus. index. $45.00. ISBN 13: 978-0-252-03321-6.

Architectural historian Sarah Allaback has compiled a thoughtful, well-organized, and insightful guide to the first generation (or two) of women licensed as architects in the United States. Acknowledging that women entering the profession well past her cutoff of 1920 (established in practice or well into training before the end of the 1920s) were often the first females to enter a firm or to practice in a city and thus worthy of the title "pioneer," Allaback profiles 76 architects and documents their training, experience, buildings, influences, biography, and bibliography in individual alphabetized entries. Many of the profiles are brief because records are poor, but most develop a solid sense of the architect and her practice. Portraits, plans, or images of buildings enliven many of the profiles. The appendixes list female graduates of architecture schools from 1878 to 1934 and female members of the American Institute of Architects from 1857 to 1950. The index, notes, and annotated bibliography make accessing the book quite simple.

Allaback cites her frequent challenges in research, such as incomplete records, tracking maiden versus married names, the practice of using initials to hide gender, misattribution to male colleagues, and similar problems typical in recovering the history of females in traditionally male activities and professions. The introductory essay, which builds a strong context for the profiles, includes anecdotes of architects receiving correspondence addressed to "Mr." and "Esq.," professional recognition in part because of gender-ambiguous names, and the unwanted title "Miss" in directories that provide no title for the men. This study builds on work by a number of researchers, and Allaback specifically cites the work of Kathryn H. Anthony, professor of architecture at the University of Illinois, who has compiled substantial oral histories of pioneering women in the profession. *The First American Women Architects* is an important, readable, and easy-to-use addition to the literature on the history of architecture in the United States. It is well produced, scholarly but not pedantic, and a useful corrective to the exclusion of women from so many tradition historical publications.—**R. K. Dickson**

Catalogs and Collections

C, P, S

327.   **Cities and Buildings Collection. http://content.lib.washington.edu/cities/.** [Website]. Free. Date reviewed: 2008.

The *Cities and Buildings Collection* database is "a collection of digitized images of buildings and cities drawn from across time and throughout the world, available to students, researchers, and educators on the Web." Established in 1995 by a professor in the Architecture and Art History Departments at the University of Washington, the site has grown substantially and now contains nearly 10,000 images that have all been scanned from original slides or drawn from documents in the public domain. Consequently, they can all be freely used in the classroom. Finally, the site is searchable by country, city, style, title, architect, data of construction, and other fields.—**Greg Byerly**

Dictionaries and Encyclopedias

C, P, S

328. **The Greenwood Encyclopedia of Homes Through American History.** By Melissa Wells Duffes, William Burns, and Olivia Graf. Westport, Conn., Greenwood Press, 2008. 4v. illus. index. $399.95/set. ISBN 13: 978-0-313-33496-2.

This four-volume set, meant for students of any age, can be used as a reference encyclopedia or as a narrative history. The set follows the "dynamic developmental process of the American home" through history (p. x). The architecture considered is the vernacular or common rather than the grand or ostentatious. In telling the story of American architecture, this set also provides the reader with cultural, political, economic, geographic, demographic, and technological context.

The four volumes are arranged chronologically. Volume 1 covers the time period from 1492-1820; volume 2 covers from 1821-1900; volume 3 discusses 1901-1945; and volume 4 from 1946 to the present. Each volume contains: an introduction to the time period, a timeline highlighting special events, architectural styles, building materials and manufacture, layout and design, furniture and design, landscaping, and outbuildings. Each section is subdivided as appropriate. For example, in volume 1 the layout and design section is divided into Native American, early Colonial Northeast, and early Colonial South. Black-and-white photographs illustrate and highlight some descriptions. Insets scattered throughout each volume give interesting information about people, technology, architectural details and motifs, society and customs, and bibliographies of resources used during the time period in question. Each section contains a glossary and an extensive resource guide including print resources, museums and repositories, films and videos, and Websites. An index completes each volume. The editor and authors include a historian, a curator, a designer/architect, and a cultural geographer. All of the contributors are credentialed in their fields and all have written in their fields.

The writing style for this work is engaging. Information included is interesting and informative. This set could be used by general readers or scholarly researchers as a starting point for almost any inquiry concerning American architecture. This set is recommended for public, high school, academic, and architectural libraries.—**Joanna M. Burkhardt**

Handbooks and Yearbooks

P

329. Kaiser, Harvey H. **The National Park Architecture Sourcebook.** New York, Princeton Architectural Press, 2008. 600p. $40.00pa. ISBN 13: 978-1-56898-742-2.

The architecture of our national parks is often overlooked, and the treasures that can be found there often left to decay. But books like this can help reverse this trend. Harvey Kaiser has written several books on architecture and is a leading voice for the preservation of American architecture. The work provides the reader with a state-by-state review of important structures, monuments, and special places that can be found in our national parks.

The book is organized by region (e.g., Far West and Pacific, Southwest, Rockies and Plains, Midwest, South, Mid-Atlantic and New England). Within these divisions each state is represented. In addition, there is a list of national parks, and the front and back covers contain a reference of parks by state with page indications. The entries tend to be brief and to the point, and often contain interesting black-and-white photographs. Each entry contains information on the official name of the park (also any alternate names), the official Website (if available), directions to the park from local highways and towns, and several paragraphs on the history, primary architectural sites, and often fascinating anecdotes concerning the establishment of the area. The book can be used as a handbook for visiting national parks and viewing the architecture found there. One failing of the work is the lack of a detailed index. Because of this it is far less important as a reference source than it might be, even though it contains a lot of detailed information. The work is recommended for both academic and public libraries, and as a personal purchase for someone planning on visiting our national parks.—**Robert L. Wick**

PHOTOGRAPHY

P

330.   Ang, Tom. **Fundamentals of Photography: The Essential handbook for Both Digital and Film Cameras.** New York, Alfred A. Knopf/Random House, 2008. 352p. illus. index. $25.00. ISBN 13: 978-0-375-71157-2.

Recent decades have seen no shortage of reference books on photography. Books on photographic theory abound, and those offering practical guidance have tended to focus either on analog or digital technique. This handbook claims to be the first to integrate the fundamentals of photography with specific instruction in both digital and analog technique and where the two intersect.

Beautifully designed with color-tabbed chapters, this book covers much ground. Topics range from the uses of photography and the fundamentals of light and color, to processing film and outputting and enhancing images. With 80 percent of its 1,000 images in color, this book is a joy to browse; each fully captioned illustration quickly explains a concept in context. Ang leaves little ground uncovered, all the while clearly integrating photographic technique with its underlying philosophy. He demonstrates traditional darkroom tricks, such as "burning and dodging," alongside digital editing effects, like those used in Adobe Photoshop software. Even peripheral topics are touched upon, such as pinhole photography. However, black-and-white photography is mentioned only in terms of developing and printing, and, disappointingly, composition and framing are only highlighted. The book closes with a helpful "References" chapter, which includes a glossary, copyright FAQ, and thumbnail libraries of common image faults, processing defects, and editing effects. Additionally, certain sections throughout on "tinted" pages denote further reading for the advanced photographer.

Tom Ang is a highly respected expert in digital photography demonstrated by earlier works such as his unillustrated *Dictionary of Photography and Digital Imaging* (see ARBA 2004, entry 940), which may now serve as a handy companion to his colorful new book. While it uniquely provides a basic understanding of photography regardless of format, the new handbook suffers in spots from an unnecessarily technical and awkward writing style. In contrast, the National Geographic Society's comprehensive and colorful handbook on digital technique, *Ultimate Field Guide to Photography* (see ARBA 2007, entry 821), uses plain and direct prose. Although sturdy and flexible, Ang's book is also physically difficult to flip through—a minor annoyance caused by its "rounded and backed" binding (no doubt necessary for the high level of durability needed out in the field). Nevertheless, this work is a gem for it price and size, and most importantly for the ground it covers in both film and digital photography. The handbook makes an essential addition for public libraries, art libraries, and most libraries in between.—**Lucy Duhon**

C, S

331.   Congdon, Kristin G., and Kara Kelley Hallmark. **Twentieth Century United States Photographers: A Student's Guide.** Westport, Conn., Greenwood Press, 2008. 384p. illus. index. $99.95. ISBN 13: 978-0-313-33561-7.

Photography is ubiquitous in modern American life, and it is easy to let it blend into the fabric of daily existence. Congdon and Hallmark's guide helps to broaden the reader's appreciation for the expansive variety of styles and influences that exist in American photographers working throughout the twentieth century. The authors use an alphabetical rather than a chronological approach to introduce early pioneers such as Alfred Stieglitz, Man Ray, Dorothea Lange, Lewis Hines, Walker Evans, Edward S. Curtis, and Ansel Adams, as well as innovators working today, including Andres Serrano, Cindy

Sherman, Mary Ellen Mark, Jeanne Dunning, Joel-Peter Witkin, Carrie Mae Weems, Mike and Doug Starn, Lorna Simpson, and Nan Goldin—and everyone in between. Each of the 75 entries includes a summary essay that incorporates biographical and career highlights along with a context for the photographer's work in photographic history. A short bibliography and a list of collections in which the work may be found are also furnished. Small black-and-white photographs accompany the entries, and a center section with select color photographs is featured. A glossary and index are provided along with a thoughtful introductory essay that reflects on the evolution of photography into its current role in modern life. Similar titles, such as *Contemporary Photographers* (St. James Press, 1995) assume a deeper level of knowledge of the field. This book serves as an excellent introduction for those seeking a framework for understanding the development of American photography and an appreciation for some of the major contributors.
—**Judy Dyki**

23 Language and Linguistics

GENERAL WORKS

Dictionaries and Encyclopedias

C

332. Crystal, David. **A Dictionary of Linguistics and Phonetics.** 6th ed. Malden, Mass., Blackwell, 2008. 529p. $39.95pa. ISBN 13: 978-1-4051-5297-6.

First published in 1980, *A Dictionary of Linguistics and Phonetics* is a standard reference work now in its 6th edition. It includes more than 5,100 terms grouped into over 3,000 entries. It is intended as an introductory text of terms for students of linguistics and as such, it includes mainly core terms. Although this work is described as a dictionary, it is also encyclopedic in nature, and this edition in particular contains more of a developed historical perspective than the previous ones. This edition also has more information concerning the usage of terms, which may be helpful to non-native speakers of English.

Main terms are listed in bold typeface and terms defined elsewhere are in small capital letters. This approach makes finding terms throughout the book relatively easy. Also included is a list of abbreviations and symbols and a chart of the International Phonetic Alphabet (2005 revision). One item that is missed by this reviewer is a CD-ROM or access to an online version to facilitate searching even more and to make the work more accessible. The author, David Crystal, is Honorary Professor of Linguistics at the University of Bangor, Wales, and has published several leading reference works dealing with language, making him a renowned scholar in the field. Overall, this dictionary is a valuable resource for general and core terms in linguistics and phonetics and should be invaluable to students and instructors alike.—**Christine Rigda**

Handbooks and Yearbooks

C, P

333. **One Thousand Languages: Living, Endangered, and Lost.** Peter Austin, ed. Berkeley, Calif., University of California Press, 2008. 288p. illus. maps. index. $29.95. ISBN 13: 978-0-520-25560-9.

One Thousand Languages identifies the major spoken languages of the world. It begins by highlighting 11 global languages spoken by the majority of the world then explores other languages arranged by region. Each description is one or two pages and features a short history of each language, the number of speakers, details on how the language has spread geographically, and colored maps. Interesting bits of information about each language are also included, such as slang, how to count to 10, and words that are derived from other languages. Near the end of the book is a section featuring large maps of each region with lists of where each language is found as well as maps showing endangered and extinct languages. The work ends with a glossary, bibliography, and detailed index. What is striking about this work is the numerous color photographs used to showcase the cultural aspects of each language. This gives it a textbook feel, but it is very enjoyable to browse. It is highly recommended as a reference resource or for anyone who wants to learn more about the world's languages.—**Christine Rigda**

ENGLISH-LANGUAGE DICTIONARIES

General Usage

C, P

334.   **Merriam-Webster's Advanced Learner's English Dictionary.** Springfield, Mass., Merriam-Webster, 2008. 2032. $34.95; $29.95pa. ISBN 13: 978-0-87779-551-3; 978-0-87779-550-6pa.

This 1st edition of *Merriam-Webster's Advanced Learner's English Dictionary* is designed to provide in-depth coverage of contemporary English vocabulary and grammar. This dictionary provides 100,000 words and phrases, with more than 3,000 core vocabulary words identified. It includes 22,000 idioms and commonly used phrases as well. Unlike many dictionaries, this edition provides usage examples to all of the words defined—160,000 usage examples in all. Also included are 32,000 pronunciation examples and subject labels with British variants. Many of the entries are supplemented with line drawings, plus an additional 16 pages of cull-color art is included. This dictionary provides a substantial amount of supplementary material, including: 30 pages of grammar, a 10-page section on style, prefixes and suffixes, irregular verbs. spelling rules, roots of English words, common first names, weights and measures, metric system, and geographical names. With purchase of the volume users will also have access to a free e-book download, a study guide for teachers, and access to the dictionary's Website (http://www.LearnersDictionary.com). At only $34.95 for the hardcover volume, this dictionary is a good deal and provides a good deal of information. It will be good for ready-reference use at school and university libraries as well as at the desk of writers and researchers.—**Shannon Graff Hysell**

P

335.   **Oxford American Large Print Dictionary.** New York, Oxford University Press, 2008. 1442p. $24.95pa. ISBN 13: 978-0-19-537125-3.

The *Oxford American Large Print Dictionary* provides concise definitions of words considered the "core" of the English language and also includes approximately 2,000 difficult literary words. Each entry term appears in bold typeface and contains the word's part of speech, a brief definition, syllabication, and, if necessary, a pronunciation guide, but word etymology is absent. In addition to definitions, the dictionary features a spelling guide, listings of words that are commonly confused or misspelled, and usage notes. The page layout was designed in association with Lighthouse International, an organization that assists the visually impaired through research, advocacy, and vision rehabilitation. This means that there are large margins and adequate spacing between entries, and that the paper on which the text is printed provides a minimal amount of glare. These resources are well suited for adults and children who are visually impaired or who prefer a larger typeface and are recommended for libraries that serve these users.—**Maris L. Hayashi**

C, P, S

336.   Sheehan, Michael J. **Word Parts Dictionary: Standard and Reverse Listings of Prefixes, Suffixes, Roots and Combining Forms.** 2d ed. Jefferson, N.C., McFarland, 2008. 286p. $55.00. ISBN 13: 978-0-7864-3564-7.

Michael J. Sheehan's *Word Parts Dictionary* is a great tool for any language and writing tool box. The volume is especially useful in conjunction with a dictionary or thesaurus. The 2d edition of the book only improves upon the 1st edition (see ARBA 2001, entry 1019). Stated well in the preface, Sheehan has two objectives: to help people broaden their vocabularies and to present word parts in a handy format for those who wish to interpret or create new words. This work is for anyone "with a vested interest in words, professional or personal" (p. 1). The book would be a great addition to any library. The volume is set up in three parts: a straightforward alphabetic dictionary (part 1); a reverse dictionary that enables one to find a word part using meanings, concepts, or actual words (part 2); and a categories section that organizes word parts by group such as animals or food (part 3). The three-way approach to finding word parts offers the user different ways with which to conduct their search. The volume focuses on prefixes, suffixes, combining forms and bases. Parts 1 and 2 indicate which of these a word part is. This 2d edition includes more terms and categories than the 1st edition. The author has added embedded etymologies and more examples to part 1; added over 1,000 new terms to part 2; and expanded old categories, and added three new categories to part 3. Sheehan has compiled a practical work that is comprehensive yet very efficient.—**Sue Ellen Griffiths**

P, S

337.   **Webster's Contemporary School & Office Dictionary.** Darien, Conn., Federal Street Press, 2008. 639p. $7.98pa. ISBN 1-59695-047-1. ISBN 13: 978-1-59695-047-4.

P, S

338.   **Webster's Contemporary School & Office Thesaurus.** Darien, Conn., Federal Street Press, 2008. 668p. $7.98pa. ISBN 1-59695-048-X. ISBN 13: 978-1-59695-048-1.

Is there any name more synonymous with dictionaries than Webster's? This 2008 edition of *Webster's Contemporary School & Office Dictionary*, published by the editors of Merriam-Webster, provides the general reader with a resource of over 70,000 definitions for words most frequently found in the English language. Among these entries are recently coined words and abbreviations. For example, *Internet*, *telemarketing*, *TGIF*, and *BYOB* are included; however, some of the latest technology words are not, including *blog*, *wiki*, or *Wi-Fi*.

The useful definitions are concise. Every entry has an example use sentence, but only some contain synonyms and cross-references. The 150 line drawings of animals, insects, birds, and objects are scattered throughout the text. The Explanatory Notes introduction explains entry meaning, grammar, phonetic information, and much more. Other sections are included, such as a Foreign Words & Phrases section that contains pronunciation guidance as well as a translation for words and phrases that occur frequently in English speech and writing; a Biographical Names section that lists a wide-range of diverse individuals from contemporary culture, history, the Bible, legends, and mythology; and a Geographical Names section that is global in nature and current in its representation of popular figures.

Webster's Contemporary School & Office Thesaurus provides more than 150,000 synonyms, antonyms, and related words. The definitions are clear and concise, making it easy to choose the right word. Many of the entries offer usage examples to help clarify meaning.

Selecting a dictionary and thesaurus for use often depends on its reliability and selecting one for purchase usually depends on the cost. These titles are good for both. With over 170 years of dictionary publishing experience behind it, these all-purpose, affordably priced dictionaries are ideal for students in middle and high school grades and for individuals in a typical office.—**Alice Crosetto**

Etymology

C, P, S

339.   **The Facts on File Encyclopedia of Word and Phrase Origins': Definitions and Origins of More Than 15,000 Words and Expressions.** 4th ed. By Robert Hendrickson. New York, Facts on File,

2008. 948p. index. (Facts on File Library of Language and Literature). $95.00. ISBN 13: 978-0-8160-6966-8.

This marvelous reference has grown by about 150 pages and 2,500 new entries from its predecessor, which was published four years ago. The grand total now exceeds 15,000 letters, words, and expressions, all alphabetized, defined, and traced to their most likely provenance(s). Here one can find slang expressions like "It's the pits," foreign terms like "fatwa," abbreviations and acronyms like "AWOL," euphemisms like "gee!," terms from Classical literature like "Sisyphean," pop culture items like "smiley face," place-names (including all 50 states), homonyms like "quail," and so on. Drawing from both historical and contemporary sources, Hendrickson's book will appeal to researchers, and with its broad range and scope, word lovers are likely to become addicted—it is hard to read just one! Of course, this information can be found in *The Oxford English Dictionary* and in the works of Bartlett, Brewer, Mencken, Partridge, Pepys, and sundry other well-established authorities, but having it in one book is hard to beat. An index of proper names mentioned in the entries adds to its value.—**Lori D. Kranz**

C, P

340.   Liberman, Anatoly. **An Analytic Dictionary of English Etymology: An Introduction.** Minneapolis, Minn., University of Minnesota Press, 2008. 359p. index. $50.00. ISBN 13: 978-0-8166-5272-3.

Anatoly Liberman's latest work follows the success of his 2005 *Word Origins . . . And How We Know Them: Etymology for Everyone* (see ARBA 2006, entry 948). As one of the world's leading scholars in the study of word origins, Liberman, with the assistance of J. Lawrence Mitchell, provides a glimpse into the world of etymology by using centuries of research as a base and adding his unique perspective on the study of etymology.

In this introductory volume, Liberman selects 55 words of questionable origins. Most of these words are nouns (e.g., boy, cub, girl, rabbit, toad). Several verbs are examined as are some adverbs and compounds. The first section provides a concise etymology of each word. The following section containing an in-depth look at the conflicting hypotheses of their origins, gives the reader an understanding of the complexity of such philological exercises. Each of the entries in the in-depth section contains information derived from 200 dictionaries and examples of the word found in articles and books. More than one-half of the entries are between one and three pages, and few entries are over eight pages. The entry *dwarf* is the longest, covering 16 pages. A substantial bibliography, subject index, personal and place-name index, and an index containing 6,000 words from over 80 languages are included.

Professional philologists may be the only group to appreciate this work; however, a casual reader may discover that words reflect history, culture, and societal trends, thus illustrating the value and importance of etymology. Academic libraries should have this resource as well as public libraries.—**Alice Crosetto**

Slang

C, P, S

341.   **Stone the Crows: Oxford Dictionary of Modern Slang.** 2d ed. By John Ayto and John Simpson. New York, Oxford University Press, 2008. 408p. $18.95. ISBN 13: 978-0-19-954370-0.

Ranging from *abaht* (used in writing to represent a Cockney or British accent) to *zowie* (expressing astonishment), *Stone the Crows: Oxford Dictionary of Modern Slang* contains over 6,000 words and phrases comprising the British, American, and Australian slang of the twentieth century. Arranged alphabetically, each entry contains the part of speech, a brief etymology, definitions, and a sentence to ensure clarity of usage and meaning. If the term has more than one meaning, each definition is listed in chronological order. The subject index provides access by various themes, such as people and society or abstract qualities and states. This authoritative guide to English colloquial speech is engaging and of interest to general users and students.—**Denise A. Garofalo**

Terms and Phrases

C, P, S

342.   **The Facts on File Dictionary of Foreign Words & Phrases.** 2d ed. By Martin H. Manser. New York, Facts on File, 2008. 469p. index. (Facts on File Library of Language and Literature). $49.50. ISBN 13: 978-0-8160-7035-0.

Just six years since the publication of the 1st edition (see ARBA 2003, entry 973), the author has increased the contents with 500 new entries, such as *retro* and *Sudoku*, proving that the English language is still a great macaronic aggregator. The entries are broken down into two types: foreign words that have become fully integrated into English (like *minimum* and *exit*) such that their origins no longer seem foreign, and others, like *kia-ora* (Maori for good luck), that have retained their foreignness. A great many of the more than 4,500 terms comes from medicine, law, and food and represent commonly used words users are likely to encounter or want to investigate. Each bolded headword is followed by pronunciation, etymology, grammatical information, definitions, and, usually, examples of use (some fabricated and some actual citations). Cross-references guide users to a more standard form, such as the referral from the plural *messieurs* to the singular form *monsieur*. The sole index, which rearranges entries by language of origin, tells us that French and Latin have been the two largest contributors. Even some relatively minor languages, like Hausa, Khoikhoi, and Salishan, have played a role in enriching the English language.

Public and academic libraries that own either the 1st edition or the complementary and more comprehensive *Oxford Dictionary of Foreign Words and Phrases* (see ARBA 99, entry 903) may want to acquire this edition so they will be *au courant*.—**Lawrence Olszewski**

C, P, S

343.   Korach, Myron, with John Mordock. **Common Phrases and Where They Came From.** 2d ed. Guilford, Conn., Lyons Press, 2008. 188p. index. $12.95pa. ISBN 13: 978-1-59921-307-1.

This collection of the stories behind the development of several common idioms is preceded by an outline of the various sources from which the information was obtained, although nowhere is there provided a thorough bibliography. A discussion of idioms in general is followed by the entries for individual expression. The expressions are grouped in basic categories focusing on areas such as work, home life, and health. At the beginning of each entry is a brief discussion of the type of topics included in that category. The entries seem to be well researched and written in a concise, matter of fact style. There are some illustrations to make the text more interesting and an index at the end. Although not informative enough for upper-level research, this listing would serve as a quick and informative reference and an excellent starting point for further research.—**Martha Lawler**

Thesauri

C, P, S

344.   **Oxford American Writer's Thesaurus.** 2d ed. Christine A. Lindberg, comp. New York, Oxford University Press, 2008. 1047p. index. $40.00. ISBN 13: 978-0-19-532284-0.

This newest edition draws on the expertise of various individuals and on resources produced by the Oxford University Press to present over 15,000 main entries, 300,000 synonyms, and 10,000 antonyms, along with notes on word associations and writing formats. A preface, foreword, and introduction explain the approach and organization of the information. An example entry is provided with explanations of the various parts of each entry. A list of the labels used to describe the origin and use of each term include a brief description of the label and how it is applied, such as format, informal, vulgar slang, technical, literary, dated, historical, rare, humorous, archaic, derogatory, and euphemistic terms. A brief discussion of the use of trademarked terms is followed by a discussion of the various featured notes that are offered as aides to choosing the right work and by a listing of note authors. These featured notes are small sidebar items that are interspersed throughout the main listing of entries often with appropriate *see* references and with background discussion on common or historical usage. In the middle of the listing of entries is a separately paged "wordfinder" section that includes an index, thematic lists (such as words about "animals," subdivided by types of animals), a listing of archaic works with definitions, and a listing of literary works that are used in poetry and other elevated forms of writing. At the end of the main listing of entries is a language guide, which discusses grammar, spelling, capitalization, and pronunciation. A very thorough examination and interesting approach makes this thesaurus different and more useful than the usual simple listing of terms.—**Martha Lawler**

NON-ENGLISH-LANGUAGE DICTIONARIES

General Works

C, P, S

345.   **Oxford Language Dictionaries Online. http://www.oxfordlanguagedictionaries.com.** [Website]. New York, Oxford University Press. price negotiated by site. Date reviewed: Mar 08.

Oxford University Press has made the *Oxford Spanish Dictionary*, *Oxford-Paravia Italian Dictionary*, *Oxford-Hatchette French Dictionary*, and the *Oxford-Duden German Dictionary* available online as the *Oxford Language Dictionaries Online* (OLDO). Released in late 2007, Russian, Chinese, and most importantly, pronunciation software, have been added in an update. Dictionaries for other languages are to be added eventually, with Japanese, Polish, and Arabic next in line. Pricing for the dictionary is reasonable and cost per student, teacher, and patron use should make the product easily justified.

Searching is simple; interpreting and extending the results are not intuitive, but libraries can help students quickly learn what to do with hits. First, users must choose which language dictionary to search. The second step is the direction of the search; for example, English-French or French-English. The browse button allows the user to search alphabetically, obviously a great feature when exact spelling is not known. One can also search by phrase by putting the words within quotation marks. Searching can be limited by choosing only headwords rather than full text, by parts of speech, level of usage, and by geographical/cultural variants. The search choices (complete with a built-in keyboard to enter diacriticals, accent marks, and other language characters) result in a list of words, example usage, and sentences that can be arranged by relevance, alphabetical order, or reverse alphabet. The search work is highlighted in each result. Boolean and adjacency advanced search options are also available. Software allows the user to hear the word pronounced with a mouse-over. The entry gives the definition, parts of speech, and phonetic pronunciation, and can be opened to show use of the words in common phrases as well as their translations. Many words have fact boxes with links to notes about grammar, verb forms, and cultural information. One feature that is helpful when trying to get an exact meaning is that the words in the definitions and phrases can be cut and pasted back into the search box. It is, therefore, very easy to refine searches to achieve the best possible translations.

Useful additions that come with the dictionary include: a word of the day vocabulary builder; a "Life and Culture" section; Weblinks that lead users to world language magazines and newspapers, museums, comic books, and radio stations; a useful "Phrases" section that provides simple greetings, civilities, directions, and traveling tips; a "Writing and Word Games" section; and a teaching and learning section for grades 6-9 and grades 9-12 that includes lesson plans, worksheets, and slide shows.

Technically, the site is set up to use with any current browser. Remote access is automatically included in the subscription price. Any library supporting language instruction needs the appropriate dictionaries from Oxford Online. Advantages such as providing access to the same excellent dictionary for the instructor and each student in a language class, as well as to all other students and parents in an online environment at the reasonable subscription price make these dictionaries first-purchase recommendations.
—**Barbara Ripp Safford**

Italian

P

346. **Oxford-Paravia Italian Dictionary.** 2d ed. New York, Oxford University Press, 2006. 2773p. $65.00. ISBN 0-19-929775-4.

The 2d edition of the English-Italian/Italian-English dictionary published by Oxford-Paravia contains more than 300,000 words and phrases and includes over 450,000 translations. In both the English and the Italian sections, a triangle before the headword denotes the 7,000 most common words in Oxford's "core vocabulary" listings, with the most frequent 3,000 words marked with a black triangle, and the remaining words with a white triangle. A distinguishing feature of the work is that entries include collocates, words that often appear with the headword in a phrase, creating a more accurate sense of how the word may be used by native speakers. Phonetic transcription of the pronunciation of the entries employs the symbols of the International Phonetic Alphabet (IPA) for both English-Italian and Italian-English. In addition to the alphabetic entries, the dictionary includes a listing of abbreviations, a guide to the use of the dictionary, and a listing of the phonetic symbols. At the end of each language section is a chapter of lexical notes that provides examples of use based on categories of words, such as age, sizes, and weights. In addition there is a guide to effective communication that addresses various forms of correspondence, such as business writing, advertising, telephone, and e-mail communications.

Unlike other bilingual dictionaries, this work serves the native speaker of either language with equal utility. While the *Harper Collins Sansoni Italian Dictionary*, as with other dictionaries, provides the IPA transcriptions only in the English-Italian section, this work offers the IPA notation in both sections. In fact, the approach here is to treat each section equally in terms of page layout and lexigraphical structure. While this dictionary could benefit the native English speaker by Harper Collins' approach of marking the main stress in the Italian headword with a sub-dot below the accented vowel for ease of use (while also including the IPA transcription), it is clearly a more comprehensive work. This dictionary provides outstanding features including well-designed page layout, the provision of collocates, and informative notes. Notations for core vocabulary terms assist in browsing the dictionary for the most frequently used words in both languages. This is a superbly constructed English-Italian/Italian-English dictionary.—**Glenn S. McGuigan**

Spanish

C, P, S

347. **Oxford Spanish Dictionary: Spanish-English, English-Spanish.** 4th ed. Beatriz Galimberti Jarman and Roy Russell, eds. New York, Oxford University Press, 2008. 1943p. $49.95 (w/CD-ROM). ISBN 13: 978-0-19-920897-5.

The *Oxford Spanish Dictionary*, now in its 4th edition, offers extensive assistance for both English and Spanish speakers by including a wide array of definitions and related information about words in both languages. The 1st edition was compiled to reflect Spanish and English as spoken or written in the 1990s. The 4th edition updates existing entries and adds new words and senses of words. A special section on practical problems in communication, especially for those living in a foreign country, has been updated and expanded. The differences between English and Spanish require a good deal of explanation when conveying both the definition of a word and the sense or senses in which it can be used. This dictionary provides an overwhelming amount of information to make those explanations available.

Abbreviations used are spelled out inside the front and back covers. A 10-page section explains how entries are structured, including headword and definitions, grammatical information, labels, examples, translations, and cross-references in both languages. This is followed by a 22-page explanation of how to use the dictionary, including the interpretation of all signs and symbols, explanation of regional and local usage, and how cross-references are constructed. The general rules of pronunciation for Spanish and English complete the introductory material.

Approximately 300,000 words and phrases in English and Spanish are defined in the body of the work. Entries are in strict alphabetic order, including acronyms. Selected words are given extended explanation and/or put in context in box insets scattered throughout the dictionary. Separating the Spanish-English and English-Spanish sections is a 68-page section entitled "Guide to Effective Communication." This section provides advice on the effective use of the language, difficulties in each language, variations in each language, transitional words and phrases, living in a Spanish/English speaking country, correspondence on various topics with sample letters, using the telephone, electronic messaging, and using the Internet.

The final section of this dictionary includes Spanish verb tables, giving the conjugation of the most common verbs, lists of irregular verbs for each language, a glossary of grammatical terms, and an index to inset boxes. The dictionary also comes with a CD-ROM.

While a beginner could use this dictionary to find a definition, the complex nature of the entries makes really understanding all the possible uses for a word a matter for more advanced linguists. The numerous abbreviations, symbols, signs, and numbers might become more meaningful with constant use, but for a casual reader, finding out how to read an entry may take longer than is worthwhile. The section of practical advice on living and communication in a foreign country is useful, but the dictionary is not the first place this reviewer would look for that type of information. The size and weight of the volume indicate that this dictionary would be used in a personal or institutional library. It is not easily portable. This Spanish dictionary is recommended for advanced students and reference collections in public, language, and academic libraries.—**Joanna M. Burkhardt**

24 Literature

GENERAL WORKS

Bibliography

C

348. Harner, James L. **Literary Research Guide: An Annotated Listing of Reference Sources in English Literary Studies.** 5th ed. New York, Modern Language Association of America, 2008. 826p. index. $37.50pa. ISBN 13: 978-0-87352-808-5.

With the increase of published content in literary studies, a researcher may often overlook or be unaware of certain useful manuals, guides, and other literature. In *Literary Research Guide*, Harner gathers invaluable resources for researchers in English Literary Studies into one collection, devoting in-depth analyses of each item. Basic research tools, such as single-author critical guides, are omitted in the presumption that users of this guide are already familiar with them. Print and electronic resources are examined.

Literary Research Guide is the 5th edition of this title. Past reference sources were re-evaluated and revised, and more electronic resources have been included while certain areas have been completely deleted to make room for the electronic sources and allow for greater focus on reference sources. A section on cultural studies was added.

This guide is a well-organized compendium laid out in a thoughtful and easy-to-use manner; a section is provided on how to use Harner's organizational system. Topics are arranged from A (Research Methods) through U (Literature-Related Topics and Sources). Each topic is subdivided into headings to include particular resources (e.g., Research Methods, Guides to Reference Works, Annals, Periodicals). Subdivided further, we see entry numbers, entries, citations, and annotations. Each entry includes pertinent information that will allow the researcher to make a well-informed decision on whether or not a particular resource will be useful in his or her search, sparing time in viewing each item individually.

There are two indexes: one of names and the other of titles. Both are comprehensive with brief instructions on how to use them. These indexes allow a researcher to flip through this resource to find out if a particular title, author, editor, or translator is reviewed in this book. The *Literary Research Guide* is a useful tool for collection development in research and academic libraries, particularly those supporting master's and doctoral programs because of the in-depth annotations provided.

Harner's analyses are well written and detailed, accomplishing his goal in providing researchers with a compilation of essential and useful resources. Harner fully explains his organizational system, providing cross-references in related areas, and the criteria used for including the reference sources he selects. This is an invaluable guide to literary researchers.—**Michelle Martinez**

Bio-bibliography

P, S

349.   **Bloom's Literary Reference Online. http://www.factsonfile.com.** [Website]. New York, Facts on File. Price negotiated by site. Date reviewed: 2008.

This generally well-received database is compiled using 70 full-text books and 12 partially included books from the significant Facts on File literature reference tools and from hundreds of Harold Bloom critical titles from series published by Chelsea House. Facts on File bought Chelsea house in 2005, and someone had the good idea to make a literature database that combined the resources of the two companies.

Searching is easy. A clear keyword search box on the home page allows keyword and Boolean combinations. Advanced search is Boolean without actually saying so, much like Google Advanced search, and very accommodating to the searcher. In addition, there is a choice to search within full text or just within titles. Also, users can browse by author, work, topic/theme, and timeline. Finally, one can browse *Bloom's Western Canon*. The list of titles that, in Bloom's mind, represent the finest in literature. Browsing is not as efficient as searching because of the depth of the database. Browsing begins by choosing a letter of the alphabet, but search results can be strung out alphabetically over many screens.

Articles are long enough to provide substantial information, contain hot-linked cross-references as well as linked related information and bibliographies. Citation information is suggested, and students can save, e-mail, or print information. Searching produces long result lists, nicely organized with folder tabs for focusing. Biographies, overviews and synopses, analyses and criticism, topics and themes are choices, or one can select to see all entries. Entries can be biography, character sketches, titles of works, or criticism and analysis. Students can keep track of their saved files and later look at the full text or delete any or all of the items.

There are a lot of duplicated entries, but this can be explained by the number of Facts on File sources that naturally deal with the same works and authors—and to their credit, the same text is not used in different titles. Each entry provides a slightly different set of facts and opinions. The Bloom critical essays are longer, more difficult to understand, and often ironic, sarcastic, and snide. This makes for interesting and proactive reading; however, it is not easy for secondary students to interpret the difference in tone of the search results. In the hands of an excellent teacher the two very different types of entries could provide a context for the style of literature and its meaning. An exceptional student would see immediately something interesting going on here. A perceptive library media specialist could help students understand that half of this database is factual and half is critical. But, unfortunately, typical students will do typical searches and paste the usual sentences into their repots, without thinking about what they are reading. Databases created from merged product lines present serious problems of retrieval and/or purpose. My advice is to look very carefully at such hybrid creations.—**Barbara Ripp Safford**

Dictionaries and Encyclopedias

C, S

350.   Cook, James Wyatt. **Encyclopedia of Ancient Literature.** New York, Facts on File, 2008. 716p. index. (Facts on File Library of World Literature). $70.00. ISBN 13: 978-0-8160-6475-5.

Written by an author of several books on world authors, the *Encyclopedia of Ancient Literature* features more than 500 entries covering the literary works, writers, and concepts of the ancient world, from the beginnings to approximately 500 C. E. The title covers authors and works from ancient Greece and Rome to China, Egypt, Japan, India, Persia, Babylonia, the Hebrew world, and more. This easy-to-read and comprehend title is designed for high school and upper-level college students needing an overview of this period of literature. Entries include writer (e.g., Aesop, Aristotle, Homer, Euclid, Zoroaster), famous works (e.g., *Aeneid*, the *Iliad*, the Hebrew Bible, the *Odyssey*, the *Ramayana*), and literary terms (e.g., epic, Rosetta Stone). Supplementary materials include an insightful introduction by the author, a list of writers by language of composition, a timeline of the authors' lives, a four-page selected bibliography, and an index.

This work will serve as a great starting-off point for high school and undergraduate students researching specific authors, key titles, or literary terms of ancient literatures. For that reason it is recommended for high school and undergraduate libraries.—**Shannon Graff Hysell**

C, P

351. **The Facts on File Companion to the World Novel: 1900 to the Present.** By Michael D. Sollars. New York, Facts on File, 2008. 2v. index. (Facts on File Library of World Literature). $126.00/set. ISBN 13: 978-0-8160-6233-1.

This attractive two-volume set is part of the Facts on File Library of World Literature series, which includes volume on the American novel, French novel, British novel, and British short story. This set contains about 600 entries, approximately 260 are on individual authors and the remainder on important novels. For example, there is an article on Franz Kafka and four separate entries for *Amerika*, *The Castle*, *The Metamorphosis*, and *The Trial*. Each article is signed. The editor, Michael D. Sellars, an associate professor of English at Texas Southern University, has assembled an impressive group of about 200 contributors whose names are listed with academic affiliations (but no indication of specific articles written) in a separate appendix. To be included for coverage, an author must have worldwide importance and have written during the twentieth century in a language other than English. There are a few exceptions to the latter. For example, the African writer Chinua Achebe and Nabokov's *Lolita* are discussed, but generally this criterion is maintained with the result that, for example, such eminent India writers as Anita Desai and R. K. Narayan are excluded (Tagore is the only Indian writer included). Each entry is about two double-columned pages in length. Again, there are exceptions, usually related to the importance of the writer (e.g., Gunter Grass is given eight pages). Although biographical material or plot summaries are included in entries, there is a concentration on interpretive material like influences, stylistic matters, unique contribution, and significance. Greatest coverage is given to writers from Europe (Germany, France, and Italy number about 25 each) and there is a good balance between writers from the beginning of the century (e.g., Proust, Pirandello, Gide) and those writing today (e.g., Eco, Haruki Murakami, Orhan Pamuk). Material is up to date (e.g., Pamuk's 2006 Nobel Prize is noted) and there are brief bibliographies for each entry. Most are English-language books, although there are some foreign-language materials and periodical articles also included. The titles tend toward the scholarly in content. Cross-referencing could be improved; for example, within articles a title in capitals indicates a separate article, but even though the title may appear many times in the entry, it is capitalized only once. The use of standard *see also* references would have helped. The book ends with a fine 15-page general bibliography and an author, title, and subject index. This is a valuable book that contains good material on many standard as well as obscure writers. The work is highly recommended for public and college libraries.—**John T. Gillespie**

C, P, S

352. **Holocaust Literature.** John K. Roth, ed. Hackensack, N.J., Salem Press, 2008. 2v. illus. index. $120.00/set. ISBN 13: 978-1-58765-375-9.

Beginning with the cover artwork of a narrow corridor surrounded by barbed wire in a concentration camp, this two-volume set introduces distinctive and provocative perspectives on the Holocaust. Edited by Holocaust scholar John Roth, the set contains over 100 reviews of notable fiction and nonfiction works that portray the Holocaust and its aftermath. The words of the poets, dramatists, novelists, historians, and first-hand witnesses whose works are reviewed in these volumes keep the memory of the Holocaust alive, and this living memory is also the purpose of *Holocaust Literature*. Through introducing multifaceted perspectives on the genocide of the Holocaust, this set is intended to give readers with a sense of responsibility to remember and to counter genocide wherever it occurs in the world.

To accomplish this purpose, each review begins with an informative abstract and contains a summary and critical analysis of the reviewed work's themes and significance. Entries range in length from three to five pages and include a selected bibliography. Their scope is comprehensive, including works from the *Diary of a Young Girl* (1947) to *Europe Central* (2005). Although all entries are written in concise and inviting prose, some of the entries do not seem to follow a clear pattern of organization. They are arranged alphabetically by title for easy access, and are indexed by author, title, and genre, although not by principal characters. Extensive bibliographies of both print and Web sources conclude the second volume, making this set an ideal choice both for teachers and for beginning and advanced students of the Holocaust.
—**Helen Margaret Bernard**

C

353.   **Oxford Dictionary of Literary Terms.** 3d ed. By Chris Baldick. New York, Oxford University Press, 2008. 361p. $29.95. ISBN 13: 978-0-19-923891-0.

From *abjection* (an explanation of the appeal of horror stories) to *zeugma* (a form of word relationships in one sentence), this book presents in one alphabetic list 1,200 literary terms whose definitions are usually understandable by the average reader but sometimes require a literary background for comprehension. The book, which is a small attractive format with good legible type, is a complete reworking of the *Concise Oxford Dictionary of Literary Terms* (Oxford University Press, 2001). The writer and editor of this volume is Chris Baldick, a University of London professor, who has been involved with other Oxford University Press publications. Entries average 10 to 12 lines in length and deal with such subjects as literary movements (e.g., Romanticism), literary forms (e.g., sonnet), literary terms (e.g., rhyme), genres (e.g., domestic tragedy), and schools of literary theory (e.g., Structuralism). The material is up to date with entries for subjects like Post-structuralism and chick lit. There are also about 10 special articles of about 2 pages each, dealing with such broad topics as detective stories, feminist criticism, metre (meter), and Post-modernism. After most definitions, there are usually examples of usage and sometimes one or two references to books for further information. The cross-referencing is excellent. A *see* reference is indicated within the entry by the use of an asterisk in front of a term for which there is a separate entry. As well, there is a generous use of *see also* references at the end of entries. Forty-five of the entries also have *see web links* indicators, which means additional information is available at the Oxford University Press Website. It was found, however, that several common literary terms were missing. Some examples include foreshadowing, cliff hanger, Robinsonnade, and poet laureate. In spite of this weakness, this is fine all-purpose dictionary for medium to large public and academic libraries. Its two chief competitors are *The Penguin Dictionary of Literary Terms and Literary Theory* (Penguin, 2000) , which contains 2,000 terms or 800 more than the Oxford dictionary, and the *NTC Dictionary of Literary Terms* (McGraw-Hill, 1991), which defines only 600.—**John T. Gillespie**

Handbooks and Yearbooks

C, P

354.   **The Victorian Literature Handbook.** Alexandra Warwick and Martin Willis, eds. New York, Continuum Publishing, 2008. 258p. index. $120.00; $29.95pa. ISBN 13: 978-0-826-49576-1; 978-0-826-49577-8pa.

The Victorian Literature Handbook is one of a series of volumes on British and American literature and culture. The introduction emphasizes the need for flexibility in defining Victorianism as it transcends chronology. The three-columned timeline, divided into Literary, Historical, and Cultural, begins in 1830 with Tennyson and the ascension to the throne of William IV and ends in 1901 with the death of Queen Victoria.

The main text begins with an overview of historical events with cross-references to appropriate succeeding chapters. Nineteen writers, from Matthew Arnold to Oscar Wilde, are alphabetically listed with dates and a brief analysis of their major works, followed by a list and discussion of genres and literary movements. Case studies for five key texts—*Jane Eyre, In Memorium, Bleak House, Middlemarch,* and *The Importance of Being Earnest*—with suggestions for further readings, are followed by case studies of six important critical texts on general aspects of Victorian literature. Key concepts and topics are then discussed presented alphabetically from Childhood to Sexuality.

The volume is especially useful for its discussion of canonical changes and differences in critical approach since 1950 with less emphasis on morals, and more on the interconnectedness with other fields, such as media, feminism, poststructuralism, politics, class, psychology, and visual arts. Drama and shorter works marginalized in the past are replacing the longer novels. Fifteen pages of works for further reading are listed by topic.

Teachers will find the appendix especially interesting for its survey of Victorian literature curricula in 50 British and American universities revealing current pedagogical trends and ending with a helpful list of Websites. The handbook is an indispensable modern guide for both students and teachers of Victorian literature.—**Charlotte Lindgren**

CHILDREN'S AND YOUNG ADULT LITERATURE

Bibliography

P, S

355.   Barr, Catherine, and John T. Gillespie. **Best Books for Children: Preschool Through Grade 8. Supplement to the 8th edition.** Westport, Conn., Libraries Unlimited/Greenwood Publishing Group, 2007. 445p. index. (Children's and Young Adult Literature Reference Series). $40.00. ISBN 13: 978-1-59158-574-9.

A supplement to the well-written 8th edition of *Best Books for Children: Preschool Through Grade 8* (see ARBA 2007, entry 886), this work continues the useful annotated bibliography of works well subdivided into eight major categories and then further, with strong multicultural coverage. After a clearly labeled table of contents Barr and Gillespie include a listing of major subjects, or the first subdivision under the eight main categories, arranged alphabetically and identified by both their starting page and the entries encompassing the topic. Each entry is identified by a consecutive number and a full bibliographic citation, including price, a brief summary, and selected book reviews. Arranged alphabetically by author's last name within each subtopic, the entries also indicate the reading level of the item. The work ends with an author/illustrator index, a title index, and a subject/grade level index. Useful for any librarian servicing children in grades kindergarten to 8, the work assists in readers' advisory for the student and in suggesting works for teachers or parents to use with children on any topic or aspect. A definite need for anyone working with the intended population, this work will help in advising others and in collection development, along with aligning literature with the curriculum.—**Sara Marcus**

P, S

356.   Barstow, Barbara, Judith Riggle, and Leslie Molnar. **Beyond Picture Books: Subject Access to Best Books for Beginning Readers.** 3d ed. Westport, Conn., Libraries Unlimited/Greenwood Publishing Group, 2008. 645p. index. $75.00. ISBN 13: 978-1-59158-545-9.

Beyond Picture Books presents access to picture books and beyond for the beginning readers via a variety of formats. At the start of the work is a list of best authors, followed by a comprehensive subject index to books annotated in this work. After the list of 3,762 annotations, organized by author, the work then presents a title index, an illustrator index, a readability index organized by category of difficulty for beginning readers as determined by the authors of the work, and a series index. Including both fiction and nonfiction titles, this volume will assist in collection development and readers' advisory for children in grades three and under. The numbering of entries so as to ease locating via the index is useful, as is the inclusion of subjects, genre, and reading levels within each annotation. The subject index includes *see* references, and refers to works by author, then title, then entry number in the annotated bibliography. A lack of guidewords at the top of the pages can hinder the use of the work, as can the poor binding, which breaks easily and will not stand up to the constant use this work surely will invite. Teachers, librarians, and parents will all appreciate the vast knowledge Barstow, Riggle, and Molnar have presented regarding what they have deemed to be the best books for beginning readers.—**Sara Marcus**

P, S

357.   East, Kathy, and Rebecca L. Thomas. **Across Cultures: A Guide to Multicultural Literature for Children.** Westport, Conn., Libraries Unlimited/Greenwood Publishing Group, 2007. 342p. index. (Children's and Young Adult Literature Reference). $55.00. ISBN 13: 978-1-59158-336-3.

Arranged in thematic groups, this volume is designed to link peoples, themes, and issues. The authors have brought together more than 400 recently published fiction and nonfiction multicultural resources for grades K-6. It will help teachers and librarians easily combine multicultural studies into their literacy programs and curriculum. Some of the topics included are: Family and Friends, Traditions, Exploring the Past in Diverse Communities, and Identity and Self Image. Each entry includes a bibliography, annotation, and practical advice on how to use the book for teaching young students about their world through projects and activities. Useful features are the suggested reading levels given for each title and the list of titles that have been given literary awards. This title could easily be used in public and school libraries as a tool for collection development, library programming, and classroom use. [R: SLJ, Oct 07, p. 191]—**Lucy Duhon**

P, S

358.   Gillespie, John T. **Historical Fiction for Young Readers (Grades 4-8): An Introduction.** Westport, Conn., Libraries Unlimited/Greenwood Publishing Group, 2008. 489p. index. (Children's and Young Adult Literature Reference). $60.00. ISBN 13: 978-1-59158-621-0.

John T. Gillespie is probably well known to librarians and school media specialists who buy books. The Library of Congress lists 47 book titles that he either authored or co-authored in its catalog; 44 of them deal with choosing young adult books to acquire. The first three chapters of *Historical Fiction for Young Readers* prepare the librarian to use the five following chapters. Chapter 1 lays out criteria for judging fiction, with an emphasis on novels for young readers. It also explains how judging historical fiction differs from judging regular fiction. Chapter 2, the longest of these three, is entitled "A Brief History of Historical Fiction for Young Readers in English." Beginning in the fifteenth century, it goes up until the early twenty first century. It is well researched and reads very well. Chapter 3 lists nine ways to interest young readers in reading. Chapters 4 through 8 each deal with a continent of the globe; however, Australia is folded into "Asia and Oceania," South America is combined with Canada into "Latin America and Canada," and Antarctica is not covered. Chapters 4 and 8, Europe and the United States respectively, are further subdivided by historic periods. Each chapter or section highlights several books giving publication information and cost for the highlighted title, followed by an introduction that covers the life of the author, followed by a historical background of the novel, and a list of the story's principal characters. The principal characters are followed by a plot synopsis, and passages for booktalking. The section on the highlighted book ends with themes and subjects. Each geographic section concludes with an annotated list of additional readings. The book has both a title and a subject index. This book can easily be used by librarians to work with history teachers and is strongly recommended for librarians who purchase historical fiction.—**Scott Alan Sheidlower**

P, S

359.   Lima, Carolyn W., and Rebecca L. Thomas. **A to Zoo: Subject Access to Children's Picture Books. Supplement to the 7th edition.** Westport, Conn., Libraries Unlimited/Greenwood Publishing Group, 2008. 191p. index. (Children's and Young Adult Literature Reference). $45.00. ISBN 13: 978-1-59158-672-2.

In response to request for more frequent editions of this essential title in children's reference, the publisher has decided to add a supplement to the 7th edition (see ARBA 2007, entry 897) approximately two years before the next full edition is expected, cutting in half the waiting time for an update. This supplement lists 2,451 titles under 769 subjects. The subject headings are drawn from the 1,350 subject headings used in the 7th edition, and the arrangement in this volume is the same as in the original. The familiar list of subjects, subject guide (which lists authors and titles only), the bibliographic guide (arranged by author, and including title, illustrator, publisher, ISBN, and subjects), title index, and illustrator index make using this volume in conjunction with the original quite easy. The introduction on the "Genesis of the English Language Picture Book" included in the 7th edition was not reprinted in this volume. School, public, and academic librarians who use *A to Zoo* regularly will consider this an essential purchase. Those who do not already own the 7th will want to buy it as well as this supplement.—**Rosanne M. Cordell**

P, S

360.   **The Newbery and Caldecott Awards: A Guide to the Medal and Honor Books.** 2008 ed. By the Association for Library Service to Children. Chicago, American Library Association, 2008. 192p. index. $19.00pa.; $17.10pa. (ALA members). ISBN 13: 978-0-8389-3574-3.

The Newbery and Caldecott Awards: A Guide to the Medal and Honor Books has been an annual publication from the Association for Library Service to Children since 1991. Each edition contains an ever-expanding collection of chronological book entries. Every entry contains the year, title, author, illustrator (if applicable), publisher, and a summary of the book. Black-and-white reproductions of the book jackets for the current medal winners are included, as well as photographs of the current Newbery author and Caldecott illustrator.

In addition to the book entries, each edition contains title and author/illustrator indexes as well as an updated version of Christine Berhmann's essay, "The Media Used in Caldecott Picture Books: Notes Toward a Definitive List." Berhmann includes a chronological list of Caldecott winners and the media used in the illustrations. She also provides a list of definitions of art terms.

Beginning in 1992 all editions contain the essay, "Newbery and Caldecott Awards: Authorization and Terms," by Bette Peltola. An added value each year is a new essay on a topic dealing with the Newbery or Caldecott awards. The newest essay is Mary Erbach's "The Art of the Picture Book." This annual publication is useful for public libraries, school libraries, and academic libraries with education or children's literature training programs.—**Cynthia Crosser**

P, S

361.   Schon, Isabel. **Recommended Books in Spanish for Children and Young Adults 2004-2008.** Lanham, Md., Scarecrow, 2009. 414p. index. $55.00. ISBN 13: 978-0-8108-6386-6.

Expert Isabel Schon, a founder of the Center for the Study of Books in Spanish for Children and Adolescents at California State University, has produced an excellent book for the public and school librarian with her guide to more than 1,200 works of reference, fiction, and nonfiction for Latino readers. Her criteria for inclusion are quality of art and writing, presentation and appeal, and support of school curriculum. Arrangement follows Dewey in summarizing books and series at varied reading levels from publishers in Argentina, Mexico, Spain, Venezuela, and the United States. For teachers and librarians, she identifies these as the best publishers of Spanish books for children and youth.

The table of contents and a straightforward 2-page introduction precede a 413-page text set up in familiar format: type of work in bold typeface, author or title in italics, translator, place of publication, date, number of pages, ISBN, paper or hardback, price, and reading level. For the non-Spanish reader, she translates each title. The text concludes with an appendix listing dealers of books in Spanish for children and young adults as well as author, title, and subject indexes.

Schon knows how to write book summaries. Without wasting words, she moves competently into the particulars of each story. Schon highlights types of illustrations, plots, and maps and comments on the quality of translation as well as themes that will benefit and entertain readers. Her reference guide, offered at a reasonable price, will make a difference between shelves with no books to serve Latino children and a long-standing relationship with young readers who deserve the best of books.—**Mary Ellen Snodgrass**

P, S

362.   Schwedt, Rachel E., and Janice A. DeLong. **Core Collection for Children and Young Adults.** Lanham, Md., Scarecrow, 2008. 207p. index. $50.00pa. ISBN 13: 978-0-8108-6115-2.

In this companion volume to *Core Collection for Small Libraries: An Annotated Bibliography of Books for Children and Young Adults* (2007), editors Rachel E. Schwedt and Janice A. DeLong, both of Liberty University, provide annotations of carefully selected children's and young adult books. Following the selection principles of the first volume, the books were chosen for annotation based on their standing as classics or their adherence to the following criteria: "positive character themes," wide appeal, quality, and reception of an award. Within these criteria, the scope of books reviewed is impressive: over 350 titles are included, most copyrighted since 1994, and none duplicating annotations in the first volume. The organization of the book is straightforward, allowing readers to access information quickly. Each chapter begins with a short description and evaluation of a particular genre, such as fantasy or picture books. A list of annotated books follows, organized alphabetically by the author's last name. Each annotation includes the target grade level of the book, a succinct plot summary, a listing of positive themes found in the work, and cross-references. Four indexes allow for targeted searching of title/author/illustrator/translator, book awards, character themes, and related subjects. Although a master index and grade level index would also have been helpful in locating a particular book or group of books, the indexes included are more than adequate for an efficient search. Due to its focused selection of positive and value-centered books, effective organization, general readability, and competitive pricing, *Core Collection for Children and Young Adults* will be a valuable resource for librarians, parents, reading group leaders, and anyone interested in children's and young adult literature.—**Helen Margaret Bernard**

Bio-bibliography

P, S

363.   **Tenth Book of Junior Authors and Illustrators.** Connie C. Rockman, ed. Bronx, N.Y., H. W. Wilson, 2008. 803p. illus. index. $120.00. ISBN 13: 978-0-8242-1066-3.

The growth of children's book publishing in recent decades has required an equally proliferate stream of authoritative, evaluative tools. Fewer offer insight into the souls of the creators. This 10th edition of the junior author book series, begun in 1934, serves such a purpose. Expanded and revised several editions ago, it is now among the only concise biographical dictionaries to offer personal views into the best of both authors and illustrators of English-language children's nonfiction and fiction—poetry, picture books, and novels alike.

Clear in its scope and closely following the layout of its predecessors, this edition comprises 240 entries gathered from awards lists and confirmed by a voting process. Each entry consists of an autobiographical essay (complete with photograph and autograph), followed by a biography, a representative list of works, and in some cases, further suggested reading. Rockman now includes a representative jacket illustration for every entry. Although the focus is on new contributors, she continues her practice of updating previously profiled distinguished creators (now neatly asterisked in the table of contents, and totaling no more than 10 percent of the entries) to include new awards of biographical updates; therefore, long-standing favorites such as Dr. Seuss and Jane Yolen share pages with relative newcomers Robert Casilla and Grace Lin. A descriptive appendix lists the awards and honors cited. Unlike earlier editions, this volume features a cover designed by one of the illustrators represented (a practice also begun by Rockman). The handy index adds value to the entire series by referencing previously profiled authors and illustrators to their respective editions.

Although there are numerous reference resources with similar aims, such as *Something About the Author, Autobiography Series* from Gale and most notably Lee Bennett Hopkins' 1995 compilation, *Pauses: Autobiographical Reflections of 101 Creators of Children's Books*, few can rival this book for both its comprehensive coverage and its compact, attractively designed format.

This series should continue to prove practical for teachers, parents, and children's librarians; but more importantly, since it offers a view into the creators themselves it also promises to be illuminating for young people and aspiring writers. It is now also available in a cumulative electronic edition.—**Lucy Duhon**

DRAMA

C, S

364.   Burt, Daniel S. **The Drama 100: A Ranking of the Greatest Plays of All Time.** New York, Facts on File, 2008. 612p. index. (Facts on File Library of World Literature). $40.50. ISBN 13: 978-0-8160-6073-3.

With this book, Daniel S. Burt, a teacher of literature at Wesleyan University, offers his third collection of what he considers to be a ranking of the 100 best examples of a featured literary subject. As in his earlier works, *The Literary 100: A Ranking of the Most Influential Novelists, Playwrights, and Poets of All Time* (see ARBA 2002, entry 1050) and *The Novel 100: A Ranking of the Greatest Novels of All Time* (see ARBA 2004, entry 1021), each of Burt's essays inter-twine criticism, biography of the author, historical context, cultural significance, and summary of the featured work to prove why this play was selected for inclusion on his list. Beginning with *King Lear* (number one) and ending with *Peter Pan* (number 100), Burt travels back and forth in time, from 485 B.C.E. to 1836 to 1991/1992 (where his time line concludes). However, with a few exceptions, his 100 greatest plays remain fixed in the Western Hemisphere. That said, in his introduction, Burt acknowledges that his selections, although researched, are based on one man's critical opinions and notes the educational value of disagreeing with his list. To demonstrate his point, at the end of the book, between the timeline of the ranked plays and the index, Burt provides the reader with an alternative listing of a second 100 (honorable mentions), casualties of his own conflicting opinions. This book would be a welcome addition to any reference collection as an introduction to the societal significance of drama upon Western culture.—**Brian T. Gallagher**

FICTION

General Works

C, P

365.   **Books and Beyond: The Greenwood Encyclopedia of New American Reading.** Kenneth Womack, ed. Westport, Conn., Greenwood Press, 2008. 4v. index. $399.95/set. ISBN 13: 978-0-313-33738-3.

In 74 lengthy, alphabetically arranged articles (about 15 pages each), this 4-volume set presents an overview of American literature and reading patterns with emphasis on developments from roughly 1980 to the present (usually 2007). As well as fiction, there is coverage on general nonfiction, biography, poetry, plays, and graphic representations like comic books and graphic novels. There are separate entries for the major literary genres (e.g., science fiction, adventure stories) and their subdivisions (e.g., time travel fiction, spy fiction) as well as articles involving important ethnic groups like Jewish American literature, current trends and fads like Chick Lit, EcoPoetry, and Flash Fiction (short-short stories), plus multimedia topics like Film Adaptations of Books, and separate entries for Children's Literature and Young Adult Literature.

Although there are no articles on electronic books and publishing, the scope and range of topics covered is otherwise amazing. All entries are signed and the contributors are listed (mostly academics), with credentials, in a separate section of volume 4. This includes the editor-in-chief who is an English professor at Penn State's Altoona College. The entries are divided into six sections: Definition, where the author defines the general nature of the topic and often describes subdivisions and related areas; History, where there is a brief history that describes the evolution of the genre with emphasis on ground-breaking development and important contributors; Trends and Themes, where current developments concerning content, attitudes, and subjects are outlined with examples for important contemporary writers; Contexts and Issues, with present-day concerns, spin-offs into other media, and exterior influences are discussed, again with numerous examples; Reception, where the size, nature, tastes, and reactions of readers of the genre are described; and Selected Authors. In this last part, currently important and/or immerging authors and their works are described. This coverage varies widely from entry to entry. For example, in the article on Contemporary Mainstream American Fiction, almost 40 writers are highlighted, whereas in Young Adult Literature there are only eight. (A separate listing arranged by genre of the authors covered in these sections can be found in volume 4 in the section Contemporary Authors by Genre section.) Each entry concludes with two bibliographies: the first is a general one (usually of works described in the article) and the second consists of additional listings of books and articles on the subject. Again the length, depth, and usefulness of these bibliographies vary considerably from article to article. The set concludes with a four-page listing of "Suggestions for Further Reading" and a combined index that includes, in its almost 100 pages, references to the most important authors and subjects (and a few titles) cited in the articles.

Despite the differences in coverage throughout this work, this set is unique in its scope and treatment of the contemporary American literary scene and will prove to be an invaluable supplement to standard references sources on American literature. It is highly recommended for academic and large public libraries. [R: LJ, Jan 09, p. 122]—**John T. Gillespie**

P

366.   **What Do I Read Next? A Reader's Guide to Current Genre Fiction. Volume 2.** 2008 ed. Farmington Hills, Mich., Gale Group, 2009. 621p. index. $200.00. ISBN 13: 978-1-4144-0019-8. ISSN 1052-2212.

Designed to help readers find fiction books, *What Do I Read Next?* is a useful and focused resource. Nine genres are covered, from fantasy to romance to inspirational fiction, just to name a few. An overview of each genre is provided, followed by a listing of the titles in that genre for the year. The indexes cover series, time periods, geography, genres, subjects, character names, character descriptions, authors, and title, allowing users to identify a book, find titles on a particular subject (e.g., law) or with certain characters (e.g., mountain man or caterer), or locate titles within a series. A key to genre terms is provided, defining what is meant by words such as anthology, historical/Tudor Period, or sword and sorcery. This title will be useful to the general reader, students, and researchers.—**Denise A. Garofalo**

Crime and Mystery

P

367.   **Critical Survey of Mystery & Detective Fiction.** rev. ed. Carl Rollyson, ed. Hackensack, N.J., Salem Press, 2008. 5v. illus. index. $399.00/set. ISBN 13: 978-1-58765-397-1.

Critical Survey of Mystery & Detection Fiction joins Salem's library of fully revised and expanded critical surveys. Accordingly to the editor, several phenomena generated this revised edition. First, the genre has become increasingly important and is receiving more attention in classrooms. Second, the domination by British, American, and European authors has weakened. Third, mystery fiction has been receiving increased recognition for its social observations. Consequently, the editor and the approximately 250 contributors of this edition made an effort to reflect these changes and to achieve greater ethnic and international diversity.

The first 4 volumes are devoted to articles on 393 authors. Each of these ranges in length from approximately 2,300 to 3,200 words. They contain: biographical information; pseudonyms; plot types; the names of principal series and principal series characters; the author's contribution to the field; analysis; principal mystery and detective fiction titles; other major works; and a bibliography. The text, which is presented in a particularly easy-to-read font, is supplemented with black-and-white photographs and illustrations. The fifth volume contains essays on past and present mystery and detective fiction, mystery fiction around the world, subgenres of mystery fiction, types of detectives, and other media. The section titled "Resources" includes a bibliography, a guide to online resources, genre terms and techniques, crime fiction jargon, major awards, a timeline, and a chronological list of authors. The volume concludes with four indexes; authors by geographical location, authors by category, character, and subject. This is an outstanding reference source that should be purchased by all but the smallest libraries.—**January Adams**

Science Fiction and Fantasy

P

368.　Herald, Diana Tixier, and Bonnie Kunzel. **Fluent in Fantasy: The Next Generation.** Westport, Conn., Libraries Unlimited/Greenwood Publishing Group, 2008. 312p. index. (Genreflecting Advisory Series). $52.00. ISBN 13: 978-1-59158-198-7.

An annotated bibliography of fantasy works from the nineteenth century to today, with a large focus on works from the past decade, Herald and Kunzel present a well-organized list of works in the fantasy genre geared toward adults. Grouping titles according to shared subgenres and themes, *Fluent in Fantasy* not only provides full bibliographic citations and annotations, but also identifies books as: award-winning, if a book has been made into a film or if the book has been made into a miniseries (particularly appealing to teenagers), and if a book is available as an audiobook. Sorted into 13 main genres, the work also includes a listing of resources and a list of award-winning and humorous fantasy works. Three indexes—author, title, and subject—enable the reader to quickly locate their desired work, while a discussion at the beginning of each section informs the novice about the subgenre of fantasy being addressed. The entries are arranged by author then series (if applicable), rather than alphabetic order. Individual entries include author, title, ISBN, year of publication, and an annotation, but no publisher is given, making this work hard for use as a collection development tool. Useful for any adult librarian who wishes to know more about fantasy works, or for the researcher who desires additional information on the genre of fantasy, this work continues the great work in the Genreflecting Advisory Series from this publisher.—**Chris Tuthill**

Short Stories

P

369.　**Short Story Writers.** rev. ed. Charles E. May, ed. Hackensack, N.J., Salem Press, 2008. 3v. index. (Magill's Choice). $217.00/set. ISBN 13: 978-1-58765-389-6.

A revision of the 1997 edition (see ARBA 98, entry 1123), Salem Press' *Short Story Writers* (published under Magill's Choice), this source still, as the previous reviewer stated, offers the users of any school or public or academic library a reference source that acts as a gateway to further research of their subject. This edition boasts an additional 44 authors, 21 of whom are female practitioners of the short story form. Like the previous edition, this three-volume set features writers who, according to the publisher, represent the most popular practitioners of the short story craft in the nineteenth and twentieth centuries, with a focus on writers from the United States (87 of the 146 authors). The organization remains the same, providing the reader with an alphabetic listing of the authors (by last name) and continuous pagination. Following a factual listing of biographical information and principle short fiction, each entry offers an essay that examines other literary forms (such as novels or poetry), achievements (during their lifetimes, after their deaths), and a biography. An analysis of the author's work is the fourth element of the essay's template. The analysis is twofold: the first part serves as an introduction to the selected stories in the second part, presenting the reader with a brief overview of the writer's background and the themes used in his/her work. The critiques that follow the first part illustrate how the writers made use of their own background and how, with each story, the themes and styles they worked with as they practiced their craft became their trademark, their signature. The critiques of "Bartleby the Scrivener" and "The Fiddler," for example, follow the analysis of Herman Melville's financial motivations and artistic strategy when he began writing short stories such as featured examples. The author of the entry weaves a narrative that directs the reader to a glimpse of the biographical and historical information, stressing the importance of examining those factors when interpreting an author's intent. The analysis, demonstrates to the reader what should be sought for in short story to pay special heed to what is not said in the narration. Each entry, like Melville's, concludes with a listing of other major works and an annotated bibliography. Volume 3 contains a glossary of literary terms and techniques, a timeline of the evolution of the short story (beginning with Giovanni Baccaccio and Geoffrey Chaucer), and an index.—**Brian T. Gallagher**

NATIONAL LITERATURE

American Literature

General Works

Bio-bibliography

C, P

370.   **American Ethnic Writers.** Hackensack, N.J., Salem Press, 2008. 3v. illus. index. $217.00/set. ISBN 13: 978-1-58765-462-6.

The 3-volume set, *American Ethnic Writers*, contains in-depth information on 225 writers, enlightening readers and researchers about their lives and literature. The volumes include a range of work from the African Americans during the time of the Harlem Renaissance through the Asian and Latino contemporary writers of the twenty-first century; many new and familiar authors are revealed within these 1,295 pages. Offerings include authors belonging to African American, Asian American, Jewish American, Hispanic/Latino, and Native American ethnicities and descents.

The volumes present the roster in user-friendly alphabetic order, listing the authors by their best-known names, then other names and pseudonyms (where applicable). Also included is information about their birth and death dates and location (if known). Following each author's name is a quote about the author, a list of principle works, phonetic pronunciation of their name, and a short biography. The most interesting feature of this three-volume set is a selection of essays by academicians and scholars about the better-known, more widely studied works of each author. Some entries are also enhanced with a black-and-white photograph of the author. Naturally, well-known authors such as Martin Luther King, Jr.,

Alan Ginsberg, or Alice Walker appear; but other, lesser-known writers, such as Chinese American, Lee Li-Young, or Cuban American, Virgil Suarez, are introduced within this resource.

Each volume gives the user a list of contents for that volume, a name pronunciation guide, and a complete table of contents covering all three volumes. Volume 3 ends with two appendixes, one a general bibliography and the other a list of electronic resources. Five indexes then follow, listing authors by name, authors by ethnicity, titles by ethnicity, titles by genre, and titles by name.

American Ethnic Writers is an invaluable resource for high school and college students seeking literature by and authoritative material about these American writers.—**Ann Howington**

Dictionaries and Encyclopedias

C, P, S

371. Imbarrato, Susan Clair, and Carol Berkin. **Encyclopedia of American Literature.** rev. ed. New York, Facts on File, 2008. 4v. illus. index. (Facts on File Library of American Literature). $375.00/set. ISBN 13: 978-0-8160-6476-2.

The revised edition of the *Encyclopedia of American Literature* is an immeasurable improvement of an already valuable and recognized reference set. There are now four renamed and more coherently organized volumes rather than three. These include close to 1,000 new entries (Don DeLillo is an obvious choice) and "more than 300 new black-and-white illustrations" powerfully impact each volume: steel engravings, portraits, signatures, photographs, and dust jackets from individual seminal works all serve to punctuate the impact these works of literature had on the world around them in which they originally emerged.

The entries themselves have been intuitively reworked; an example entry contains a sample quotation, indication when a work is cross-referenced in the same volume, an illustration, and a substantial section of "studying" this person, which will be especially valuable for high school and undergraduate readers. Several entries (e.g., Ayn Rand) are revised to be more even-handed, whereas others (e.g., Philip K. Dick) could be expanded on in later editions.

While there are works that are finally added (The Constitution as an example), there are others that, given the expansive inclusivity of the extra volume, might not have been dropped (for example, where is Paine's *Common Sense?*). The editors recognize that the landscape is changing, however, and aver that this present edition is itself "a work in progress."

This four-volume set is necessary for community colleges, institutions supporting undergraduates, and high school libraries. The clarity, additions, and clear annotations make this worth considering even if it would replace the earlier edition. [R: VOYA, June 08, p. 182]—**Stephen J. Shaw**

C, P

372. **Masterplots II: African American Literature.** rev. ed. Tyrone Williams, ed. Hackensack, N.J., Salem Press, 2009. 4v. index. $404.00/set. ISBN 13: 978-1-58765-438-1.

Masterplots II: African American Literature is a four-volume collection that has been revised from the original 1994 publication. The collection covers works from the earliest known colonial writings through the start of the twenty-first century, providing essays about bodies of work and individual works by novelists, playwrights, poets, memoirists, orators, and more. Each entry takes care to include information specific to each piece while maintaining a basic familiar outline. Essays referring to works of fiction include sections discussing its contents, its themes and meanings, and, optionally, one or more of its main characters. Essays referring to works of nonfiction include discussions about its form and content as well as an analysis of the text. All essays include their own annotated bibliography and conclude with a section discussing the critical context of the work, including information about its writing or publication, influences, reception, and place within the canon of literature.

Whereas the original *Masterplots* publication is a 12-volume set covering all aspects of literature, *Masterplots II: African American Literature* is able to expand on the works of African American Literature, providing an in-depth and much more thorough account of the genre. Of the 367 original essays, 101 have been newly added and 20 overviews have been updated. Additionally, two annotated appendixes, a bibliography, a list of electronic resources, and a chronological list of titles have been added. Although the contents list is included in each volume, the other resource lists are only provided in the final volume of the set. By excluding most of the resource lists from the first three volumes, the collection does make navigation amongst the volumes slightly more difficult.

Each essay within this collection includes a surprising amount of both factual and subjective information about a large number of African American works of literature. The essays appear to be well written and understandable by a college-age audience. Because of the great amount of supplemental information presented simultaneously with informative essays, this publication is an exceptional starting point to any research into the genre.—**Tyler Manolovitz**

C, S
373. Samuels, Wilfred D. **Encyclopedia of African-American Literature.** New York, Facts on File, 2007. 626p. index. (Encyclopedia of American Ethnic Literature). $75.00. ISBN 13: 978-0-8160-5073-4.

Facts on File's *Encyclopedia of African-American Literature* covers African American literature from the eighteenth century through the twentieth century. The author has even included some of today's best-selling authors and rap artists. The dictionary includes many biographical entries (e.g., Maya Angelou, James Baldwin, Frederick Douglass, Jamaica Kincaid) as well as entries for critically acclaimed writings and literary terms (e.g., *A Raisin in the Son*, *Beloved*, the civil rights movement, black arts movement). The volume includes more than 500 entries, including fiction and nonfiction writers, poets, critics, and dramatists. The entries are several pages in length; unfortunately, no photographs are provided. This title is written at a level that high school students and undergraduate students will find useful.—**Shannon Graff Hysell**

C, S
374. **Student's Encyclopedia of American Literary Characters.** Matthew J. Bruccoli and Judith S. Baughman, eds. New York, Facts on File, 2008. 4v. index. $340.00/set. ISBN 13: 978-0-8160-6498-4.

This student's encyclopedia, focusing mainly on American classic fiction, presents literature for study and enjoyment in four engaging volumes. The volumes offer an extensive collection of descriptive and educative entries on popular literary characters organized first alphabetically by the author's last name, second by the title of the work, and third by the character. Approximately 900 entries averaging 1,200 words each provide analysis and commentary on characters and their roles. The in-depth coverage was furnished by over 300 contributors.

According to the encyclopedia's introduction, the work intends to distinguish itself from many other literary reference resources in that it delivers knowledge, understanding, and entertainment via the vehicle of one of the most interesting elements of a work of fiction—the character. The characters chosen are readily recognizable. Students will already be familiar with many of the personas, such as Tom Sawyer, Huckleberry Finn, The Wizard of Oz, Tarzan, Brer Rabbit, Hannibal Lecter, Ichabod Crane, Rip Van Winkle, and many more. Furthermore, a perusal through the names and titles in the expanded table of contents in each volume will whet the literary appetite for further discovery. Important to note is that many fictional works presented have also been produced in film, such as *The Talented Mr. Ripley*, *The Color Purple*, *The Accidental Tourist*, *The Godfather*, *The Shipping News*, *Charlotte's Web*, and much more.

Pertinent questions follow each entry and are designed to stimulate discussion in a group or a class. Readers will find helpful character and title indexes at the end of the last volume. Suitable for grades 9 and up, students, teachers, and general readers will find this encyclopedia educational, refreshing, and stimulating.—**Glenda Irene Griffin**

Handbooks and Yearbooks

C

375. Courtney, Angela. **Literary Research and the Era of American Nationalism and Romanticism: Strategies and Sources.** Lanham, Md., Scarecrow, 2008. 251p. index. (Literary Research: Strategies and Sources, no.2). $45.00pa. ISBN 0-8108-6035-X. ISBN 13: 978-0-8108-6035-3.

The basic criteria for any guide to scholarly research include specificity, conciseness, and elucidation of general research principles. Courtney's excellent guide to American literature from the end of the colonial period to the beginning of the Civil War does all this and adds to its usefulness with practical advice about dealing with possible bumps in the road during the research process. While many such studies begin with essential tools, Courtney, aware of the most pressing needs of her readers, starts by explaining the basics of online searching because effectively using the resources described later depends upon understanding the importance of keywords and the creation of Boolean search statements. She goes on to cover the essentials of online catalogs, print and electronic bibliographies, and scholarly journals before dealing with more elusive sources such as period journals and newspapers, manuscripts and archives, and microform and digital collections. While not discouraging the use of Google, Courtney points her readers toward Google Scholar while stressing its limitations. She brings everything together by showing how a researcher might use these techniques and resources to examine Edgar Allan Poe's reputation during the years immediately following his death. Courtney concludes with an annotated appendix of resources in linguistics, music, philosophy, and other related disciplines; a short bibliography of important literary research guides; and a detailed index.—**Michael Adams**

British Literature

General Works

Biography

C, P

376. **Arthurian Writers: A Biographical Encyclopedia.** Laura Cooner Lambdin and Robert Thomas Lambdin, eds. Westport, Conn., Greenwood Press, 2008. 401p. index. $95.00. ISBN 13: 978-0-313-34682-8.

Arthur, his queen Guinevere, Merlin, and the Knights of the Round Table have been enduring themes throughout Western literature since Nennuis first made reference to Arthur in a ninth-century text. Carol Cooner Lambdin and Robert Thomas Lambdin, authors and editors of *A Companion to Old and Middle English Literature* (see ARBA 2003, entry 1074), *Encyclopedia of Medieval Literature* (see ARBA 2001, entry 1068), *Chaucer's Pilgrims: An Historical Guide to the Pilgrims in The Canterbury Tales* (see ARBA 97, entry 989), have compiled *Arthurian Writers: A Biographical Encyclopedia*, an excellent collection of essays regarding writers who have employed Arthur or associated individuals and related themes in their own literary works.

Thirty-four writers, beginning with Gildas (c. 490-570) to the contemporary Canadian writer, Margaret Atwood, have been profiled by scholars. Boccaccio, Chaucer, Dryden, Twain, C. S. Lewis, Steinbeck, and Mary Stewart are among the expected writers. Also worth noting are the early writers who laid the groundwork for Arthur, such as Wace, Geoffrey of Monmouth, and Chrétien de Troyes. Each chapter contains a respectable biography, and good coverage of the writer's entire literary opus, particularly addressing those works in which Arthur and others are present. A comprehensive listing of each writer's primary works and exemplary secondary sources are also included in each chapter. Collections, editions, papers, play productions, translations, papers, and other works are listed when appropriate. The chapter titled "Arthurian Art" provides an excellent overview of the artistic representation of Arthur and related themes found in sculpture, stained glass, decorative boxes, metalwork, tiles, wall hangings, illuminated manuscripts, and much more. An index and a list of selected readings are included.

The question of Arthur's historical authenticity may never be answered. This legendary figure, the lure of Camelot, and its royal residents continue to fascinate Western culture. The Lambdins' latest exceptional volume should be in academic and public libraries.—**Alice Crosetto**

Handbooks and Yearbooks

C, P, S

377.   **Oxford Concise Companion to English Literature.** 3d ed. By Margaret Drabble and Jenny Stringer. New York, Oxford University Press, 2007. 804p. $18.95pa. ISBN 13: 978-0-19-921492-1.

Updated and expanded, this new concise edition is based on the *Oxford Companion to English Literature* (6th rev. ed.; see ARBA 2007, entry 955). More non-British writers have been added, although American writers such as the Alcotts are omitted and only British black writers are discussed in a major essay.

The 796 pages of entries consist of not only English-language literature, which includes the United States, Canada, Australia, New Zealand, the Caribbean, and India, but also Classical, Icelandic, and influential foreign-language authors. Current writers such as J. K. Rawlings and Maggie Gee have been added, but not entries for winners of recent literary awards.

In addition to authors, titles, and major characters, there are definitions of terms from the familiar to the lesser known (e.g., anachrony, galliambic, amphibrach). Societies, literary groups (such as Lake Poets and Transcendentalists), places (such as Drury Lane and National Theatre), and even influential nonliterary figures (such as Capability Brown, Beau Brummel, and William Hogarth) are also included. Expanded two-page essays, printed against a gray background, cover broad topics like spy novels, gothic fiction, and biography. The volume concludes with five lists. The Chronology of Literary Works and Historical Events begins with "The Owl and the Nightingale" (1200) and the Norman Conquest, and ends with McEwans's *Atonement* (2001) and the 2001 terrorist attack on the United States. Prize Winners to 2006 include the Poets Laureate, Nobel Prize for Literature, the Pulitzer Prize for Fiction, and the Man Brooker Prize for Fiction. Beautifully organized, replete with valuable information, and small enough to be easily handled, this inexpensive paperback volume is an ideal reference book.—**Charlotte Lindgren**

African Literature

P, S

378.   Killam, Douglas, and Alicia L. Kerfoot. **Student Encyclopedia of African Literature.** Westport, Conn., Greenwood Press, 2008. 339p. index. $85.00. ISBN 13: 978-0-313-33580-8.

The *Student Encyclopedia of African Literature* is a good starting point for those doing research on African authors, literary works, and related subjects. The authors have put together 598 entries on major writers, works, and subjects in African literature. Some of the subjects include censorship and apartheid, as well as more general categories such as drama and literary criticism. Entries are clear and concise, and will give students a good overview as they begin their studies. There are references at the end of many of the entries as well as a selected bibliography at the end. The book is meant as an introduction to student research, and those interested in more in-depth study will need to consult other sources, such as those in the bibliography, or more advanced resources like the *Encyclopedia of African Literature* from Routledge (see ARBA 2004, entry 1059). This work is recommended for school and public libraries. [R: BL, 1 & 15 June 08, pp. 138-140]—**Chris Tuthill**

Latin American Literature

C, P

379. **The Greenwood Encyclopedia of Latino Literature.** Nicolás Kanellos, ed. Westport, Conn., Greenwood Press, 2008. 3v. illus. index. $299.95/set. ISBN 13: 978-0-313-33970-7.

This three-volume encyclopedia, a project of editor Nicolás Kanellos' Recovering the U.S. Hispanic Literary Heritage, provides basic biographic, bibliographic, and critical information on more than 700 authors and topics written by 60 contributors, although the bulk of the entries are penned completely or jointly by the editor himself, a renowned expert and scholar in the field and author of the title *Hispanic Literature of the United States: A Comprehensive Reference* (see ARBA 2005, entry 1065). The time covered ranges from the earliest colonists (e.g., the seventeenth-century Sor Juana) up to the present day, including authors with forthcoming works. The work uses the terms Latino and Hispanic interchangeably; its broad coverage of authors writing exclusively in English or in Spanish or both reflects the hybrid nature of the genre. Only "creative" writers are included—poets, novelists, playwrights, essayists; pure literary critics are excluded, but occasionally they creep in if they have also contributed to the creative literature, like Gustavo Pérez-Firmat or Ilán Stavans. As usual in a reference work of this type, some users will question the inclusion and exclusion of authors, but the work's main value lies in its emphasis on Anglophone Latinos; those writing in Spanish are more adequately covered elsewhere. Entries also include two or three citations to further reading, and occasionally photographs, although some verge on the antiquated side of quaint. Cross-references to full articles are indicated with an asterisk; actual translated titles appear parenthetically in italics. Although its primary focus is individual authors, the encyclopedia also includes some rather lengthy thematic articles, such as the mini-monograph surveys on the aesthetic concepts of Latino literature and on women writers. An extensive bibliography and valuable index, with page numbers for main entries bolded, conclude the set.

The closest competitor is Salem's *Notable Latino Writers* (see ARBA 2006, entry 1062), with a similar format (e.g., short biographies, pictures), but which is aimed at a less academic audience. A more scholarly alternative is the two-volume *Latino and Latina Writers* (see ARBA 2004, entry 1068), which, although with fewer authors and thematic essays and an Anglophone emphasis, provides longer and more scholarly critical essays of 57 major authors, with a 100 percent overlap here. *The Greenwood Encyclopedia of Latino Literature* will be most useful in public libraries and as a springboard for further study in undergraduate libraries. [R: LJ, Jan 09, pp. 128-130]—**Lawrence Olszewski**

C, P, S

380. Ramirez, Luz Elena. **Encyclopedia of Hispanic-American Literature.** New York, Facts on File, 2008. 430p. index. (Encyclopedia of American Ethnic Literature). $75.00. ISBN 13: 978-0-8160-6084-9.

As used in this volume, the term Hispanic American refers to people of Spanish-speaking cultures who live or have lived in the United States. This definition of residence is somewhat slippery, however; some stays are permanent but others, like Fidel Castro's, were very brief. Although labeled an encyclopedia, entries are relatively short, averaging a page, with bibliographies of key primary and secondary works. The 250 or so entries are evenly split between authors and works, with several articles about themes and movements thrown in. The entries about authors, who flourished from the colonial era (Cabeza de Vaca) to the present, include a biographical sketch and a brief analysis of major works; emphasis is on those of Mexican, Cuban, Dominican, and Puerto Rican descent. The articles about works, which include mostly titles in today's curriculum, provide a plot summary followed by critical highlights. Information is very current; the Castro entry says "former president of Cuba" and several bibliographies include works with 2007 publication dates. Cross-references are effectively and consistently indicated by majuscules. A useful addendum is the bibliography of major works by the writers included. Contributors all hail from mostly U.S. academic institutions, including the editor Luz Elena Ramirez (California State San Bernadino). Its most obvious competitor is the recent *Greenwood Encyclopedia of Latino Literature* (see entry 379); although there is overlap with major writers and a similar focus on creative works, the *Encyclopedia of Hispanic-American Literature* differs in its equal coverage of individual works. This volume is appropriate for public and undergraduate collections, and for high schools with sizeable Latino populations or courses.—**Lawrence Olszewski**

NONFICTION

P, S

381.   Drew, Bernard A. **100 Most Popular Nonfiction Authors: Biographical Sketches and Bibliographies.** Westport, Conn., Libraries Unlimited/Greenwood Publishing Group, 2008. 438p. illus. index. (Popular Authors Series). $65.00. ISBN 13: 978-1-59158-487-2.

100 Most Popular Nonfiction Authors: Biographical Sketches and Bibliographies is the latest volume in a series that includes authors of popular and genre fiction. Just as nonfiction authors are curious about any number of subjects, many readers are eager to know more about their increasingly complex world and the writers who explore it in articles and books.

l00 Most Popular Nonfiction Authors is arranged alphabetically by author with the genre covered by the subject, ranging from Edward Abbey, environment, politics, travel, to Tobias Wolff, memoir. Each article contains a brief biography, works by the author, and a "For More Information" bibliography. A useful comprehensive title/author index follows the listings. Black-and-white portraits of most authors are included.

The reader of *100 Most Popular Nonfiction Authors* will find useful information on researchable subjects and could be surprised to see how many nonfiction writers like Anne Dillard also produce fiction. This volume is easy to use and should be of wide interest and value to students and leisure readers alike. It is highly recommended.—**Kay O. Cornelius**

P

382.   Rainey, David. **Faith Reads: A Selective Guide to Christian Nonfiction.** Westport, Conn., Libraries Unlimited/Greenwood Publishing Group, 2008. 370p. index. $55.00. ISBN 13: 978-1-59158-602-9.

Designed as a reader's guide to Christian nonfiction books, this volume provides access to a bibliography of 646 annotated titles and over 1,000 additional books. The author seeks to satisfy two audiences: the librarian and the general reader. For the librarian, especially in a public library, this work can be used as a readers' advisory tool to suggest relevant books. The general reader can also use the work as a guide for exploration and discovery of different topics from a Christian point of view. All the books are either by Christian authors or are published by Christian publishers or imprints. Protestant and evangelical publishers and authors predominate although some Catholic and a few Eastern Orthodox can be found. A few older, classic works are included, but the main emphasis is on books that have been first published over the last 20 to 30 years and are still in print. Although some books are academic or scholarly, most have been written for the general reader, such as those using public or church libraries. Arrangement is by broad topic such as life stories, Christian self-help, business, science, and bible and theology. Complete author/title and subject indexes provide alternate access to the contents. Although some academic libraries that collect broadly in the areas of modern Christian culture may wish to add this work, it is most appropriate for public, church, and Protestant seminary libraries.—**Gregory A. Crawford**

POETRY

Dictionaries and Encyclopedias

C, S

383.   **The Facts on File Companion to British Poetry Before 1600.** By Michelle M. Sauer. New York, Facts on File, 2008. 514p. index. (Facts on File Library of World Literature). $85.00. ISBN 13: 978-0-8160-6360-4.

C, S

384.   **The Facts on File Companion to British Poetry: 17th and 18th Centuries.** By Virginia Brackett. New York, Facts on File, 2008. 488p. index. (Facts on File Library of World Literature). $75.00. ISBN 13: 978-0-8160-6328-4.

C, S

385.   **The Facts on File Companion to British Poetry: 1900 to the Present.** By James Persoon and Robert R. Watson. New York, Facts on File, 2009. 568p. index. (Facts on File Library of World Literature). $85.00. ISBN 13: 978-0-8160-6406-9.

These books from the Facts on File Library of World Literature serve as three parts of a four-volume set on British poetry. *The Facts on File Companion to British Poetry Before 1600* focuses specifically on British poetry written during the Anglo-Saxon, Middle English, and early Renaissance (Tudor) literary periods. Whereas more general literary works may be forced to greatly summarize or ignore parts of this period, *The Facts on File Companion to British Poetry Before 1600* provides a focused and thorough discussion. Sauer concentrates on providing an academic research tool by including topics most often found in high school and college classrooms. The book comprises approximately 600 entries of varied length that discuss multiple aspects of the age, including poems, poets, themes, topics, and terms. All entries are intermixed and arranged alphabetically, often containing information for additional readings and/or related entries within the book. The entries appear to be well written and easily understandable by a general audience. Also included is a short glossary of poetic terms, a selected bibliography, and a thorough index.

The Facts on File Companion to British Poetry, 17th and 18th Centuries is a guide to British poetry from 1600 to 1800. With more than 400 entries ranging in length from 300 to more than 2,500 words, this resource covers some of the finest and most popular poetry in the English language. Poets and terms in this title include: John Donne, John Dryden, Thomas Gray, John Milton, Alexander Pope, Jonathan Swift, *carpe diem*, Cavalier poets, Metaphysical poets, and Sons of Ben. Appendixes include a general bibliography and a glossary of poetic terms.

The Facts on File Companion to British Poetry: 1900 to the Present provides 450 entries on modern-day British poets and poetry. The entries range in length from 300 to more than 2,500 words and cover such topics as poets (e.g., Thomas Hardy, William Butler Yeats, Seamus Heaney, Robert Graves), famous poems (e.g., "Anthem for Doomed Youth," "September 1, 1939," "Do Not Go Gentle into That Good Night") , and important themes and movements. As with the other volumes, this title includes a general bibliography, and a glossary of poetic terms.

Considering that any one poet or poem in this work could constitute an entire library of materials, the authors of these titles do an excellent job of providing the essential information on a wide variety of topics within the stated boundaries. As the titles suggest, these volumes are probably best suited as companions to a larger collection of literary resources. In that role, however, they can serve as an excellent resource for individuals interested in British poetry, including students, teachers, librarians, and casual researchers.—**Tyler Manolovitz**

Indexes

C, P

386. **Index of American Periodical Verse 2006.** Rafael Catala and James D. Anderson, comps. Lanham, Md., Scarecrow, 2008. 737p. $125.00. ISBN 13: 978-0-8108-6176-3.

The primary purpose of this *Index* is to provide an important resource for research to more than 6,900 contemporary poets whose work has graced the pages of some 232 periodicals published in the United States, Canada, and the Caribbean during 2006. A concomitant inference indicates that poetry is flourishing through North America.

Selection of periodicals was a responsibility of the editors based on recommendations from literary scholars and critics, librarians, and publishers. Chief among the editors' criteria for inclusion were the reputations of the poets and the quality of their recent poems. Within these broad and subjective guidelines, the editors have come up with 20,185 poems, the listing of which reveals trends and influences.

Poets are arranged alphabetically by surname, and under each entrant's name poems are set up alphanumerically by title, or if lacking a title, by first line. An appended index provides access to poems by title or first line. Being that this *Index* is the only reference tool of its kind, it deserves a place in large literature collections, especially in those that have reason to believe that the annually published volumes that preceded this latest addition to the series have been put to use.—**G. A. Cevasco**

25 Music

GENERAL WORKS

Bibliography

C, P

387.   Clifton, Keith E. **Recent American Art Song: A Guide.** Lanham, Md., Scarecrow, 2008. 310p. index. $70.00; $45.00pa. ISBN 13: 978-0-8108-5940-1; 978-0-8108-6210-4pa.

The reference source, *Recent American Art Song: A Guide*, is a well-researched directory of U.S. songwriters and their music since 1980. The resource contains a foreword by Paul Sperry, a preface, an introduction titled "American Art Song Today," information on how the songs were selected and how to use the entries, additional resources, future goals, a list of abbreviations, composer entries A to Z, a discography, a bibliography, and indexes. The music cataloged in the book is restricted to solo songs in English along with pianos.

The author is a world authority on the topic and arranged the inventory in alphabetic order by the songwriters' last names. Each section devoted to the songwriter consists of a paragraph detailing the songwriters' birthdays, deaths, famous notable songs, present employment, life history, and a bibliography. Any songwriters' Websites are given in the bibliography. The songs mentioned include the publisher, the year published, and how to conduct the song.

Some 81 discs are detailed in a discography. The book provides a index of composers, poets, song titles, voice type (e.g., soprano, tenor), and songs by difficulty. Any patron at an academic, public, school, or music library will discover this publication is the choice quality informant.—**Melinda F. Matthews**

Catalogs

P

388.   Rickards, Steven L. **Twentieth-Century Countertenor Repertoire: A Guide.** Lanham, Md., Scarecrow, 2008. 400p. $100.00. ISBN 0-8108-6103-8. ISBN 13: 978-0-8108-6103-9.

A countertenor is a male alto voice that sings in the falsetto, above the range of the tenor. The purpose of this book is to catalog and compile information about repertoire composed for the countertenor from 1950 to 2000. Over 600 entries represent 350 composers from 30 countries in 31 languages.

Each entry is identified by a reference number, which makes accessing specific compositions more convenient. Each of these entries includes the composer's name; birth/death dates; nationality; the title, medium, date, and duration of the composition; the instrumentation, voicing, range, and tessitura of the piece; and the author and language of the text. All of these categories are explained briefly in a prefatory "Organization of Data and Definition of Terms." Rickard actually identifies the medium as the form or genre of the piece; Samuel Adler's *The Binding*, being an oratorio. Instrumentation is a list of instruments used in performances. For Range and Tessitura (the portion of the vocal range most exploited in the composition), Rickard uses a system slightly variant to the standards for pitch identification.

Particularly useful are the 16 appendixes. The first two list the titles and authors of text, respectively. Then follow nine appendixes that link the performing ensemble, such as countertenor with three accompanying instruments. The author presents several combinations of instruments with the voice, such as music for countertenor and double bass, or countertenor and temple blocks. Three more appendixes list cantatas, oratorios, dramatic works, and song cycles. Completing the appendixes are the addresses of music publishers, including physical and e-mail addresses, and a list of international music information centers.

Performers will find the ranges, tessitura, and durations very useful in planning programs. Steven Rickards is a countertenor singer who has recorded and premiered some of the works listed in this catalog, like *El Nino* by John Adams.—**Ralph Hartsock**

MUSICAL FORMS

Classical

P

389.   Green, Jonathan D. **A Conductor's Guide to Nineteenth-Century Choral-Orchestral Works.** Lanham, Md., Scarecrow, 2008. 336p. $67.50. ISBN 0-8108-6046-5. ISBN 13: 978-0-8108-6046-9.

Conductors of choirs use a myriad of resources to assist them in choosing music appropriate for their ensembles' abilities, vocal ranges, rhythmic awareness, and ability to change time signatures quickly. Green presents useful data on 28 significant nineteenth-century composers, from Ludwig van Beethoven and Franz Schubert to Horatio Parker and Samuel Coleridge-Taylor.

Green begins each composer's section with a brief biography of that composer, highlighting his or her major works, teachers, students they influenced, and a select general bibliography. Works, such as Gabriel Faure's Pavane, op. 50, are described in detail, with attention to performance forces required. Green presents the duration, source of text, performers required, performance history, and location of manuscript materials.

He then describes "performance issues": factors that may determine whether a given choir and orchestra should perform this work. Sometimes, as in the case of Amy Beach's Grand Mass in Eb, "all of the choral parts are doubled by the orchestra. The vocal writing for the choir and the soloists is fairly athletic. A large choir is demanded to balance the orchestration" (p. 3). Green also presents the ranges of each soloist, in a format similar to that described in Don Michael Randel's *New Harvard Dictionary of Music* (Belknap Press of Harvard University Press, 1986): c' is middle C, and the use of more prime signs (?) indicates higher pitch. He then rates the orchestral and choir parts for level of difficulty. Sometimes he comments on the solo parts or the tessitura portion of the range, that which is used the most. For Beethoven's Fantasia in C minor, op. 80, "the tessitura of the choral soprano part is fairly high and narrow" (p. 18). The author concludes each selection with a discography, and a bibliography that lists not only articles and books, but pinpoints pages relevant to the composition.

The only minor complaint is one of navigation—the volume lacks headers or footers that identify where one is in the alphabet of composers. Nonetheless, this reference source will assist conductors of professional, university, or community choruses in selecting appropriate repertoire. It can also serve as a basic guide for those researching these specific compositions.—**Ralph Hartsock**

Popular

Country

P

390. **The Billboard Illustrated Encyclopedia of Country Music.** Bob Allen and Tony Byworth, eds. New York, Watson-Guptill, 2007. 320p. illus. index. $50.00. ISBN 0-8230-7781-0.

Billboard's contribution to reference works on country music is to produce a big panoramic scrapbook of this popular music with emphasis on its commercial artists. As the title blares, it is abundantly illustrated with color as well as black-and-white photographs, mostly featuring the artists. The text is organized by the myriad styles that constitute the big tent of country music, in a rough historical line from "the early years of hillbilly music" to the pop crossover, neo-traditional, and alternative country genres. These are common labels, but some of the artists included may raise eyebrows to hard-core country fans. Appendixes and sidebars pepper each section, including a lead quote providing a keynote for the chapter, key track, key artists, and an A to Z list of notable artists. Still, the text is descriptive rather than interpretive, and written with fans in mind. The text appears secondary to the photographs, and researchers will be disappointed by the lack of detail and annotation in the A to Z list and stylistic discussions. It pales as a thematic overview to the more sophisticated *Encyclopedia of County Music* (2004) from the Country Music Hall of Fame edited by Paul Kingsbury and as a biographical dictionary to *Country Music: The Encyclopedia* by Irwin Stambler (2000). Considering that Billboard's brand on this encyclopedia, many users will be surprised by the absence of an appendix for or reference to Billboard's country charts over the years, which would have been of significance to historical and cultural researchers. In its attractive presentation and broad coverage, if not detail, it will be appealing to country music fans and uninitiated popular music buffs rather than researchers. [R: LJ, 15 June 07, p. 94]—**Simon J. Bronner**

P

391. **Joel Whitburn Presents Hot Country Albums: Billboard 1964 to 2007.** Menomonee Falls, Wis., Record Research, 2008. 341p. illus. $49.95. ISBN 0-89820-173-X. ISBN 13: 978-0-89820-173-4.

If you are a serious country music fan, then you will want a copy of *Joel Whitburn Presents Hot Country Albums: Billboard 1964 to 2007.* Not only does this book provide interesting details about individual albums, but it also shows how the trends in country music have evolved over the last four decades.

Every album that appeared in Billboard's Country Albums Chart from 1964 to 2007 is in this book. Information includes number of weeks charted, peak position, as well as any gold or platinum status. Brief biographical information is also included for each artist. Songs released as singles are bolded. The charts also identify the biggest-charted album for any artist with 10 or more albums.

Every cut from every Billboard-charted album is categorized into one A-Z track listing for each artist. Billboard started charting country albums in 1964; to add a broader historical perspective, the author has also included groundbreaking pre-1964 albums by country greats, such as Eddy Arnold, Johnny Cash, George Jones, and Marty Robbins. The back matter provides interesting compilations. such as the Top 200 artists; artists with the most charted albums; artists with the most top-40, top-10, and number-one albums; and most weeks at the number-one position.

There is an incredible amount of country music history packed into these lists and numbers, including the short careers of hot bands that ruled the charts for a year or less. If you are the kind of person who would enjoy knowing Bobby Bare was born in Ironton, Ohio, and his song "Drop Kick Me Jesus" peaked at the number 17 spot in 1976, this is the book for you.—**Mark J. Crawford**

Folk

C, P

392.   Cohen, Norm. **American Folk Songs: A Regional Encyclopedia.** Westport, Conn., Greenwood Press, 2008. 2v. index. $149.95/set. ISBN 13: 978-0-313-34047-5.

Folk songs survived in a community without the need for commercial media. Transmission was orally, or by sheet music, song sheets (broadsides), recordings, or public concerts. Cohen presents songs associated with individual states or regions of the United States. Travelers, both seagoing and pioneers of land traverses, wrote songs. Newspapers often printed songs and poems, especially during the nineteenth century.

The author begins with a useful political chronology from 1607 to 1912. Each chapter begins with a regional overview, then state overviews, in the context of history. Cohen selected examples from cheap print in the nineteenth century because: these are hard to find today; printed versions had older and more complete texts; and they are in the public domain. His theory is that folk songs indicate attitudes and opinions of the people rather than mundane historical facts found in textbooks. For instance, some folk songs that commemorate a war battle will reflect the sentimental emotions toward the heroes or tragedies of those close to the writer, and not the political or tactical implications of the conflict.

Cohen's collection emphasizes the songs as text. He makes reference to books, recordings, and online sources, especially for tunes that are not commonly known. Types of folk songs include War songs, Songs about Local Events, Crimes, Disasters, Songs of Praise, and Ethnic Songs. He provides a statistical chart by type and region of those used in these volumes. For instance, in West Virginia, the songs can reflect its history. "The Battle of Point Pleasant" (p. 213) reveals sentiments about the 1774 conflict called Lord Dunmore's War. One finds the attitudes of northerners after a failed raid at Harper's Ferry in "John Brown's Body" (p. 214). The 1907 disaster at the Fairmont Coal Mines is symbolized in the song "The Explosion in the Fairmount Mines" (p. 220), with variant spelling indicated by Cohen. In North Carolina (p. 237) is a song about the murder of Emma Hartsell. The author then presents a context for each of the texts printed, including the person or event. Cohen retains the texts used by the original writers, as in "De Free Nigger" (pp.189-191); he then comments on the tune, noting that the term was not always a racial epithet—that function occurred more towards the twentieth century. Even Woody Guthrie was unaware of the offense it could cause. (See note 8 on page 284.)

Interspersed throughout the volumes are broadsides, sheet music covers, and an image from a newspaper. Endnotes are at the end of regional chapters. The volumes conclude with two indexes: a song index lists those used in the books, directing one to the state and region in which it is located; a general index lists persons, specific events, laws, and associated songs, and selective topics of songs (e.g., Revolutionary War, Cajun music, Chicago fire); but not mining disasters or earthquakes.

The one drawback is navigability. The table of contents is scanty, and needs more elaboration, such as states to be listed. Some states may be applied to different regions, and Cohen does not delineate which states are in each region. Where to divide the country into regions is opened for interpretation, and each book should delineate its regional contents. West Virginia, in this case, is classed in the "Upper South," after Virginia, and followed by North Carolina. "The Deep South and The Ozarks" ends with Arkansas and Missouri. The "Appendix: Songs Excluded" provides some semblance of sequence, but lists only 41 states. However, the volumes are easily used with known-item searches.—**Ralph Hartsock**

Hip-Hop and Rap

C, P, S

393.   Gulla, Bob. **Icons of R&B and Soul: An Encyclopedia of the Artists who Revolutionized Rhythm.** Westport, Conn., Greenwood Press, 2008. 2v. illus. index. (Greenwood Icons). $175.00/set. ISBN 13: 978-0-313-34044-4.

Icons of R&B and Soul is the sixth publication in the Greenwood Icons series of reference works on popular culture. The 2-volume set covers 24 artists that span the chronological evolution of rhythm & blues and soul from Fats Domino to Prince. Preceding the entries is a timeline from 1940-1983 containing important events and amusing facts related to the development and maturation of R&B. Entries average 20 pages in length for each artist and are well written, easy to read, and engaging. The key people and events that shaped the life of an artist as well as the influence they had throughout their careers are told from a variety of cultural and personal perspectives. Entries end with a selected discography of three to six recordings and a short bibliography of three to six sources for further reading. These bibliographies and discographies are gathered together at the end of the set to create a single bibliography and discography. There is a short list pointing to broad music Websites, such as *All Music Guide* and *YouTube* rather than sites particular to individual artists. There is also a short list of films dealing with R&B and soul artists. The entire set is indexed appropriately with relevant cross-references. Photographs are sparse with only one black-and-white photograph of each artist. While ample material can easily be found on all 24 artists from other sources, this source brings some depth to the lives of the artists in a concise, readable format. The one drawback to the set is the somewhat high cost. It is recommended for school and public libraries.—**Mike Burgmeier**

Rock

C, P, S

394.   **Joel Whitburn Presents Rock Tracks 1981-2008.** Menomonee Falls, Wis., Record Research, 2008. 400p. illus. $49.95. ISBN 0-89820-174-8. ISBN 13: 978-0-89820-174-1.

The 3d edition of this resource compiled by the chart guru Joel Whitburn provides numerous lists of top-rated rock songs, otherwise known as tracks. The main section is an alphabetic listing by artist of all tracks reaching *Billboard Magazine*'s "Mainstream Rock" and "Modern Rock" charts. Under each artist is a brief biography, followed by the tracks, which are grouped by album and placed in chronological order. Additional data includes the date of the track's debut, the chart in which the track appeared, the highest chart position, total weeks charted, peak position on Billboard's Hot 100, and album label and number. Additional symbols, highlighting, and underscoring provide more information, although the meaning is unclear unless one consults the user's guide at the beginning of the book. Following the artist section is a title listing, with a simple code to indicate the chart in which the track appeared, the highest chart position, and year the track peaked. Finally, Whitburn provides groupings such as the top 100 artists in rank order, artists with most charted tracks, top tracks of all time and by certain periods, and more. Also included in this 3d edition is an expanded Classic Rocks Tracks, which lists tracks from 1964-1980 that are still being played today on classic rock radio stations. For the serious music lover who frequently peruses charts in old issues of *Billboard Magazine*, Whitburn's book is an invaluable timesaver. More casual fans will likely get lost with the details provided in the main artist listing, and simply use the book to identify the most popular songs from their favorite rock bands, or entertain themselves with some of Whitburn's "Top Artist" or "Top Tracks" lists. This work is recommended for school and public libraries.—**Kevin McDonough**

C, P, S

395.   Schinder, Scott, and Andy Schwartz. **Icons of Rock: An Encyclopedia of the Legends Who Changed Music Forever.** Westport, Conn., Greenwood Press, 2008. 2v. illus. index. $175.00/set. ISBN 13: 978-0-313-33845-8.

In 1992, Bob Dylan commented that "People today are still living off the table scraps of the sixties. They are still being passed around—the music and the ideas." Scott Schinder and Andy Schwartz, authors of the encyclopedia *Icons of Rock*, appear to share his estimation of the decade's musical legacy. Of the 24 recording artists they profile, over one-half either began their careers or released their most influential albums during the 1960s. The emphasis is less a symptom of bias than recognition of the creative spirit that flourished in that decade. Between 1964 and 1968 the Beach Boys, Beatles, and Rolling Stones released a cumulative total of over 20 full-length studio albums. Frank Zappa, Pink Floyd, and the Grateful Dead detoured rock music into realms aesthetically informed by contemporary classical music and jazz, changing forever audiences' perceptions of the genre's stylistic possibilities.

Schinder and Schwartz indeed are at their best when they conjure the energy and innovation of rock music's formative years. They wisely acknowledge the oft-overlooked importance of sound in defining the music (the echo effect on "That's All Right, Mama" by Elvis Presley) and of the recording industry in establishing artists' careers (Atlantic Records producers Jerry Wexler and Ahmet Ertegun's support of Ray Charles). They also convey the commitment and vision of rock's trailblazers. James Brown and Elvis Presley, for example, appear as hardworking bandleaders in command on stage and in the studio, not as eccentric has-beens.

Icons of Rock contains enough meaty details to engage neophytes and aficionados alike. It is a fine introduction to a select group of artists whose music begs discovery and rediscovery.—**Craig Mury Keeney**

P, S

396.   Smith, Kerry L. **Encyclopedia of Indie Rock.** Westport, Conn., Greenwood Press, 2008. 400p. illus. index. $75.00. ISBN 13: 978-0-313-34119-9.

From Kerry L. Smith comes the one-volume *Encyclopedia of Indie Rock*, offering information on more than 150 singers and songwriters, producers, labels, icons, and subgenres as it follows independent rock's (indie rock's) rich history. Beginning with Frank Zappa and up through 2007, the *Encyclopedia of Indie Rock* details the do-it-yourself determination, ingenuity, and contributions of bands such as R.E.M., Nirvana, Talking Heads, Ani DiFranco, and the Ramones as they fight to retain most of the creative control over their songs. Indeed, the introduction, called "How Indie Rock Shaped and Inspired Generations of Do-It-Yourselfers," focuses solely on this theme. Yet, after reading it, one might argue the reverse is also true, as we see how the artists and genres were influenced and how they influenced others. Also included are a timeline from 1952-2007, appendices (Top 10 Influential Indie Rock Artists" and "Most Significant Indie Rock Albums," and a resource guide that includes books and additional references.

Each artist's entry covers the artist's background and their evolution, influences, instruments, and dress, and ends with a further reading section. Frank Zappa's influence and importance to indie rock is covered in his entry along with two additional entries: B.Z.—"Before Zappa" and A.Z.—"After Zappa." The sub-genre entries include: emo, post-punk, indie pop, math rock, Twee pop, and sadcore. The author makes a significant error by failing to define the phrase, "DIY" (Do-It-Yourself), which is used incessantly throughout the volume—almost to the point of annoyance.

While the *Encyclopedia of Indie Rock* is a fun read, it is difficult to imagine the audience for whom this reference book was intended. It is definitely not a definitive work on the subject and is written for the average reader. Perhaps a K-12 or a public library would be the most appropriate place for this work. —**Linda W. Hacker**

26 Mythology, Folklore, and Popular Culture

FOLKLORE

Catalogs and Collections

C, P, S

397.   **Tales Online. http://www.talesunlimited.com.** [Website]. May Brottman, ed. Price negotiated by site. Date reviewed: Jan 08.

Tales Online, the database on comparative folk literature, has the highest of credentials, developed partially through a grant from the National Endowment for the Humanities and work at Indiana University, where Stith Thompson created the foundation folklore motif index. This life undertaking is designed to index folklore from around the world by theme and variations as well as make it possible for all of us to recognize the commonalities of experience expressed through folk literature. The sterling academic qualifications linked to the database should not make us think it is too difficult for K-12 students. The project director was a library media specialist, and library media specialists and teachers have been part of the advisory and testing groups from the beginning.

Tales Online contains 2,000 folktales (of the more than 4 million out there). The tales include fables, tall tales, fairy tales, sagas, legends, and myths. Many are in full text from standard folktale sources that are now in public domain; others that are still under copyright are presented in long summaries. Searching is simple and flexible, there is a list of all titles, although it is too long and too badly organized to be of much use ("A" and "The" are used as entry words; "The" entries are repeated by the first main word, but "A" entries are not). Separate hierarchical searches by countries, ethnic groups, and languages allow easy access for everything from world culture units in high schools to Native American studies in elementary schools. The keyword search responds to themes such as events, emotions, family members, character roles, title, and genre. Users could even begin their research on an animal by reading the folktales to see how the animal has been portrayed, and then do their research to see if the portrayals are at all accurate, or if they can explain why the folktale animal has such a reputation.

Navigation throughout the Website is easy, although some revisions should be made. An occasional page is missing a back button, some pages have live links that are plain text rather than colored, and the heading links change without warning. While searching, the toolbar headings include Search, Help, Glossary, and Previous Screen. During a search, navigation links lead to more results and to top of page. Information can be printed and text size can be enlarged, but there are few other special features to be found.

When tales appear as search results, each is labeled with its title, the collection from which it comes, age appropriateness, length, original source, and genre indication. There is also a short summary. Clicking on the title leads to the full text of the tale. Folktale entries can be very brief or many screens for complex stories. When a tale is found, the toolbar expands to include Bibliographic Information, Notes, Performance Information, and Variant Titles. The latter is most important because it leads to stories with similar motifs. Some of the other categories are incomplete, however.

As the database grows and adds more tales it will become even more valuable. It is certainly easier to use than the standard paper folk and fairy tale indexes and provides an authenticity to versions of the folktale all too often lost in this age of innocuous Disney-like retellings.—**Barbara Ripp Safford**

Dictionaries and Encyclopedias

C, P
398. **The Greenwood Encyclopedia of Folktales and Fairy Tales.** Donald Haase, ed. Westport, Conn., Greenwood Press, 2008. 3v. illus. index. $299.95/set. ISBN 13: 978-0-313-33441-2.

Yet another title in Greenwood Press's series of multi-volume reference sets, these three tomes contain a wide ranging scope to studies in folk and fairy tales. Covering tales from the entire globe and with a timeframe from antiquity to the present, presenting information useful to a panoply of disciplines and including media tellings of the stories, and emphasizing the new ideas brought forth since 1970, the 670 entries point in any direction you may want to research. This set uses Antti Aarne's 1910 and Stith Thompson's 1961 enlarged classifying systems for folktales. Also, the 2004 overhaul of those systems by Hans-Jorg Uther is incorporated into the entries. The three volumes are continuously paged with a complete list of the topics printed at the beginning of each book. It is disconcerting that these entries are not given page numbers; however, the 8-page list of related topics that follows, plus the 64-page bibliography, and the 20-page index found at the end of volume 3 do make the text quite usable. There is a smattering of small black-and-white photographs, drawings, and reproduced paintings that add interest to the research. The books are well made for a long shelf life. What is most useful is that each of the entries has a further reading bibliography with complete citations, which makes it easy to move onto other titles without having to have the last volume in hand. A 15-page list of contributors at the end of the third volume does give proof to the large scope and well-written essays found in the text. Since the Tolkien revolution in the 1960s fairytales and folktales have experienced a resurgence in popularity both in the mass market press and in academic studies. This set is a good starting place to anywhere on the map to the "Land of Faire" and "Once Upon a Time."—**Kennith Slagle**

C, P
399. **The Greenwood Library of World Folktales: Stories from the Great Collections.** Thomas A. Green, ed. Westport, Conn., Greenwood Press, 2008. 4v. index. $299.95/set. ISBN 13: 978-0-313-33783-3.

This valuable collection of folktales provides an engaging introduction to cultural themes and stories from around the globe. The tales are organized by country and then by region (or people group when appropriate), allowing readers to encounter the stories without categorizing them according to western genres or labels. Chosen to give researchers a selection that is both representative and foundational, the tales range from classic to little known. The section from Germany, for example, includes both the familiar "Hansel and Grettel" and the less well known "The Nixy."

A comprehensive index at the end of each volume allows easy access to the tales by title, author, region, country, theme, or term. Because it allows readers to compare stories that have similar motifs (such as the trickster figure) across countries, regions, and time periods, this index is one of the most helpful features of the set. Each volume also offers a short bibliography at the end of each volume; these bibliographies are combined at the end of the fourth volume. However, the bibliographies are a disappointing aspect of the set: they are too short to be comprehensive resources for scholars and are not subdivided by country or region, making it difficult to access works on specific topics.

The tales themselves range from 1 to 10 pages. Each begins with a helpful introduction that situates the tale within the most relevant aspects of its context: historical, cultural, religious, and literary. These introductions are extremely concise, sometimes at the expense of flow and readability. The language of most of the tales has been modified for the modern reader, providing reading ease but at times resulting in an uneven or choppy tone. Despite these disadvantages, this set is an invaluable resource for high-school or beginning college students who are researching in the fields of literature or cultural studies.—**Helen Margaret Bernard**

Handbooks and Yearbooks

P, S

400. Tucker, Elizabeth. **Children's Folklore: A Handbook.** Westport, Conn., Greenwood Press, 2008. 164p. index. (Greenwood Folklore Handbooks). $55.00. ISBN 13: 978-0-313-34189-2.

Tucker's overview of child lore contains much valuable analysis. She flourishes at categorization of play mode, thought, and genre. Her models disclose a postmodern truth—a child milieu that can be charming, ribald, coarse, and disturbingly violent. In text and photograph, the underlying psychology reveals an aggressive, competitive survivalism blended with aspects of a universal spontaneity of whim and fancy. Succinct passages, 54 glosses, and ample bibliography over a broad historical span make connections with child consciousness essential to the homeschooler, teacher, researcher, and student of early childhood education, psychology, sociology, or literature. Tucker extends research to multiple races. The main weakness of her study is an absence of commentary on gender-specific games and taunts. This volume is highly recommended.—**Mary Ellen Snodgrass**

MYTHOLOGY

P

401. **Storytelling: An Encyclopedia of Mythology and Folklore.** Josepha Sherman, ed. Armonk, N.Y., M. E. Sharpe, 2008. 3v. illus. index. $299.00/set. ISBN 13: 978-0-7656-8047-1.

Every now and again you find a publication that lives up to its name. Josepha Sherman has edited contributions from three dozen writers into an excellent three-volume set about the subjects and aspects one needs to not only tell stories, but to understand where they come from, how they work, and why all cultures have them. The volumes are numbered continuously and each tome has an index to the entire set. Volume 1 has a table of contents to the three parts; however, volumes 2 and 3 only have tables of contents to themselves. Each of the entries covers a character, a theme, or germane aspects found in a story and the entries are worldwide in scope. There are small "For Further Reading" bibliographies after each entry. These titles refer to the basic information one needs to understand each topic and is not overwhelming for the nonspecialists. Attractive black-and-white illustrations and photographs are found throughout the set. At the end of volume 3 users will find 49 retellings of major stories that represent both the large scope of the set and that stand as examples of what users are studying. Following these stories is a list of schools throughout the world that have courses or a specialty in the storytelling field. The list gives addresses, Websites, and e-mail contacts for the reader to follow up on. The bibliography is separated into sections on "Storytelling Books," "Folktale Books," and "Tale Type and Motif Indexes" that direct users to their chosen subject. The set is oversized for easy reading and is well bound to stand up to continued use. I recommend this set to undergraduates, graduates, the professors, and anyone who wants to understand storytelling or who is interested in becoming a storyteller.—**Kennith Slagle**

P, S

402. **U*X*L Encyclopedia of World Mythology.** Farmington Hills, Mich., U*X*L/Gale Group, 2009. 5v. illus. index. $305.00/set. ISBN 13: 978-1-4144-3030-0.

Encyclopedia of World Mythology is arranged in five volumes whose contents are alphabetic and page numbers continued from volume to volume. No editor is given and individual articles are not signed. The five types of entries are character (e.g., heroes), deity, myth, the stories' themes (e.g., reincarnation), and culture (the overall cultural setting as mythological cause and effect). Each volume contains the same alphabetic index and research and activity ideas and limited "words to know." More volume-related activities and glossaries would aid classroom use; "mummifying a chicken" will appeal to young students, but the more mature students might prefer to go beyond that and "storytelling" for meaningful activity. Teachers of Myth and Legend could be invited to contribute to a future enhancement of the set. The pronunciation guide and timeline are helpful, as is the limited but modern bibliography, which includes Internet sources, television, movies, and gaming. The mostly black-and-white illustrations are helpful, and each volume also has a special section of other illustrations, including color reprints of important mythological-based art.

Knowledge of world mythology is basic to a study o f literature and history. For that reason, *U*X*L Encyclopedia of World Mythology* should be available in every school library from fifth grade up. It offers excellent broad overviews of large topics like Greek and Egyptian mythology as well as defining more arcane subjects such as trolls and Golem. As with any large undertaking, this encyclopedia is not all-inclusive. It omits Druids, Stonehenge, and vampires, but includes Atlantis, dragons, and witches. All volumes look the same. The set is sturdily bound and should stand up well to the use it deserves to have. While cost is always a factor, *U*X*L Encyclopedia of World Mythology* contains such a wealth of information it should rank high on all school libraries' must-have list.—**Kay O. Cornelius**

POPULAR CULTURE

Bibliography

P

403.   Weiner, Robert G. **Marvel Graphic Novels and Related Publications: An Annotated Guide to Comics, Prose Novels, Children's Books, Articles, Criticism and Reference Works.** Jefferson, N.C., McFarland, 2008. 385p. index. $49.95. ISBN 13: 978-0-7864-2500-6.

Since Superman first leapt over a tall building in a single bound, comic books have changed drastically. Their maturation has marked them for inclusion into library collections, as well as the classroom, usually in the form of a graphic novel (GN). *Marvel Graphic Novels and Related Publications* operates as an annotated bibliography for graphic and prose novels, books, articles, scholarly publications, and reference material that relate to Marvel Comic titles from 1965 to 2000.

Robert Weiner, a reference librarian, should be applauded for trying to incorporate every publication concerning Marvel-related graphic novels in his research. It is apparent that he tried, but even he admits that limits had to be placed. The book is divided into five sections, beginning with a brief analysis of comic books and graphic novels in general and moves to a history of Marvel Comics. The next two sections, one of which is dedicated to special volumes, list GN's and focus on mainstream Marvel characters. Anomalies such as children's books and GN's based on film characters or musicians, and prose novels are covered throughout the last half of the book. The last 100 pages are a selector's delight. Listed are critical articles, guides, indexes, and scholarly material on Marvel Comics-related subjects.

Appendixes and title, author (artist), and subject indexes are included. For each item listed in the book, a brief description is given with a bibliographic citation and where appropriate, the description will include what individual comic issues the GN comprises. Most of the sections are subdivided by main character.

The one disappointment of the book is that the descriptions of the novels themselves are mostly play by plays of the story action and any philosophical or social commentary about the content for book selectors is limited. However, Weiner compensates for this in the chapters featuring reference material and scholarly criticism. While much of the GN summary content can no doubt be found online, the reference material and critical works would be highly valuable to book selectors.—**Brian J. Sherman**

Dictionaries and Encyclopedias

P, S

404.   **Encyclopedia of World's Fairs and Expositions.** John E. Findling and Kimberly D. Pelle, eds. Jefferson, N.C., McFarland, 2008. 474p. illus. index. $125.00. ISBN 13: 978-0-7864-3416-9.

A handsome summary of 106 global expos, this encyclopedia compiles succinct details dotted with onsite commentary, photographs, maps, and graphics of events. Coverage extends from 1851 to a prospectus of the Shanghai fair of 2010. Entries feature names, dates, places, exhibits, and controversies, and conclude with annotated bibliography.

The editors provide superb bibliography divided into archives, collections, and electronic sources. Following a list of 74 contributing authors, the 13-page index connects events to famous people (e.g., Charles Lindbergh, Walt Disney, Susan B. Anthony), architecture (e.g., Palais d'Electricité, Crystal Palace, Eiffel Tower), and inventions (e.g., robotics, electricity, prefabricated construction).

Missing from the entry on the 1964 fair in New York City are the sit- ins that James Farmer orchestrated on April 23 to increase employment opportunity for black applicants. This is a worthy addition to the reference shelves of public and school libraries and museums.—**Mary Ellen Snodgrass**

C, P, S

405.   Hill, Jeff, and Peggy Daniels. **Life Events and Rites of Passage.** Detroit, Omnigraphics, 2008. 498p. illus. index. $64.00. ISBN 13: 978-0-7808-0735-8.

Unlike other reference materials on holidays and events, this takes a far more personal approach to religious and secular celebrations and commemorations observed by groups in the United States. The volume is organized chronologically by life event, rather than by culture, facilitating cross-cultural comparisons of events from before birth ("Conception and Pregnancy") , to after death ("Memorials and Later Commemorations") . Some interesting inclusions fall outside the scope of other reference works: "First Dates," "Debutante Balls," "Purchasing a House," and "Sidewalk and Other Public Shrines."

While the entries provide a general comparison of observances, there are a few entries that could contain more information. For example, the Buddhist forty-ninth day memorial is given its own full chapter (albeit short), while the Jewish Yahrzeit entry is noted briefly as part of a general chapter on "One-Year Memorials," and describes only the first observance with no mention of the subsequent annual observations.

Each entry includes information on customs and symbols associated with the event, observances, as well as its history and cultural significance. Overall, the information is well documented, with relevant Website references and a list of further readings at the end of each chapter. The volume concludes with a bibliography and index. This resource is appropriate for public, high school, and undergraduate libraries.—**Amanda Izenstark**

P, S

406.   **Holiday Symbols and Customs.** 4th ed. Helene Henderson, ed. Detroit, Omnigraphics, 2009. 1321p. index. $94.00. ISBN 13: 978-0-7808-0990-1.

Holiday Symbols and Customs, now in its 4th edition, includes information on the origins, symbols, and customs of holidays, festivals, and celebrations across the world. The secular and religious events covered in this work include both ancient and modern celebrations, and 50 new entries have been added since this book was last published. Some of these new entries, such as Cinco de Mayo and the ancient Celtic celebration of Mabon, are more typical of what you would expect to find in a reference work such as this. However, other more modern entries, such as the Academy Awards and the Iditarod dogsled race, are a bit more unusual. Several new appendixes are available in this updated edition. One of these new appendixes, a listing of holidays by type (e.g., religious, national, seasonal), seems like a useful addition. However, the inclusion of a section on world calendar systems and another appendix with tourist information seem less useful and do not appear to match the overall purpose of this reference work. Those with the 3d edition of this book (see ARBA 2004, entry 1126) may not feel the need to update their collections. Otherwise, *Holiday Symbols and Customs* seems to be a useful resource for school and public library collections.—**Larissa Anne Gordon**

C, P, S
407.   Lenburg, Jeff. **The Encyclopedia of Animated Cartoons.** 3d ed. New York, Facts on File, 2009. 738p. illus. index. $85.00. ISBN 13: 978-0-8160-6599-8.

Jeff Lenburg's *The Encyclopedia of Animated Cartoons*, now in its 3d edition (see ARBA 2000, entry 1161, for a review of the 2d edition), remains the most comprehensive book on American cartoon history. Prefaced by an abbreviated history of American cartoons, the book is divided into seven categories, among which include silent cartoons, theatrical sound cartoons, full-length animated features, television specials, and cartoon television series. Academy and Emmy Award listings for cartoons, as well as other cartoon milestones, are also featured. The update is expanded to include detailed information on every cartoon that was broadcast between 1999 and 2007 on more than 60 major U.S. commercial and cable networks. This information includes cartoon imports from countries such as Japan and Canada. Where applicable, each entry includes film or series history, voice credits, dates produced or broadcast, and complete filmographies. This title is recommended for all libraries.—**Brian J. Sherman**

C, P, S
408.   **Pop Culture Universe. http://greenwood.com/PCU/default.aspx.** [Website]. Westport, Conn., Greenwood Press, 2008. Price negotiated by site. Date reviewed: 2008.

Icons, Idols, Ideas is the subtitle of this digital library of American and world popular culture that supports the history, literature, and social studies curriculums. It contains more than 250 volumes, thousands of images, and Decades Pages that give instant access to important news items, movies and television shows, fads, fashion, and so forth. This site contains thousands of topics that will appeal to all levels of students, but without the bias, suggestive content, or questionable sources of most commercial and fan sites. This is a product that combines scholarship with the best in reference Web technology, thereby allowing students easy access to a wide range of pop culture topics, both current and historical. This site was recognized as the leading reference source of 2009, winning the prestigious Dartmouth Medal. —**Catherine Barr**

P
409.   Prono, Luca. **Encyclopedia of Gay and Lesbian Popular Culture.** Westport, Conn., Greenwood Press, 2008. 310p. illus. index. $85.00. ISBN 13: 978-0-313-33599-0.

With nearly 100 entries, the author of the *Encyclopedia of Gay and Lesbian Popular Culture* aims to survey the influence of gays and lesbians in film, television, entertainment, popular literature, and music. A few entries are thematic (e.g., "AIDS," "Beat Generation," "Camp") , but the vast majority of them focus on well-known twentieth and twenty-first century American and British individuals whose contributions resonate in contemporary modes of queer representation. These individuals may be gay/lesbian or alleged to be (e.g., Edward Albee, Richard Chamberlain, Agnes Moorehead), although a few are heterosexual icons who have had enduring influence on queer audiences, such as Judy Garland and Barbra

Streisand. Given the vastness of popular culture and the limited number of entries, the author has been highly selective in his material. Some readers may find his emphases unusual; for example, basically the same amount of text is devoted to Divine, the Harlem Renaissance, Freddie Mercury, and Gore Vidal. All will find the numerous black-and-white photographs appealing and the bibliographic citations useful. The use of bold font for cross-referenced entries makes them easy to locate. With one of its announced purposes being to chronicle the battle of gays and lesbians to achieve visibility against forces that might closet them or render them invisible, this encyclopedia has a political agenda as well as an informative one. It is recommended for all general collections.—**G. Douglas Meyers**

Handbooks and Yearbooks

C, P, S

410.   **African Americans and Popular Culture.** Todd Boyd, ed. Westport, Conn., Praeger/Greenwood Press, 2008. 3v. illus. index. $300.00/set. ISBN 13: 978-0-275-98922-4.

This compact three-volume set contains essays exploring the wide range of African American contributions to popular culture in the United States. The first volume covers "Theater, Film, and Television," and includes essays on racism and stereotypes in the media, but also information on pioneers in early cinema and contemporary filmmakers. The second volume, "Sports," covers major inroads and accomplishments by African Americans, from barrier-breaking baseball players and boxers to Venus and Serena Williams and Tiger Woods. The final volume, "Music and Popular Art," includes the expected essays on jazz and hip-hop, but surprises with an essay on "Superheroes and Comics." Each essay is followed by endnotes containing bibliographic information, making the essays a good starting point for further research.

Each volume contains its own index, and does not reference the other volumes. While this allows each volume to stand on its own, users of the "Theater, Film, and Television" volume might miss the essay "Standup Comedy," which is included in the "Music and Popular Art" volume. That said, the series is a good addition to high school, public, and undergraduate libraries.—**Amanda Izenstark**

P, S

411.   **Celebrity Culture in the United States.** Terence J. Fitzgerald, ed. Bronx, N.Y., H. W. Wilson, 2008. 183p. index. (The Reference Shelf, v.80, no.1). $50.00pa. ISBN 13: 978-0-8242-1078-6.

Celebrity Culture in the United States is the latest book in H. W. Wilson's Reference Shelf series that analyzes American society's infatuation with the celebrity universe. The work is divided into four main sections, and includes an index and annotated bibliography for further research. The editor brings together two dozen articles from a variety of publications in order to discuss different aspects of celebrity culture and its place in society.

The book opens with "The Cult of Celebrity," a section devoted to the history and evolution of celebrity culture, including how it has grown into such an overwhelming part of people's lives. The second section, "Celebrity Activism and American Politics," discusses how celebrities and politics have become increasingly intertwined. The third section, "The Price of Fame," brings together a collection of writings that focus on the negative aspects of celebrity, including public scrutiny, personal struggles, and society's fascination with celebrity downfalls. The book concludes with "The Democratization of Celebrity," which focuses on how technology and society have enabled nearly anyone to attain celebrity status.

Considering the rapidity in which celebrity news comes and goes, this book does a respectable job of balancing the nature of celebrity culture with current celebrity news and events. The entries that mention current news risk becoming quickly outdated, but much of the book will remain useful by focusing on concepts, ideas, and history. Despite the potential timeliness issue, this book is a suitable introductory research tool for works related to the topic of celebrity culture.—**Tyler Manolovitz**

27 Performing Arts

GENERAL WORKS

Directories

C, P
412. **The Grey House Performing Arts Directory, 2009.** 6th ed. Millerton, N.Y., Grey House Publishing, 2009. 1100p. index. $185.00pa. ISBN 13: 978-1-59237-376-5.

The 6th edition of this directory has over 9,000 listings of performing arts resources and organizations, including everything from large production companies to small troupes and nonprofits. The depth of information continues to be impressive: contact information includes name, address, telephone and fax numbers, e-mail and Websites (if available), and mission statements. Other information, if provided, includes size of staff (both paid and volunteer), size of stage and seating capacity, budget information as well as where the organization performs. Entries are divided by chapter: dance, instrumental music, vocal music, theater, series and festivals, and theatrical facilities. Each chapter is then organized by states, subdivided by city. Entries are listed alphabetically by category; under Theatre, for example, we find Dinner Theatre and Theatre for the Deaf. Under dance, we find everything from Belly Dance, Liturgical Dance to Mime. The indexes are alphabetic listings of all organizations, executive name index, facilities, geographic breakdown, and the impressive information resource index. Three articles on event promotion are reprinted from *The Music & Sound Retailer*. This will be of great interest to those looking to increase attendance at not only at performances, but also foot traffic in underused stores. This impressive directory is recommended as a solid resource to any public or academic library.—**Stephen J. Shaw**

FILM, TELEVISION, AND VIDEO

Catalogs

P
413. Atkinson, Michael, and Laurel Shifrin. **Flickipedia: Perfect Films for Every Occasion, Holiday, Mood, Ordeal, and Whim.** Chicago, Chicago Review Press; distr., Chicago, Independent Publishers Group, 2008. 337p. index. $16.95pa. ISBN 1-55652-714-4. ISBN 13: 978-1-55652-714-2.

Movies, aside from being sources of entertainment, can also have therapeutic value, as shown by this reference work, including over 1,300 recommendations tailored for everyday and for special occasions. Most are available on DVD, VHS, and On Demand. The book aims to enhance the readers' range of film options, serving the filmgoer and movies themselves. Inclusion depends on a policy of "selective subjectivity" formed by the author, a film reviewer, and his wife.

Entries are broadly arranged by experience (e.g., *Home for the Holidays*, *World Traveler*), and then subdivided by type (e.g., Christmas, Family Trip). Each has title, year, plots summary, and review. "Resources" has online information and addresses of rentals, downloads, retailers, and distributors. An index of film titles and an index of names offer further access. Cinema is such a part of our lives, and will doubtless continue to be, in all its ramifications. Any insights into its uses will be welcome.—**Anita Zutis**

C, P

414.   Keaney, Michael F. **British Film Noir Guide.** Jefferson, N.C., McFarland, 2008. 261p. illus. index. $55.00. ISBN 13: 978-0-7864-3805-1.

Keaney makes a strong case for the need of a guide to British film noir. While American noir and even its French cousin have received considerable critical attention, the British version has been unfairly neglected. By looking at 369 films, including 116 not covered in other studies, released between 1937 and 1964, Keaney proves that the same combination of moody lighting and moral ambiguity on display in countless American films was also strong in the UK, if not quite so prevalent. Each entry includes both British and American titles, a subjective rating of the film's quality (one to five stars), release date and length, quotation of representative dialogue, cast, production company, director, cinematographer, screenwriter, synopsis, and Keaney's view of a film's significant noir qualities and its entertainment value. In addition to obvious choices such as *The Third Man* and *Night and the City*, he calls attention to such worthy examples of the genre as *Seven Days to Noon* and *They Made Me a Fugitive*, offering excellent analyses of each. Keaney includes many titles clearly not films noir, straining to find justification for *Great Expectations* and offering no rationale for *Black Narcissus*. He also neglects several titles in the Hammer Film Noir DVD series. While appendixes list the titles by year, director, cinematographer, and quality rating, there could also have been ones for screenwriters and actors. The index indicates Herbert Lom appeared in these films most frequently, but all 20 references must be consulted to compile a list of his titles. The *British Film Noir Guide* is nevertheless full of interesting facts, and the 48 well-chosen photographs capture the genre's hypnotic style. [R: BL, 1 &15 Jan 09, p. 122]—**Michael Adams**

C, P

415.   **Magill's Cinema Annual 2008: A Survey of the films of 2007.** 27th ed. Hilary White, ed. Farmington Hills, Mich., Gale Group, 2008. 604p. index. $165.00. ISBN 13: 978-1-558-62611-9.

The 27th volume in the series, *Magill's Cinema Annual 2008* continues to offer an in-depth retrospective for over 250 domestic and foreign films released in the United States. Designed for film enthusiasts, students, and the entertainment industry as a single source of information on the theatrical releases of 2007, this guide's features include its extensive credits, awards and nominations (including the Golden Raspberries), obituaries, nine indexes, a bibliography of selected film books for the year, and most importantly its critical reviews with author bylines.

Entries are alphabetically arranged by film title and each review contains up to 16 items of information, ranging from taglines and film reviews to trivia and film quotes. A number of separate indexes allow the reader to quickly scan through the guide for specific directors, screenwriters, or subject matter. Of particular strength is the cumulative title index, including all of the films reviewed in the previous 26 volumes of the series.

The guide's only weakness comes from the list of contributing reviewers, many of whom are listed as freelance reviewers or publishing professionals. Analysis from noted film reviewers such as *Chicago Sun-Times* film critic Roger Ebert, among others, are cited in the individual film entry, but the full review is left to the series contributors. Although many of the contributing reviewers will not be well known to even the most dedicated of moviegoers, the newest installment in the ongoing series is still a valuable overview of the year in film. This work is recommended for any academic library supporting a film studies program.—**Josh Eugene Finnell**

C

416.   Wlaschin, Ken. **The Silent Cinema in Song, 1896-1929: An Illustrated History and Catalog of Songs Inspired by the Movies and Stars, with a List of Recordings.** Jefferson, N.C., McFarland, 2009. 388p. illus. index. $49.95pa. ISBN 13: 978-0-7864-3804-4.

The author of this work, the director of creative affairs at the American Film Institute, offers a history of theatric music during the time of silent films in the early part of the twentieth century. Without speaking roles oftentimes the musical score could make or break the film for moviegoers and at time the music was just as popular as the film. Therefore, music was a big part of the popular culture of the time and songs were associated with and written about many of the major stars of the day. This title, divided into three sections, provides a history of those songs and the movies they were used in. Part 1, "Movies and Moviegoing," describes the songs used in movies between 1896 and 1929, while part 2, "Movie Personalities and Their Films," provides biographical information about the stars and the songs that were created for their movie roles. Part 3, "Recordings," provides reviews of the songs as well as their availability today on LP, CD, DVD, and the Internet. This is a valuable addition to any film library because it includes biographical and historical information not found in other resources. Large public libraries will want to consider it as well because of its well-written, educational, and eminently readable look at the early history of the entertainment industry.—**Shannon Graff Hysell**

Dictionaries and Encyclopedias

C, P

417.   Armes, Roy. **Dictionary of African Filmmakers.** Bloomington, Ind., Indiana University Press, 2008. 397p. index. $65.00. ISBN 13: 978-0-253-35116-6.

Armes (Professor Emeritus of Film, Middlesex University) specializes in African filmmaking, having previously published two reference works on the subject. His new volume covers the entire range of feature film on the continent, from the earliest days through the present, listing 5,415 films made by 1,253 filmmakers in 37 countries. Each director must have made at least one feature film to be included, so not all are necessarily known for the genre. Entries in part 1, the biographical dictionary, provide data on date and place of birth, training or film experience, other creative activities, and a list of feature films produced. Biographical data is very brief, normally a sentence or two, with the lists making up the body of this section. Part 2 lists the films by country and then by year, to see how productive a particular nation has been. The longest section, part 3, indexes the film titles and provides English and French translations where appropriate. A final secondary bibliography aids in future research. As a quick guide to feature filmmaking in Africa, Armes is a welcome addition to the comprehensive film reference collections, to support Leaman's *Companion Encyclopedia of Middle Eastern and North African Film* (see ARBA 2002, entry 1207).—**Anthony J. Adam**

P

418.   Leslie, Roger. **Film Stars and Their Awards: Who Won What for Movies, Theater and Television.** Jefferson, N.C., McFarland, 2008. 282p. index. $49.95pa. ISBN 13: 978-0-7864-4017-7.

In this title the author has listed all film stars and the awards that they either won or for which they were nominated. The awards include film, theater, television, and tributes. The groups giving awards for film include the Academy of Motion Pictures Arts and Sciences (Oscar), the Berlin International Film Festival, the National Board of Review, the British Academy of Film and Television Arts, the Broadcast Film Critics Association, the Cannes Film Festival, the Hollywood Foreign Press Association (Golden Globe), Los Angeles Film Critics Association, New York Film Critics Circle, Screen Actors Guild, National Society of Film Critics, Film Independent (Independent Spirit Awards) and the Venice International Film Festival. The group giving the award for theater is the American Theater Wing (Antoinette Perry "Tony"

Award), while the groups giving the television awards include the American Television Arts & Sciences (Emmy), the Hollywood Foreign Press Association (Golden Globe), and the Screen Actors Guild. Organizations who give out tribute awards include the American Film Institute, the Kennedy Center for the Performing Arts, the Film Society of Lincoln Center, and the Emmy Hall of Fame.

The entries are listed alphabetically by the actor's last name and include the actor's name, the type of award or recognition with movie awards being listed first, followed by theater, television, tributes, records, and highlights. The records refer to acting or other awards. The highlights include interesting background information about the actor's award histories. Not every entry has all categories, but a movie award must be included in order to be listed in this work.

There is a very detailed index. It includes the actors, films, plays, and television shows listed by name. The only problem with that index is that when something other than the actor's name is mentioned one is given a page number, which means that one must scan the whole page to find the entry that lists the mentioned item. It would also have been useful to have a listing by film award and then by year.

This book makes finding awards for actors in films very easy. There are Websites that list these awards, but nowhere is it made so convenient. This will be useful in most collections.—**Robert L. Turner Jr.**

C, P

419.   Terrace, Vincent. **Encyclopedia of Television Shows, 1925 Through 2007.** Jefferson, N.C., McFarland, 2009. 4v. index. $145.00pa./set. ISBN 13: 978-0-7864-3305-6.

Terrace is arguably the most prolific developer of television reference material, with more than 30 books to his credit, including *Television Characters* (see ARBA 2006, entry 1137) and *Television Sitcom Factbook* (see ARBA 2001, entry 1126). His latest work documents the entire history of U.S. television shows aired between 1927 and 2007, including network, cable, syndicated prime time, late night, daytime, and Saturday morning programs. The 9,350 shows featured here cover all genres, from talk shows to documentaries to sitcoms, but what distinguishes Terrace from other resources is the inclusion of failed pilots. Each alphabetically arranged entry includes network and genre data, airing dates, a basic plot synopsis (but no episode information), and cast/character names. For some longer entries, Terrace includes trivia and additional production information. A useful index completes the final volume, and entries reference prequels and spinoffs. However, Terrace does not include BBC shows often found on PBS, and no locally produced shows (e.g., "Garfield Goose and Friends") are included. Although the Internet Movie Data Base (http://www.imdb.com) features much of the cast information found in this volume, readers will still want to purchase the set for the plot synopses and other data. This set is highly recommended for all libraries to complement *The Complete Directory to Prime Time Network and Cable TV Shows, 1946-Present* (9th ed.; Ballantine, 2007).—**Anthony J. Adam**

C, P

420.   Varner, Paul. **Historical Dictionary of Westerns in Cinema.** Lanham, Md., Scarecrow, 2008. 259p. (Historical Dictionaries of Literature and the Arts, no.26). $80.00. ISBN 13: 978-0-8108-5589-2.

For a dictionary-style reference work, Paul Varner manages to weave a surprisingly strong narrative about the history of Western cinema. As Varner points out in his introduction, Western films and television shows have generally been more about mythmaking (or myth busting) than history telling. Yet, it is still important for viewers to understand the historical context of the genre, as analyzed in such entries as "Manifest Destiny" and "Racial Others as Threats to White Women." John Wayne and Clint Eastwood loom large here, partly due to their large bodies of work. They also serve as examples of the two main Western film styles: the classic Western and the anti-myth Western. Varner presents John Ford's *The Searchers* as something of a turning point between the two styles. Featuring one of Wayne's most complex and flawed characters, the film uses the classic American myths of the West to explore contemporary concerns. As the collective consciousness changed throughout the twentieth century, the tone of Westerns gradually changed from nostalgia for what American viewers saw as an age of endless possibility to criticism of a bygone era that was never as innocent or as noble as the movies once made it seem. An extensive bibliography divided by category and a chronology of events spanning from 1890 to 2007 help round out the book as an excellent resource for researchers, yet the book has plenty to offer for the casual user as well. Current fans of the genre will appreciate the lighthearted entries discussing famous movie horses and early cowboy creeds (which all included being kind to women, children, and animals), while novice viewers will learn about every aspect of the genre, from the importance of landscape to the impact of television Westerns on American life. This work is highly recommended for public and academic libraries.—**Alan K. Pannell**

Filmography

C, P

421.   Pitts, Michael R. **Western Film Series of the Sound Era.** Jefferson, N.C., McFarland, 2009. 474p. illus. index. $95.00. ISBN 13: 978-0-7864-3529-6.

The author of this title has written over 30 books on entertainment, including another title on Westerns from McFarland, *Western Movies: A TV and Video Guide to 4,200 Genre Films* (1997). This title covers 30 western film series that appeared from 1930 to the early 1950s. Pitts includes both long-running and short-running series, such as *Hopalong Cassidy*, *The Durango Kid*, *The Singing Cowgirl*, and *The Texas Rangers*. The book is arranged in alphabetic order by series name and each includes a three- to five-page synopsis and analysis of the series, black-and-white photographs, and a detailed filmography. A name/title index concludes the volume making the title easy to use for reference purposes. This work could be used as a supplement in film history sections of public and academic libraries.—**Shannon Graff Hysell**

Videography

P

422.   **VideoHound's Golden Movie Retriever.** 2009 ed. Jim Craddock, ed. Farmington Hills, Mich., Gale Group, 2008. 1923p. index. $24.95pa. ISBN 13: 978-1-4144-0004-4. ISSN 1095-371X.

With "VideoHound" in the title, it is tempting to toss out analogies such as "man's best friend" or "faithful companion." Clichés aside, *VideoHound's Golden Movie Retriever 2009* is an addictive source of facts and reviews of almost 29,000 videos and DVDs with plenty of attitude to make it fun. Published annually since 1991, this guide just keeps getting better. The 2009 edition provides short, snarky reviews with ratings of 0-4 bones (four bones will make one "want to recommend to complete strangers on the street") . Cast, director, writer, and cinematographer; format; MPAA rating; and much more are listed for each film. The category index provides a subject arrangement of the films—and not just the conventional categories. Where else could one find films classified by "Bad Bosses," "Fatsuit Acting," "Nuns with Guns," "Penguins," and numerous other equally odd headings. Other sections include the alternate titles index, kibbles and series index (adaptations and sources), awards index, cast index, director index, writer index, cinematographer index, composer index, video sources (e.g., mail order, retail), and an extensive Website guide for film information. At 1,923 pages, it is hard to find a more comprehensive guide. Leonard Maltin's annual *Movie Guide* comes the closest, but with only 17,000 entries in the 2008 edition, shorter reviews, and less factual information, the award goes to *VideoHound*. The large format in paperback with very thin pages may make it awkward for heavy use in a busy reference department (it resembles a telephone book), but that is a small inconvenience for extensive information with attitude.—**Judy Dyki**

THEATER

Biography

C

423.   Fliotsos, Anne, and Wendy Vierow. **American Women Stage Directors of the Twentieth Century.** Champaign, Ill., University of Illinois Press, 2008. 461p. index. $60.00. ISBN 13: 978-0-252-03226-4.

Although Shakespeare accorded them equal status when he said, "All the world 's a stage, and all the men and women merely players," the history of theater has not been so generous in its treatment of women directors. This fascinating study by Anne Fliotsos and Wendy Vierow focuses on the lives and careers of American women stage directors who were active during the twentieth century. The authors selected 50 women for whom stage directing comprised a significant portion of their careers. Each informative essay provides brief biographical material, a chronology of the woman's career in directing, excerpts from reviews, a description of the director's approach to casting and rehearsal, and a summary of the director's legacy or contribution (including major awards). A short bibliography is included for each entry. Portrait photographs of the women are clustered at the center of the volume. The introductory material for the book includes a brief literature review, plus insightful essays exploring the history of women's involvement in theater and the obstacles and prejudices women have faced in pursuing the role of stage director in a field that still favors men. Appendixes include a chronology of women directors by birth date, lists of women nominees and winners of Tony Awards for Best Direction, plus a general bibliography on women directors. Fliotsos and Vierow, with academic backgrounds in theater and performance studies, respectively, have crafted a solid volume that fills a gap in the literature and will prove valuable for collections in theater history and gender studies. [R: BL, 1 &15 Jan 09, p. 120]—**Judy Dyki**

Dictionaries and Encyclopedias

C, P

424.   Fisher, James, and Felicia Hardison Londré. **Historical Dictionary of American Theater: Modernism.** Lanham, Md., Scarecrow, 2009. 570p. (Historical Dictionaries of Literature and the Arts, no.23). $120.00. ISBN 13: 978-0-8108-5533-5.

Compiled by two U.S. theater professors, this dictionary is a very comprehensive and rather unique resource covering the five-decade Modernism era of American theater (1880-1930). Dealing exclusively with legitimate theater only (no musicals or variety shows), it focuses mostly on the people (dramatists, actors, directors, designers, and critics) and the major plays of the era, although terminology and other miscellaneous categories are included. Biographical entries include birth and death dates and their major productions. Entries for plays include length of run, major performers, and skeletal plot summaries, but, like the entries for people, lack bibliographic references. The entries are informative, objective, and brief. Cross-references follow a complicated but effective system; basically those within the volume appear in bold and those that extend into the yet-to-be-published companion volume on contemporary theater are marked with an asterisk. The dictionary is enhanced by a 15-page chronology, a 10-page introduction that provides context, and a comprehensive bibliography. This worthy companion to the *Historical Dictionary of the Broadway Musical* (see ARBA 2008, entry 1041), in the same Scarecrow series, is appropriate for both public and academic reference collections.—**Lawrence Olszewski**

C, P

425.   Hill, Anthony D., and Douglas Q. Barnett. **Historical Dictionary of African American Theater.**
Lanham, Md., Scarecrow, 2009. 542p. (Historical Dictionaries of Literature and the Arts, no.31). $115.00.
ISBN 13: 978-0-8108-5534-2.

This much-needed and appreciated reference work is part of a historical dictionary series published
by Scarecrow Press. It deals with the history and development of the African American theater from the
seventeenth century to the present. Even though black theater in America started in 1821, it has had a var-
iegated history. The heart of the dictionary consists of over 600 alphabetically arranged entries dealing
with black playwrights, actors, production organizations, directors, plays, and historical events and trends.

Surrounding the entries is a short chronology compilation, a detailed acronym and abbreviation
list, and an excellent historical overview of black theater by the authors. A solid bibliography follows
the entries and is divided up by topics (e.g., historical studies, playwrights, autobiographies, biographies, criticism, interviews). There are also 18 interesting illustrations and photographs of social importance in the history of black theater. This reference work will be a boon to social and theater historians,
libraries, teachers, students, directors, critics, and dramaturges, as well as the casual lover of all theater
and theater history.—**Charles Neuringer**

C, P

426.   **The Oxford Companion to the American Musical.** By Thomas Hischak. New York, Oxford
University Press, 2008. 923p. illus. index. $39.95. ISBN 13: 978-0-19-533533-0.

Hischak (SUNY Cortland) has an impressive list of publications, many of them reference works related to the performing arts. A recent example is his revision of the 3d edition of *The Oxford Companion to
American Theatre* (see ARBA 2005, entry 1220). In this new volume he furnishes a separate guide to
American musicals, but with a difference: he does not limit himself to the stage but also includes film and
television musicals. There are approximately 2,000 entries arranged in one alphabet: by name of individual or organization; title of show; or subject (e.g., "Revue Musicals") . Individual entries range in length
from 250 to some more than 1,000 words. Hischak cross-references items by use of "caps and small caps"
for words or names within entries to show there is a link to another entry. Small icons indicate whether the
show discussed is a stage, film, or television musical.

The scope is broad, ranging from the earliest musicals (a production of Gay's *Beggar's Opera* in
1750 to 2008s *In the Heights*). One finds performers from Lillian Russell (1861-1922) to Sutton Foster (b.
1975), composers from John Philip Sousa (1854-1932) to Adam Guettel (b. 1964), and producing organizations like Playwrights Horizons and the Ohio Light Opera. Performers identified with screen musicals
(Joan Blondell and Nelson Eddy) are featured as are those with the stage (Karen Ziemba and Alfred
Drake), not to mention those who found careers on stage, screen, and television (Danny Kaye and Bob
Hope).

As the work is not limited to one medium, the reader can follow the course of a particular show. For
Oklahoma! information is given on casts of four major stage productions as well as the film. In a few cases
the show began as a film. For *Singin' in the Rain* you first have information and cast of the 1952 movie and
then the 1986 stage version. There are some productions that had life only on the screen (*Gold Diggers*,
Moulin Rouge). Hischak does a fine job treating the individual versions a particular show might have.
With *Peter Pan* there is a basic story but two different stage versions plus a movie and then a television
production. Or consider O'Neill's *Ah, Wilderness!* It had one incarnation as a film musical, *Summer Holiday*, and then a completely different life on stage as *Take Me Along*. Hischak adeptly handles what might
otherwise be confusing situations.

The subject entries give an extra dimension to this work; for example, "Business and Politics in Musicals" and "Shakespeare Musicals" address these very specific topics. Unfortunately, those using the
work solely as a ready-reference tool may miss these valuable additions. Hischak enlivens many entries
with his own personal comments, which give this work particular warmth. The volume concludes with
several appendixes: a chronology of the musicals (1750-2008), a chronological list of Academy and Tony

Awards, a guide to recordings, a comprehensive bibliography, and an index. For many shows Hischak features as a sidebar lists of casts (original and revival productions and movie and television versions). For some musicals he also includes a sidebar with musical numbers. The photographs throughout the volume are a good addition.

Aficionados may question a few statements or regret the omission of some favorite performers and shows; but they should take a cue from those *South Pacific* Seabees, singing about the "dames" they miss, "Be grateful for the things they got." Like the latest edition of Gerald Bordman's *American Musical Theatre: A Chronology* (see ARBA 2002, entry 1242), this volume is an essential reference work on the shelves of all performing arts collections, large public libraries, academic libraries, and the personal libraries of individuals committed to the American musical.—**Richard D. Johnson**

Handbooks and Yearbooks

C

427.   **Women in American Musical Theatre: Essays on Composers, Lyricists, Librettists, Arrangers, Choreographers, Designers ....** Bud Coleman and Judith A. Sebesta, eds. Jefferson, N.C., McFarland, 2008. 282p. illus. index. $45.00pa. ISBN 13: 978-0-7864-3382-7.

This work is a collection of essays that chronicle the history of women in musical theater. Each selection provides biographical information, and a detailed description of the career of the individual or individuals. While the selections vary in length and detail, each provides valuable information and complete notes at the end. Some of the selections include "Twentieth-Century Women Choreographers: Refining and Redefining the Showgirl Image," by Anna Wheeler Gentry; "The Rise of the Female Director/Choreographer on Broadway," by Mary Jo Lodge; and "Will You Remember: Female Lyricists of Operetta and Musical Comedy," by Korey R. Rothman. The book also includes an introduction, which provides a valuable overview of women in the American musical theater and a detailed index. One important aspect of the work is its ample documentation, but it lacks a bibliography. Looking at the notes at the end of each selection makes this reader long for a detailed bibliography that could have been developed from the works documented in the individual selections. All-in-all Professor Coleman has done an excellent job bringing all of these articles together in one volume. The work is recommended for all public and academic library collections, and would certainly be a must purchase for all scholars of American musical theater. —**Robert L. Wick**

28 Philosophy and Religion

PHILOSOPHY

Dictionaries and Encyclopedias

C

428. Burbidge, John W. **Historical Dictionary of Hegelian Philosophy.** 2d ed. Lanham, Md., Scarecrow, 2008. 253p. (Historical Dictionaries of Religions, Philosophies, and Movements, no.90). $75.00. ISBN 0-8108-6051-1. ISBN 13: 978-0-8108-6051-3.

This resource begins with a chronology of Hegel's life in the context of his published writings and the writings of other philosophers with special focus on his tenure as professor at Heidelberg, 1816-1831. The chronology continues long after his death regarding editions of his collected works. The introduction describes the love-hate reaction to Hegel, some viewing him as a savior, others as a heretic. The term dialectic is explained as a hallmark of Hegelian thought. The dictionary is comprised of terms used by Hegel and these terms are defined as Hegel understood them as well as in the broader realm of philosophy. All terms include their original German translation. A shorter glossary follows of German terms used by Hegel along with their English translation. The volume concludes with a lengthy bibliography of known works by and about Hegel. This dictionary is a fine resource for students and professors engaged in the study of Hegel and Hegelian thought.—**Arthur Quinn**

C

429. Gensler, Harry J., and Earl W. Spurgin. **Historical Dictionary of Ethics.** Lanham, Md., Scarecrow, 2008. 362p. (Historical Dictionaries of Religions, Philosophies, and Movements, no.91). $95.00. ISBN 0-8108-5763-4. ISBN 13: 978-0-8108-5763-6.

This resource begins with a chronology of milestones in the study of ethics, dating back to the Code of Hammurabi, 1780 B.C.E. The introduction simplifies ethics as understanding and making choices relevant to all concerns. The field of ethics is divided into three areas: metaethics (moral judgments), normative ethics (general principles), and applied ethics (specific moral issues). The bulk of the dictionary entries more closely resemble articles that address historical, biographical, and practical aspects related to the entries. The bibliography is divided into sections and is very comprehensive, including resources in all media (e.g., print, electronic, audiovisual) and appropriate in all adult contexts (e.g., scholarship, pedagogy, multi-disciplinary pursuits). This resource would make a fine addition to any collection in higher education and could easily bear the title, "Historical Encyclopedia of Ethics."—**Arthur Quinn**

C

430. Michelman, Stephen. **Historical Dictionary of Existentialism.** Lanham, Md., Scarecrow, 2008. 379p. (Historical Dictionaries of Religious, Philosophies, and Movements, no.82). $90.00. ISBN 0-8108-5493-7. ISBN 13: 978-0-8108-5493-2.

Existentialism remains one of the most popular and least well understood areas of the western intellectual tradition. Stephen Michelman sifts through mountains of material in order to produce an extraordinarily valuable reference work. In his historical dictionary, he deftly traces the development of existential thought from its roots in French and German philosophies of existence into the European strands of thought known in pop culture as existentialist. Despite its popularity, many misconceptions about existentialism remain in the minds of the public. Michelman clearly demonstrates that existentialism is not identical to atheism or nihilism, and he addresses some of the lingering questions about Sartre and Heidegger's troubling connections to political movements.

The dictionary will be of great value to undergraduate and graduate students, and serve as a useful reference for their instructors. Michelman provides a chronology, a preface and introduction, and a helpful bibliography, which gives recommendations for both introductory texts and more scholarly commentaries on the major existentialist texts.

Entries include brief discussions of significant critics and rivals of existentialism, such as logical positivism. Heidegger and Sartre, the major existentialist thinkers, receive attention for their texts, political activities, and concepts they introduced, including concepts over which they disagreed, such as Sartre's definition of existentialism. Kierkegaard, Husserl, and Nietzsche, whose works influenced the later existentialists, also receive careful attention. The dictionary covers both the well-known and lesser-known figures, philosophical and literary works, and controversial topics such as the relationship between Heidegger and Hannah Arendt. It is both meticulous and readable.—**Delilah R. Caldwell**

C

431. Pike, Jon. **Political Philosophy A-Z.** Edinburgh, Edinburgh University Press; distr., Irvington, N.Y., Columbia University Press, 2007. 178p. $70.00; $20.00pa. ISBN 13: 978-0-7486-2269-6; 978-0-7486-2270-2pa.

This entry in the Philosophy A-Z Series is primarily intended for undergraduate students to be used as a supplement to political philosophy course texts. The book aims to serve as both a reference resource and an introductory overview to the subject. Despite the broad and interdisciplinary scope of political philosophy, the book manages to be both concise and comprehensive. Through the use of encyclopedic entries, Pike succinctly covers the most significant concepts and figures in the field, while also discussing and evaluating key criticisms of political theories. While remaining reasonably neutral, he interjects just enough opinion to make the book a compelling read. Although most entries are less than a page in length, the suggestions for further reading and an extensive bibliography make this an excellent starting point for anyone unfamiliar with this area.

A book of this type faces increasing competition from the Internet for readers, yet one of the techniques it employs will seem very familiar to students who have grown up in the age of hyperlinking. Key terms and names in each entry appear in bold type, directing the reader to related entries. This system of cross-referencing greatly extends the value of this slim volume by helping those who fully explore these related ideas to gain an understanding of the larger context. As with Web browsing, there can be an addictive quality to following the often unexpected trail of these cross-references. In showing how the diverse concepts fit together, the book succeeds in its goal of providing the philosophical framework needed by new students of this subject. This work is recommended for academic libraries.—**Alan K. Pannell**

RELIGION

General Works

Atlases

C, P

432. **Atlas of the World's Religions.** 2d ed. Ninian Smart and Frederick Denny, eds. New York, Oxford University Press, 2007. 272p. illus. index. $110.00. ISBN 13: 978-0-19-533401-2.

Using maps, charts, timelines, photographs, and text, this atlas presents a historical geography of religion. From Paleolithic beginnings with Beijing Man (500,000 B.C.E.) to the present day, the changes in the world of religion have been traced by reference to broader traditions. In this work, Smart and Denny, have edited the writings of several highly qualified authors, all professors at universities around the world.

More than 200 carefully drawn maps are cleverly marked, with icons setting forth the specifics of each. These maps are found in chapters of up to 15 double-page spreads dealing with each religion. New to this edition are spreads on Mormonism, Charismatic Christianity, religion and ecology and the environment, contemporary pilgrimage routes around the world, languages of religion, religious personal and place-names, Christianity in South America, and contemporary diasporic religious communities.

It is interesting to note how similar celebratory rites and views about a deity existed in different locales around the world although they were widely separated geographically. The text and maps in the section on historical geography begin this concept that is expanded in the larger section on the world's religions and amplified with timelines and photographs of sacred sites, figures, and objects. Furthermore, it continues to describe how various beliefs were transmitted to different areas of the world. Because of this work's inclusiveness and easy-to-read maps and text, it will be appreciated by both specialists and generalists.—**Sara R. Mack**

Biography

C, P, S

433. **Icons of Unbelief: Atheists, Agnostics, and Secularists.** S. T. Joshi, ed. Westport, Conn., Greenwood Press, 2008. 463p. index. (Greenwood Icons). $75.00. ISBN 13: 978-0-313-34759-7.

This biographical collection offers in-depth, essay-format profiles of 27 iconic figures of "unbelief," intellectuals who have advocated for atheism, agnosticism, or secularism, from the historical (e.g., Voltaire, the Founding Fathers) to the contemporary (e.g., Ayaan Hirsi Ali, Sam Harris). Intended to foster debate, *Icons of Unbelief* provides an overview of each individual in the context of their religious philosophy related to atheism, agnosticism, and secularism. The political and social implications of religious thought are woven throughout the essays, as these domains are not easily separated from religion and everyday life. This is an excellent starting point for research and paper writing, but the casual reader will find the book engaging as well. This reviewer was caught up in the content and found the profiles to be well written, clearly presented, and very informative. The essays present minimal personal biographical information and do not aspire to comprehensive coverage of the subjects' lives, rather the essays mostly focus on the subject's religious philosophy. Each essay includes a primary and secondary bibliography representing works cited within the essay plus a few other major publications. The bibliography is not intended to be comprehensive as many of the icons profiled are, or have been, quite prolific. The expertise of each of the contributors is outlined in brief biographies following the main entries. A comprehensive keyword index completes the volume. This set is recommended for public, high school, and academic libraries. —**Polly D. Boruff-Jones**

Bible Studies

Atlases

C, P

434.   **Oxford Bible Atlas.** 4th ed. By Adrian Curtis. New York, Oxford University Press, 2007. 229p. illus. maps. index. $35.00. ISBN 0-19-100158-9.

The aim of this new edition, as in previous editions, is to help the reader perceive the setting and context of the Bible by using maps accompanied by abundant descriptive text. The text of this edition has been considerably revised and updated. All illustrations, maps (27), and photographs (81) are now in color (except for three photographs). These include two spectacular satellite photographs of the southern Levant region. Also new to this edition is a chronology table adapted from *Oxford History of the Biblical World* (1998) beginning approximately 43,000 B.C.E. and ending 330 C.E. The editor, a Methodist lay preacher, chose to avoid the terms "Holy Land" and "Promised Land" in this edition due to religious and politically charged connotations. "Palestine" is used in the geographical sense for the southern part of the east Mediterranean coastal strip. Arrangement of this edition begins with a section that orients the reader to the lands of the Bible, including climate, plants, and animals, as well as the great civilizations of the ancient Near East which form the backdrop to the events of the Bible. The next two sections cover the Hebrew Bible and the New Testament. Then finally, a section on archaeology in Bible lands outlines the contributions of archaeology to the understanding of ancient cultures and their influence on the peoples of Israel and Judah. A general index follows an index of place-names (many entries include alternative names). [R: LJ, 1 Sept 07, p. 166]—**Linda M. Turney**

Bibliography

P

435.   Worth, Roland H., Jr. **Biblical Studies on the Internet: A Resource Guide.** 2d ed. Jefferson, N.C., McFarland, 2008. 378p. index. $49.95pa. ISBN 13: 978-0-7864-3625-5.

This is an amazing, massive directory of mostly free English and non-English Bible resources on the Internet, including Bible translations (102 non-English translations), simultaneous multiple translations, audio Bibles, and downloadable Bible programs (mostly free). The volume also includes commentaries on the Bible as a whole and on individual books as well as concordances, dictionaries, encyclopedias, and Greek, Hebrew, and other ancient language resources. In addition, the author includes apologetics and religious debates, theological studies, hermeneutics, private Bible studies, sermons, devotionals, hymns, recreational activities, Apocrypha and Deuterocanonical literature, non-canonical materials and pseudo-authoritative writings, writings by church-related authors, and non-Christian Jewish authors. Web pages that have multiple entries are noted as major sources, indicated by "M," and are listed in the appendix. Special instructions on how to use a Website are included when needed. An index is included.

A heavy-duty bookmark is recommended to keep one's place while turning to the appendix in the back of the book and typing in Web addresses. This reviewer frequently lost her place while visiting a sampling of Web pages. The addition of a CD-ROM with the book's Web addresses and links already typed and ready to click would be beneficial to the reader. Overall, this book is an excellent resource for locating Bible-related materials on the Internet.—**Linda M. Turney**

Biography

P

436.   Losch, Richard R. **All the People in the Bible: An A-Z Guide to the Saints, Scoundrels, and other Characters in Scripture.** Grand Rapids, Mich., William B. Eerdmans, 2008. 578p. $26.00pa. ISBN 13: 978-0-8028-2454-7.

The Christian Bible is like a Russian novel: full of characters, with each character having multiple, hard-to-pronounce names. It is no wonder that many people have problems keeping the 31 Azariahs or even the several Jameses that appear in the New Testament straight. Even the most seasoned biblical scholar needs a well-written, organized guide to the people of the Bible.

The main purpose of *All the People in the Bible*, is to not only give the reader a brief biography of many of the characters in the Bible, but to include others, who influenced the events of the Bible but were not mentioned in it. By including the Roman and Seleucid emperors, and the Maccabean leaders, the reader not only grasps the importance of each biblical character, but also understands the historical perspective of each person.

Another strength of this work, is its in-depth treatment and the unique perspective of the Herod family. Traditionally in Christian literature, Herod Agrippa I, is portrayed as a merciless persecutor of the early church; Losch, however, depicts Agrippa as a devoted Jew, whose primary goal was to preserve the Jewish religion and way of life. Even though Richard R. Losch is a retired rector of the Episcopal Church, he nevertheless successfully reaches out to other religious traditions, Christian and otherwise, by including the characters from the Catholic Apocrypha and using the dating system of B.C.E. and C.E. instead of the traditional B.C. and A.D.

Losch's organized treatment of the characters in the Bible, as well as his respect for other traditions and enthusiasm for the Judeo-Christian scriptures, makes *All the People in the Bible* a must for any church or seminary library.—**Theresa Lynn Bruno**

Dictionaries and Encyclopedias

P

437.   Porter, J. R. **The Illustrated Guide to the Bible.** New York, Oxford University Press, 2008. 288p. illus. index. $24.95pa. ISBN 13: 978-0-19-534233-8.

This book has many colorful illustrations throughout its pages. There are color maps, photographs, and other illustrations that are eye catching. The maps have the appearance of having been hand drawn. There are many sidebars throughout the book on various subjects connected with the chapter they are in. There are several charts like lists of rulers and family trees. At the beginning of each chapter is a short list of the various sections in the chapter with its page number. Toward the back of the book is a short summary of all of the books of the Bible, including the Apocryhpal and Deuterocanonical books. There is a one-page glossary, a one-page list of abbreviations, a two-page bibliography, and an index. This book is highly recommended to libraries looking for an inexpensive guide to the Bible. It is not a reference book for small or medium-sized libraries. It is a colorfully illustrated introduction to the Bible.—**Benet Steven Exton**

Buddhism

C, P, S

438.   Irons, Edward A. **Encyclopedia of Buddhism.** New York, Facts on File, 2008. 634p. illus. index. (Encyclopedia of World Religions). $67.50. ISBN 13: 978-0-8160-5459-6.

The *Encyclopedia of Buddhism* is one of six titles in the Encyclopedia of World Religions series that introduces and profiles the world's major religious traditions—Buddhism, Hinduism, Islam, Judaism, Roman Catholicism, and Protestant Christianity—with comprehensive coverage of each religion's historical beginnings, defining events, and faith traditions. Similar to the other books in the series, this *Encyclopedia* provides explanation and description of key terminology, individuals, places, and theological concepts. Although this title is focused specifically on Buddhism it also includes introductions to Daoism, Shinto, and Confucianism. The introductory essay outlines significant concepts and describes Buddhism's development and spread from India to Southeast Asia, China, Korea, Japan, and Tibet. As Buddhism spread across Asia variant schools developed due to differences in geography and doctrine and several of the major schools are profiled. Other themes include art, historical events, modern traditions, festivals, globalization, martial arts, psychology, war, and Buddhism in the West. Users will likely find the introduction sections on the Romanization of foreign terms and pronunciation helpful to read before moving into the body of the book. Approximately 700 fascinating entries are arranged alphabetically with coverage ranging from brief (one to two paragraphs) to in-depth entries several pages in length. Maps, tables, and a chronology covering the years 3000 B.C.E. to 2007 provide additional information that enriches the text. The index is not cross-referenced, but the body of the text does include *see* references, which usefully include alternate spellings. For example, looking up "Tai Chi Chuan" refers the researcher to the entry "Taijiquan," but there is no "Tai Chi Chuan" listed in the index. The contributors are well-credentialed experts; the coverage is academic and very readable. Each entry concludes with further readings for the reader wishing to expand their research. This book is highly recommended for public, high school, and academic libraries.—**Polly D. Boruff-Jones**

Christianity

Chronology

C

439.   Bowden, John, with Margaret Lydamore and Hugh Bowden. **A Chronology of World Christianity.** New York, Continuum Publishing, 2007. 529p. illus. index. $70.00. ISBN 13: 978-0-8264-9633-1.

What does a monk, a prostitute, a king, and a poor carpenter have in common? This isn't the beginning of a bad joke—these characters and many others have played a role in the history of Christianity. A favorite religion instructor of mine once told me that the history of Christianity is much like a soap opera, only it is filled with more sex, lies, and intrigue. Trying to follow all of this intrigue, however, can be confusing even for an expert. There are 13 Pope Leos, 16 King Louis's of France, and endless ecumenical councils, so how is any novice suppose to keep them all strait? To help novices and experts alike find the Pope Leo who had his eyes gorged out by assassins or the King Louis whose head was chopped off, John Bowden wrote *A Chronology of World Christianity*. This book attempts to list in chronological order the events, people, and ecumenical counsels and disputes until the present day. The book is divided into centuries, with an introduction to each chapter with a brief summary of events and important developments during the century. In addition, major events, people, and movements in Christianity receive a more detailed description about their influence on the history of Christianity.

John Bowden's book has many positive aspects, from the in-depth explanations of major events to the illustrations found in the book. I most appreciated, however, that Bowden includes all the sects that considered themselves Christians, such as the Gnostics, Arians, and Cathars. No group or sect is considered a heretic by Bowden and are all treated with respect and dignity.

Unlike other books I have reviewed, I have no real criticism of the book. Bowden's book is what it is, a chronology of the events, persons, and movements that have shaped Christianity. This book would be a perfect addition to any college or seminary library.—**Theresa Lynn Bruno**

Dictionaries and Encyclopedias

C, P

440. Bitton, Davis, and Thomas G. Alexander. **Historical Dictionary of Mormonism.** 3d ed. Lanham, Md., Scarecrow, 2009. 319p. (historical Dictionaries of Religions, Philosophies, and Movements, no.89). $99.00. ISBN 0-8108-5814-2. ISBN 13: 978-0-8108-5814-5.

This dictionary, one in the Historical Dictionaries of Religions, Philosophies, and Movements series from Greenwood Press, defines the terms associated with the Church of Jesus Christ of Latter-Day Saints, better known as Mormonism. This religion, organized in 1830, has an interesting history and, although mainly based in the United States, is growing in South America, Asia, and even Africa, with a congregation of about 13 million members worldwide. The terms defined in this work include historical regions, leaders and prominent individuals, beliefs, events, and activities associated with Mormonism. The entries range from one paragraph for easily understood terms to several pages for others (e.g., Joseph Smith, polygamy, Brigham Young). The book has four appendixes—a list of church presidents, reprints of "The Family: A Proclamation to the World" and "The Living Christ," and a list of temples dedicated through February 2008. The volume concludes with a 60-page bibliography of books and periodical articles. As Mormonism is one of the world's most misunderstood religions, this title will be a useful title in many public and academic libraries.—**Shannon Graff Hysell**

C, P

441. Chryssides, George D. **Historical Dictionary of Jehovah's Witnesses.** Lanham, Md., Scarecrow, 2008. 169p. (Historical Dictionaries of Religions, Philosophies, and Movements, no.85). $80.00. ISBN 13: 978-0-8108-6074-2.

The author, who is head of religious studies at the University of Wolverhampton, England, has produced a work that will help a layperson understand better the Jehovah's Witnesses. He starts the book with a brief chronology of events that are important in their history, with a caution that the dates given for biblical events are contested by historians and other religious groups.

The next part of the work is a 40-page introduction that looks at the history of the movement, mentioning the key people and important events both within the movement as well as outside world events that influenced the Witnesses' doctrines and beliefs. It is a good overview of the organization from its beginning up to the twenty-first century. There are then about 250 entries that discuss doctrines, people, beliefs, and organizations. Within each entry words that are elsewhere defined are printed in bold type making it very easy to determine which other ideas to pursue. There are many *see* references to send the reader to the correct term. For example, door-to-door ministry sends the reader to the preferred term house-to-house ministry where that practice is explained.

Then there is an extremely detailed bibliography that lists primary sources, mainly those published by the Jehovah's Witnesses themselves. Next there is a section on writings that had an early influence on the movement and a section on things written by Jehovah's Witnesses that are unofficial writings. There is a section on non-witness publications that are recommended by Witnesses and one that lists secondary sources, including those written by ex-witnesses and a section listing critiques of Jehovah's Witnesses. There is also a section on electronic resources including CD-ROMs, videos, DVDs, and Websites that have both anti and pro viewpoints.

This is an evenhanded, comprehensive look at the Jehovah's Witnesses and their history. It will be a good place to start studying their religion and world view.—**Robert L. Turner Jr.**

C, P

442. **Global Dictionary of Theology.** William A. Dyrness, Veli-Matti Karkkainen, Juan Francisco Martinez, and Simon Chan, eds. Downers Grove, Ill., InterVarsity Press, 2008. 996p. index. $50.00. ISBN 13: 978-0-8308-2454-0.

The *Global Dictionary of Theology* reviews emerging theological perspectives in World Christianity. Taking a "broadly evangelical and ecumenical perspective" (p. viii), the editors regard theology as inherently contextual, arising within specific contexts. A global perspective takes place as these multiple local contexts engage in conversation and enrich each other. As the introduction states, "The way forward in a globalizing world, we believe, is to acknowledge this diversity of Christian difference" (p. ix). The key strength of this resource is the editors' skill in selecting the voices of difference, orchestrating the conversations, and providing readers with an opportunity to hear "global theology" in the process of construction.

Thus the editors recruited scholars from around the world to discuss theological issues and produce articles that illustrate the rich diversity of perspectives endemic to a global resource. These articles mirror the constructed nature of theological knowledge—readers will observe points of unresolved tension, diversity of perspective within articles, and tentative statements that signal the need for further dialogue. And this is the authentic nature of global theology—dynamic voices from around the globe, building knowledge through multiple perspectives.

Readers will not find articles on individual theologians, but on communal aspects (e.g. themes, traditions, doctrines, theological trends in geographical regions). These substantial articles are proportional to the prominence of the topic in the current "state of the art" in theology. Articles on regions include African, Indian, Latin American, and North American native theology. Each article has been carefully organized with a topical outline; appropriate topics include sections on biblical theology and historical foundations. Others divide topics according to their respective nature. There are also a number of articles related to the Church's global mission.

The editors' own traditions, Evangelical and Pentecostal-Charismatic, may have modestly influenced the inclusion of some topics, including Baptism in the Holy Spirit, Healing and Deliverance, and Miracle. However, these belong to any resource that claims to be global in perspective, since Pentecostalism comprises the second largest group in World Christianity. Besides, the editors have exercised their ecumenicity in the selection of a broad array of contemporary scholars and thus transcended particular traditions. The end result is a monumental achievement of ecumenical conversation.—**Barry Hamilton**

C, P

443.   **The New Westminster Dictionary of Church History. Volume I: The Early, Medieval, and Reformation Eras.** Robert Benedetto and others, eds. Louisville, Ky., Westminster/John Knox Press, 2008. 691p. $59.95. ISBN 0-664-22416-4. ISBN 13: 978-0-664-22416-5.

The original *Westminster Dictionary of Church History* (1971) has been succeeded by a two-volume work (of which this is the first volume), continuing its ecumenical orientation and four-part historical organization (Early, Medieval, Reformation, and Post-1700). This newer work enjoys a broader diversity of contributors and greater attention to the modern period (in volume 2). Each of the more than 1,400 articles is now signed, with a brief bibliography for further reading. An alphabetic list of entries and table of abbreviations is provided. Besides referencing people, places, events, and movements, the volume offers helpful entries on wider concepts such as "Devotional Images" and "Early Christian Rhetoric." Broader issues are treated in linked entries, such as the 6 on Historiography and 10 on the Reformation. While the work declares itself neither definitive nor exhaustive (p. ix), readers may miss some familiar names. Among English figures we find John Donne and John Tillotson but not Lancelot Andrewes, Jeremy Taylor, Richard Crashaw, Thomas Traherne, or Robert Southwell. Nevertheless, as a ready source for scholars, pastors, researchers, and general readers of the earlier eras of church history, this volume should prove as helpful as (and more affordable than) the venerable *Oxford Dictionary of the Christian Church* (3d ed.; see ARBA 2006, entry 1234).—**Christopher Baker**

Handbooks and Yearbooks

C

444.   Hess, Peter M. J., and Paul L. Allen. **Catholicism and Science.** Westport, Conn., Greenwood Press, 2008. 241p. illus. index. (Greenwood Guides to Science and Religion). $65.00. ISBN 13: 978-0-313-33190-9.

It is difficult, if not impossible, to consider the development of science in the Western world without exploring the continuing influences of the Catholic Church on scientific belief and inquiry. From Coperni-cus and Galileo to today's debates on stem cell research and cloning, the Church has been and continues to be right at the forefront of scientific debate. In *Catholicism and Science*, authors Hess (St. Mary's College) and Allen (Concordia University, Montreal) explore the interaction between the Catholic tradition and sci-ence over the past 2,000 years. The book is organized chronologically, by topic, discussing in some depth the doctrines and figures that exemplify each topic and time period. Each chapter covers a different topic: "Introduction to Science in the Catholic Tradition," "From Cosmos to Unbound Universe: Physical Sci-ences from Trent to Vatican I," "From the Garden of Eden to an Ancient Earth: Catholicism and the Life and Earth Sciences," "Catholicism and Science at Mid-Twentieth Century," "The Legacy of Vatican II in Cosmology and Biology," and "Catholicism, Neuroscience and Genetics." Each chapter has an introduc-tion to the topic, followed by entries on people and events that illustrate it. Important primary sources, including a letter written by Galileo and documents from several popes and other Church figures, round out the resource.

Catholicism and Science is an outstanding reference resource. It is authoritative and mostly free from bias. The entries are well written, with enough detail for deeper understanding yet not overwhelming as many works on theology, philosophy, and science can be. The illustrations are appropriate, and each en-try has a list of works cited for further research. The index is useful for locating information quickly, and the extensive bibliography provides even more suggestions for further research. It is highly recommended for academic libraries supporting theology, science, and philosophy programs. Larger public libraries might also find it useful.—**Mark T. Bay**

Islam

C, P

445.   Glassé, Cyril. **The New Encyclopedia of Islam.** 3d ed. Lanham, Md., Rowman & Littlefield, 2008. 718p. $99.95. ISBN 13: 978-0-7425-6296-7.

The maps, chronologies, charts, and genealogical tables, along with the plates that adorn rather than illustrate the text, make this work visually appealing and easy to consult. The many brief translations from Islamic classics are an especially attractive feature, and the entries (especially the shorter ones) are simple, clearly written, and accessible to readers with no prior knowledge of Islam. The main subject categories include paradigmatic figures in the Koran, early Islamic history, Islamic rituals, some practical legal top-ics (e.g., abortion, birth control), selected historical dynasties, and institutions. There are also a few techni-cal terms from various Islamic intellectual and legal traditions; a sampling of various Islamic creeds, schools, and sects; and some discussion on Muslim contribution to the arts and science is covered only as far as it pertains to religious thought.

The entries on Hajj and other rituals, Koran recitation, and other practices of the faith discuss not only the mechanics of these rituals but also the deeper spiritual significant they carry. Unfortunately, en-tries related to the Islamic intellectual traditions (such as theology and philosophy) and diverse Muslim communities and societies (especially Shia Islam), are lacking in depth and can sometimes be misleading. Most of the definitions provided are much too basic to satisfy those who want to undertake a serious study of Islam, making it inadequate for undergraduate level work. This work is best suited as a first place to start that leads to more in-depth research as the readers' interests dictate.—**Muhammed Hassanali**

Judaism

C, P

446. Mandel, David. **Who's Who in the Jewish Bible.** Philadelphia, Jewish Publication Society, 2007. 422p. $30.00pa. ISBN 13: 978-0-8276-0863-4.

In this volume David Mandel describes the biographies of 3,000 individuals mentioned in the Tanakh, using the Hebrew Bible as his sole source. The author does not take a theological approach, but bases his entries upon a literal reading of the *Tanakh*, treating it as an historical document. Some of the characters mentioned are spiritual or non-human (Satan), others are of legend. There are major articles on David, Solomon, Moses, and Abraham. He begins with a useful chronology, beginning with the 20th century B.C.E., and Abraham, and ending with a post-biblical chronology, ending in 73 C.E., with the fall of Masada.

Instead of a syndetic structure, where the Hananiah of the 6th century BCE mentioned in Daniel is given a *see* reference from his Babylonian name of Shadrach, Mandel repeats the information in both entries' locations. In many instances, more than one person had the same name. Here Mandel orders the names according to their first appearance in the Bible. For each name, he provides the Hebrew origin of the name, the scriptural reference of the first occurrence, and chronological period, usually by century B.C.E. Some, such as Job are listed as an unspecified date. Satan, whose date does not apply, is surprisingly first mentioned in the minor prophet Zechariah. Some names of those prior to Noah are listed as Antediluvian (before the flood). Through the entries, he cites other biblical scripture that describes the character.

The book is very useful in providing basic chronological data and biographical information about biblical characters, and should be a welcome addition to all academic and religiously sponsored libraries. [R: BL, 1 & 15 June 08, p. 140]—**Ralph Hartsock**

Part IV
SCIENCE AND TECHNOLOGY

29 Science and Technology in General

BIBLIOGRAPHY

C, S

447. **eLibrary Science. http://www.proquestk12.com/eLibrary_Science.shtml.** [Website]. ProQuest K-12. Price negotiated by site. Date reviewed: 2008.

C, S

448. **ProQuest AP Science. http://www.proquestk12.com/productinfo.shtml.** [Website]. ProQuest K-12. Price negotiated by site. Date reviewed: 2008.

The ProQuest *eLibrary Science* service gathers information from more than 400 worthy science publications and provides continually updated science news links, facts on well-known scientists, and educator-approved Websites.

ProQuest AP Science is a database of higher-level materials to support advanced placement and college-level studies in the areas of earth, life, physical, medical, and applied sciences. There is content from more than 500 magazines, full-text from scholarly and professional journals, and images.—**Catherine Barr**

DICTIONARIES AND ENCYCLOPEDIAS

C, P, S

449. **Access Science. http://www.accessscience.com.** [Website]. New York, McGraw-Hill. Price negotiated by site. Date reviewed: 2008.

A total redesign of the online science platform for Access Science was rolled out in the fall of 2007-2008. Based on the 10th edition of the *McGraw-Hill Encyclopedia of Science and Technology* (10th ed.; see ARBA 2009, entry 1130), this site has detailed content and many user-friendly options that address the needs of today's teachers, students, and librarians.

The database's new features include e-mail forwarding, multiple saving options, and visual and audio learning tools such as flash animations, tutorials, and podcasts. Similar to other online encyclopedias, this source addresses the need for keeping up with current events through the Access Science Explorations feature. It offers highlights of newsworthy topics and provides an exhibition of each topic with accompanying images, video, and audio resources. Users can make the following choices from the homepage: insert a search item in the search box, select a predetermined topic, or go to an alphabetic list of topics to conduct a search. A semantic search engine increases the relevancy of the results by looking for associated words such as synonyms of the identified terms. Another improvement in the searching feature helps students identify and select relevant topics through browse options that have suggested topics or alphabetically linked topics. The content coverage available to users with these new search options include updates from the *Yearbooks of Scientific and Technical Terms*, over 100,000 definitions from the *Dictionary of*

Scientific and Technical Terms, and over 2,000 biographies from the *Hutchinson Dictionary of Scientific Biography.*

Although there are many sections and subject categories on the homepage screen, it is still well-organized and clear. The use of high-contrast black, white, and red colors prevent the homepage from appearing too cluttered and overwhelming. *Access Science* can easily be used as a ready-reference resource for science questions—specifically those difficult questions posed on scientific innovations or equations. The prominent tab on the homepage labeled "Librarians" includes many useful resources for library professionals. Current information is available on this page regarding content updates, contact information, and helpful marketing and instructional tools.

Access Science is an excellent resource for upper grades, teachers and librarians. Not only is *Access Science* a terrific resource for strengthening information literacy skills, it is an outstanding online resource that library media specialists can use to encourage collaborative relations with classroom teachers.—**Meghan Harper**

C, P, S

450.   **Battleground: Science & Technology.** Sal Restivo and Peter H. Denton, eds. Westport, Conn., Greenwood Press, 2008. 2v. index. $175.00/set. ISBN 13: 978-0-313-34164-9.

Battleground: Science & Technology is one of the titles in the Battleground series, published by Greenwood Press. (Other titles address topics such as religion, the environment, immigration, sports, and the media.) The intent of the series is to provide nonbiased coverage of topics presented, examining the main points of each side of the issue. *Battleground: Science & Technology* examines more than 100 hot-button science and technology-based topics in essay form, offering an overview of each topic and their scientific, technological, and societal implications. Topics range from autism, cloning, fossil fuels, geothermal energy, and medical ethics, to pesticides, UFOs, and video games. The series editors state in the introduction that "these two volumes are designed to give you a better appreciation of the complexities involved in what might be called the 'science-technology-society' nexus."

Entries are signed by guest authors and average two to four pages in length. Entries offer historical and legal perspectives on topics, as well as key names, dates, and events as appropriate. Some entries have sidebars outlining important events or people. Some entries have additional series editors' comments at the end of the entry. Entries conclude with *see also* references to other entries and a further readings list. At the end of volume 2, there is a comprehensive bibliography and index.

Battleground: Science & Technology offers a basic introduction and overview to the topics addressed. A minor criticism would be the lack of a comprehensive subject index at the end of volume 1. This set is most appropriate for high school libraries, public libraries, and community college library that have a need for introductory material on the topics presented.—**Caroline L. Gilson**

S

451.   **Britannica Illustrated Science Library.** Chicago, Encyclopaedia Britannica, 2008. 16v. illus. maps. index. $425.00/set. ISBN 13: 978-1-59339-382-3.

This new 16-volume set from Encyclopaedia Britannica is designed for students in the middle grades, 5-9. Each volume covers a specific area of science: Birds, Volcanoes and Earthquakes, Universe, Technology, Space Exploration, Rocks and Minerals, Reptiles and Dinosaurs, Mammals, Invertebrates, Human Body I, Human Body II, Fish and Amphibians, Evolution and Genetics, and Energy and Movement. Each volume provides an overview of the subject and uses graphics and photographs to explain details of the science. The simplified text and more than 16,000 images explain the more complicated concepts of each topic and encourage further research. Each volume contains an index and a glossary with full definitions. [R: LJ, 1 April 08]—**Shannon Graff Hysell**

P, S

452.   **Inventors and Inventions.** Tarrytown, N.Y., Marshall Cavendish, 2008. 5v. illus. $399.95/set. ISBN 13: 978-0-7614-7761-7.

Presented in A-Z format, *Inventors and Inventions* provides information on the life and accomplishments of 151 inventors, primarily from the nineteenth and twentieth century. In addition to the inventors, 21 overview articles cover technological developments within various broadly defined themes, such as communication, entertainment, and transportation. While the intended audience is not indicated this set would be most appropriate for middle school through high school students. The first volume contains a table of contents for all five volumes in addition to each volume having its own table of contents. Volume 1 also has a thematic outline grouping the inventors into 14 themes. The set concludes with a glossary, a list of resources for further study, both a name and an inventors index, and a comprehensive index.

Entries for each inventor are 5 to 8 pages in length, while the overview articles range from 6 to 12 pages long. The entries provide brief information on the early life of the inventor and continue with details on the developments and applications of the various inventions. There are sidebars and other highlights throughout the work that provide descriptions of how various technologies work. Pictures, charts and graphs, timelines, and schematics are used throughout the text and contribute to the overall attractiveness and readability of the work. The impact of each invention on society is discussed and a short list of further reading concludes each entry. The majority of inventors come from the United States but a variety of other countries are represented. About 10 percent of the inventors are women. The overall quality of this work is high and would make a nice addition to a school library collection lacking information on inventors and inventions.—**Mike Burgmeier**

C, P, S

453.   Krebs, Robert E. **Encyclopedia of Scientific Principles, Laws, and Theories.** Westport, Conn., Greenwood Press, 2008. 2v. illus. index. $199.95/set. ISBN 13: 978-0-313-34005-5.

This book is a greatly expanded version of the author's *Scientific Laws, Principles, and Theories: A Reference Guide* (see ARBA 2002, entry 1332). It consists of over 600 articles arranged alphabetically by name of the originating scientist. There are a few medical articles, but coverage is largely pure science and mathematics. Each entry has a short biographical identification of the originator, a brief statement of the theory, and a paragraph. There is an extensive glossary, a list of entries by discipline, lists of Nobel laureates, and a short bibliography with a list of relevant Websites (without titles or annotations). There is a detailed index. The work is aimed at high school and college students.

There many serious errors in articles on evolutionary topics. We are told that Mendel published "long before" Darwin. The Gould/Eldredge punctuated equilibrium theory is equated with catastrophic mass extinction. There are said to be two animal kingdoms and three plant kingdoms. Wallace's line is confused with his theory of natural selection. Cuvier's catastrophism is seen as a theory of evolution. Many of the evolutionary articles are confusing. Articles outside evolutionary biology are clearer and more accurate. This title is recommended for public, high school, and college libraries.—**Frederic F. Burchsted**

S

454.   **The New Book of Popular Science.** 2008 ed. Danbury, Conn., Grolier, 2008. 6v. illus. maps. index. $299.00/set. ISBN 13: 978-0-7172-1226-2.

This set has been a reliable science reference source with annual or biennial revisions since 1978. The publisher has retained the six-volume format with thematically arranged topics. The set now contains 15 major topics: astronomy, space science, mathematics, past and future, earth sciences, energy, environmental sciences, chemistry, physics, biology, plant life, animal life, mammals, human sciences, and technology. Articles are signed and written by noted academic scientists. Each topic provides a thorough introduction from a historical perspective to the present of that scientific area. Subheadings and sidebars are used to assist the reader and provide additional related information. New articles are included on portable media players, scientific illustration, and computer graphics. Standard measurements are used throughout the text with metric equivalents in parenthesis. The 5,000-plus illustrations include photographs, maps, computer graphics, art work, and diagrams and comprise approximately one-third of the set. Nearly all illustrations are in full color. The table of contents of each volume is broken into subtopics to assist the reader in rapidly locating specific information. Each volume contains a comprehensive index to the set and a bibliography of suggested resources on the topics within that volume. Volume 6 contains an appendix of 15 lists, which include Subatomic Particles, Mathematical Symbols, Notable Volcanoes, and Units and Symbols. The heavy duty bindings are colorful and illustrate the topics within that volume. A list of the topics within the set is included on the back of the binding with the topics within highlighted in red. The language is jargon free and is directed to middle school and high school students. The set will also be useful in public libraries. The content within this set is also available through Grolier Online, Scholastic's online reference resource. This general science resource is recommended for libraries needing this information in a traditional print format.—**Elaine Ezell**

S

455.   **The New Book of Popular Science. http://auth.grolier.com/login/go_login_page.html?bffs=N.** [Website]. Danbury, Conn., Grolier. Price negotiated by site. Date reviewed: 2008.

The New Book of Popular Science, available both online and in print, offers upper elementary, middle, and high school students and their teachers an important resource for researching curricular-based science topics. Revised editions appear approximately every two to four years, and this latest edition of *The New Book of Popular Science* contains 270 articles, 3,870 pages with 2,750 revised pages, and 5,000 photographs, maps, and pieces of art. The publisher's Website states that "more than one-third of the set is devoted to descriptive illustrations."

The online version of this reference has all of the information from the print set in a component called the SciClopedia with the same thematic topics as the print set. However, since there is no need to combine topics as in the six printed volumes, the online version lists 13 separate areas in a left side navigation bar and available from any page within the online product. These 13 areas are Animal World, Astronomy and Space, Biology, Chemistry, Earth Science, Energy, Environment, Human Life, Mathematics, Past and Future, Physics, Plant World, and Technology. Each topic links to a hyperlinked table of contents with a list of subsections for that topic.

The drawback of using the print set is that all students assigned to the same general topic area, such as Technology or Environment, for research would need to use the same volume at the same time. The online version preserves the thematic arrangement that is so helpful for inquiry, while providing for multiple users and outside school use. A text-only version toggle switch makes the product accessible for those using text readers. The online version, however, does not have any video or audio components as do other Grolier online products. A school's intended use, computer circumstances, and budget will help determine the most useful format for each library media center setting.

The product employs a basic search, "Find It Fast," and an "Advanced Search." The advanced search provides limiters not available in the basic search. In addition to limiting the search to article titles, searchers may also add two additional terms using the Boolean operators and, or, and not. Students can also use this option to narrow and focus their topics. A metasearch of all seven titles simultaneously is available for any or all of the additional Grolier Online titles to which the school subscribes.

Like many other electronic reference sources that include news updates, online lesson plans, and other interactive features, *The New Book of Popular Science* online is no exception. Besides SciClopedia, the main menu lists these additional components: NewsBytes, Projects, Biographies, SciZone, SciFiles, Sky Watch, and Ask Pop Sci.

While this online product will predictably create more student interest in searching and teacher interest in the article Lexile levels, the encyclopedia information on both the print and electronic sets is detailed, authoritative, and clearly written with students' interests and reading level taken into consideration.

Even though the publisher indicates this resource is for seventh through twelfth grade students, it is included in H.W. Wilson's Children's, Middle and Junior High, and Senior High School Core Collections, thus extending usage to the upper-elementary grades.—**Karla Krueger**

C, P, S

456. **Scientific Thought: In Context.** K. Lee Lerner and Brenda Wilmoth Lerner, eds. Farmington Hills, Mich., Gale Group, 2009. 3v. illus. index. $385.00/set. ISBN 13: 978-1-4144-0298-7; 978-1-4144-1085-2 (e-book).

This 3-volume set in the In Context series from Gale features contributions by 59 researchers and scholars who write about science, the history of science, and specific scientific disciplines. The content is aimed primarily at young readers—high school and undergraduate college students—to introduce them to concepts surrounding the relationship of scientific thought to society. As the editors state, "Students not exposed to the intellectual heritage (and baggage) of scientific thought will be unable to make tempered and rational decisions regarding the appropriate application of scientific thought to modern issues."

The content is authoritative and provides a collection of entries on diverse scientific topics, especially as they relate to general science studies. The entries could be used easily in a ready-reference setting in libraries, or could be understood by anyone curious about science, inquiry, and springboards to critical thinking. Each volume has a table of contents; a section describing the books and ways to cite entries; a section about using primary sources such as letters, newspaper articles, speeches, interviews, and personal quotations; and a 55-page glossary of terms.

Volume 1 deals with astronomy and cosmology, space science, biology and genetics, biomedicine, and biotechnology. Volume 2 continues with chemistry and biochemistry, computer science, earth science, mathematics, physics, science philosophy, and practice from ethical principles to the scientific method. Volume 3 contains a general chronology of science beginning 4.6 billion years ago, and continues with milestones through 2008. The chronology is followed by a 47-page section listing the sources consulted in putting together this ambitious reference resource. A general index follows the source list.

Each chapter also contains a chronology specific to the scientific discipline being discussed. In addition to the general glossary found at the beginning of each volume, there are terms within entries and individual "Words to Know" sidebars designed to stimulate deeper research into the topic at hand. At the end of each chapter is a bibliography specific to the chapter's content. The writing is clear and designed to encourage readers not to be intimidated by scientific terminology and research. The editors quote Dr. Richard Feynman: "We do not know what the rules of the game are; all we are allowed to do is to watch the playing. Of course, if we watch long enough, we may eventually catch on to a few of the rules." This reference is highly recommended for high school, public, community college, and academic libraries.—**Laura J. Bender**

HANDBOOKS AND YEARBOOKS

C, S

457. **Research and Discovery: Landmarks and Pioneers in American Science.** Russell Lawson, ed. Armonk, N.Y., M. E. Sharpe, 2008. 3v. illus. index. $299.00/set. ISBN 13: 978-0-7656-8073-0.

This useful work comprises about 650 biographical and topical articles covering American science, medicine, and technology from its beginnings to the present. Articles are arranged under 14 subject sections, such as geography, biology, and mathematics. Each section has three or four integrative essays (three to four pages each) followed by briefer articles (one to two pages) on particular persons, disciplines (e.g., ichthyology, psychiatry), concepts, events, organizations, and more. Biographical coverage is most complete for pre-twentieth-century figures; coverage of the twentieth century is necessarily more selective. A few living figures are included. Each of the 14 sections concludes with 3or 4 short extracts from primary works. Each volume has a Topic Finder that lists all the articles under general headings (e.g., Natural Phenomena and Features), thus grouping articles independently of the subject arrangement. The work is illustrated with pictures of scientists, instruments, inventions, and more. Also included are lists of American Nobel laureates in science by date under subject and giving brief statement of their work. A substantial terminal bibliography of books on the history of American science plus short list of Websites are included.

There is a great deal of interesting and well-done material here, but there are also real problems with evenness, accuracy, and coverage. The only comparable work is Marc Rothenberg's one-volume *The History of Science in the United States: An Encyclopedia* (see ARBA 2003, entry 1285), which is more even and accurate, and has longer article bibliographies. *Research and Discovery* (RD), however, includes many topics omitted by Rothenberg. It is good to see many lesser-known nineteenth-century scientists included. Unfortunately, there are major omissions. Among those not receiving articles in RD are: A. Agassiz, S. F. Baird, C. E. Bessey, G. D. Birkhoff, W. K. Brooks (also missing from Rothenberg), F. E. Clements, T. Dobzhansky, Clarence King, E. Mayr, N. S. Shaler, G. G. Simpson, E. B. Wilson. RD usefully includes geography and a section on history and philosophy of science. Also, RD has more emphasis on medicine and technology, as opposed to pure science, and includes more social and behavioral science (i.e., F. Boas and J. B. Watson were omitted from Rothenberg). Neither work has cross-references, but RD does a much better job grouping articles by broad subject.

Some of the disciplinary articles are disappointing, devoting much space to describing the general nature of the discipline and its European history but leaving its American history sparse and vague. References are often to general textbooks rather than to disciplinary histories. For example, the article on ecology cites none of the several available books on the history of ecology in America. The disciplinary articles in Rothenberg are often much better.

There is a scattering of minor errors and omissions: Alpheus Hyatt moved to Boston in 1870, not 1879, and did not study with Louis Agassiz in Italy. There is a more recent biography of William Beebe and Winsor's History of the Museum of Comparative Zoology is not cited in the article on Harvard museums. Despite these flaws, this is a worthwhile purchase for high school, college, and public libraries.
—**Frederic F. Burchsted**

C, P

458. Roberts, Michael. **Evangelicals and Science.** Westport, Conn., Greenwood Press, 2008. 303p. index. (Greenwood Guides to Science and Religion). $65.00. ISBN 13: 978-0-313-33113-8.

In *Evangelicals and Science* author Michael Roberts attempts to present and examine the historical and contemporary contexts of evangelicals and their varied and often contentious relationships with science, from theories of creation and evolution to stem cell research. Roberts carefully defines evangelicals and describes their responses and justifications for those responses to scientific developments beginning in the early 1700s, focusing on Britain and the United States. He addresses the major court cases associated with evangelicals and their objections, devoting an entire chapter on the Scopes trial and its aftermath. He also devotes an entire chapter to the development of and study of the issue of creationism and the various movements that have resulted: Young Earth Creationism, intelligent design, and theistic evolution. Roberts admits in his introduction to not being an entirely "detached and disinterested" outside observer of evangelicals and their interactions with science. However, he does an admirable job of presenting his material as objectively as possible. He also candidly admits that his focus on scientific issues is dominated by the two fields in which he is familiar: geology and the history of science. This limits the scope of the book necessarily, but Roberts is so thorough in his examination that it is understandable that narrowing the scope makes the material much easier to manage for lay readers and students. In conclusion, it is important to note that Roberts does his best to give his readers as much information with as little interference as possible. He provides a chronology of significant events in the development of evangelicalism and its intersections with significant scientific developments. The book includes a rather lengthy list of Roberts' resources, which could also function as a "Further Reading" directory. He also describes his audience; he directs his work at students, clergy, educators, the scientific community, and anyone interested in the topic. Consequently, this makes the book ideal for public libraries and academic libraries alike, and this reviewer highly recommends it for those libraries.—**Megan W. Lowe**

P, S
459.   Sullivan, Megan. **All in a Day's Work: Careers Using Science.** 2d ed. Arlington, Va., NSTA Press, 2008. 140p. illus. index. $15.94pa. ISBN 13: 978-1-93353-145-8.

This 2d edition of *All in a Day's Work: Careers Using Science* is a collection of nearly 50 "Career of the Month" columns from *The Science Teacher*, a publication of the National Science Teachers Association (NTSA). The target audience is students in grades 9-12, but this could be appropriate for middle school students as well.

Careers are grouped together in categories such as The Adventurous Life (e.g., deep-cave explorer, astronaut), Environmental Issues (e.g., volcanologist, ethnobotanist), Technology and Toys (e.g., video game level designer, GIS specialist), and What We Eat (e.g., food technologist, plant geneticist). Entries are two to three pages long and highlight a specific person in each career. Entries include an overview of the field, how the person found themselves choosing this career, description of a typical day, and words of advice for students. Most entries have a black-and-white photograph of the profiled scientist. Each entry concludes with a chart of educational degrees needed, Website(s) for further information, and a related careers list. There is also an alphabetic list of all the careers profiled in the book with corresponding page numbers. Following all the entries is a brief reference list and a keyword index.

All in a Day's Work is an easy-to-read and easy-to-use guide to help students learn more about jobs and careers in the sciences. The price makes this an affordable option for the career sections of public and school libraries.—**Caroline L. Gilson**

30 Agricultural Sciences

FOOD SCIENCES AND TECHNOLOGY

Atlases

C, P, S

460.   Millstone, Erik, and Tom Lang. **The Atlas of Food: Who Eats What, Where, and Why.** rev. ed. Berkeley, Calif., University of California Press, 2008. 128p. illus. maps. index. $19.95pa. ISBN 13: 978-0-520-25409-1.

This small volume is divided into 4 parts: an outline of contemporary challenges (8 chapters); farming and all its ramifications (15 chapters); international food trade (6 chapters); and lastly food processing, retail, consumers, and consumption (11 chapters). Each chapter is highly illustrated with colored maps, pictures, graphics, and each chapter covers approximately two pages. The writing is concise, readable down to middle school grades, and easy to understand. The data tables compare the world's countries by agriculture and consumption. The sources bibliography is for Websites on the Internet and lists the Internet addresses. Unfortunately, if a Website is taken down or a broken link develops there is no way to trace where the information came from at a later date. There is also an alphabetic index by subject. This title is recommended for middle school and high school libraries and public library collections.—**Betsy J. Kraus**

Dictionaries and Encyclopedias

C, P

461.   **The Oxford Companion to American Food and Drink.** Andrew F. Smith, ed. New York, Oxford University Press, 2007. 692p. illus. index. $49.95. ISBN 13: 978-0-19-530796-2.

This panoramic view of the culture and history of food and drink in the United States contains nearly 1,000 articles arranged alphabetically. Readers will find entries about unique dishes, modes of preparation, methods of food distribution, and the usual and unusual ways Americans eat. Discover the history of A&W Root Beer Stands, the origins of Bloody Marys, funnel cakes and jambalaya, the man behind Duncan Hines, Good Humor, and Howard Johnson, and food products like Tang, Natchitoches Meat Pies, and MoonPies. Entries conclude with *see also* listings and a short bibliography. One of the over 200 specialist contributors signs each entry. Editor Andrew F. Smith teaches culinary history and professional food writing at The New School University in Manhattan. Many historical and bright color images illustrate the entries. Food-related events, Websites, and museums, along with technological developments and social movements that have shaped how Americans understand and consume their food and beverages are included. Interesting stories and histories of the practice of veganism, celebrity chefs, regional and ethnic cuisines, and historical food traditions will entertain readers searching for fascinating tidbits. Concisely written and presented, chefs, culinary students, foodies, and historians will enjoy the three centuries of food and drink in the United States. [R: LJ, Aug 07, p. 123]—**Susan C. Awe**

C, P

462.   **The Oxford Companion to Food.** 2d ed. Tom Jaine, ed. New York, Oxford University Press, 2006. 907p. illus. index. $65.00. ISBN 0-19-280681-5.

This dictionary of foods and related topics is composed of four major categories and groups. These groups include food plants; animals, birds, fish, and more; cooked foods and beverages; and lastly culture, religion, meals, diet, and regional cuisine. This second edition has 72 new entries. The entries are arranged alphabetically, each has a definition, some have drawings of the item, a history of the item, its origin, how it is prepared, where it is grown and used, and a description of its flavor and texture. The entries are informative as well as fun to read. There are maps showing how foods traveled throughout the world, an extensive bibliography, and an index with cross-references. This is not a traditional stuffy dictionary; it is a history and geography book of food combined. The only drawback to the book is the very light green print for cross-references within the entries. It is a definite purchase for any library with a culinary program or public library with cooking schools in their towns or cities. [R: LJ, 15 Sept 06, p. 87]—**Betsy J. Kraus**

Handbooks and Yearbooks

P, S

463.   Deutsch, Jonathan, and Rachel D. Saks. **Jewish American Food Culture.** Westport, Conn., Greenwood Press, 2008. 141p. illus. index. (Food Cultures in America). $49.95. ISBN 13: 978-0-313-34319-3.

Jews living in the United States are a diverse lot. They vary in there degree of religious observance from ultra-orthodox to secular. They come from all over the world and bring with them the culinary traditions of their ancestors. This book from Greenwood's Food Cultures in America series looks at how American Jews eat. It begins with a timeline of Jewish history from Abraham to 2007 and a chapter on the history of Jewish food. Chapters on major foods and ingredients, cooking, typical meals, eating out, and special occasions follow. The Jewish dietary laws, *kashrut* or keeping kosher, are mentioned throughout the book, but not explained in detail until the final chapter on diet and health. The authors provide explanations of traditional prayers, holidays, and rituals connected with meals as well as recipes to demonstrate the rich food heritage of the Jews. They include a glossary and a resource guide of books and Websites as well as a bibliography. *Jewish American Food Culture* offers a good introduction to American Jewish culinary traditions. It is a good addition to high school, public, and synagogue libraries.—**Barbara M. Bibel**

C, P, S

464.   Janer, Zilkia. **Latino Food Culture.** Westport, Conn., Greenwood Press, 2008. 174p. index. (Food Cultures in America). $49.95. ISBN 13: 978-0-313-34027-7.

American food culture is and has always been founded on a global perspective coming from the settlers of this country. This book on Latino food is an example of one segment of this internationalization of American food. Eating at international restaurants has become a hallmark of mainstream American culture and despite the fact that many food items have been Americanized, the foundation is still from the country of origin. This book is divided into chapters, including introduction, chronological historical overview of Latino food, major foods and ingredients, cooking, meals, eating out, special occasions, diets and health, glossary, resource guide, bibliography, and an index. Recipes are interspersed throughout the volume and sufficient diagrams of ingredients are also included. In the 2000 census, Latinos constituted 12.5 percent of the U.S. population and many of them come from ancestors of indigenous people who were here long before the United States came into existence. The text is easy to read and very enjoyable in its content; the glossary is extremely helpful for new arrivals to this type of cuisine. The chapter has a bibliography to obtain more information on the subject matter. It is well indexed. The book has appropriate binding, the paper is average; and font size is sufficient. This book should be in all food-oriented libraries. It will be particularly useful for students studying in food culture since the Latino population is growing in this country and consequently will be important in their future.—**Herbert W. Ockerman**

C, P, S

465.   Thursby, Jacqueline S. **Foodways and Folklore: A Handbook.** Westport, Conn., Greenwood Press, 2008. 204p. illus. index. (Folklore Handbook Series). $55.00. ISBN 13: 978-0-313-34173-1.

Food is one of the few truly universal requirements in life, but the diverse customs, traditions, and interpretations surrounding it in each culture show that it takes on a meaning far beyond simple sustenance. Jacqueline Thursby's handbook provides a clear path to explore "foodways," the folkloric study of foods. Her focus is primarily on the United States, but the melting pot character of the country makes it necessary to investigate origins in other countries as well. The text, part of Greenwood Press's Folklore Handbook Series, provides a general overview of the topic, including a brief history of food over the centuries. The author describes some of the most significant types of food-related folklore and traditions and offers numerous examples of stories and practices within the various American traditions, including Native American, African American, English American, Jewish, South Asian Indian American, and Chinese American. Thursby summarizes the work of various scholars and their methodologies and finishes with a discussion of foodways in the context of literature, drama, art, music, film, television, and other cultural venues. The guide includes an extensive bibliography to facilitate the further study of the topic and a short glossary. Jacqueline Thursby, professor of English at Brigham Young University, has her Ph.D. in American Culture Studies and has written extensively on folklore.

Thursby has fashioned an excellent framework for the exploration of foodways by offering the basic knowledge and scholarly apparatus needed for formal study along with enough fascinating stories and examples to pique anyone's interest in learning more.—**Judy Dyki**

C, P

466.   Toussaint-Samat, Maguilonne. **A History of Food.** new ed. Hoboken, N.J., John Wiley, 2009. 756p. illus. index. $34.95. ISBN 13: 978-1-4051-8119-8.

This is a translation of the 2d edition of this book. The book covers man's relationship with food from published time the present. The book is a social evolution of food and describes a transition from a vegetable-based to an increasingly meat-based diet. It also explores the relationship between people and what they eat, between particular foods and social behavior, and between dietary habits and methods of cooking. The first section covers collecting, gathering, and hunting, and chapters under this section explore collecting honey, the history of gathering, and the history of hunting. Section 2 looks at stock breeding, arable farming, meat, milk, and cereals. Section 3 looks at three sacramental foods—oil, bread, and wine. Section 4 evaluates economy of the market and is subdivided into the history of fish and poultry. Section 5 examines luxury foods, and chapters under this include treasures of the sea and forest. Chapter 6 discusses the era of merchants. Under that, essential food and spices are discussed. Section 7 evaluates new needs, sugar (confectionary and pastries), chocolate and divinity, coffee, tea, and philosophy. Section 8 discusses orchards and kitchen gardens and chapters under this section looks at the tradition of fruits, evolution of vegetables, and the potato revolution. Section 9 describes science and conscience in the diet. Chapters under this section evaluate preservation by heat, cold, reassurance of dietetics, and a reassuring future. The author is well qualified to author this title; he has written 17 books on cuisine, history, and French regional culture. The book has excellent binding, quality paper, and the font is of adequate size. It also includes a number of plates and colored photographs. Each chapter is adequately referenced and the index is sufficient for the purpose. This book should be in all libraries where history and food are a concern. It gives information that is not available anywhere else. It is well written and fascinating reading.—**Herbert W. Ockerman**

HORTICULTURE

Dictionaries and Encyclopedias

P

467.   Toensmeier, Eric. **Perennial Vegetables: From Artichoke to 'Zuiki' Taro, a Gardener's Guide to Over 100 Delicious, Easy-to-Grow Edibles.** White River Junction, Vt., Chelsea Green, 2007. 241p. illus. index. $35.00pa. ISBN 13: 978-1-9331498-40-.

In *Perennial Vegetables* users will find information and tips on how to grow less-common vegetables that will make any garden a perpetual source of food. The vegetables found in this volume product require no annual tilling or planting—they are unusual in that they grow back each year with a minimal amount of gardening. Inside users will discover how to grow their favorites—asparagus, rhubarb, and artichoke—as well as some soon-to-be new found favorites—ground cherry and wolfberry. The author not only explains how to grow these in a garden but also how to harvest and cook them. This title profiles more than 100 species, each with color photographs, illustrations, growing tips, recipes, and additional resources. This title will be useful in the gardening and horticulture collections of public libraries. —**Shannon Graff Hysell**

Handbooks and Yearbooks

P

468.   Calhoun, Scott. **Designer Plant Combinations: 105 Stunning Gardens Using Six Plants or Fewer.** North Adams, Mass., Storey, 2008. 239p. illus. index. $18.95pa. ISBN 13: 978-1-60342-077-8.

Calhoun's colorful garden groupings favor the romantic style of sprawling flower beds. A sprightly, appealing mélange of 105 layouts, the text showcases bright juxtapositioning—indigo sage and red oriental poppies with lamb's ears—and the layering of textures that blend blue spruce fescue, prickly pear, yucca, and mountain laurel with ground huggers like portulaca, ice plant, plumbago, and rock rose. Color combinations tend toward purples and lavenders offsetting orange, gold, pink, and fuchsia. Designs offer no modeling of plantings against residences or fencing and suit the tastes of xeroscapers and naturalizers rather than classic landscapers or planters of fragrant, edible, or bird and butterfly pleasing varieties. This title is heartily recommended for public collections as well as the shelves of home builders and site developers.—**Mary Ellen Snodgrass**

P

469.   Tozer, Frank. **The Organic Gardener's Handbook.** Felton, Calif., Green Man, 2008. 247p. illus. index. $24.95pa. ISBN 13: 978-0-9773489-1-6.

P

470.   Tozer, Frank. **The Uses of Wild Plants: Using and Growing the Wild plants of the United States and Canada.** Felton, Calif., Green Man, 2007. 263p. illus. index. $24.95pa. ISBN 0-9773489-0-3.

A perfect blend of clarity and content, the *Organic Gardener's Handbook* is a compendium of useful, real-world information that should be in the library of every gardener. Intended for the novice organic vegetable gardener, the book offers ideas that will benefit everyone who works the soil, including flower gardeners. For instance, the tips on garden shape and exposure, instructions for different methods of composting, and ideas for soil improvement are useful to all. So, too, are the lucid tabulations, such as the way to quickly appraise soil by its color. Not everyone will be so keen to improve soil that they will be attracted to human urine or composting toilets. But the inclusion of those ideas is illustrative of the comprehensiveness of the volume. From the shelf-life of common vegetable seeds to descriptions of the best soil-improving crops, along with line drawings of the same, coverage is broad and deep. Strategies for thwarting common pests of all kinds, including insects, deer, and rats, are given. Success in vegetable gardening requires plans for storage and use of the harvest; and there are instructions for that happy outcome, too. One wishes the illustrations were credited. Otherwise, each page is a superb offering, much like the ideal loamy soil with abundant earthworms to support it.

Similarly, *Uses of Wild Plants* is a great addition to the gardening and horticultural reference sources. The work covers the uses and cultivation of some 1,200 species of wild plants in more than 500 genera. It covers all of the basics of cultivating wild plants and more. Included is the history of how Native Americans and European settlers used wild plants for food and medicine and how they can be used today to enhance health and nutrition. The book also discusses eco-friendly concepts, such as using wild plants to create an ecologically sustainable society through their use as food, medicine, fuels, and building materials. More than just providing natural beauty, this book explains how theses plants can be used to keep the environment clean and help lower the rate of global warming. Both titles will be welcome in any public library reference collection.—**Diane M. Calabrese**

VETERINARY SCIENCE

P
471.   Eldredge, Debra M., Delbert G. Carlson, Liisa D. Carlson, and James M. Giffin. **Cat Owner's Home Veterinary Handbook.** 3d ed. Hoboken, N.J., Howell Book House, 2008. 626p. illus. index. $34.99. ISBN 13: 978-0-470-09530-0.

This book includes chapters on emergencies, gastrointestinal parasites, infectious diseases, each of the bodily systems of the cat (e.g., respiratory, circulatory), nutrition, tumors and cancers, and medications. Each chapter describes a series of ailments common to cats. Each entry in a chapter includes a definition of the term/condition. The causes are listed. The condition is described, with accompanying pictures and drawings where appropriate. This is followed by advice on treatments that can be administered by the pet owner, and when the owner should seek professional advice. Prevention and public health concerns complete each entry.

Appendixes include data on normal cat physiology, a chart comparing the age of cats with humans, a description of lab tests commonly required, useful resources (e.g., associations, veterinary schools, Websites, cat registries), and a glossary of terms. Biographical information about the authors and a list of tables are followed by the general index. An index of signs and symptoms appears inside the front and back covers.

This work is written in easy-to-understand language. Pictures and diagrams help to provide clarity and a basis for comparison. The indexes and cross-references make it easy to find the information sought. Chapter 1 on emergencies is particularly useful as it provides step-by-step instructions that could save a pet's life when medical help is not readily available. This handbook is reasonably priced and is recommended for cat owners and public libraries.—**Joanna M. Burkhardt**

P
472.   Eldredge, Debra M., Liisa D. Carlson, Delbert G. Carlson, and James M. Giffin. **Dog Owner's Home Veterinary Handbook.** 4th ed. Hoboken, N.J., John Wiley, 2007. 628p. illus. index. $34.99. ISBN 13: 978-0-470-06785-7.

An excellent reference tool for dog owners, handlers, and groomers, this handbook has earned respect for accuracy and readability. The end papers anticipate first aid needs by listing common complaints, such as pawing at ears, limping, or coughing, that could indicate disease or accident. Division into 20 chapters begins with emergencies, parasites, and infection before branching into particulars of coat, eyes, ears, nose, mouth, and internal systems. Extensive details of reproduction, birthing, and pediatrics precedes end-of-life information on cancer, geriatrics, and medication. Appendixes on physiology, aging, and laboratory tests extend to a list of 33 electronic resources. A seven-page glossary clarifies valuable terms. Indexing offers both common queries (e.g., obesity, milk fever) and medical terms (e.g., osteoma, epidermis). The most serious weakness is poor quality photography, which does little to enlighten the reader. This guide is highly recommended for public, home, and school libraries.—**Mary Ellen Snodgrass**

31 Biological Sciences

BIOLOGY

Biography

C, P, S

473.   **Icons of Evolution: An Encyclopedia of People, Evidence, and Controversies.** Brian Regal, ed. Westport, Conn., Greenwood Press, 2008. 2v. illus. index. $175.00/set. ISBN 13: 978-0-313-33911-0.

The editor notes in the preface to this excellent pair of volumes that there is another book called *Icons of Evolution*. It, however, is just the opposite of the work reviewed here—it is a text that claims to refute evolutionary theory in favor of some cryptic creationism. This juxtaposition of titles makes for an excellent comparison of the scientific and anti-scientific genres. One is honest, diverse, interesting, and designed to show the complexities of the scientific enterprise; the other is just the opposite and need not be mentioned again.

These two volumes contain 24 long articles on some of the most intriguing topics in evolutionary studies today and, not coincidentally, the topics that most often appear in the ongoing creation-evolution wars. Each article is written by an expert in the discipline and directed toward an educated layperson. About one-third of the book covers historical subjects such as the rise of the evolutionary paradigm, where the "survival of the fittest" formulation came from and why it is still problematic, the development of Neodarwinism, and the fascinating stories behind famous frauds such as Piltdown Man. There are also biographies and critical analyses of key figures in evolution, from Charles Darwin through Louis Leakey.

The rest of the articles in these volumes are about particular evolutionary narratives and how they have been used and misused. Hominid evolution is well covered with separate sections on Lucy, the Taung Child, Java Man, Peking Man, and the Neandertals. The best chapter is probably the detailed analysis of the famous peppered moth experiments, followed closely by useful articles on dinosaurs (and how they are often misunderstood), the dinosaur-bird Archaeopteryx, and the horse fossil series. The articles on Radiometric Dating and Cladistics are models of clear prose, which could easily be used to teach the topics to undergraduates.

Icons of Evolution holds its own as an introduction to some of the most interesting aspects of evolutionary theory and history. It will be most useful, however, as a resource for those lonely soldiers on the frontlines of science education who find themselves besieged by pseudoscientific claims that evolution is a failing concept. The candor of these volumes is refreshing, showing evolutionary studies to be a dynamic, human science that produces astonishing insights about our world and our places in it. This work is highly recommended for all libraries.—**Mark A. Wilson**

Dictionaries and Encyclopedias

C, S

474.   **Dictionary of Biology.** 6th ed. New York, Oxford University Press, 2008. 717p. $17.95pa. ISBN 13: 978-0-19920462-5.

As part of the Oxford paperback reference series, the 6th edition of the *Dictionary of Biology* from Oxford University Press focuses on biology and biochemistry and exhibits some changes in format and coverage from previous editions (see ARBA 2001, entry 1343, for a review of the 4th edition). The dictionary is updated and expanded with every new edition. Some 400 new entries appear within its 717 pages, bringing the total to more than 5,500 entries. The concise entries, generally less than a few hundred words, are presented in an easy-to-read, two-column format. Many entries are cross-referenced to related entries within the work. Drawings, graphs, timelines, and chemical structures of some compounds facilitate understanding. The dictionary uses British spelling. This edition adds a short table of contents, three appendixes, and six feature articles on topics such as bioinformatics, genetically modified organism, and microarray technology. The editors, advisors, and contributors are the same as for the previous edition and all have degrees ranging from bachelors to doctorates. A paragraph at the beginning of the book explains how to access the Web links that appear after some definitions. These links provide expanded coverage for users requiring more information. The dictionary is recommended for all libraries, especially college and university libraries.—**Ignacio J. Ferrer-Vinent**

C, P, S

475.   Moore, Randy, and Mark D. Decker. **More than Darwin: An Encyclopedia of the People and Places of the Evolution-Creationism Controversy.** Westport, Conn., Greenwood Press, 2008. 415p. illus. maps. index. $85.00. ISBN 13: 978-0-313-34155-7.

Although there are many books that discuss the theories of evolution and creationism, this 415-page encyclopedia is unique in emphasizing the people and places that have played an important role in the evolution-creationism debate over the years. Over 500 scientists, religious leaders, organizations, and locations are discussed. Access to the main part of the text is alphabetical by entry, although a detailed index is provided. Entries range from as few as 30 words to over 6 pages, with mid-length to longer descriptions being more common. Less familiar individuals or places are present, but only if they played an important role in the evaluation-creationism controversy. Entries are well written, descriptive, and take an objective tone. Text predominates, although approximately 80 illustrations are included, consisting primarily of photographs of key individuals or places. More illustrations would be preferable, but space constraints likely limited their inclusion in this single-volume encyclopedia. References are occasionally provided at the end of an entry, but there is an extensive bibliography of 160-plus references at the end of the book. The references serve to provide additional reading on a topic or entry and for the most part do not attempt to document primary literature. An appendix provides a brief guide to the sites of the Scopes Trial, but in this reviewer's opinion, it does not provide much value. Overall, this book meets its stated goals and is recommended for a general audience through first-year college students.—**Kevin McDonough**

ANATOMY

S

476.   Balaban, Naomi E., and James E. Bobick. **The Handy Anatomy Answer Book.** Canton, Mich., Visible Ink Press, 2008. 362p. illus. index. $21.95pa. ISBN 1-57859-190-2. ISBN 13: 978-1-57859-190-9.

This book is another in a series of handy reference books presented in a question-and-answer format. Designed for the general reader, the 1,000-plus questions cover all the major body systems. Chapter 1 provides background information on the scientific disciplines and their subdivisions, history of tissue types, organ systems, anatomical terminology, and imaging techniques. Chapter 2 covers basic biology, which is followed by chapters on each of the 12 body systems. The book concludes with a chapter on human growth and development. The information is concise, clearly written, and easy to understand. Photographs and illustrations supplement the information and are in color with captions and identifying labels. Many lists are provided, such as the parts of the eye and their function, cranial nerves and their function, and types of joints with their movement and an example of each. Historical and biographical trivia information is given at the top of the page in a color-coded box. Trivia questions include the first organ to be transplanted, the earliest known vaccination, and the individual who performed some of the earliest studies on digestion. The book has a thumb index at the upper right of the page with each chapter denoted by a different color. A glossary and index assist the reader in locating information. Photographs and illustrations are also noted in the index. This is a handy reference tool, but due to the lack of depth in the information it may be better suited to the regular circulating collection in school and public libraries.—**Elaine Ezell**

BOTANY

General Works

C, P

477.   Gledhill, David. **The Names of Plants.** 4th ed. New York, Cambridge University Press, 2008. 426p. index. $95.00; $45.00pa. ISBN 13: 978-0-521-86645-3; 978-0-521-68553-5pa.

This is the 4th edition of a standard glossary of plant names, providing translations or the source of the scientific names of both cultivated and wild plants. It is aimed at both gardeners and plant biology students and is in two sections. The first section provides background information on the rules of plant nomenclature and the reason why formal naming rules are necessary. Gledhill discusses everything from Latin declension to the special rules for naming cultivated plant varieties. The only topic dealing with scientific names that is not covered is pronunciation, which is often a source of anxiety for both students and gardeners.

The glossary has more than doubled in size over the 3d edition—from about 7,500 names to over 17,000. The words include terms for color, shape, and people or places commemorated by the scientific name. In the case of people's names, Gledhill includes dates and a brief explanation of the person's importance. The words are largely Latin or Greek but come from many other languages as well. The majority of terms are from plant names, but a few major algae, fungi, and plant pest names are also included. In addition, there are eight pages of figures illustrating leaf or flower shapes that are often used as scientific names.

The glossary is recommended for horticultural and academic libraries as well as public libraries that serve large numbers of gardeners. The greatly expanded size makes this edition useful even for libraries that have previous editions.—**Diane Schmidt**

C, P

478.   Meuninck, Jim. **Medicinal Plants of North America.** Guilford, Conn., Falcon Guides, 2008. 159p. illus. index. (A Falcon Guide). $16.95pa. ISBN 13: 978-0-7627-4298-1.

This field guide identifies and provides information on the medicinal use of 120 common species of plants in North America. This includes several species that the author does not recommend using because they are rare (such as orchids) or dangerous (such as sassafras or evening primrose). It could be argued that these dubious plants should not be included in a guide such as this, but it is safer to include them in order to warn against their use. The author also strongly suggests not self-medicating using these plants without checking with an expert holistic practitioner.

The guide is arranged by habitat and region, such as eastern forests, wetlands, or deserts. Each species account includes a color photograph of the plant and detailed description, but most of the text covers the use of the plants. There are sections on edibility for humans, traditional and modern medicinal uses, wildlife or veterinary use, general notes, and warnings. The author has consulted the major resources on medicinal plant use including the *German Commission E Monographs* that provide authoritative guidance on the use of medicinal plants. Taking into account all the caveats and warnings the author provides about the use of medicinal plants, this is an attractive and very user-friendly guide to common medicinal plants and is a good purchase for public and academic libraries.—**Diane Schmidt**

Trees and Shrubs

C, P

479.   Rodd, Tony, and Jennifer Stackhouse. **Trees: A Visual Guide.** Berkeley, Calif., University of California Press, 2008. 304p. illus. index. $29.95. ISBN 13: 978-0-520-25650-7.

Again and again, it remains perfectly clear life on earth would in no respect, be like we know it today, without trees and related flora. Tony Rudd and Jennifer Stackhouse, both Australians, have provided us with a stunning visual illustration of only a miniscule sampling of the tree-world around us. Not content to covering trees on this planet favoring us today with their presence, they dug into those that existed millions of years ago in prehistoric time. One cannot help marvel at the wealth of information and science modern man has squeezed out of mother earth in just a few millennia.

The book leads off with a discussion of what is a tree, followed by form and function, diversity and design, communities of life, trees and the human world, and ends up in a blaze of glory with "Factfile." Punctuated on each page are photographs of intriguing diversity, clarity, and appropriateness augmented with textual material. Where necessary, explicit illustrations add depth to the discussions. For example, on pages 262 and 263 there is a double-page photograph of a stack of timber cut in four foot lengths of a variety of species with the ends showing. The photograph was so clear that I was tempted to try my luck in identifying the species

While this book was certainly not intended as a reference source for specific species of trees, it has fulfilled its objectives nobly as a reminder of the vital importance of a life-sustaining resource. From this wide world of ours the authors selected 99 species of the world's trees and did a credible job in this selection. The mundane (with no intent to demean our Australian authors) Australian species black wattle, *Acacia mearnsii*, to the rare Franklin Tree, *Franklinia alatamaha*, a U.S. species, received the honor to be mentioned. This very appropriate mix are all judicially described with botanical and historic data.

In today's world, where a keen understanding of the fragility of our environment is so important, we are finally awakening to the need for a deeper respect for the trees we live amongst. This outstanding publication is worthy to stand with and become a part of this continuing education.—**James H. Flynn Jr.**

NATURAL HISTORY

C, P

480.   Mackay, Richard. **The Atlas of Endangered Species.** rev. ed. Berkeley, Calif., University of California Press, 2009. 128p. illus. maps. index. $19.95pa. ISBN 13: 978-0-520-25862-4.

The ever-increasing threat of extinction has raised interest and concern for almost 20 percent of the Earth's species. This compact guide provides excellent overviews of the endangered flora, fauna, and ecosystems. It is a very visual reference with colorful maps, charts, and photographs throughout. The text is up to date with quantified reports (e.g., deforestation rates, animal import trade, and conservation efforts). Biodiversity "hot spots," such as the Galapagos Islands and Madagascar, are given particularly in-depth assessments. From bats to fish and seabirds and snakes, this global review vividly summarizes threatened life. The author is a well-known ecologist specializing in environmental policy.—**Charles Leck**

ZOOLOGY

Birds

P, S

481.   **Birds of the World.** Tarrytown, N.Y., Marshall Cavendish, 2009. 11v. illus. maps. index. $359.95/set. ISBN 13: 978-0-7614-7775-4.

This encyclopedic view of the world's birdlife has 139 entries based on three thematic categories: general ornithological topics, with 28 entries (e.g., avian adaptations, conservation, behavior, human interactions); bird orders and families overviewed, with 48 entries; and single species accounts, with 63 entries on common or noteworthy North American birds. The editor, an ornithologist, has coordinated professional accuracy throughout. The text is engaging and informative for middle school age students and up. The set concludes with a glossary, resources for further study, and a 34-page comprehensive index. All parts of the set are beautifully illustrated with color photographs and range maps.—**Charles Leck**

Insects

C, P

482.   Klotz, John, Laurel Hansen, Reiner Pospischil, and Michael Rust. **Urban Ants of North America and Europe: Identification, Biology, and Management.** Ithaca, N.Y., Cornell University Press, 2008. 196p. illus. index. $27.95pa. ISBN 13: 978-0-8014-7473-6.

Most of the World's ants, over 12,000 species, live obscure lives under stones, in rotten wood, and a myriad of other habitats. A few species have invaded human habitations and have made nuisances of themselves. Many North American pest ants are invasive species; others are natives who have adapted to live with people. This interesting and useful book presents biological and control information for some 40 species of pest ants. After introductory chapters on the biology of pest ants, individual species accounts cover identifying characteristics, distribution, biology and habits, and control. There are keys to subfamilies (species accounts are arranged in subfamily chapters) and to genera and species of pest interest. There are chapters on treatment and diagnosis of ant stings and bites and on ant management.

Although substantial information on control is given, emphasis is on understanding the biology so as to optimally direct control efforts. Although aimed at pest control workers and entomologists, it has much to offer for anyone interested in invasive species. This title is highly recommended for public and academic libraries.—**Frederic F. Burchsted**

Mammals

C

483.   **Mammals of South America. Volume 1: Marsupials, Xenarthrans, Shrews, and Bats.** Alfred L. Gardner, ed. Chicago, University of Chicago Press, 2007. 669p. maps. index. $85.00. ISBN 0-226-28240-6. ISBN 13: 978-0-226-28240-6.

Reviewers rarely receive volumes so obviously destined to become indispensable for specialists in their field of coverage. Editor and author Gardner and 36 other mammalian authorities have produced such a volume as the first of a series of three on mammals of South America. Introductory units on account authors, preliminary comments, and museum acronyms and abbreviations are followed by detailed taxonomically sequenced accounts on marsupials, shrews, armadillos, anteaters, sloths, and bats. Characterization comments and dichotomous identification keys introduce higher taxa (e.g., orders families). The keys lead to included taxa (e.g., subfamilies, tribes, genera), their descriptions, synonymies, and additional keys that, if followed correctly, will take readers to accounts of individual species. Key characters assume familiarity and are not illustrated.

Species accounts include scientific and vernacular names, lists of nomenclatural synonyms, comments on distribution, marginal localities, and subspecies (if any). Lists of synonyms are provided for subspecies. Natural history and remarks sections complete each species account. The volume closes with a comprehensive literature cited list, gazetteer of marginal localities, lists of taxa and contributors, and an index of scientific names.

While a superb contribution of South American mammalogy, this book is written to serve the needs of specialists and is not likely to appeal to a general readership. It is recommended for purchase by museum and institutional libraries serving students staff, and faculty having interests in South American fauna.—**Edmund D. Keiser Jr.**

C, P, S
484.   Redmond, Ian. **The Primate Family Tree: The Amazing Diversity of Our Closest Relatives.** Richmond Hills, Ont., Firefly Books, 2008. 176p. illus. index. $35.00. ISBN 1-55407-378-2. ISBN 13: 978-1-55407-378-8.

A survey of our cousins the primates, this attractively illustrated book offers general information on the taxonomy, distribution, behavior, and adaptations of primates from prosimians such as lemurs to great apes. We humans are covered in a very brief discussion of hominid paleontology. As well as covering primate behavior and evolution, the author discusses conservation and primate tourism and includes a list of the 14 best sites for watching primates in the wild. Each chapter covers one of the major primate groups, and includes a list of species, their conservation status, and a general distribution map. The author also discusses the behavior and biology of the primate species, and there are excellent photographs on almost every page. The photographs illustrate primate behavior as well as highlighting the often attractive or bizarre appearance of the animals. An appendix lists books, Websites, and organizations for further information. Jane Goodall wrote the foreword.

Primate Family Tree is not a book for primatologists, but it provides a great introduction to primates and their evolution for students and the general public. It would be a very good purchase for high school, academic, and public libraries.—**Diane Schmidt**

Reptiles and Amphibians

C
485.   Reichling, Steven B. **Reptiles & Amphibians of the Southern Pine Woods.** Gainesville, Fla., University Press of Florida, 2008. 252p. illus. index. $29.95pa. ISBN 13: 978-0-8130-3250-4.

This is a book about the dependence of many amphibian and reptilian species on the rapidly disappearing habitats within the pine forests of the southeastern United States. It is an easy-to-read, superbly narrated, highly informative volume describing the habitats, habits, and status of 26 species of southern pine woods amphibians and reptiles. The majority of the species discussed have populations rapidly approaching threatened or endangered status. All are dependent upon the continuing existence of the pine woodlands. Author Steven Reichling, curator at the Memphis Zoo and adjunct professor at the University of Memphis, is an acknowledged authority on this subject.

The southern pine woods at one time included disjunct forests in eastern Texas and central Louisiana and more extensive forests extending from near the eastern bluffs of the Mississippi River flood plain to North Carolina and north-central Florida. These pine woodlands have been decimated in recent years to about five percent of their former size.

The text is organized into a preface, acknowledgments, introduction, and eight narrative chapters. Species survival probabilities and problems interpreting range maps are outlined in the introduction. Ecological subdivisions within the southern pine woods and the woodlands themselves are discussed in chapter 1, while chapter 2 is concerned with locating amphibians and reptiles within these woodlands. Chapter 3 focuses on generalist species, such as the Louisiana Slimy Salamander, Pine Woods Treefrog, Oak Toad, and Slowinski's Corn Snake. Chapter 4 covers flatwoods specialists (e.g., the Flatwoods and Mabee's salamanders, Gulf Coast Box Turtle, Brownchin Racer, the Apalachicola Lowland Kingsnake). Chapter 5 describes savanna specialists, including the Dusky Gopher Frog, Mimic Glass Lizard, Pine Woods Snake, and Tan Racer. Ridge specialists, such as the Striped Newt, Pine Barrens Treefrog, Florida Worm Lizard, Bluetail Mole Skink, and six snake species are detailed in chapter 6, while chapter 7 relates details on the Key Ringneck Snake and the Rim Rock Crowned Snake. The final chapter concerns frog, turtle, lizard, and snake species associated with, but not restricted to, the defined pine woodlands.

Distribution maps are included for species in chapters 3 through 7. Some 100 color plates, ranging from excellent quality to too dark to discern details, illustrate the animals and various pine woods habitats discussed within the narrative. The volume closes with a bibliography and index. This is a fascinating book on rapidly disappearing species of a rapidly disappearing ecosystem. This title is highly recommended for a general readership and, in particular, for individuals concerned about perpetuating flora and fauna for future generations.—**Edmund D. Keiser Jr.**

32 Engineering

BIOMEDICAL ENGINEERING

C

486. **Sourcebook of Models in Biomedical Research.** P. Michael Conn, ed. Totowa, N.J., Humana Press, 2008. 778p. illus. index. $229.00. ISBN 13: 978-1-58829-933-8.

Conn, a distinguished scientist at the Oregon National Primate Research Center and the Oregon Health and Science University, has created one of the most significant and comprehensive model reference tools in recent years. He states that the book is " . . . an effort to reflect the diversity and utility of models used in biomedicine . . . because observations made in particular organisms will provide insight into the workings of other, more complex, systems." He has drawn on the expertise of over 150 contributors, the majority from the United States, to describe the models found in their areas of research. The majority of the articles are found in three sections: Well-established Models, Models of Behavior, and Models of Other Human Diseases. Each is further broken down into subsections. For example, the essays found in Models of Behavior are grouped into Cardiovascular, Reproduction, Drug Development and Research, Physiology, Genetics, and Immunology and Virology. Most essays are 8 to 12 pages. Each describes its model and provides a system of relevancy that leads the serious student to adapt the model to their own different and perhaps unique research applications. The essays have a sufficient number of tables and overwhelmingly black-and-white figures and photographs to assist in comprehension. A significant list of references is appended to each. Very useful for libraries serving upper-division and graduate students in the life sciences.—**John M. Robson**

CHEMICAL ENGINEERING

Dictionaries and Encyclopedias

C

487. Schramm, Laurier L. **Dictionary of Nanotechnology, Colloid and Interface Science.** Hoboken, N.J., John Wiley, 2008. 290p. $145.00. ISBN 13: 978-3-527-32203-9.

This work is an expanded version of the author's *Dictionary of Colloid and Interface Science* (2nd ed.; see ARBA 2002, entry 1445), with more terms and longer entries, an expanded set of tables, a brief historical introduction, and more references (270 rather than 181). Definitions are paragraph-length, and may include equations and references to the tables and to the references at the end of the book. Abbreviations have *see* references for entries. Biographies of some important scientists are included.

Criteria for inclusion are not clear; not found for example are Supramolecular Chemistry, Molecular Recognition, or Atomic Layer Deposition. Astonishingly, for a work emphasizing nanotechnology, Gerd Binnig and Heinrich Rohrer, whose invention of Scanning Tunneling Microscopy launched nanotechnology, are not among the biographees. Nevertheless, this is a useful dictionary.—**Robert Michaelson**

Handbooks and Yearbooks

C, P

488.　**Handbook on Household Hazardous Waste.** Amy D. Cabaniss, ed. Blue Ridge Summit, Pa., Government Institutes, 2008. 269p. index. $59.00pa. ISBN 13: 978-0-86587-163-2.

Interest in managing old and unwanted consumer products with hazardous waste, including household cleaners, pesticides, paint products, and automotive products, emerged in the late 1970s. However, even today, it is estimated that more than 1.6 tons of household hazardous waste is produced each year by the American public. Consumer products are exempt from federal and most state regulations because of their household origin, and many communities still lack the basic information, guidance, and planning support for HHW management. This book provides solid waste management professionals, municipal officials, chemical waste handlers, and environmental students with a comprehensive look at the state of household management. It discusses such issues as: what hazardous household waste is and why we collect it; what are the main environmental concerns; how are the collections of such waste materials managed; how can we motivate consumers to change their behavior; and what can be done to increase responsible management of hazardous waste materials and create and promote healthier product use. —**Shannon Graff Hysell**

GENETIC ENGINEERING

P, S

489.　Yount, Lisa. **Biotechnology and Genetic Engineering.** 3d ed. New York, Facts on File, 2008. 364p. index. (Library in a Book). $45.00. ISBN 13: 978-0-8160-7217-0.

Since the 1st edition in 2000 (see ARBA 2001, entry 1354), Yount's comprehensive overview of the biotechnology revolution has proven to be a foundational tool for undergraduates looking at the components of this discipline from a social science perspective. The Facts on File series, Library in a Book, has been an important first step in a great number of freshmen term papers over the last 16 years and this title is very representative. Yount's work leads with an extensive overview that helps the reader to appreciate the complexity and interrelationships present between biotechnology and genetic engineering. Subsections like genetically altered animals, DNA fingerprinting, human cloning, and future trends allow students begin to develop a focus for research. The chapters devoted to chronology and key individuals are useful to the beginner; however, part 2, "Guide to Further Research," is outstanding and essential, particularly for the distant learner. In 15 pages she explains avenues for research, online resources, strategies for organizing data, metasites, legal aspects, and effective use of bibliographic tools. The annotated bibliography is up to date and the index is very user friendly. The series in general and this title specifically advances the researcher from similar content in the Opposing Viewpoints and Current Controversies series. This work is highly recommended.—**John M. Robson**

MECHANICAL ENGINEERING

C

490.　**Encyclopedia of Statistics in Quality and Reliability.** Fabrizio Ruggeri, Ron S. Kenett, and Frederick W. Faltin, eds. Hoboken, N.J., John Wiley, 2007. 4v. index. $1,150.00/set. ISBN 13: 978-0-470-01861-3.

This source aims to be an international, peer-reviewed collection of statistical methods for quality and reliability in the many fields of design. It succeeds admirably except that it is less an encyclopedia, as the term is usually used, than a handbook. Since the latter is more sorely needed, this is not a significant criticism except that users might not immediately find the resource given the name. With that small caveat aside, this is a solid and well-designed resource. Entries in the 4-volume set range from 2 pages to more than 10. Bolded subheadings break the longer entries into more digestible chunks, a feature that makes an equation-heavy resource like this much easier to skim. Illustrated with charts and diagrams as needed, each ends with a short bibliography and cross-references to other articles. The set begins with a list of common abbreviations and a list of authors and affiliations and ends with author and subject indexes. Despite the rather specialized subject area, this resource would likely be useful in any library that supports a design program, coursework, or design itself; advanced students, faculty, researchers, and practitioners will find these volumes useful.—**Peter Larsen**

33 Health Sciences

GENERAL WORKS

Dictionaries and Encyclopedias

C, P

491. **Encyclopedia of Global Health.** Yawei Zhang, ed. Thousand Oaks, Calif., Sage, 2008. 4v. illus. index. $425.00/set. ISBN 13: 978-1-4129-4186-0.

This four-volume reference work consists of over 1,200 articles contributed by 247 scholars from all over the world. The articles cover a broad array of health topics encompassing 19 key themes: Children's Health, Africa, the Americas, Asia, Europe, the Pacific area, Cancers, Localized Diseases, Systemic Diseases, Drugs and Drug Companies, Health Sciences, Men's Health, Women's Health, Mental Health, Organizations and Associations, People (in health), Procedures and Therapies, Research, and Society and Health. The general editor of the *Encyclopedia* possesses an ideal background to oversee the editorial role for this project. Yawei Zhang holds both an M.D. and Ph.D. in Public Health from Yale University. She has been involved with epidemiological studies and biostatistics in projects investigating environment interactions in several types of human cancers. She works closely with other researchers within her department at Yale, as well as with faculty at Johns Hopkins University. Yale and Johns Hopkins are considered to be the leading centers of global health research in the United States.

Volume 1 contains a reader's guide to help researchers find articles by category or theme. For example, the Systemic Diseases section contains articles on topics from Acquired Mutation, through Wilson's Disease. The list of articles follows the guide, which in turn is followed by the list of contributors. Readers and students will find the chronology of particular interest. Health-related discoveries and activities are listed from 10,000 B.C.E. through 2007. A 64-page index can be found in every volume, as well as the complete list of articles. At the end of each article is a *see also* section and a bibliography for further research. A glossary of terms can be found in volume 4 on pages 1763-1840. Also in volume 4 is an appendix of statistical data compiled by the World Health Organization, verified and validated by the ministries of health of member states. The editor cautions the reader that various data may not be as complete as others due to the limitations of data collection and differences in definitions provided by some national health information systems. Most of the statistics are current only through 2005.

The articles are written in a clear, authoritative, straightforward style, and a spot-check in all four volumes yielded only two small typographical errors. The *Encyclopedia of Global Health* provides useful information for researchers, students, and laypersons. It is recommend for high school, public, community college, and academic libraries.—**Laura J. Bender**

Directories

P

492.   **Encyclopedia of Medical Organizations and Agencies.** 18th ed. Farmington Hills, Mich., Gale Group, 2008. 1950p. index. $470.00. ISBN 13: 978-1-4144-0692-3. ISSN 0743-4510.

This volume is a directory of various health and medical entities. The bulk of the *Encyclopedia* is the "List of Medical Organizations and Agencies," subdivided by subject areas such as aging, biomedical engineering, environmental health, genetics, health care industry, and nutrition. Each category lists federal government agencies, foundations and other funding organizations, national and international organizations, research centers, and state and regional organizations. The entries provide a brief description and contact information. In addition, there is a helpful subject cross-index and an alphabetic name and keyword index. This reference contains much of the information in the *Medical and Health Information Directory*, which is also from the Gale Group (21st ed.; see ARBA 2009, entry 1128), but is only one volume instead of three, and about half the price. In addition, the descriptions are more helpful. This reference is an adequate resource for most public, academic, and health libraries. For a wider array of organizations, but without many of the useful descriptions, consult the *Medical and Health Information Directory*.
—**Elaine Lasda Bergman**

Handbooks and Yearbooks

S

493.   **Fitness Information for Teens: Health Tips About Exercise, Physical Well-Being, and Health Maintenance.** 2d ed. Lisa Bakewell, ed. Detroit, Omnigraphics, 2009. 432p. index. (Teen Health Series). $62.00. ISBN 13: 978-0-7808-1045-7.

The subject of keeping our young people fit and healthy has never been so important than today. We need every source of information provided by the professionals in the medical, health, and fitness fields for variety in the health choices we provide to our teens.

Fitness Information for Teens is an excellent source for general information on why teens should be active, making time to exercise, the equipment people might need, various types of activities to try, how to maintain health and wellness, and how to avoid barriers to becoming healthier. (See ARBA 2005, entry 1428, for a review of the 1st edition.) Comparing the two editions, in the table of contents the same areas are covered in six parts; however, in the 2d edition the topics are combined into fewer chapters. Some of the topics in the older edition have been shortened to brief entries. An example is the Aerobic Dancing chapter from the 2004 edition, which explains the history of aerobic dance and in the 2008 edition it is renamed "Aerobic Step Bench Training" and the article is shortened to a brief 2 ½ pages explaining how to begin and the proper techniques. Unfortunately, getting library patrons so seek out paper books for quick information is becoming less of a trend since a great deal of this information can be found on the Internet. This would still be an excellent addition to a public library ready-reference collection or a high school health library collection. The book ends with suggestions of Websites and organizations and a bibliography for additional readings, which were updated from the 1st edition to include more books focusing directly on teens, including yoga for teens and teen guides to fitness and nutrition. Variety is the key to keeping teens interested in fitness and staying healthy and this book has many ideas to help achieve fitness goals.—**Amy B. Parsons**

C, P

494.   **Health Care State Rankings 2008: Health Care Across America.** Kathleen O'Leary Morgan and Scott Morgan, eds. Washington, D.C., CQ Press, 2008. 539p. index. (CQ Press's State Fact Finder Series). $65.00pa.; $99.95 (CD-ROM and database). ISBN 13: 978-0-87289-928-5.

Where would a person go to locate the birthrate, number of registered nurses, and number of new cases of tuberculosis in a particular state? Any one of those statistics could be readily found online, but all three, together, would require an extensive search over different Websites. An alternative would be the new edition of this reference, which provides all of those statistics, and more, in one easy-to-use source. Now published by CQ Press (although the editors and layout of previous editions remain the same), this book is comprised of over 500 identically organized tables on various aspects of health, illness, and health care in each American state. Specific tables are organized under seven general chapters: births and reproductive health; deaths; health care facilities; financing of health care; incidence of diseases, particularly cancer and infectious diseases; health care professionals; and physical fitness (primarily information on health behaviors). The data provided come from reliable sources and is current to 2005, and in some categories, to January 2007. Each item is presented in at least two tables: one organized alphabetically by state name and the second in rank order for the particular statistic. One can readily evaluate health in a particular state, compare one state to others, or compare a state to the national average. It would take hours searching the Internet or hard copy resources to find the wealth of health statistics in this book. An absolute must for public libraries and libraries serving health science schools. This work is highly recommended.—**Mary Ann Thompson**

MEDICINE

General Works

Dictionaries and Encyclopedias

P, S
495.   Berlan, Elise. **Encyclopedia of Family Health & Wellness.** Edited by Patricia Therrien. Vestal, N.Y., AlphaHouse, 2008. 10v. illus. index. $356.60 (list price); $249.95 (school library price). ISBN 13: 978-1-934970-00-3.

Unlike many medical reference sources, this 10-volume set provides clear and concise information about health issues for the lay reader. Not only are the entries written in straightforward, nontechnical language, each entry has a corresponding drawing or photograph to illustrate the definition, condition, or treatment of the subject being described.

The content is authoritative and written by a physician who specializes in pediatric and adolescent medicine. There are over 500 entries arranged alphabetically in the 10 volumes. "Ask the Doctor" sections feature questions posed by young people and serve to relate the entries to real-life health situations without oversimplifying the issues. Topics covered include basic hygiene, HIV/AIDS, puberty, mood swings, sunburn, and sexual activity, just to name a few. There is a well-developed section on alternative medicine, which is gaining in importance and popularity among health professionals and medical school curricula. Each volume contains a list of informative Web sources for further research, a helpful index, a glossary of important terms, and "Did You Know?" boxes scattered throughout, with interesting historical information to complement the medical facts.—**Laura J. Bender**

C, P
496.   **The Gale Encyclopedia of Surgery and Medical Tests: A Guide for Patients and Caregivers.** 2d ed. Brigham Narins, ed. Farmington Hills, Mich., Gale Group, 2009. 4v. illus. index. $520.00/set. ISBN 13: 978-1-4144-4884-8.

Editor Narins, along with a 3-member advisory board, oversaw the work of 102 contributors (including the advisors) for this 4-volume encyclopedia. The contributors are all members of the medical profession, and include medical doctors, medical writers, pharmacists, science researchers, and registered nurses. Because the medical field is constantly growing and changing, and differences of opinion exist among medical professionals, the publisher offers an important advisory to readers of this reference source. They strongly recommend that readers seek professional diagnosis and treatment for any medical condition, and state that this resource "is intended to supplement, not replace, consultation with physicians or other healthcare practitioners."

Each volume in the set contains an alphabetic list of entries, a list of entries by body system (e.g., cardiovascular, endocrine, neurological, respiratory), an introduction, advisory board members, and contributors. Volume 4 also features an alphabetic list of organizations associated with the medical profession and the specific medical systems outlined in the encyclopedia. These organizations provide more contact information for readers. In addition, volume 4 has a glossary beginning on page 1785, and a general index beginning on page 1865.

To facilitate use of this resource, each entry follows a standardized format to provide information at a glance. Readers can read portions or the entire entry for their research. Most topics include a definition, description, purpose, demographics affected by the topic, diagnosis/preparation, aftercare, precautions, risks, side effects, possible interactions, morbidity and mortality rates, alternatives for the patient, normal results, questions to ask the doctor, types of doctors who perform certain procedures and where the procedures are performed, resources for patients, and key terms. There are well-placed illustrations to help users better understand the diseases and procedures described.

Readers will find the scope of entries to be broad and informative. Not only are there specific entries related to conditions, diagnosis, surgery, and aftercare, there are topics of general interest too. For example, readers will find entries about exercise, long-term care, patient rights, powers of attorney, Medicaid and Medicare, and private insurance plans to help them round out their understanding of these medical issues. This reference is recommended for ready reference in public, community college, medical school, and academic libraries.—**Laura J. Bender**

P, S

497.   **Health Reference Center. http://factsonfile.com/.** [Website]. New York, Facts on File. Price negotiated by site. Date reviewed: 2008.

As of January 2008 Facts on File launched a redesigned and updated version of their *Health Reference Center* database. The new format is more visually appealing than the older edition and will appeal to students doing quick research on specific subjects or browsing general health care topics.

The first thing users will notice that is new about this database is the updated interface. It has been redesigned to provide quicker access to the database's content. The site offers both search and browse tools. The search terms are now highlighted within the results making it easier for users to find their specific terms within an entry. Results also offer hyperlinks to related sites as well as suggested searches for further research. Search results are organized using a tabbed interface and are listed by relevancy. Other new material added to the site includes more than 570 new educational videos that will be of interest to students as well as 1,000 new images; news articles that feature the latest in health research topics; and an "Editor's Feature of the Month," which highlights a timely topic. The site also offers "Explore Subjects" and "Health Centers" sections that introduce topics of interest to school and public library users. Content is organized into five subjects: Body Systems, Conditions and Diseases, Drug Abuse and Addiction, Mental Health and Developmental Disorders, and Nutrition and Wellness. Some interesting new features on this site are the clickable food pyramid, conversion calculator, BMI calculator, and hotline listings that will be of interest to teens. The content of this site comes mainly from Facts on File's and Chelsea House's print titles, which address general health topics as well as specific topics (e.g., learning disabilities, family issues).

This is a unique database with deep content with great browse searching, good illustrations and videos, and useful learning centers. I would recommend it for middle and high schools as well as for larger public libraries.—**Shannon Graff Hysell**

Handbooks and Yearbooks

P

498.   **Disease Management Sourcebook.** Joyce Brennfleck Shannon, ed. Detroit, Omnigraphics, 2008. 621p. index. (Health Reference Series). $78.00. ISBN 13: 978-0-7808-1002-0.

The organization of this book is by parts and chapters. The eight parts cover broad areas of the health care system with chapters covering very specific topics within each category. The broad areas include serious and chronic illnesses, health care providers and systems, health literacy, drugs (whether prescriptions or over-the-counter), chronic diseases, children and chronic diseases, and financial and insurance issues. The book was written to help the consumer become a savvy health advocate of their own or on their family's behalf. Each section lists numerous other sources for finding information on the specific topic, including patient's rights, using medicines correctly, managing chronic illness and disease, Hospice, Medicaid, medical studies, and many others. The last part includes a glossary, information resources for disease management, directory of health insurance information, directory of groups that provide financial assistance for medical treatments, and an index. Consumers need to know how to manage their health care the same way they manage anything else in their lives. The text is very readable and is written for the layperson and consumer. The cost is not prohibitive. This book should be in all collections of health care libraries and public libraries.—**Betsy J. Kraus**

C, P

499.   **The Healthy Woman: A Complete Guide for All Ages.** Washington, D.C., Government Printing Office, 2008. 500p. illus. index. $24.95pa. ISBN 13: 978-0-16077-183-5.

This guide, offered from the Office on Women's Health, is intended to provide women of all ages, economic backgrounds, and ethnicities with general health information. It serves more as a guide to keeping women healthy and safe than a guide that will help women deal with long-term health issues, although these are addressed here as well. Numerous medical experts from government agencies helped create this volume, including: the Centers for Disease Control and Prevention, the U.S. Food and Drug Administration, Indian Health Service, and National Institutes of Health. The work is arranged into more than 20 chapters that address diseases (e.g., heart disease, type 2 diabetes, blood disorders, HIV/AIDS), woman-specific health concerns (e.g., reproductive health, pregnancy, breastfeeding), well-being (e.g., healthy aging, mental health, nutrition, fitness), and very specific concerns (e.g., violence against women, alternative medicine). The chapters are well written and will be easily understood by women with a high school education. There are many illustrations, charts, lists, and sidebars that add both interest and additional information. Users will find practical advice and tips to deal with a wide range of common health concerns among women of all ages. Each chapter is supplemented with lists of additional resources, Websites, and organizations to contact for more information.

This guide will appeal to a wide range of women. It should be found in most public libraries of all sizes as well as consumer health collections. The information is timely, easy to comprehend, and lends itself well to further research if needed.—**Shannon Graff Hysell**

S

500.   **Stress Information for Teens: Health Tips About the Mental and Physical Consequences of Stress.** Sandra Augustyn Lawton, ed. Detroit, Omnigraphics, 2008. 392p. index. (Teen Health Series). $58.00. ISBN 13: 978-0-7808-1012-9.

This title, one in the Teen Health Series from Omnigraphics, addresses health and hygiene issues that teens face during the adolescent years. Much like Omnigraphics' Health Reference Series, this series pulls together excerpts from government organizations such as the Centers for Disease Control and Prevention, the National Center for Complementary and Alternative Medicine, the National Center for Posttraumatic Stress Disorder, and the Substance Abuse and Mental Health Services Administration. The articles selected will specifically appeal to young adults and are designed to answer their most common questions.

Part 1 is a short section designed to help teens understand the concept of stress and how it is experienced. Part 2 covers the common causes of stress, including school violence, bullying, test anxiety, sports, and sleep deprivation. Part 3 discusses how stress affects the body, including chapters on insomnia, irritable bowel syndrome, weight gain, and depression. Part 4 provides chapters on managing stress, including boosting self-esteem, controlling anger, and journaling. The work concludes with Websites that discuss stress management and addition reading materials that cover the topic.

This work is an optional purchase for high school libraries and many larger public libraries. This title is recommended.—**Shannon Graff Hysell**

C, P, S

501.   Youngerman, Barry. **Pandemics and Global Health.** New York, Facts on File, 2008. 353p. index. (Global Issues). $45.00. ISBN 13: 978-0-8160-7020-6.

Pandemics and Global Health is one of ten titles in Facts on File's Global Issues series, a new series that covers contemporary issues from a global perspective. This specific title covers global health issues by examining historical perspectives, primary sources, and case studies.

The book is presented in three sections, with multiple chapters in each section. Part 1 introduces the issues and global health challenges and offers background information on international issues, including a review of major types of infectious agents and modes of transmission, as well as national and international governmental reaction to health concerns. Examples of topics covered include malaria, influenza, AIDS, and SARS. Part 2 provides primary sources (historical and contemporary) that give readers a starting point for their own investigations on public health issues. Part 3 includes research tools, including brief biographies of key international players, facts and figures, an annotated bibliography, and a list of relevant international organizations and agencies. A chronology, glossary, and topic index are also provided. There are no photographs or illustrations. Sources consulted throughout the book are footnoted.

Pandemics and Global Health is a useful resource for researchers wanting to learn more about important health issues from a global perspective as well as the history that has led up to their present state. This is a well-organized, well-cited source. It is appropriate for academic, public, and high school libraries.—**Caroline L. Gilson**

Alternative Medicine

P

502.   Ninivaggi, Frank John. **Ayurveda: A Comprehensive Guide to Traditional Indian Medicine for the West.** Westport, Conn., Praeger/Greenwood Press, 2008. 349p. index. $49.95. ISBN 13: 978-0-313-34837-2.

Ayurveda, which technically means "life wisdom," is probably one of the least known and least understood forms of alternative or complementary medicine. The author, a medical doctor and psychiatrist, points out in the introduction to this volume that he has attempted "to write a book that both intelligently and accurately embodies the essence and spirit of Auerveda in a form that is logical, plausible, and understandable to the Western thinker." Ayurveda originated in India and is considered to be the oldest medical tradition that exists. It endeavors to promote physical and mental health by targeting threats from acute and chronic stress to today's disorders, such as obesity and diabetes. There is an emphasis on self-inquiry, self-realization, and self-actualization; one must take an active part in one's own well-being.

This comprehensive volume has 12 chapters, covering such topics as the history and theoretical foundations of Ayurveda; anatomy and physiology; health, nutrition, and diet; lifestyles and behavior regimes; and Ayurvedic therapies. In a brief epilogue the author points out that his aim was to present elements of Ayurveda from its original forms to its modern developments, but that in recent years numerous peer-reviewed studies have been made available that show great promise for new evidentiary-based applications of Ayurvedic medicine. Some of these are briefly described. Included also in the volume are three appendixes (one of which describes clinical case examples), a glossary, an extensive reference list, and an index.

Although it is claimed that this volume can be used by any health-oriented layperson, it would seem to be most beneficial for those in a seminar or class with a qualified professional. It is very scholarly and should be a useful addition to any library having an alternative health collection.—**Lucille Whalen**

Dentistry

P

503. **Dental Care and Oral Health Sourcebook.** 3d ed. Amy L. Sutton, ed. Detroit, Omnigraphics, 2009. 619p. index. (Health Reference Series). $84.00. ISBN 13: 978-0-7808-1032-7.

There are few people who do not cringe at the thought of a dental drill, but few who understand basic dental care and are willing to take preventative measures to pre-empt problems. This book could serve as turning point in the battle to educate consumers in issues concerning oral health.

Tightly written in terms the average person can understand, yet comprehensive in scope and authoritative in tone, it is another excellent sourcebook in the Health Reference Series. This book has an informative style yet its material has not been overly simplified. Many of the entries are reprinted from national associations and federal organizations (e.g., National Institute of Child Health and Human Development, National Institute on Aging, American Academy of Periodontology). The editor has compiled information on topics in dental care important for infants to the aged, dental concerns from caries to periodontal disease, and dental procedures from brushing and flossing to oral surgery. Controversial subjects like holistic dentistry and mercury toxicity from amalgam fillings are also covered. There is a special section on surgical, orthodontic, and cosmetic dental procedures, which will be useful due to the popularity of these procedures. True to its name, this volume contains contact information to help the needy and those with special needs find appropriate dental care. All of the articles have been updated for this new edition and users will find a lot of new information here. This book should be in the reference department of all public libraries, and in academic libraries that have a public constituency.—**Susan K. Setterlund**

Ophthalmology

P

504. **Eye Care Sourcebook.** 3d ed. Amy L. Sutton, ed. Detroit, Omnigraphics, 2008. 646p. index. (Health Reference Series). $78.00. ISBN 13: 978-0-7808-1000-6.

This volume is the 3d edition of *Eye Care Sourcebook*, part of the Health Reference Series from Omnigraphics. The series in general is very well done. The book is divided into various sections covering: "Facts about the Eyes and Eye Diseases and Disorders" (discussing eye care facts and myths, eye care professionals, and vision impairment and blindness); "Refractive Problems and Procedures" (information about how vision can be corrected by glasses, contacts, or various surgical procedures); "Cataracts" (discussing the facts about cataracts and intraocular lens implantation); "Glaucoma"; "Macular Degeneration" (juvenile and age-related macular degeneration, the role of nutrition); "Disorders of the Cornea,

Retina, and Lacrimal Glands (Tear Ducts)"; "Eye Infections, Muscular Problems, and Malignancies"; "Disorders with Eye-Related Complications" (e.g., allergies, diabetes); "Protecting Vision by Avoiding Injury"; "Living with Low Vision or Blindness"; and "Additional Help and Information" (a glossary of terms, frequently asked questions about eye donation, a directory of state libraries for people with vision problems, a list of organizations). The text materials are well written and at a level consumers can understand. With no diagrams, photographs, or drawings, consumers might not find the book appealing; it has a very plain appearance in comparison to other consumer health books. While the book is not a must-have and does not have the visual appeal of a book from the Mayo Clinic, it is a solid reference tool for eye care and a valuable addition to a collection.—**Leslie M. Behm**

Specific Diseases and Conditions

Arthritis

P

505.　Hohler, Sharon E. **Arthritis: A Patient's Guide.** Jefferson, N.C., McFarland, 2008. 254p. index. $35.00pa. ISBN 13: 978-0-7864-3450-3.

This well-written guide is a timely and valuable resource. It is likely to be useful to individuals, including healthcare providers, who are involved or interested in learning more about topics related to arthritis. The graphic on the cover is eye-catching as it shows a person's hand using a computer's mouse. This imagery is unique as arthritis can impair or reduce the use of joints, including the use of the hand.

The contents of the guide are comprehensive. It begins with a table of contents that lists the book's 17 chapters. The chapters include: "Understanding Osteoarthritis," "Coping with Rheumatoid Arthritis," "Remembering the Past," "Taking Charge of Your Life," "Prevent Arthritis," "Dealing with Pain," "Eating Healthy," "Exercising with Arthritis," "Drug Therapies," "Alternative Therapies," "Preparing for Surgery," 'Total Hip Replacement," "Total Knee Replacement," "Elbows/Shoulders/Fingers/Toes," "Before/During/After Surgery," "Caregivers Need Care Too," and "Researching Arthritis." This text also includes a glossary, appendix, chapter notes, bibliography, and index. Each is detailed and easy to use. Pictures are included throughout the text and are black and white. Tables and other graphics are easy to follow and are user friendly.

This text is likely to be useful to individuals with arthritis or their relatives. It is also a resource that a variety of healthcare providers may find helpful, especially if they are involved in providing arthritic care specifically.—**Paul M. Murphy III**

Autism

P

506.　**Autism and Pervasive Developmental Disorders Sourcebook.** Sandra J. Judd, ed. Detroit, Omnigraphics, 2007. 603p. index. (Health Reference Series). $78.00. ISBN 13: 978-0-7808-0953-6.

Autism and related disorders appear to be increasing in the United States. One out of every 166 children, mostly boys, receives such a diagnosis. The cause is still unknown, but genetics plays a role. Since the diseases that make up the autism spectrum are incurable, parents, teachers, and family members must learn to help affected children and develop coping skills to help themselves. The *Autism and Pervasive Developmental Disorders Sourcebook*, a new title in Omingraphics' Health Reference Series, offers information to help.

The book has eight parts: understanding autism spectrum and pervasive developmental disorders; causes of autism spectrum disorders; conditions that may accompany autism spectrum disorders; diagnosing and evaluating autism spectrum disorders; treatments, therapies, and interventions; family and lifestyle issues for people with autism; and additional resources. The information contained in these sections comes from government and nonprofit agencies as well as periodicals. The government information is from the Centers for Disease Control and Prevention and various branches of the National Institutes of Health. The nonprofits include professional organizations, such as the American Psychiatric Association and the American Music Therapy Association, as well as groups such as Autism Outreach. The book includes a glossary, a chapter on evaluating health information found on the Internet, and a resource list of organizations.

This book provides a current overview of disorders on the autism spectrum and information about various therapies, educational resources, and help for families with practical issues such as workplace adjustments, living arrangements, and estate planning. It is a useful resource for public and consumer health libraries.—**Barbara M. Bibel**

Obesity

C, P

507.   **Encyclopedia of Obesity.** Kathleen Keller, ed. Thousand Oaks, Calif., Sage, 2008. 2v. illus. index. $250.00/set. ISBN 13: 978-1-4129-5238-5.

This 2-volume encyclopedia contains around 475 entries and covers a wide range of issues related to obesity. Medical complications, social implications, policies affecting nutrition and health, and various treatments and diets are among the included topics. The articles presented apply mainly to obesity in the United States, although an appendix with international statistics is included. An international selection of pioneering scholars in the study of obesity—medical doctors, psychiatrists, nutritionists, and other university scholars—provide relatively detailed entries, which include bibliographies. The work also includes a resource guide of books, journals, and select Websites. Other types of eating disorders, such as anorexia and bulimia, are also covered to a limited extent. Most current trends in the treatment of obesity are included; however, research on at least one type of treatment (12-step "Anonymous" programs) is absent. The terminology used is mainly appropriate for high school readers and older. The broad cross-section of medical, cultural, and societal topics makes this a worthwhile resource for most high school, public, and academic libraries.—**Elaine Lasda Bergman**

Sexually Transmitted Diseases

P, S

508.   **Sexual Health Information for Teens: Health Tips About Sexual Development, Reproduction, Contraception ....** 2d ed. Sandra Augustyn Lawton, ed. Detroit, Omnigraphics, 2008. 430p. index. (Teen Health Series). $58.00. ISBN 13: 978-0-7808-1010-5.

Part of the Omnigraphics Teen Health Series, this updated edition presents information related to the emotional, physical, and biological development of both males and females that occurs during puberty. It also strives to address some of the issues and questions that may arise. The work is intended as a reference set for teens in middle and high school who may be seeking factual information on puberty, sex, pregnancy, or STDs. The text is easy to read and understand for young readers, with satisfactory definitions within the text to explain new terms. Small fact boxes are interspersed throughout the text. The information presented is brief and, in some areas, may be too brief to adequately provide the help intended. In other areas, assumptions are made that may be perceived as out-dated such as the comment that today's parents may not have received any education about sex or reproduction. While the language and brevity may be helpful for young readers, the list of agencies to contact for further information appears to be more intended for adults than for adolescents seeking information relevant to their needs. Given the sensitive nature of the book's content, the plain text, and minimal black-and-white illustrations, the text may not be heavily used by its intended audience who may be more inclined to surf for this information on the Internet.—**Susan E. Thomas**

Sports Medicine

C, P

509.   **Sports Injuries Guidebook: Athletes' and Coaches' Resource for Identification, Treatment, and Recovery.** Robert S. Gotlin, ed. Champaign, Ill., Human Kinetics, 2008. 288p. illus. $24.95pa. ISBN 13: 978-0-7360-6339-5.

The chapters in this handy reference title were written by 25 leading sports physicians and therapists. The writing style is clear and free of overly technical medical jargon; therefore, it will appeal to those in the field of sports medicine as well as athletes doing their own research. It is organized into 16 chapters, with the first 3 covering introductory material such as body conditioning and maintenance, prevention and treatment, and injury type and assessment. The remaining chapters cover specific parts of the body (e.g., Concussions and Head Injuries, Arm and Elbow Injuries, Lower-Back Injuries). Each chapter begins with an overview of the anatomy being discussed and then goes into specific injuries. Each injury is given one to two pages of description and includes common causes, identification, treatment, the recommended "downtime" an athlete should take to heal, and a full-color illustration of the part of anatomy affected. The volume includes supplementary materials add greatly to the resource, including a chart to identify an injury based on type and location of pain, skin color, and active symptoms; a list of works consulted for each chapter (located at the back of the book); and a discussion on integrative medicine treatments (e.g., mind-body practices, supplements, yoga and East Asian medicine).

As any athlete knows, injuries happen. This book would be a great one to have access to when you need it. It provides useful information in an easy-to-search and easy-to-read format. This work will be useful in university libraries with sports medicine programs and in large public library collections. —**Shannon Graff Hysell**

PHARMACY AND PHARMACEUTICAL SCIENCES

Bibliography

P

510.   Snow, Bonnie. **Drug Information: A Guide to Current Resources.** 3d ed. New York, Neal-Schuman, 2008. 546p. index. (Medical Library Association Guides). $165.00pa. ISBN 13: 978-1-55570-616-6.

Drug information and pharmaceutical research and development are rapidly growing fields. Whether searching for information about a prescription drug or conducting a literature review for a researcher, knowing the best places to find data and the most efficient search strategy to employ will help to find the information quickly. Bonnie Snow, who has more than 30 years of experience in pharmaceutical information management and research, has updated her comprehensive guide to the field. It profiles the most current print and electronic resources as well a subject-specialty news services.

The chapters of the book cover broad subject areas: drug nomenclature and identification, laws and regulations, pharmacology and therapeutics, adverse reactions and interactions, drug formulation, analysis, and compounding, evaluating information sources and developing search protocols, and competitive intelligence resources. Each chapter contains an introductory overview of the subject area followed by a list of resources with extensive annotations. There are notes at the end of every chapter as well. This edition of the guide has expanded coverage of international resources and of regulatory information. This includes information on animal welfare and alternatives to animal testing as well as surveillance of adverse reactions to newly marketed drugs. A glossary and a detailed subject index make it easy to locate material. This is an outstanding resource for academic, health sciences, and special libraries. Independent information brokers will appreciate it as well. [R: LJ, Jan 09, p. 126]—**Barbara M. Bibel**

Directories

P

511.   **PDR for Nonprescription Drugs, Dietary Supplements, and Herbs 2008.** 29th ed. Montvale, N.J., Thomson Healthcare, 2007. 1v. (various paging). $59.95. ISBN 13: 978-1-56363-662-2.

The 29th edition of *PDR for Nonprescription Drugs, Dietary Supplements, and Herbs* provides entries and information on hundreds of over-the-counter medications, supplements, and herbal remedies. Entries are presented according to therapeutic categories, and both by scientific name and common name. The guide provides complete descriptions of the most common OTC drugs, with additional information on ingredients, indications, interactions with other drugs, and recommended dosages for symptomatic relief. Two new sections have been added to this edition: a listing devices, diagnostics, and nondrug products; and two full sections on dietary supplements and herbs (fully cross-referenced and alphabetically organized for ease of use).

Indexing herbs by both botanical name and common name is appreciated for the academic as well as general public audiences. Language within can get technical, so a cautionary note to public libraries considering this source: have a chemistry or medical dictionary handy. *PDR for Nonprescription Drugs, Dietary Supplements, and Herbs* is becoming a standard reference sources in the medicinal field. This new edition is recommended to college and university libraries supporting medical and botanical collections and to public libraries supporting advanced alternative medicine information.—**Caroline Gilson**

P

512.   **PDR Guide to Drug Interactions, Side Effects and Indications.** 63d ed. Montvale, N.J., Thomson Healthcare, 2009. 2100p. index. $74.95. ISBN 13: 978-1-5-6363-711-7.

This volume was developed to be used in conjunction with the 2009 *Physicians' Desk Reference* (63d ed.; see ARBA 2009, entry 1278) and other PDR publications to help with the safe management of drugs for patients. The largest section of the volume is the Interactions Index, which lists the drug name/product in bold as it appears in the PDR, interactions of generic drugs and dietary items followed by brand drugs with their generic components, and a page number that refers one back to other publications in the PDR group. The "Food Interactions Cross-Reference" covers not only food interactions but also alcohol interactions with drugs. This section is alphabetized by the food or liquid component with drugs listed alphabetically below and the page number to the corresponding PDR volume for more information. The third section is the Side Effects Index, which alphabetically lists the condition, such as "aggression," and then lists all the drug names with the corresponding page number for the volume of PDR publication. The Indications Index lists in alphabetic order all the indications found in the PDR publications and the drug names with the corresponding page number to the PDR publication. There is also a Contraindications Index, which follows the same format as the previous index. The International Drug Name Index lists the foreign drug name, the countries using that name, and then gives the U.S. equivalent drug along with the page number to the appropriate PDR publication. This index also lists the 37 countries that are used in the index. The "Generic Availability Guide" lists the proprietary drug and if there is a generic available and the strengths available. The last major section is the "Imprint Identification Guide" for the health care professional whose patient brings them one pill from each bottle. This index gives the imprint that's on a pill and then tells you the brand name, strength, and color so one can determine exactly what the patient is taking. The volume also includes a list of poison controls centers for the 50 states and Puerto Rico. There is a key to the abbreviations used in the text along with a key at the bottom of each section to determine which PDR is being referenced for further information. This resource is recommended for all health care professionals' offices and bookshelves and all medical and hospital libraries.—**Betsy J. Kraus**

Handbooks and Yearbooks

P

513.   Maxmen, Jerrold S., Sydney H. Kennedy, and Roger S. McIntyre. **Psychotropic Drug: Fast Facts.** 4th ed. New York, W. W. Norton, 2008. 260p. index. $42.50pa. ISBN 13: 978-0-393-70520-1.

The 4th edition of this handbook for medical professionals reflects the recent major advances in psychopharmacology. The authors are Canadian psychiatrists with academic appointments who carry on the work of the late Dr. Maxmen.

The eight chapters of the book are devoted to different classes of psychotropic drugs: antipsychotics, agents for treating movement disorders, antidepressants, dementia-treating agents, mood stabilizers, antianxiety agents, hypnotics, and stimulants and stimulant-like agents. Each chapter begins with an overview of the drug class followed by sections about dosing, dose form, and color; pharmacology; clinical indications; side effects; drug and food interactions; effects on laboratory tests; discontinuation; overdose (toxicity, suicide, and treatment); special populations (children, adolescents, pregnant and lactating women, and seniors); precautions; key points to communicate to patients and families, and therapeutic application. Four appendixes cover drug identification by generic name, drug identification by trade name, drug interactions with cytochrome P450 enzymes, and measurement-based care. A bibliography and an index round out the work.

This is a very useful resource for pharmacists, psychiatrists, and other practitioners working in the mental health field. It would be a good addition to health science library collections.—**Barbara M. Bibel**

34 High Technology

GENERAL WORKS

Dictionaries and Encyclopedias

C, P

514. **Encyclopedia of Multimedia Technology and Networking.** 2d ed. Margherita Pagani, ed. Hershey, Pa., Information Science Reference, 2008. 3v. index. $965.00/set. ISBN 13: 978-1-60566-014-1.

This is an excellent encyclopedia set that is a valuable resource. Individuals that are either interested in or directly involved with advanced multimedia technology and networking should find this most useful.

The encyclopedia set consists of three comprehensive volumes. The cover of each includes graphics that clearly relate to the theme of technology. Each volume begins with a list of the Editorial Advisory Board and is followed by an extensive List of Contributors. Subject matter experts from around the world have been consulted for this encyclopedia set.

The contents are impressive, comprehensive, and timely. The page count exceeds 1,500 pages. Volume 1 includes more than 40 topics, beginning with "Accessibility, Usability, and Functionality in T-Government Services" and ending with "Evolution of Technologies, Standards, and Deployment for 2G-5G Networks." Volume 1 has more than 60 topics and begins with "Examination of Website Usability" and ends with "New Technology for Empowering Virtual Communities." Volume 3 includes more than 60 topics ranging from "Online Communities and Social Networking" to "World of Podcasting, Screencasting, Blogging, and Videoblogging." Black-and-white tables and figures can be found throughout the volumes.

This encyclopedia set is likely to complement any library, especially those of students, professionals, and researchers that are involved in multimedia technology and networking.—**Paul M. Murphy III**

C, P

515. Kock, Ned. **Encyclopedia of E-Collaboration.** Hershey, Pa., Information Science Reference, 2008. 725p. index. $345.00; $280.00 (online access only). ISBN 13: 978-1-59904-000-4.

The *Encyclopedia of E-Collaboration* is a compilation of articles related to e-collaboration technologies, their implementations, and group activities and behaviors of individuals using the technologies. Contents of the articles are based on a specific definition of e-collaboration wherein individuals are engaged in collaborative activities using electronic technologies not restricted to Internet-mediated technologies. There are 109 articles contributed by nearly 200 authors from all over the world. Articles follow a certain format that includes introduction, background, conclusion, references, and key terms with definitions. Definitions of the key terms are clearly cited in the references of each article. Articles cover a wide range of topics concerning gender and cultural imperatives in e-collaboration as well as use of e-collaboration in the fields of finance, virtual project management, health, education, research, and detection of occupational fraud. Although contents of articles do not thoroughly investigate every aspect of e-collaborations, they provide theoretical models of collaborative e-learning and various applications of e-collaboration technologies. In other words, contents of the encyclopedia offer a range of topics related to

e-collaboration but they do not offer in-depth investigations of those topics. This encyclopedia provides a list of contributors along with the names of institutions they are affiliated with. This may help readers in contacting writers of articles for further information. References of the articles indicate that the contents of the articles are relevant to current issues and practices of e-collaboration. The drawback of the encyclopedia lies in its organization of materials. Articles are organized alphabetically by article title. As a result, readers have to go through all 109 titles of the articles to learn if the encyclopedia has any article of their interest. However, there are keywords for each article and, therefore, it would be easier for readers to find articles on an e-book format. The index is not complete. Readers may not be able to find topics such as e-learning and theoretical models using the index. Since the encyclopedia covers implementation and use of e-collaboration technologies in fields such as education, computer science, business, health, management, and finance it may be useful to researchers, students, and professionals from these fields.
—**Anamika Dasgupta**

COMPUTING

C, P

516.   **A Dictionary of Computing.** 6th ed. New York, Oxford University Press, 2008. 579p. $50.00. ISBN 13: 978-0-19-923401-1.

The 1st edition of this venerable Oxford University Press *Dictionary of Computing* was published in 1983. Its primary audience was computer science professionals and engineers in business, industry, and workplace settings, working on industrial strength computing systems, using complex programming languages such as COBOL, FORTRAN, and even bit-level machine language. To put this in a historical perspective, 1983 was the year the C++ programming language was introduced. The 2d edition's publication in 1986 coincides with the introduction of the Intel 80386 microprocessor. Tim Berners-Lee was proposing the World Wide Web in 1989; the 3d edition of this dictionary came out the next year, 1990. The publication year for the 4th edition, 1996, would have found Larry Page and Sergey Brin deep in development work on their fledgling search engine, Google. By the 2008 edition, microprocessors, PCs, handheld devices, multimedia computing, and social networking of all types on the World wide Web are fully available and proliferating in types of hardware, software, cloud computing, and various other open access means and methods.

Two general editors and 52 contributors worked to update the almost 600-page 6th edition of *A Dictionary of Computing*. Over 6,500 entries comprise the fully updated work, including 250 totally new entries. Beside the mathematical and computer science entries and a myriad of abbreviations, acronyms, and cross-references, short biographical entries of selected computer science/Internet personages are included. Entry size ranges from one sentence to short and longer paragraphs, interspersed with six two-page entries (i.e., pages 100-101, "Computer Graphics") . Graphics other than formulas and short tables are kept to a minimum throughout the work. This work has a decidedly British bent; for example, the "Copyright" entry mentions the WTO agreement from "all nations" with no mention of Title 17 of the U. S. Code, the usual U.S. reference point. Newer entries include Web 2.0 concepts such as Facebook, Ruby on Rails, the blogosphere, and Second Life. The dictionary concludes with seven appendixes, including lists of Generic Domain Names, Country-Code domain Names, File Extensions, a Greek/American alphabet, and a brief computing chronology table, from 1821/Charles Babbage, through 2007. The physical book has an accompanying URL of 85-plus Websites referenced in the dictionary. This scholarly, highly scientific, no-nonsense dictionary is recommended for the bookshelves of college students, undergraduate, and graduate science/math libraries, as well as computing/Internet professionals and seriously math/science-oriented hobbyists.—**Linda D. Tietjen**

C

517.　**The Handbook of Information and Computer Ethics.** Kenneth Einar Himma and Herman T. Tavani, eds. Hoboken, N.J., John Wiley, 2008. 671p. illus. index. $125.00. ISBN 13: 978-0-471-79959-7.

The field of information and computer ethics is vast and continues to grow in today's electronic world. This handbook of 27 topical articles written by an international team of academic subject experts aims to provide a robust introduction to the discipline and largely succeeds.

The *Handbook* is divided into six issue-oriented sections: "Foundational Issues" covers some general history and methodology matters; "Theoretical Issues" comprises intellectual property, privacy, anonymity, and hacking; "Professional Issues' examines the ethical concerns of librarians, business people, health professionals, software designers, and Internet researchers; "Responsibility Issues" deals with virtual reality, genetic information, cyber warfare between nations, and risk assessment; "Regulatory Issues" analyzes Internet governance, information overload, spam, plagiarism, and file sharing software; and "Access and Equity Issues" considers censorship, gender, the digital divide, and intercultural questions.

Each article opens with an introductory summary and concludes with a bibliography of sources. In outline format, the articles provide an overview of opposing positions on the issue at question and include both supporting arguments and objections to those positions. From this balanced basis, the author offers his own informed take on the subject.

This book should be of interest to students and scholars in computer science, philosophy, communications, business, library science, and law. It offers a thorough evaluation of important and timely ethics issues and is recommended for all academic libraries.—**John Maxymuk**

C, S

518.　Henderson, Harry. **Encyclopedia of Computer Science and Technology.** rev. ed. New York, Facts on File, 2009. 580p. illus. index. $87.50. ISBN 13: 978-0-8160-6382-6.

This is an excellent encyclopedia that is a valuable resource. Individuals that are interested in, or those that are directly involved with, technology are likely to find this to be useful. The cover includes graphics that clearly relate to the theme of technology. The contents of the text includes acknowledgements, an introduction to the revised edition, A–Z entries, four appendixes (a bibliography and list of Web resources, a chronology of computing, some significant awards, and computer-related organizations), and an index.

The page count exceeds 500. The text begins with an introduction to the revised edition. This is a useful section that provides a brief overview of recent changes in technology that prompted the revised edition. The author also provides a listing of the text's contents by category. The content of the topics included in this text range from "abstract data type" to "Zuse, Konard." Throughout the text black-and-white pictures, tables, and figures are included. They are easy to read and clearly printed. Appendix 4 is especially valuable, offering a list of computer-related organizations by the following general categories: general computer science organizations; industry-specific groups; government, standards, and security organizations; and advocacy groups. The index is comprehensive.

This encyclopedia is likely to complement any professional or personal library. Individuals that are looking for a contemporary resource on technology are likely to find this to be useful. This text is also likely to be useful for individuals who may not be as familiar with various aspects of technology.—**Paul M. Murphy III**

TELECOMMUNICATIONS

C, P

519.　**Handbook of Research on Mobile Multimedia.** 2d ed. Ismail Khalil Ibrahim, ed. Hershey, Pa., Information Science Reference, 2009. 2v. index. $495.00/set. ISBN 13: 978-1-60566-046-2.

This two-volume handbook contains the latest research on mobile multimedia systems such as e-mail, text messaging, cell phones, Internet access, video conferencing, streaming video, GPS systems, and other mobile personal communications systems. The 1st edition of the handbook was published in 2006 and is held by 98 libraries according to WorldCat. These 98 libraries for the most part are at universities that have major engineering programs. A few non-U.S. library holdings are shown in WorldCat for the 2008 edition. The 2006 edition is also available in an electronic edition through NetLibrary and IGI Global is offering a "complementary" free electronic copy of the 2008 edition to libraries who purchase the new edition.

The *Handbook* is organized into six sections: Basic Mobile Multimedia; Standards and Protocols; Multimedia Information; Mobile Networks; Applications and Services; and Further Readings (a section on next generation systems). Typical chapter titles are: "Business Model Typology of Mobile Computing," "Routing Algorithms for Mobile Ad Hoc Networks," "Adaptive Retransmission Scheme for Video Streaming Applications," "Advanced Mobile Multimedia Services with IMS," "Creating Successful Mobile Viral Marketing Strategies," and "Spatial Data on the Move." The later article gives a summary of recent research on mobile spatial data indexing techniques; for example, how do systems answer the query "Give me the names of the restaurants that are in five miles of my mobile device?" The authors of the chapter discuss the algorithms that mobile system can use to locate both the device and the nearby restaurants. Exciting research in this area include algorithms that predict not only where the mobile device is, but where it will be going (i.e., a list of upcoming restaurants based on your direction of travel). Another exciting chapter is entitled "Towards a Taxonomy of Display Styles for Ubiquitous Multimedia." This section looks at how humans determine where we are and how these sensations can be blended/converted into computer generated output. Overall, the *Handbook* gives a survey of the exciting research being conducted into the development of the next generation of mobile interfaces. Despite the high cost, most university libraries would benefit from the purchase of this encyclopedia of emerging technologies.—**Ralph Lee Scott**

35 Physical Sciences and Mathematics

PHYSICAL SCIENCES

Chemistry

C

520.   **CRC Handbook of Chemistry and Physics, 2007-2008.** 88th ed. David R. Lide, ed. Boca Raton, Fla., CRC Press, 2008. 1v. (various paging). index. $125.96. ISBN 13: 978-0-8493-0488-0.

The *CRC Handbook of Chemistry and Physics* provides a wealth of numerical data, constants, and other scientific information of interest to scientists and engineers. (See ARBA 2000, entry 1473, for a review of the 80th edition.) The *Handbook* is probably the first reference resource to which chemistry students are exposed, and it is often found in the offices of science professionals. It has grown from the thin, 116-page pocket book manual of 1913 to the familiar, authoritative, and massive volume containing a plethora of physical science data distilled from the work of innumerable scientists. David R. Lide has been its editor-in-chief for close to 20 years. A list of current contributors appears at the beginning of the work. The handbook is expanded and updated with every new edition. Additional new tables of data in the 88th edition are on the subjects of ionic liquids, solubility of organic compounds in pressurized hot water, solubility of hydrocarbons in seawater, nutrient values of foods, and properties of organic semiconductors. This essential compendium of physical science data should be in every college and university library as well as in any chemistry, physics, or engineering research lab.—**Ignacio J. Ferrer-Vinent**

Earth and Planetary Sciences

General Works

Dictionaries and Encyclopedias

C, P, S

521.   Allaby, Michael, and others. **The Encyclopedia of Earth: A Complete Visual Guide.** Berkeley, Calif., University of California Press, 2008. 608p. illus. maps. index. $39.95. ISBN 13: 978-0-520-25471-8.

"One could make the case that geology, the science of the Earth, is the most critical of all the sciences for the 21st Century." This is the opening line of Walter Alvarez's foreword to this very impressive volume, and the book indeed makes the case. It is comprehensive, well written, beautifully and luxuriously illustrated, very up to date, and, as far as I can tell, scrupulously accurate. To top it, the value for the price is simply unbeatable.

This is a visual encyclopedia, so the emphasis is on images, both photographic and diagrammatic. Each page is brilliantly colored with modest text essentially filling in the spaces between pictures. There are so many images, however, that users still trace a narrative through the captions alone. These illustrations are of the very highest quality.

The volume is divided into six elemental sections: Birth, Fire, Land, Air, Water, and Humans. Each has a series of articles within it. Each article has a consistent set of features for easy orientation and navigation. Global and regional maps ensure that the reader can locate the many examples used for the topic. Charts and graphs are often inset to provide critical information but not distract from the photographs and graphic images. These latter are often complex block diagrams with cross-sections showing internal details. Some of the articles are quite detailed, even to the point of describing each major tectonic plate separately. There is a glossary at the end, along with a long index.

The coverage of geological topics in this book is so thorough that some teachers and professors will be tempted to use it as a textbook. The publishers might even consider selling the illustrations separately as images for projection in classrooms. This book is highly recommended for all libraries with Earth and environmental sciences collections.—**Mark A. Wilson**

Astronomy and Space Sciences

Dictionaries and Encyclopedias

C, P

522.   **Cambridge Illustrated Dictionary of Astronomy.** By Jacqueline Mitton. New York, Cambridge University Press, 2007. 397p. illus. $35.00. ISBN 13: 978-0-521-82364-7.

This is a beautiful volume with about 1,300 individual entries, hundreds of clear color photographs and charts, and very high production values. It is easy to use and just the right size for easy access. This dictionary is so well done and so reasonably priced that I can make the unusual recommendation that everyone should own a copy. After all, astronomy is the science with the largest (and oldest) subject, so we each need a simple, clear source for term definitions, maps, biographies, and images.

Like most dictionaries, the entries in this volume are concise and cross-listed. Here, however, the text is mostly black with bright blue words highlighted for cross-referencing. The effect is attractive and drives the reader onward to more and more links between subjects. The brilliant color photographs have an atlas-like quality remarkable for their relatively small size, and they too encourage browsing. (My favorite image is a composite of Comet Wild 2 showing jets and surface details.)

The content of this dictionary is up to date, which is easy to check these days by quickly seeing if Pluto is listed as a "dwarf planet." Current and proposed spacecraft are also included, along with the latest discoveries of moons, extrasolar planets, asteroids, and other heavenly objects. In addition to the standard astronomical terminology there are also many short biographical entries and new star maps by the famous stellar cartographer Wil Tirion. This astronomical dictionary is well worth its modest cost to have in at least every library with a science or natural history collection.—**Mark A. Wilson**

Handbooks and Yearbooks

P

523.   Dickinson, Terence, and Alan Dyer. **The Backyard Astronomer's Guide.** 3d ed. Richmond hills, Ont., Firefly Books, 2008. 368p. illus. index. $49.95. ISBN 1-55407-344-8. ISBN 13: 978-1-55407-344-3.

A magnificently illustrated and superb guide to astronomy is contained in the newest edition of *The Backyard Astronomer's Guide*. The title is divided into three parts. The first is choosing equipment, which covers stargazing tools from binoculars to telescopes. Observing is the second part. Topics include what can be seen with the "naked-eye sky," observing conditions, and the geography of the night sky. Advanced tips and techniques comprise the third section, and covers digital astrophotography, polar alignment, and technology. Next is a Milky Way atlas that depicts the part of "the night sky with the majority of most-observed deep-sky objects," which has side-by-side photographs and charts. The title concludes with an epilogue to provide inspiration to continue to observing, a further reading list, and an index. Overall, this title is a beautiful and informative resource for the amateur astronomer, both the beginner and the experienced.—**Denise A. Garofalo**

P, S

524.   Liu, Charles. **The Handy Astronomy Answer Book.** Canton, Mich., Visible Ink Press, 2008. 332p. illus. index. $21.95pa. ISBN 1-57859-193-7. ISBN 13: 978-1-57859-193-0.

The Handy Astronomy Answer Book offers clear, detailed explanations of the many fascinating and diverse aspects of astronomy with over 100 illustrations and photographs. Topics include the fundamentals of astronomy, the universe, galaxies, stars, the solar system, the Earth and moon, space programs, exploring the solar system, life in the universe, and astronomy today (e.g., use of telescopes, photometry, spectroscopy). The book is written in understandable language, but the answers are not over-simplified and provide sufficient detail for understanding the concept or feature described, making this book appropriate for readers from high school to college. Unfamiliar terms are briefly explained within the text and a comprehensive subject index is provided as well. This book covers many aspects of astronomy and the space sciences that will be of interest to students and general readers, including facts about planets and stars, information on space mission programs, and the latest science behind the new discoveries in space. This title will be useful for high school and public library reference collections.—**Polly D. Boruff-Jones**

Climatology and Meteorology

Dictionaries and Encyclopedias

C, S

525.   **Climate Change in Context.** Brenda Wilmoth Lerner and K. Lee Lerner, eds. Farmington Hills, Mich., Gale Group, 2008. 2v. illus. maps. index. $245.00/set; e-book available. ISBN 13: 978-1-4144-3614-2; 978-1-4144-3708-8 (e-book).

The key phrase in the title of this two-volume set is the words "in context." De-emphasizing clinical data, statistics, and scientific jargon, this work's focus is the history, politics, and ethical debates related to climate change, including the impact of climate change on daily life, trade and commerce, travel, and the future of both industrialized and impoverished nations. Geared toward high school students, the entries include sidebars of possibly unfamiliar terms as well as a separate glossary. The terms and entries included in the work are those that will spur critical thinking about the impact of environmental issues, such as Abrupt Climate Change, Arctic Melting, Carbon Footprint, Heat Waves, Environmental Protest, and Sustainability. The 250 articles have been written by scientists in the areas of physics, geology, earth science, environmental science, sociology, and more. Interspersed within the entries are 250 color photographs, illustrations, maps, and tables that help clarify the text. Each entry offers references for further research. A chronology is included that provides significant events in the history of environmental study and advances of science. Written from a global and socially conscious perspective, this is fascinating reading. The work would be useful for any science reference collection from junior high through adult levels. It is highly recommended.—**Elaine Lasda Bergman**

P, S

526.   Davis, Lee. **Natural Disasters.** new ed. New York, Facts on File, 2008. 464p. illus. index. (Facts on File Science Library). $75.00. ISBN 13: 978-0-8160-7000-8.

The 2d edition of this reference work includes 50 new entries, while others have been updated. Also new in this edition are eight pages of color photographs, joining the black-and-white photographs that continue to illustrate some entries. The ARBA review of the previous edition was not favorable, in fact going so far as to label the book "a natural disaster on its own" (see ARBA 2003, entry 1528). The reviewer's major points of contention were that Davis' intended audience was unclear, the coverage accorded to different disasters apparently inconsistent, and the arrangement of articles confusing. Although the target audience is not specified in or on this edition either, the publisher's press release does say that the book is "indispensable for students, Earth scientists, historians, and others seeking current or historical information on cataclysmic natural occurrences and their consequences" and suitable for grades 9 and up. It seems unlikely, however, that Earth scientists and historians at the graduate level and above would in fact use *Natural Disasters* as a source, since it lacks references and citations in the individual articles (although there is a general bibliography at the back of the volume). Secondary and lower-level undergraduate students, as well as general readers, would appear to be the more appropriate target audience.

The comparative length of articles appears to be determined largely by the number of human casualties caused by a given disaster, regardless of when or where it happened. In this reviewer's opinion, such a method appears the best way to assure unbiased and consistent coverage. The organization of entries does remain confusing at times. Hurricanes, for example, are apparently listed by where they first made landfall, with the result that while the article on Hurricane Katrina focuses mostly on Louisiana and Mississippi, it is found only under the heading "Florida (Louisiana, Mississippi)," without even a cross-reference under the latter two states. The geographic organization scheme may be necessary (and in keeping with the other chapters) since hurricanes only started receiving names in the 1960s, but logic suggests that readers will search for disasters under the states or regions with which they are most closely associated. There is an index that can be used to point readers to articles not found under the expected heading. *Natural Disasters* would be a worthwhile addition to high school, public, and possibly undergraduate library collections, with the caveats that the articles lack citations and may be difficult for readers to find without using the index.—**Maren Williams**

C, P, S

527.   Gunn, Angus M. **Encyclopedia of Disasters: Environmental Catastrophes and Human Tragedies.** Westport, Conn., Greenwood Press, 2008. 2v. illus. index. $175.00/set. ISBN 13: 978-0-313-34002-4.

This work is an interesting compendium of tragedies that are perhaps the least predictable events in human history. Starting in 74000 B.C.E. with the eruption of a volcano in Indonesia, the work chronicles in a long series of disasters ending with the Greensboro, Kansas tornado in 2007. The entries, which vary in length from a page for minor events up to 10 pages for Hurricane Katrina in 2005, are well written. The author obviously has a great interest in the topic of disasters. He defines "disasters" as "a calamitous event at one point of time causing great damage, loss and destruction." Gunn is Professor Emeritus of Educational Studies at the University of British Columbia and is known for his 2004 book entitled *Evolution and Creationism in the Public Schools* published by McFarland. Disasters covered in the two-volume set can be both natural and manmade. A large number of these disasters are illustrated by photographs. Early disasters are illustrated by historical prints and twenty-first century line drawings.

A typical entry is the one for the Charleston earthquake of August 31, 1886. The entry begins with two different summary paragraphs. The first paragraph is a small capsule listing of the type of disaster. The second summary paragraph goes into greater detail but still consists of six sentences. The two summaries are set in four different type styles. Next follows the main article on the earthquake, which goes on for three pages with two nice photographs of the event. The entry ends with four "References for Further

Study." Unfortunately, the references do not appear to deal with the Charleston earthquake. Two references deal with barrier islands and two are general works on plate tectonics and "Forces of Nature." References in other articles vary from specific ones cited for the Johnstown Flood of 1889 to the more general ones cited in the Japan earthquake article of 1890.

Gunn has written a good introduction to the book, and the entries are preceded by a "Guide to Thematic Entries," which lists events by type of disaster. The main entries are arranged by date of event. Also included in the front part of the book is a list of credits for the illustrations. Appendixes include: A United States Geological Survey list of worldwide earthquakes (i.e., those greater than 5.0 on the Richter scale), 1500-2007; "U.S. Natural Environment," which is a list of the largest earthquakes, hurricanes, and tornadoes in the United States; "World's Deadliest Disasters"; and "Measuring Natural Disasters" (scales used in disasters). There is a two-page bibliography that does not appear generally to include items cited in the individual chronological entries. The bibliography does not include either Websites or periodical articles. The book is a fascinating read, and libraries will want to add this title to their general reading collections.
—**Ralph Lee Scott**

S

528.　**World Book Library of Natural Disasters.** Chicago, World Book, 2007. 15v. illus. maps. index. $329.00/set. ISBN 13: 978-0-7166-9801-2.

The new World Book set, *Library of Natural Disasters*, not only satisfies curiosity, but uses the science of disasters to ground fascination in knowledge. It is similar in coverage to U*X*L's *Dangerous Planet: The Science of Natural Disasters* (see ARBA 2002, entry 1544), but this serves as an excellent reference source for younger readers. Many library media specialists will want an extra set to circulate.

The first of the 15 volumes acts as an introduction to the three categories of disasters covered in the set: those caused by weather conditions, by shifts in the earth, and by disease. The information in the first volume sets the pattern of presentation for all volumes. Each subtopic is presented on a two-page spread with many headings and simple sentences in a clear font with lots of white space. Photographs, diagrams, and other illustrations accompany the text with informative captions that extend the narrative. Technical words are bolded, explained in the narrative, and listed in a volume glossary. Each volume also contains an activity page with experiments that are reasonable for children to accomplish. The list of additional resources includes children's books that might actually be available, usually an adult book that advanced students or a teacher might want to use, and Websites from government and other respected scientific organizations. In addition, each volume has a colorful, appealing cover.

The remaining volumes cover blizzards, ice storms, and heat waves; floods and droughts; thunderstorms and tornadoes; volcanoes, earthquakes, and tsunamis; wildfires and landslides; and hurricanes and pandemics. Since many of these are related, there are some illustrations that are repeated in different volumes, and some overlap in explanations.

While it is intended to be used in science instruction, it is also a good set for complementing social studies units on community and geography. It could also be used as a motivation for reading and writing, a resource for vocabulary terms for spelling and definition lists, or a link to booktalks and fictional accounts of various disasters. Best of all, the set is ideal for cross-curricular research units to provide motivation, information, and suggestions for further investigation. World Book suggests the interest level for this set is third grade and up. While some younger students might well be interested in the disasters covered, the reading levels of the text sampled for this review range from fifth to seventh grade. It seems most appropriate for grades four through eight. This is a good set that most elementary and middle school library media centers should own.—**Barbara Ripp Safford**

Oceanography

C, S

529.   Nichols, C. Reid, and Robert G. Williams. **Encyclopedia of Marine Science.** New York, Facts on File, 2009. 626p. illus. index. $85.00. ISBN 13: 978-0-8160-5022-2.

This is a handy one-volume encyclopedia that covers concepts in marine science in a series of concise articles. Also included are 20 additional essays covering topics in more depth such as: Marine Embedment Anchors; Jacques-Yves Cousteau; Glomar Challenger; Sargasso Sea; Icebreaking; Radioactive Waste Disposal at Sea; Robert D. Ballard; and NOAA's PORTS system. Five appendixes cover: further resources (print, Web, and associations); a list of major marine oceans, seas, gulfs, and bays; classification of marine organisms; periodic table of elements; and geologic timescale. Some encyclopedia entries have additional bibliographies appended at the end of the article. The additional essays were written by invited contributors; for example, the essay on Dr. Ballard was written by the president of the Marine Information Resources Corporation in Ellicott City, Maryland. The work is illustrated with numerous black-and-white photographs, line drawings, and tables. The articles and essays are well written and provide basic information on the topic. While not written at an advanced scientific level, the articles will provide most general readers and students with the basic facts.—**Ralph Lee Scott**

MATHEMATICS

C

530.   **Handbook of International Research in Mathematics Education.** 2d ed. Lyn D. English, ed. New York, Routledge/Taylor & Francis Group, 2008. 925p925p. index. $99.95pa. ISBN 13: 978-0-8058-5876-1.

The 2d edition brings together important new mathematics education research that makes a difference in both theory and practice. It updates and extends the *Handbook*'s original key themes and issues for international research in mathematics education. The book touches on four key themes: advances in research methodologies, influences of advanced technologies, access to mathematical ideas, and priorities in mathematics education research. Each of these themes is examined in terms of learners, teachers, and learning contexts, with theory development being an important component of all these aspects. This new edition also examines the recent strong focus on teacher and teacher practice, theory development, the need for mathematics in work place settings, and research designs and methodologies that have provided opportunities for investigating and improving mathematical teaching and learning. Of the 32 chapters in this volume, 10 are brand new that the remainder have been revised and updated.—**Shannon Graff Hysell**

36 Resource Sciences

ENERGY

Handbooks and Yearbooks

C, P, S

531.   Peacock, Kathy Wilson. **Natural Resources and Sustainable Development.** New York, Facts on File, 2008. 392p. index. (Global Issues). $45.00. ISBN 13: 978-0-8160-7215-6.

This newest addition to Facts on File's Global Issues series covers a popular political, economic, and scientific topic—the impact of overconsumption and destruction on natural resources in Brazil, China, Germany, India, and the United States. The Global Issues series is an excellent place for high school and beginning college students to start research. The volumes are similar in organization, each containing three sections that provide an excellent background on a given topic, in this case natural resources and sustainable development. Section 1 introduces the topic and provides case studies showing the impact of the issue on the regions covered; section 2 brings together primary sources from a variety of countries; and section 3 provides valuable research tools, such as names of key players, facts and figures, a annotated bibliography, and names of agencies and organizations. The source includes a broad variety of perspectives on sustainable development from global organizations, government, and business. It provides the student with the background needed to develop his or her own decisions and viewpoint. Although her subjects (e.g., OPEC, overpopulation, global climate change) are complex and controversial, Kathy Wilson Peacock's volume is written in an easy-to-read, straightforward style. This book is recommended for high school, public, and academic libraries.—**Diane J. Turner**

C, S

532.   Smith, Zachary A., and Katrina D. Taylor. **Renewable and Alternative Energy Resources: A Reference Handbook.** Santa Barbara, Calif., ABC-CLIO, 2008. 323p. index. (Contemporary World Issues). $55.00. ISBN 13: 978-1-59884-089-6; 978-1-59884-090-2 (e-book).

Another handbook in the Contemporary World Issues series from ABC-CLIO, *Renewable and Alternative Energy Resources* aims to present the range of renewable and alternative energy options, the arguments for and against the adoption of each technology, and the various policy measures that exist to encourage their use. The renewable and alternative energy technologies are broken down into their history and current use, how the energy is utilized, its advantages, and the prospects for meeting world energy demands. This is followed by a presentation of the problems and controversies surrounding the energy transition debate and a look at the policy ideas that have been developed to help push toward an expanded use of alternative energies. There is a chronology of events leading up to the current situation, brief biographical sketches of 39 individuals in the field, a directory of organizations, and a list of print and electronic resources related to alternative and renewable energy.

The handbook would provide a good starting point for research by high school and college students or others approaching the topic for the first time. While no one particular aspect of renewable and alternative energy is addressed in great detail, this source does a good job of identifying and explaining the range of technologies and the variety of policy measures that can help them succeed. The inclusion of the current state of alternative and renewable energy, along with statistical data, from countries around the world, contributes to the value as a single source of coverage on renewable and alternative energy resources.
—**Mike Burgmeier**

ENVIRONMENTAL SCIENCE

Dictionaries and Encyclopedias

C, P, S

533. Collin, Robert William. **Battleground: Environment.** Westport, Conn., Greenwood Press, 2008. 2v. index. $175.00/set. ISBN 13: 978-0-313-33865-6.

This two-volume reference covers in a very down to earth way some of the most interesting and controversial environmental topics. The many relatively recent changes to the environment have impacted human beings in a multitude of lesser-known ways, such as hormone disruptors, childhood asthma, cancer rates, genetically modified food, as well as the familiar ones like polluted water and soil. Each entry explains some of the social, political, and cultural dimensions of that topic and provides cross-references, Web resources, and a short bibliography for further research. Three appendixes provide leads to environmental databases programs, applications, and portal Websites and an index of chemicals. A glossary of environmental terms, plus a general bibliography and alphabetic index, enhance the set. There are many readily available books about the environment, including the *Encyclopedia of Environment and Society* from Sage (see ARBA 2008, entry 1338) and the *Encyclopedia of World Environmental History* from Routledge (see ARBA 2004, entry 1547) but this insightful, easy-to-read reference set is a great starting point for the consumer, student, and teacher who wishes to understand any of over 100 of the hot topic environmental issues that face us now and will continue to impact us in the future. This set is recommended for high school libraries, public libraries, and academic libraries.—**Diane J. Turner**

C, P, S

534. **Environmental Science in Context.** Brenda Wilmoth Learner and K. Lee Learner, eds. Farmington Hills, Mich., Gale Group, 2009. 2v. illus. index. $245.00/set. ISBN 13: 978-1-4144-3617-3.

This two-volume encyclopedia, one of the In Context series by Gale, was written with high school students in mind and is cross-disciplinary. It is a great place for students to begin research about various environmental topics. Approximately 250 alphabetically arranged articles cover subjects such as alternative fuel impacts, electronic waste, factory farms, invasive species, the ozone hole, and weather extremes, to name just a few. Some primary documents are included. The articles, written by experts in their fields, allow students to come to their own conclusions about a variety of social, economic, political, and environmental issues that scientists and other world leaders face every day. Since scholars have been discussing how to balance economic and environmental concerns and related ethical debate s for several years, a great deal of related material is available. Students who wish to supplement their research may also consult *The Encyclopedia of the Environment* (Houghton Mifflin, 1994), the *Green Encyclopedia* (Prentice Hall, 1992), and the *Encyclopedia of Environment and Society* (see ARBA 2008, entry 1338). This new, easy-to-read source, written especially for the high school population, updates the older sources and provides excellent illustrations, timelines, a glossary, bibliographies at the end of each entry, and an easy-to-use index. This set is recommended for high school libraries, public libraries, and community college libraries.—**Diane J. Turner**

S

535.　**Living Green.** Chicago, World Book, 2009. 9v. illus. maps. index. $279.00/set. ISBN 13: 978-0-7166-1400-5.

These volumes are designed to introduce young people, especially middle and high school students, to the principles and pragmatic details of living sustainably in an increasingly complex world. They are effective in communicating why and how we can "live green," although as with all books written for a juvenile audience, there are necessary simplifications.

These nine volumes can be divided into two groups: those that are environmentally based (e.g., Forests and Wetlands; Mountains, Deserts, and Grasslands; Oceans, Islands, and Polar Regions) and those that process and materials-oriented (e.g., Consumable Goods; Durable Goods; Green buildings; Green Transportation; Pollution; Producing and Obtaining Food). The environmental volumes begin with the definitions and origins of these particular habitat systems, usually starting with geology and geography, and then move quickly into issues such as industrialization, climate change, agriculture, and tourism and how they affect these systems. The process and materials volumes begin with historical analyses and then discussion of various greener alternatives.

Each volume is colorful and well illustrated. The prose is simple and there are many text boxes with "Green Facts" and section summaries. Each volume has a brief glossary of critical terms, all of which are bold-faced in the text. There are also "What You Can Do" and activities chapters for practical work. The sources in the back of each volume include books and Web pages, most of which are also general and child-friendly.

Sometimes the text simplifies issues too far (one caption claims that electric motorcycles are "emissions free" when we know that electricity has to be generated somewhere which likely is not so clean), but this is why we have teachers and active parents. These volumes can be important additions to any middle or high school library with environmental studies collections. They will challenge students with new knowledge and interesting ideas.—**Mark A. Wilson**

Handbooks and Yearbooks

C, S

536.　**Great Debates in American Environmental History.** By Brian Black and Donna L. Lybecker. Westport, Conn., Greenwood Press, 2008. 2v. illus. index. $175.00/set. ISBN 13: 978-0-313-33930-1.

This is a very useful set of volumes to have available to any college environmental studies program, although maybe not always in the ways the authors intended. This is an ambitious environmental history of the United States and its precursor colonies presented in a topical format with a "debate" arrangement.

These two volumes begin with a list of entries generally arranged chronologically. The entries are listed by topic as well, although maddeningly this guide has no page numbers. Each entry has a short introductory table with the time period, an often vague account of who is in "this corner" and the "other corner," and tags of the general environmental issues. The "debate" within many topics is unclear, however, because there are often no clear debatable questions and the pro and con sides, such as they are, are rarely evenly balanced. Nevertheless, the range of discussion is broad and will provoke many actual debates among students and professionals. The first topic is whether the Roanoke Colony was lost because of environmental factors, and the last is on wolves in Yellowstone National Park.

The authors make the odd claim that to do environmental studies such as this, it is required "that we attach blinders to our view of history." This is unfortunate because environmental history is as much about economics, religion, and politics as it is ecosystems. A primary value of modern environmental history is its integrative nature, not this type of reductionism. The authors know this, of course, and their articles all actually do have a framework of interdisciplinary history. The problem is that this history is sometimes incomplete, unbalanced, or just wrong. (They have Daniel Boone dying at the Alamo, for goodness sake.) Most articles are well referenced so they can be used to plant intellectual seeds in environmental studies courses.

These volumes are recommended for libraries that have science and contemporary policy collections, especially those accessed by faculty and students in environmental studies programs. [R: BL, 1 &15 Jan 09, pp. 124-125]—**Mark A. Wilson**

C, P, S

537.   **Water Supply.** Richard Joseph Stein, ed. Bronx, N.Y., H. W. Wilson, 2008. 195p. index. (The Reference Shelf, v.80, no.2). $50.00pa. ISBN 13: 978-0-8242-1079-3.

Seventy percent of the earth's surface is covered with water, but only three percent of this water is fresh, and much of that is locked up in the polar ice caps. As a result, the availability of adequate water is very unevenly distributed, and only one-half of the planet's people enjoy regular access to safe water. (The Middle East has the best oil supply but the worst water supply.) This work, like all the titles in the series, is a collection of recent periodical articles looking at the issue of water supply from economic, political, and health perspectives. The articles are grouped into five main categories: an overview of global water supply; water wars; polluted waters; climate change and the water supply; and water management. As in any anthology there is some unevenness in quality of writing and some repetition, but overall this is a well-chosen collection of writings that will be accessible to the general reader. The issues raised are certainly of worldwide significance.

The bibliography includes both books and Websites, and an appendix provides abstracts of additional relevant journal articles. This book is suitable for public, college, and high school libraries of all sizes.—**Paul B. Cors**

C, P

538.   **The World's Protected Areas: Status, Values and Prospects in the 21st Century.** Stuart Chape, Mark Spalding, and Martin Jenkins, eds. Berkeley, Calif., University of California Press, 2008. 359p. illus. index. $54.95. ISBN 13: 978-0-520-24660-7.

This volume is a combination of a high-quality photography book with a serious accounting of protected areas across the globe. It is an edited work with over 80 contributors from around the world, and the work it represents has been supported by international agencies and private foundations.

The first half of the book is a detailed overview of the history of protected areas, their influence on biodiversity, how they are managed, and the various threat they face. It is very rich in charts and tables, the tedium of which is broken up by frequent colorful photographs and maps. As might easily be imagined, the acronyms for the dozens of relevant organizations flow freely here, but the reader can eventually track down all definitions.

The second half is a regional analysis of protected areas covering most of the globe. There are 15 zones assessed by group, all with maps showing various levels of protection. (For some reason the key to these complex maps is only found at the end of the table of contents.) Each section has a historical perspective and then a discussion of national and international agreements and an assessment of the future. The prose is a bit stilted, reading like it was produced by a United Nations committee at times, but the information is first-rate and the accompanying photographs are brilliant. Each region has a set of graphs showing cumulative number and area of protected sites over time. These naturally turn out to look almost identical with most sites appearing in the last 20 years. The book ends with a bibliography and index. There is no other book on protected areas with this global coverage and consistent statistics; therefore, it is recommended for all libraries with holdings in the natural sciences and international relations.—**Mark A. Wilson**

37 Transportation

AIR

C, P

539. **Aviation Security Management.** Andrew R. Thomas, ed. Westport, Conn., Praeger/Greenwood Press, 2008. 3v. index. $375.00/set. ISBN 13: 978-0-313-34652-1.

Editor Andrew R. Thomas, author of several other titles in aviation safety and air travel, brings together a group of 10 contributing authors who offer essays on the current trends, issues, and practices in aviation security. With the threat of air terrorism, the globalization of international travel, and advances in aviation technology, air travel is more complex and the security surrounding it more serious than ever. These three volumes highlight emerging practices in the industry and illustrate the current trends in air travel.

The book is arranged into three volumes, each with its own distinct purpose. Volume 1, "The Context of Aviation Security Management," focuses on basics of aviation security and includes chapters on the benefits of security measures, aviation security practice and education, modern terrorist threats to the industry, and the legal aspects of providing aviation security. The second volume, "The Elements of Aviation Security Management," discusses passengers' rights, response management, passenger screening, air cargo security, and selection of aviation security screeners. The third and final volume, "Perspectives on Aviation Security Management," discusses passenger profiling, the "growing pains" of transportation security, in-cabin security, and an assessment of the cost of providing safe air travel.

Together the three volumes cover the major areas of focus for anyone in the aviation security business, and provide a basis for educational programs. This set will be an essential reference for those practicing or studying aviation security management.—**Shannon Graff Hysell**

GROUND

P

540. Flory, J. Kelly, Jr. **American Cars, 1946 to 1959: Every Model, Year by Year.** Jefferson, N.C., McFarland, 2008. 1037p. illus. index. $75.00. ISBN 13: 978-0-7864-3229-5.

This ready-reference volume is by the author of *American Cars, 1960-1972* (see ARBA 2004, entry 1566), and features the same expertise and attention to detail as its predecessor. The preface clearly states the inclusion criteria (for example, because they were not available for dealer sale, Checker cars are excluded) and provides useful explanatory data notes. The extensive range of data is laid out in an effective format within a year-by-year treatment allowing comparisons of models across as well as within years. Every make is clearly illustrated by small monochrome photographs. The volume has been carefully proofread, with the only error noted being blind footnote symbols on page 1,030. Finding aids comprise a table of contents, an index of makes and models, and page edge blocks corresponding to each year. These combine to provide ready answers to both general and specific queries.

This volume serves three major uses: as a reference source for the cars themselves; as a source of industry information (e.g., market share by company by year); and as a guide to collectors and restorers interested in paint colors, serial numbers, and option lists. Crisply printed on good quality matte paper, the weight and size of this title demands and gets a sturdy binding. The book will appeal to any library supporting automotive interests.—**John Howard Oxley**

Author/Title Index

Reference is to entry number.

Subject Index

Reference is to entry number.